ERNEST JONES
Freud's Alter Ego

ERNEST JONES
FREUD'S ALTER EGO

VINCENT BROME

Norton

W · W · NORTON & COMPANY   NEW YORK · LONDON

ISBN 0-393-01594-7

Printed in Great Britain

Contents

	Preface	i–iv
	Prologue	v–vii
1	Early Years	1
2	Medical Studies	18
3	Success and Failure	24
4	His Relationship with Maude Hill	30
5	His Affair with Loe Kann	36
6	Psycho-Analytic Beginnings	43
7	First Meetings with Freud	52
8	Canada and America	63
9	Loe Kann, Jones and Freud	80
10	Canadian and American Troubles	90
11	The War Years	99
12	First Marriage	111
13	Re-union with Freud	121
14	Second Marriage	124
15	Conflict with Freud	130
16	Private Life	140
17	The Arrival of Melanie Klein	149
18	The American Scene	159
19	The Break with Ferenczi	166
20	Family Life	179
21	Jones Rescues Freud	192
22	The Melanie Klein Schism	200
23	He writes the Biography	210
	Appendix – His Work	219

I have especially to thank Mrs. Katharine Jones for permission to quote from her husband's papers, letters and diaries, Diana Riviere for permission to reproduce the letters from her mother to Ernest Jones and the Sigmund Freud Copyrights Ltd for permission to quote from the unpublished correspondence between Freud and Ernest Jones.

Also I gratefully acknowlege the help given me by the Institute of Psycho-Analysis, and especially John Jarrett and Ms. Jill Duncan for access to files and dossiers.

Preface

THE SON of Thomas Jones, a clerk in a South Wales coal company, Ernest Jones rose to become President of the International Psycho-Analytical Association, a figure known internationally who not only manipulated many phases of psycho-analytical history but became the power behind the Freudian throne and actually made a great deal of that history. A close associate of Freud for thirty years, he contributed over two hundred theoretical papers, wrote eleven books and finally crowned his writing career with his three-volume biography of Freud described by the *New York Times* as "one of the outstanding biographies of the age."

Preparing a biography of Ernest Jones presented special problems since part of the Freud Archive in the Library of Congress is still unavailable, but I was — very generously — given access to Ernest Jones' papers, letters and diaries by his widow, Mrs. Katharine Jones. Otherwise the usual research processes were rigorously pursued in many directions, but I would not claim that this work is definitive. What, in any case, does definitive mean? A man's life contains an infinite perspective which stretches far beyond personality and events into unconscious motive and no multiplication of volumes can ever satisfactorily condense the whole of his experience. A certain amount of evidence about Jones' life has been destroyed and his diaries are little more than formal appointment books. Mrs. Jones' diaries yielded more extensive entries.

Crucial to the undertaking was the collection of over four hundred unpublished letters between Freud and Jones, held at the Freud Archive in the Library of Congress with copies in the Freud Archive at Colchester. These threw new light on Jones' life, his relationship with Freud and the history of psycho-analysis. There were many other letters and documents from Jones' early correspondence with Putnam, Brill, Jung, Ferenczi and the authorities at Toronto University, Canada. A whole range of letters to and from members of the Viennese and American societies were available from the Jones Archive in the Institute of Psycho-Analysis, including Jones' correspondence with Anna Freud about his biography of Freud. Listing such sources makes tedious reading and the interested reader is referred to the

Notes and Sources which give a detailed and comprehensive account.

I have for over fifteen years been pre-occupied with the nature and history of psycho-analysis, which led me to write three other books in the field — *Freud and His Early Circle, Jung, Man and Myth,* and *Havelock Ellis — Philosopher of Sex.* Research on Havelock Ellis first began thirty years ago and brought me into touch with some of the veterans of the psycho-analytic scene including Jones himself, Carl Jung, Anna Freud, Dr. J. Moore, Dr. Alan Maberly, Dr. Edward Glover, Dr. William Gillespie, Alix Strachey, Eva Rosenfeld, Paula Heimann, Dr. Gerhard Adler, Dr. Michael Balint, Adler's daughter Alexandra Adler, Judith de Taves the daughter of Izette de Forest, Dr. E. A. Bennet and Professor Manfred Bleuler. Among more contemporary people were Dr. Charles Rycroft, Anthony Storr, Diana Riviere the daughter of Joan Riviere and Lancelot Whyte. Once again any list would proliferate and specific references are given in the *Notes and Sources.*

I have specially to thank the time and patience given to my questions by Mervyn Jones, the son of Ernest Jones, and his wife Jeanne. There were many gaps which they alone could fill and this biography would have been incomplete without their help. Lewis Jones, Ernest's second son, was also very helpful. Above all for four long years Mrs. Katharine Jones patiently waited while the biography developed and in that time gave irreplaceable evidence. Throughout the early stages of the exercise Ricardo Steiner brought me to heel on certain inadequacies, but he is in no way responsible for the contents of this book. Professor Greenland of McMasters University went to considerable trouble to research the Canadian period of Ernest Jones' life and provided invaluable evidence.

It remains to say that Jones' vivid fragment of autobiography, *Free Associations,* was indispensable to an accurate account of his early and middle years. Finally Dr. Charles Rycroft took considerable trouble to read the manuscript, which led to the removal of a number of inaccuracies.

There were many amongst those I met who disliked Jones but frequently their reactions were sharpened by the recollection of fierce exchanges in which they were either involved or of which they became involuntary spectators. Such "highlights" were not representative of the long stretches of relative calm when his life ran its course with no more than the customary upheavals which accompany anyone playing the role of collaborator in a pioneering field. My reactions when I emerged from my long pilgrimage were mixed, but the reader may be interested to discover these reactions in the text which follows.

Prologue

THIRTY YEARS have gone by since I first met Ernest Jones and memory of details has become dim but the image which leaps to mind is of a short, dapper man, immacutately dressed, whose quick, military movements belied his seventy-two years. Almost at once I was aware of the double vision which he automatically brought to bear on new visitors, everyone falling to some degree into the category of potential patients, but in what precise way this became evident I cannot recollect. Possibly, I myself created the sense of being scrutinised analytically. Physically it was the face which remained most vividly in my mind, a face marked by every kind of experience, a face which spoke among other characteristics of austerity and dedication to duty.

The obligatory pleasantries were rapidly exhausted and then he said "I don't envy you the task of writing about Havelock Ellis. He could be as imprecise as Jung." I was at the time attempting to write a biography of Havelock Ellis and we quickly swung into a detailed comparison of Freud and Ellis whose early paths followed such closely similar patterns. I made careful notes of the conversation which followed, but some are indecipherable and the record probably suffers from some manipulation in the gaps which remain.

Looking back over the years it was possible to establish identities between Ellis and Freud as remarkable as the differences on which they finally split. Socially and scientifically their backgrounds were opposed, but both came to medicine in the same period, both had no special sense of vocation and Freud frequently wished "that he could retire from medical practice and devote himself to unravelling cultural problems," a desire close to the heart of Havelock Ellis.

So far Jones agreed with my analysis but now he swung away in critical mood. At a very advanced stage of the subtle relationship which developed between these two men, Jones told me Freud burst out in exasperation one day: "It's not so much Havelock Ellis' ignorance that matters — it's his knowing so many things that are not so." Driven to this attack by the tenacity with which Ellis insisted that Freud under-estimated hereditary factors in homosexuality, the words left a sardonic echo in Jones' memory, but he finally decided to exclude them from his biography of Freud.

Slowly it became clear in our conversation that Jones found it incongruous to associate the name of a man like Havelock Ellis – "a literary essayist turned sexologist" – with a man like Freud who was "an original scientist." "After all" he said "all Ellis ever did was to compile an encyclopaedia of sexual behaviour – a whole polymorphous dictionary. But when he tried to interpret the evidence, or organise it in theoretical form, he became hopelessly lost."

In the middle of my protests that Ellis had not only broken open the conspiracy of silence surrounding sex in Victorian days which was no mean feat and . . . tea was served and Mrs. Katharine Jones joined us. Gracious, charming, she played the hostess with skill but the conversation quickly turned away from psycho-sexual matters. Viennese by origin, university trained and obviously very intelligent, I felt that the ventriloquist voice of Victorian England required that men talked about matters which automatically changed when they were joined by ladies like Mrs. Jones. When I tried to turn the conversation back to Ellis, Jones adroitly side-stepped the attempt and insisted on giving full attention to a discussion about the state of his highly prized garden which, through the window, revealed a wonderful profusion of every kind of plant and shrub.

After tea he selected one of a number of sticks and marched me round the garden giving me an elaborate introduction, with Latin names, to such a variety of plant life that I felt I would be neglecting my psycho-analytical duty if I did not read into it a significance beyond the normal. Was all this the symbol of the ordered life he would like to impose on the family – if not society – where his diagnostic labels and careful treatment held sickness at bay, or did he simply revel in the orgy of colour as a riotous libidinal indulgence. Absurd of course: he did neither; but I remember vividly such images running through my mind as the conversation at last came round to intellectual matters again.

Did Ellis' work on infantile sexuality, sexual repression in religious mania and dream interpretation coincide with, anticipate or follow Freud's equivalent work? Only the very daring would have formulated the question in such a way before the grey eminence of the whole Freudian movement, and I was uneasily aware of becoming positively reckless when I added: "I think Ellis won by a couple of months on sex and religious mania."

Characteristically Jones replied "Oh no, you are quite wrong." Suitably chastened I still persisted: "I think you will find" I said "that if you look at *The Journal of Mental Hygiene* for the relevant dates that Ellis wrote an article which was first in the field."

Just what followed is obscure in my memory. Certainly Jones went in search of the reference, and although he seemed to have a "run" of the *Journal of Mental Hygiene,* by an unlucky chance the relevant volume was missing. Unlucky chance — or had the ghost of Freud temporarily removed the evidence? What did it matter: enormously, it seemed to Jones who continued to worry at the point for some minutes. Then we moved on to broader issues.

Alert, incisive, with endless references retrieved from memory by the merest flick of thought, Jones for a man of seventy-two was remarkably well-preserved intellectually. Words were never wasted. Naively I asked him whether he had ever read Westermark's *History of Marriage* and with remarkable restraint for such a paragon of psychological erudition he said in the gentlest manner "Why of course."

Mrs. Jones came and went in the conversation which followed, a charming background figure who never failed to satisfy if not anticipate her husband's needs and occasionally confirmed or denied details from the past. The main thrust of the conversation quickly became evident: two opposing champions of equally dead masters, one trying to preserve the image of Ellis as a reasonably original thinker and the other assuming that such foolhardiness required no more than a minimum of effort to defeat it.

Yes — Freud and Ellis read each other's works and their early books followed close on the heels of one another, *Man and Woman* preceding *Studies über Hysterie* by one year, *The Stuff That Dreams are Made Of* coinciding with the publication of *The Interpretation of Dreams*. Yes, Freud acknowledged that the facts contained in the first Contribution to *Three Contributions to the Theory of Sex* had been gathered from people like Kraft Ebing, Moll and Havelock Ellis. Yes, Havelock Ellis had given a number of autobiographic reports of normal persons recording their sexual feelings in childhood and Freud had cited Havelock Ellis as a reliable witness for cases of sado-masochism. As for homosexuality there were more points of coincidence between the two men than differences but — Jones protested — over all these areas Ellis not only failed to penetrate the unconscious motives which conditioned their expression, he could not bring the evidence into a cohesive whole. What was the use of stressing the innate characteristics of homosexuality when the existence of two other classes of homosexual — absolute homosexuals and bi-sexuals — made it difficult to believe that "intrinsic" homosexuality was congenitally based? In many inverts, Jones said, Freud argued that homosexuality developed not at birth or in the first years but later in life as a result of some "affective sexual impression."

But, I said, there is a common fallacy which says that if you analyse homosexuality deeply enough you will find waiting for release at the bottom of the well, heterosexual impulses. Could not the reverse also be the case — heterosexuality concealing unrealised homosexual impulses? There was a long pause and then Jones said "There's no need to be too delicate about these matters nowadays, is there. Can I ask you — are you in any way homosexual?"

I sensed that he had made a tactical mistake since he probably expected me to be either a practising homosexual or owe an allegience to the cause.

"No" I said. "I am not homosexual, but I don't regard it as a perversion as I believe Freud did."

I cannot give precise verbatim responses from now on but he replied something like: The three stages leading to maturity would in Freudian terms be the oral, anal and genital and the inability to assimilate the homosexual level to the heterosexual Freud would certainly consider a perversion.

Momentarily roused, I exclaimed that perversion was a word Ellis desired to remove from the psychological dictionary because if one observed the polymorphous perverse in children they encompassed such a variety of sexual patterns, all occuring naturally to the developing organism, that such a word was utterly misplaced.

Jones leant forward in his chair and emphasised his reply with a pointing finger. Yes, but the underlying pattern driving relentlessly to its natural end was the evolutionary need for reproduction and that conditioned what we mean by maturity.

Maturity, I said, was a term open to infinite misunderstanding. Many married men and women with children who satisfied evolutionary requirements remained emotionally immature.

We are not, Jones said, in Freudian analysis, concerned with elaborate definitions in search of precise meanings because we have found in our case histories satisfactory meanings which we attach to the clinical terms we use.

So it went on for nearly two hours and then Jones said something like "Where do you place yourself in all this — are you Freudian, Jungian, or what are you?"

"I find Freud the most sympathetic" I said and he at once responded "Well that at least makes you a man of some sense."

He then launched into an attack on Ellis' belief in pantheistic monism which he said he had picked up from Schelling and the Germans and never managed to shake off. Freud, he said, had the sense to break out of that mystical rubbish, if he ever believed it.

Suddenly a change overtook him. The eager alertness slackened, his voice was less vigorous and his manner less combative. Sitting back in his chair, his eyes momentarily closed, his face seemed paler and for the first time he had the air of slight exhaustion which haunts many men in their seventies. I waited and the silence lengthened. "I'm tiring you" I said at last, and at once he sat up and replied "Certainly you are not. Would you like a drink?" For the life of me I cannot remember what it was we drank but as the conversation became more desultory I said: "Psycho-analysis apart, do you embrace any particular kind of philosophy?"

"Oh, I'm a terribly old-fashioned materialist" he said. "But I agree with Bertrand Russell. The most we can do is to get a working hypothesis.

Materialism's the one I prefer." I remember we discussed the difficulties of reconciling the id, ego and super-ego to strict materialist equivalents, and I recall the ingenuity with which he redeemed psychic reality from materialist reality, but the details escape me.

At last, coming to his feet he said "What does it matter, anyway. I'm too old to let it matter any more."

The first impression of a too disciplined, somewhat sharp personality had softened as our conversation deepened. That he was concerned for the welfare of humanity went without saying: that his devotion to Freud admitted few concessions had equal inevitability: that he could be acerbic, even abrasive on occasion came through clearly: but there was also an underlying kindliness, a warmth of response which somehow seemed overlaid by too much — was it psycho-analytic probing?

He again expressed concern for my task of writing a biography of such a "relatively woolly-minded man as Ellis" but he appreciated the contribution he had made to liberating sexual knowledge. He expressed admiration for anyone so foolhardy as to earn a living by writing and wondered how anyone survived the hazards of such a way of life: he offered to retrieve Ellis' letters to Freud for me and said he was prepared to read my chapter comparing the two men: but before I wrote it, I simply must read his review of the seventh volume of the *Studies in the Psychology of Sex,* because there he gave his carefully considered evaluation of Ellis and his work.

In the end I came away feeling that I liked him, but that was a broad and dubious generality. Only twenty years later did I begin the long pilgrimage into his life which uncovered the changing faces, moods and motivations which made up a man no less complex than the Master he had once served.

CHAPTER I

Early Years

BORN ON the 1st of January 1879 in the village of Gowerton, Wales, Alfred Ernest Jones firmly believed, in the first few years of life, that the blasts on the factory hooters celebrating New Year's Eve were proper recognition of his glorious appearance among the living. Equal precocity distinguished his sexual life and he stated that the *practice* (my italics) of coitus was "familiar to me at the age of seven."[1]

Both experiences were overtaken by a similar disillusion. "I still recollect my shamefacedness at the age of four or five on learning that the world in its [greeting of hooters] was concerned with thoughts transcending my self important personality."[2] And infantile coitus obviously failed to yield satisfactory results since he "did not resume [the practice] till [he] was twenty-four."[3]

Against all expectation Jones' father Thomas Jones was tall, blond and handsome and his mother's genes were obviously dominant in his own physical make-up since she combined the ideal characteristics of the Iberian Welsh — short, dark, and very pale. Thomas Jones, the father, was twenty-five and Mary Ann May Lewis twenty-three at the time of Ernest's birth and Jones later committed himself to a statement about their marriage which those who knew him as a sceptical analyst would regard as almost reckless. "The marriage was" he said "a completely happy one."[4] He went even further. "I never heard a cross or even impatient word pass between them."[5] In retrospect his commitment to one or other of his parents fluctuated and whatever elements of an Oedipus complex he could rescue from conscious recollection never came through clearly. "My mother" he wrote "was the more openly affectionate of the two and had little of my father's noteworthy restraint of emotion. Save for some deep inner reserve which probably no one ever penetrated, I should say he was as mentally normal as one could reasonably expect."[6] A man of humble origins, he began his career as a clerk in the locally famous coal company of Messrs. Cory, but quickly found that way of life unsatisfactory. Assembling a relatively small handful of books he began studying on his own account, qualified as a colliery engineer, and soon rose to the post of colliery manager

1. Jones: *Free Associations,* 31.
2. Ibid, 12.
3. Ibid, 31.
4. Ibid, 21.
5. Ibid.
6. Ibid.

in the town of Gowerton.

Ernest's birth coincided with another major change in his father's career. He became accountant to the big steel works Wright, Butler & Co., where once again his promotion was swift. Appointed General Secretary to a company whose holdings extended into iron ore mines in Italy and Spain, the horizons of a small Welsh community were soon expanded by continental journeys, but he quickly discovered that mining communities have under- lying characteristics in common wherever they are based. Always an independent spirit, when the partnership in Messrs. Wright Burley & Co. which had long been promised him did not materialise, he promptly resigned, but to him idleness was another form of hell, and he immediately joined the directorial boards of a number of companies in Cardiff and London, returning to his first love – coal.

As much the product of Freudian paternalism as of his Welsh origins, when Ernest Jones came to write the unfinished fragment of autobiography he tended to underestimate his mother, Mary Ann May, nee Lewis (1855– 1909). "Of my mother I shall say less" he said because her influence "though more profound" was "less tangible." Surprisingly, in a man steeped in the Freudian belief that the first years of life are vital to a person's future development, he stated that his mother's influence "did not continue much beyond the age of eight."[7] His intellectual development he attributed to his father's influence between the ages eight to thirteen: "My father had a good grasp of the fundamentals of science, and was also pretty well read in the main English classics of prose and poetry." A sense of duty and efficiency he also inherited from his father, who believed that "business was business," chaos being the only alternative to efficient organisation. So strong was the imprint of this precept that when a big company in the neighbourhood made a present of a turkey to each employee at Christmas, the young boy found himself wondering what would happen to the efficiency of their universe "if that sort of thing was allowed to go on." However, Jones' confidence in tackling the problems with which reality quickly presented him – as witness seven-year-old coitus – was as much due to his mother's tender, loving care as any abstract paternal principle. Psychologically all was well in his relationship with his mother but physiologically a bout of rheumatic fever attacked her when he was three months old and stopped her breast feeding the boy. Falling a victim to patent medicine advertising, she substituted a series of patent milk foods which effectively deprived Jones of all vitamins. "In consequence I was a puny and ailing infant with pronounced rickets and a not very happy disposition."

It is interesting that this disturbance did not produce a deeper neurosis than later became evident, but there was already a sharpness of tongue which his mother early discovered. "I can still see her warning me by pointing at my tongue which she maintained was sharp as a needle."

7. Ibid, 26.

The realities of domestic life which surrounded his boyhood came close to being primitive. The house consisted of eight rooms with a kitchen, dining room, front and back parlour downstairs, and four bedrooms upstairs. It was lit by oil lamps, unlike the houses of the poor which never rose above candles, and meat was cooked on a spit before the open fire. Bread they baked at home and young Ernest took over responsibility at an early age for collecting the yeast. A big cask of rainwater provided washing water but drinking water had to be carried from a well a mile and a half away. The multiple burden which descended on Mrs. Jones can be imagined when washing, mangling and ironing alone occupied the greater part of two days a week.

A touch of snobbery in his mother's outlook expressed itself as a desire to see her son aspire to higher social status and intensive chapel-going suggested to her that he should enter the church as one stepping stone into the professional classes. At a very early age he apparently rejected this with a confident assertion that he was going to become a doctor.

A servant who also acted as nurse to the family remained vividly in Ernest's mind for the rest of his life but although she spoke no English he seems to have learnt very little Welsh. Despite the dread of burning hell-fire with which she inspired him, religion never really took hold of him and he remembered her mainly because she taught him "two words to designate the male organ, one for it in a flaccid state, the other in an erect."[8] Unaccountably he commented, later in life, "It was an opulence of vocabulary I have not encountered since."

Sex discussions ran their usual course among the boys at school and one boy revealed the facts of life with customary crudity. He also shocked young Ernest by expressing a desire to sleep with Mrs. Jones, not out of boyhood lust but for actual procreation. Prematurely sophisticated, his school friends were fully aware of a surprising range of sexual activity and clothed their knowledge in the current vernacular. "A boy of nine" Jones later wrote "rolling on the floor with acute belly-ache, groaned aloud 'Oh God it hurts so much I don't think I could fuck a girl if she was under me at this minute.' The same youngster asked me once if I believed that men ever thought of anything other than their cocks when they were alone. He was the son of a minister."

Only once in his writings does Jones remark that his early sexual indocrination was proof, if it were needed, of the proposition which he later encountered in Freud − that sex permeated most areas of life. Certainly practising coitus at the age of seven anticipated one of Freud's most resisted discoveries: the theory of infantile sexuality.

Two other analytic precursions in early childhood anticipated later clinical experience. At the age of three or four years he frequently slept between his father and mother and one night he was awakened by the sensation of

8. Ibid. 30.

"something hot and hard in contact with my leg." A little reflection disclosed the true nature of this object and with it a sense of having experienced something similar before, the memory of which he had repressed. In his autobiography Jones claims that at this very early age he formulated the principle of repression with the throught − "So an unwelcome idea could be repressed."[9] It reads suspiciously like the retrospective interjection of adult sophistication into the raw material of childhood experience.

Similarly he recalled having several sexual dreams about his sisters and records his childhood bewilderment that in the dream it was pleasurable and repellent to his awakened consciousness. Once again he claims that "I concluded the moral part of one's moral nature slept more profoundly than more primitive ones."[10] This, at the age of eleven, he alleged, went even further. "In this I anticipated an interesting part of Freud's celebrated theory of dreams and paved the way for a readier acceptance of it."

Experiences after the birth of his two younger sisters also had resonances into Freudian theory but here he remained content with the subjective facts. His older sister was born when he had reached his twenty-second month and he grew fiercely jealous, frequently appealing to his mother to "put the baby down in the cradle to cry, and nurse *me.*" Compensation took the place of challenge when another sister was born, after the same interval of 22 months. He swiftly made the baby his own child, singing her to sleep, but he took the precaution of "rocking her at the end of a cord that reached almost the length of the house."

It is now possible to penetrate the surfaces and document Jones' innermost thoughts about his relations with his sister and mother from the unpublished Freud−Jones correspondence. For instance, twenty-six years later, two letters to Freud are very revealing. In one he says[11]: "From about the age of twelve until almost the present I had the obsession never to write anything, a letter, address an envelope, school task, etc. without undersigning it thus ➤⊙. I always interpreted it to myself as standing for Science, which I greatly idealised. I know that it stands for Sybil, the name of my younger sister. I have found out by dream analysis that when she was born, when I was three years, eight months old, I had the double fantasy that she was my child (a) from my mother and myself, (b) from the doctor and myself. . . . All my life I have treated my sister as my father treated me, i.e. very impatiently and arrogantly, and although I am very fond of her have never been able to live with her, until last year, without quarrelling, on this account. In writing, which with me is very directly sexually symbolic, I therefore put her *below* me, in a double sense (a) as my child, (b) erotically."

Jones son Mervyn, recalls that of his two sisters his father preferred Sybil a gay jolly child who quickly developed a malicious sense of humour and indeed fulfilled the impossible cliche of − dying of laughter. She was in the middle of eating one day when she found something hilariously funny,

9. Ibid, 32.
10. Ibid.
11. Jones to Freud, March 30, 1910.

roared with laughter and suddenly choked on her food.

While complicated sexual urges were disturbing him at the age of three Jones went to the village school where unimaginative teachers taught him by rote and the A.B.C. was learnt to the accompaniment of simple but effective tunes.

When the question of baptisms arose the headmaster was anxious to increase his chances of ecclesiastical promotion by multiplying their number and it caused him great annoyance that this small boy Ernest stubbornly peristed in claiming that his parents were Baptists who would raise objections. Thus Jones remained a heathen but that did not prevent the headmaster from becoming a Bishop. "As a result of all this" Jones later wrote "I have never passed through any religious ceremony, at birth, puberty or marriage. . . ."[12]

Jones quickly revealed the requisite capacities for passing examinations. In no time he was reading widely, easily memorising, and reproducing elementary facts on paper. Mr. Edmunds, the headmaster, was a friend of his father who quickly saw the boy's potential and took a special interest in him. All three would sometimes go for bicycle rides on those monstrous spidery contraptions called penny-farthings, where the front wheel was inexplicably six times as large as the rear.

It was his mother who pressed his father, when the boy reached his ninth year, to send him to another, better, school in Swansea, called the Higher Grade School. Mr. Edmunds even descended to bribery in an effort to keep the boy in his own school, hinting that because of his abilities he would promote him by two classes at one stroke. Ernest was unimpressed. The allure of the great steam engine carrying him twelve miles to a "mysteriously superior" school within the vast city of Swansea was overwhelming. In the event the glamour and excitement quickly faded. Relatively undersized, Jones found himself the butt of his schoolfellows some of whom were skilled bullies presented with a ready-made victim. It did not interfere with his intellectual development. Dull though his teachers were they slowly realised that he was exceptionally intelligent and he quickly mastered the elements of one subject after another. According to his autobiography, by the age of ten he was steeped in the works of Euclid, had grasped the elements of Italian grammar and within a single week mastered enough shorthand to enable him to pass the standard examination of that subject. However, his school reports of the time spoke of his tendency to talk incessantly during school hours and spoke of his mathematics deteriorating at the age of twelve.[13]

His career at the Higher Grade School was suddenly interrupted when scarlet fever attacked him so severely that he remained delirious for several days. Later Jones claimed that this constituted the only serious illness in his life but in fact he underwent a number of operations and before he died suffered from cancer.

12. Jones: *Free Associations,* 24.
13. *Ernest Jones,* T. G. Davies, 19.

Both parents feared that scarlet fever would kill him and nursed him devotedly but once again it was his mother who discussed the future of his education with him as he slowly recovered. She seems to have held out the bait of "higher education" partly in the hope that it would stimulate his recovery and partly because of her belief that progress from lower to higher standards meant progress in hygiene and health.

Jones was to become the living contradition of Marx's theory that a man cannot escape his class but his first encounters at Swansea Grammar School with boys of a higher social class revealed deficiencies in speech which were at first embarrassing. He learnt not to drop his aitches, he replaced "ay mun" with "yes" but he continued to use the word "bool" meaning a round door handle, far into life. Swansea's urban proletariat quickly revealed characteristics alien to the friendly working class of his village. On his daily walk from the railway station to the grammar school the town boys would frequently run after him, taunting him with phrases like "Quack! Quack! Grammar ducks!" Sometimes they tried to knock off the symbol of class superiority represented by his school cap, and more seriously there was a scuffle one day when two town boys fought over possession of a peg-top and one stabbed Ernest's friend in the face with the spike of the top.

Anna Freud believed that Ernest Jones never quite escaped from his working class roots and thought that certain shortcomings she found in his character originated from this conflict. Certainly he seemed worried in his autobiographical fragment that he had not received a classical education, a remarkable concern for a doctor involved in the allegedly classless mores of psycho-analysis.

In fact his father Thomas Jones with his responsible white collar job would have been firmly marked off from what was strictly regarded as the South Wales working class. Ernest Jones son, Mervyn, remarked, "I'm not even sure that Thomas Jones had absolutely working-class roots – he came more from the artisan-craftsman class."

Against the evidence of his school report he claimed that he developed a certain aptitude in mathematics before he was twelve and mastered the whole of Euclid in which his pleasure remained primarily aesthetic. This he regarded as a misfortune because it drew him away from classics and left him with little Latin and less Greek. "After two years of it I got my complacent father to beg me off further study. . . . It was certainly galling in later years to have analytical friends in Vienna quoting Latin or Greek passages and being astonished at my blank response."

In later life he believed that he mixed with all kinds and classes on equal terms but although he may have called the gardener Fred it is unlikely that he would have survived the test of allowing the gardener to call him Ernest. None of these complications troubled the schoolboy, nor did they stop him emerging at the top of his form, which won him a scholarship to Llandovery College.

The world in which he was fast growing up was a world where Gladstone's Home Rule campaign had lost its impetus and Jones became torn between sympathy with the Irish and mistrust of their loyalty to the Commonwealth. One day at Singleton Park, Swansea, Gladstone made one of his rolling oratorical utterances which lasted a full hour and afterwards young Ernest was restrained, when they all filed past the Grand Old Man, from shaking his hand because the ordeal had plainly become painful to him.

It was a world where the D'Oyly Carte Company toured the countryside and their rare visits to Swansea were a marvellous feast of colour, music and wit to the fast-growing boy. The family could, between them, thrum on the piano and sing considerable extracts from many Gilbert and Sullivan operas, the Welsh aptitude for music simplifying descant problems which troubled their English counterparts. *The Silver King,* by another Jones − Henry Arthur Jones − typified the drama of the day and equally delighted Ernest. It was a well made play with a beginning, a middle and end, enlivened by suitably placed dramatic climaxes which did not trouble the intellect too much. Occasionally he went to concerts given by the world-famed Madame Patti at the Albert Hall, Swansea, but there were no late trains home, and every outing meant a six-mile country walk at midnight. Music may be in the blood of the Welsh and there is no doubting their musical prowess but whatever gene conditioned this gift it was deficient in Ernest whose efforts to play the piano quickly drove him to despair.

In his autobiographical fragment this revealing passage occurred about these years: "I begged permission to give it up. In the early days I had regaled my sisters − *we still slept together* − with tales of my future appearances on concert platforms."[14] (My italics.)

At this time his father continued to manage the steelworks of a friend, and acquaintance with all its parts brought home to Jones the ugliness of industrial waste which polluted the country in all directions. His father did not share his aesthetic scruples. When, later in life, he visited his son's beautiful house, the Plat, in Sussex, "he made the monstrous suggestion that it would be a good place for a cement works!"[15]

The world where everyone knew his place and class distinctions were regarded as inevitable was undergoing change, but young Ernest remained quite unaware of his role in minimally increasing class mobility by passing from relatively inarticulate beginnings to higher education.

The nightmares which had troubled him in early years now revived and one in particular was to have lasting repercussions. His father developed a habit of playfully tugging his moustache while snapping at the boy and this connected in his developing imagination with a fear that from nearby woods some wolves would one night descend and devour him. His own analytic

14. Jones: *Free Associations,* 36.
15. Ibid, 38.

interpretation later read: "It was no doubt a projection on to my innocent father of some oral-sadistic phantasies. . . ." A natural dog-lover, Jones from that time on made an exception of the wolf-like Alsatian, and when, years later, he first met Anna Freud's Alsatian, an interesting incident occurred. Unfortunately named Wolf, the dog immediately flew at Jones and tore a piece of his thigh. Jones's reaction in his autobiographical fragment aptly reflected the reverence he then brought to Freud. "Freud who was present, *sagely* remarked on how dogs instinctively recognise those who dislike them and are afraid of them and at once treat them as enemies." (My italics.) In view of later events there was some evidence for reflecting that perhaps Anna's dislike of Jones at the time had been picked up and projected by the dog.

It was a new doctor, the first to come to the developing village of Rhosfelyn, who not only presented Jones with his first dog but inspired his choice of profession. Handsome, dashing, with a fund of lurid stories about his medical student days in Dublin, the doctor epitomised for the growing boy an independent spirit who flashed on the wing from person to person bringing magical substances which remained inexplicable. Jones saw all this at close quarters because the young doctor could not at first acquire a house and lodged with the Jones family, inevitably taking a great interest in this lively young boy who eagerly absorbed every word he heard. Ernest's mother explained to him, at the birth of his younger sister, that "Queen Victoria, an assiduous Queen Bee, had sent us the new baby"[16] but that did not correspond to the young doctor's activities before, during and after the birth. Moreover the doctor seemed able to cope with his mother's painfully evident distress during the birth while the father was excluded, and this, in Jones' infantile hierarchy, placed a doctor above a father. One resolution formed and grew in his mind. He must become a doctor. Even when, at an early age, he was told that his delicate health made such an arduous profession difficult if not impossible, he did not give up hope.

The glamour of engine-driving never held any particular interest for Ernest and his mother's continued attempts to lure him into the church were staunchly resisted. Doctors . . . medicine . . . curing the sick . . . helping mankind . . . this was the chain of thinking which continuously recurred in his mind. The prolonged delaying action practised by adolescents today who sometimes reach their early twenties without selecting a career would have met with severe censure in the Jones family. A man must make up his mind: life began in earnest as early as fourteen or sixteen and any shilly-shallying was regarded as weakness of character, but Jones in his autobiography did not reveal the true nature of his medical inspiration.

In a letter to Freud much later in life he wrote[17]: "In the last two years I have found out the motive that made me go in for medicine; to do so was a sudden decision at the age of fifteen, never having previously thought of it. It

16. Ibid, 41.
17. Jones to Freud, June 28, 1910.

was a lucky decision, for I cannot imagine myself happy at any other work. *As a boy I had greatly admired our family doctor, a handsome dare-devil fellow. We were in a small country place, and he lived with us till I was three years old. He never much liked me, owing chiefly to my disturbing him then, by crying, etc. One day in a rage he hung me in a high water-butt, which with other traumata formed the later basis for a phobia of heights.* Three special memories stand out, as a sort of *Deckerrinerung*. (1) I was impressed by a remark of another boy's that the doctor was loved by all the women of the neighbourhood, a fact confirmed by the enormous crowd of weeping women I saw at his funeral, when I was about twelve. Now I have always been conscious of sexual attractions to patients; my wife was a patient of mine. (2) When the doctor died, my mother cried, and I heard her tell my father how kind he had always been to her, and how he had kissed her consolingly the last time he attended her. I recall feeling jealous, or, to be more accurate, wondering if my father was jealous. (3) *Intense* angst at having the doctor thrust a spoon down my throat to examine it – several times in early child-hood; and also on two occasions when he pulled a tooth.

"From several dreams, especially No. 7 in my article on dreams, I have no doubt that I was in love with him, and that at the age of three years, eight months old, when my younger sister was born, I had the double phantasy that she was the child (a) of the doctor and myself, (2) of myself and my mother."

At this early age, the narrative reads somewhat extravagantly, but the patient reader, once taken through his Freudian paces, may or may not see it otherwise.

At any rate by 1895, at the age of sixteen, Jones became one of sixteen boys from Glamorgan who competed for scholarships offered by the County Council which paid the fees for Llandovery College and an extra £40 a year for other expenses. There he returned from an English world to a Welsh world since most of the boys were recruited from the neighbourhood, but it was a Welsh world dominated by English masters from English public schools who drummed home on too many occasions the inferiority of the Welsh. Despite this Jones' attitude towards the English was somewhat at odds with his mastery of the English language and his reproduction of English behaviour patterns. "The English" he wrote, "are notoriously hard to understand – they really are a peculiar people – and I must be one of the few foreigners who have entered into their arcana." However, few Welsh-men were to become more internationalised than Dr. Ernest Jones.

There is some confusion about the results of his education at Llandovery College. Jones himself tends to smother the record with reminiscence about the masters, most of them inadequate teachers. Only two won his respect, the Reverend McClellan who taught Latin and preached matter of fact sermons, and T. S. Richards who escaped the ridicule cultivated for most masters by preserving an implacable reserve. It became customary for the Housemaster to slip his hand into one or other of the "pretty boys" pockets, a habit which led to his dismissal. He finished his career begging on the streets of a Northern town.[18] One major relaxation which ran far into life figured large in Jones' days at Llandovery. The town adjoined a river and in the bitter – described by Jones as superb – winters of 1893–1895 he skated up and down its surface indulging a romantic dream which came within an ace of realisation. Absorbed in the purple haze of adolescent romanticism, his conception of the ideal experience conjured up a beautiful Viennese maiden who skimmed across the ice in his arms performing a Viennese waltz with such skill that their feet scarcely touched the surface and their identical rhythms perfectly matched the Strauss music which emanated from an enchanted island set in an equally beautiful lake. Realisation of the dream seemed imminent forty years later when Baron Frankenstein gave a musical evening at the Austrian Embassy and Jones was asked to take charge of an "entrancingly beautiful damsel" who revealed an enthusiasm for skating but later disclosed that she could not waltz.

Llandovery was a mixed college and in these advanced circles chaperones were no longer necessary and love affairs commonplace. Jones became involved with a "plump young student" whose looks were "vivid but not beautiful" and who quickly revealed a great fear of pregnancy. Whether he in fact slept with the unnamed girl is in doubt but if his statement that he did not resume coitus until twenty-four was true, then he did not. His involvement was "exceedingly romantic and adoring" but within a year or two they sadly concluded that they were not really made for each other. The college was non-residential, which gave him the wonderfully new freedom of returning to his room at any hour of the night, a freedom made more exciting by its dangers. It was not in fact a single room but a suite of rooms including a sitting room and bedroom, with service, i.e. cooking, all included for six shillings a week, roughly 30p today.

According to the reports made on his work at the time Jones showed little sign of the brilliance which carried him so swiftly through his later academic career. T. G. Davies who wrote a very useful small study which touches on these years said: "It may well be that psychological conflicts which devastated him at the time, and which arose mainly from his religious doubts were partly responsible for this."[19] The whole trend of Jones' early reminiscences anticipated his eventual atheism but – "From ten years of age for seven years he was greatly worried by his uneasiness over religious matters. In the midst of attacks of intense self-criticism and the profound feelings of guilt that followed he would pray regularly, attend church services and would read widely the works of believers and non-believers."[20]

However, at seventeen, he decided that there was only one course of spiritual commitment open to him – atheism. Recollecting his seventeenth

18. Jones: *Free Associations*, 47.
19. *Ernest Jones*, T. G. Davies, 21.
20. Ibid, 21.

year sixty-three years later he claimed that his religious struggles concealed
sexual emotions which may have been retrospective injection of Freudian
doctrine rather than actual truth.

Despite the conflicting evidence and the obvious stress of emerging
adolescence, within six months of entering Llandovery, Ernest had passed
what was then called the Lower Oxford and Cambridge Board Examination,
taking second place to a boy who – uniquely – won eight distinctions. By
now the question of a career was pressing, and Ernest's mathematical skills
automatically qualified him for a place in the sixth form with the aim of
training him for a Cambridge scholarship. "I was only sixteen" he wrote
"and baulked at the idea of hanging about in school for another three
years." Instead he decided to renounce the Headmaster's plans for his future
and train for the London matriculation which would automatically bring
him closer to his real ambition – medical studies.

When he arrived at Cardiff for the examination his immature appearance
provoked a sotto voce remark which he clearly overheard: "My God, I
didn't know they allowed babes-in-arms here." Of course he passed in the
first class. Returning to school he was furious to find that the Headmaster
expected him to re-study and re-pass the Higher Board Examination for a
second time, a device which gave the Head a record of "passes" higher than
any other local school. Refusing to collaborate in what he regarded as a
corrupt practice, Ernest was subjected to a severe dressing down on the ethos
of loyalty to the school, but remained unrepentent.

Two lessons about life emerged from his years at Llandovery, one about
cruelty, the other obscenity. It was part of the accepted fun of school life that
a selected victim should be laid flat on his back while six or seven other boys
squashed themselves flat on top of him. "All would go on breathing except
the victim whose chest was immobilised and whose only hope of escape from
the sense of panic lay in being able to hurt one of the tormentors in a vital part
and thus transform the scene into one of general confusion."[21] Refinements
of this led to boys being ruthlessly upended and their heads immersed in the
none-too-clean lavatory bowls, producing near asphyxiation if not
vomiting. This according to Jones helped prepare him for some of the more
disturbing discoveries about human nature revealed by his later psychological researches and rendered the horrors of the Nazi concentration camps
less inexplicable.

The universality of sexuality and its distortion in obscenity became
apparent to him at school where graffiti and other practices combined to
produce every "perversion", which he found in the course of later studies in
a series of portentous tomes called *Anthropophyteria* by an Austrian anthro-
pologist named Krauss.

There were mild affairs between a number of boys, but no instance of
pederastia came to Ernest's knowledge and "homosexuality apeared to have

21. Many years later the University College of South Wales gave him an honorary Doctorate of
    Science.

no serious vogue . . . . Even mutual masturbation was strongly frowned on."
What he most regretted was learning no Welsh.

His first vacation on leaving Llandovery had to be spent in coaching for a
county maintenance scholarship, a necessary preliminary according to his
father, before he could take up his medical studies. Then, at last, the first
insignia was set on his medical career. He registered at the University College
of South Wales, Cardiff, as a fully fledged medical student. Some conflict
about his career still remained in his mind and for the first six months he
continued to develop his mathematics with the intention of somehow
combining a degree in science and medicine. After six months the strain
became too great and he abandoned science proper to his lifelong regret.[22]

Inevitably the move from Llandovery to University changed his life
intellectually, emotionally and socially. Still a gangling adolescent of sixteen
years, there was yet a certain emotional stability which rapidly developed
and characterised large parts of his life. Where before, at school, he had
sensed the intrinsic inferiority of his teachers, here at University, men like the
Principal, Viriamus Jones actually possessed that ultimate intellectual
distinction an F.R.S., and immediately commanded Jones' respect, with one
qualification. A skilled negotiator, Viriamus Jones could trim his sails to
opposing winds with such ease that the young Jones, full as yet of ultimate
integrity, did not completely trust him. Another teacher who interested
Jones was Professor Parker, a biology teacher who carried the reflected glory
of T. H. Huxley since he was known to have been one of his prize pupils.
Professor Parker's distinguished assistant was also a very shrewd gentleman
who one day remarked of H. G. Wells' *Textbook of Biology* which they used
in class, "His zoology is poor, I know his botany is bad but I am told that he
writes quite passable novels."

It was another member of the staff, Professor Thompson, the Professor
of Chemistry, who broke into Ernest's life with unfortunate consequences.
Playing the part of the Oxford don, Thompson would loll in his professorial
chair, deliver himself of a lecture with grace, fluency and occasional wit and
then become inaccessible to the students until the time for the next lecture
arrived. Between one and the other a tedious German controlled the
laboratory work and their mutually exclusive activities led to a complaint
from the students when they faced one of the more difficult parts of organic
chemistry. "There was a joint conference between the Principal and the
Professor on one side and the students on the other at which some plain
speaking took place." Intolerant of democratic procedures, Professor
Thompson did not suffer criticism gladly and when the students organised
against him a vindictive streak became apparent behind his splendid F.R.S.
Jones was one of the victims. When he failed to supply a medical certificate
to cover two days of absence due to some minor illness the Professor
exploited this to exaggerate Jones' "irregular attendance" as a result of

22. Jones: *Free Associations*, 56.

which his scholarship was temporarily suspended. This upset him for two weeks and led to an unpleasant scene with his father. Remembering Jones senior's sense of duty it is not difficult to imagine the tone in which it was conducted.

Towards the end of the first year's training a new found friend, J. F. Jennings and Ernest decided to take a six weeks' intensive training course in the University Tutorial College in Red Lion Square, London, where H. G. Wells was one of the tutors. Wells had no great faith in the establishment's ability to teach anyone anything and said it was known as a tutorial college for the mutual reassurance of its teachers, but the prospect held out much promise to Ernest.

Inevitably his first taste of the "great metropolis" was exciting and London a very different place in the years 1896/7 from the London he came to know later. Buses and trams were horsedrawn, women wore skirts to the ground, hansom cabs weaved a leisurely way from place to place, the Admiralty Arch and Kingsway had not yet been built and it was a very short walk from Golders Green to the actual countryside. The streets were gas-lit, the sexes in many areas of life segregated, chaperones widespread among the middle classes and sex still regarded by many people in high places as an unfortunate prerequisite of reproduction.

Poverty imposed considerable rigours on Ernest's life. He lodged above the old Carrera's cigarette factory in Mornington Crescent but was forced to walk the several miles to Red Lion Square and back every day because he could not afford the bus fare. More embarrassing, every sortie into the more expensive areas of the West End drove him to avoid entering even an A.B.C. in Regent Street in case he could not pay the bill. On one occasion, risking a long expedition to the Oval, as Ernest held up a solitary penny to pay the conductor he looked at it sarcastically and said "Wouldn't like ter buy the bus would yer?" The boy shrank into himself.

Cockney humour became a familiar lingua franca. "Drunk" a friend said to a policeman about his mate lying prone in the gutter — " 'e ain't drunk, I saw 'is 'and move." Another Cockney, a prostitute, said to a middle class woman holding her skirts above her knees to avoid the mud "Play the game."

The following term Jones entered Cardiff medical school proper and encountered a number of colourful teachers, among them the Professor of Anatomy A. W. Hughes, who drove up to college every day in a dashing four-in-hand. His successor was a red-haired Irishman who could never, to his embarrassment, rid himself of the habit of blushing. Jones invoked an almost scarlet response when in answer to a question he said "the direction of the vagina is upwards and backwards" in place of the more acceptable "forwards and downwards". That a professor of anatomy could raise a blush at such a revision of received wisdom was some measure of the relative prudery still operating in those days even among medical men. On another occasion the women − relatively few − in the mixed group were asked to withdraw while the Professor of Physiology, J. B. Haycroft, gave a short sharp lecture on the taboo subject of masturbation, stressing the dire results of over-indulgence. Jones later commented "It was the only time in the whole of my medical career that I heard a teacher refer to a sexual topic and if they had nothing better to say it was just as well."

Jones found anatomy and physiology heavy going, a grinding process of memorising material facts many of which tended to bore him. It was the brain which fascinated him from the start. How could anyone bother to concentrate on limbs, heart and lungs when the infinite complexity of that essential organ the brain controlled, directed and evalued all the rest. When the students set up the mock trial of a man accused of malpractice Jones automatically became the brain specialist who gave clinical evidence. In a word, neurology already dominated his thinking, but as a result of too much concentration on one organ, in the examination which followed he did not pass in the first class, and this was the only occasion out of five in his university career when he did not do so.

It already seemed to the eager, sparkling intelligence of the still very earnest young student that the central problem of philosophy and therefore of science was the mind-body or mind-matter relationship. Hume's empirical assertion that metaphysical entities like mind and soul should be subjected to the most sceptical scrutiny were already familiar to Jones. Based on a grossly atomic picture of matter which has since been refined out of all recognition, Jones found it hard to regard mental processes as anything but chemical and electrical changes in the neurological structure of the brain. Such subtle sub-divisions of the problem as to whether mind-brain processes were correlative, parallel or identical phenomena, did not trouble his teachers. His own position even at this early age was clear. The joke about "no mind − never matter, no matter, never mind" could only be considered a joke in his view by metaphysicians carried away by their personal need for another dimension in life. For Jones, "no matter never mind" far from being a jest represented the most serious fact of all experience . . . . "Such was the fundamental conviction I won at the age of seventeen and the one to which I have since adhered." He had, in effect, become a confirmed atheistic posivitist "not of course in the popular sense of someone who denies any possible existence of a deity, but of one who sees no good reason for believing in the concept."[23]

His reading at this time inevitably included Huxley's great debates with Mr. Gladstone, Dean Wace and Bishop Wilberforce. The evolutionary explanation of man's development from the amoeba seemed to Jones irrefutable and Huxley's reply to Wilberforce when he said that he would rather have an ape for a grandmother than a man who deliberately trivialised

23. Ibid, 59.

serious scientific debate, delighted him.

In a last gesture of tolerance towards his opponents Jones went one night to a lecture called "Why I Gave up Agnosticism" by a well-known biblical scholar, Dr. Rendall Harris, but it simply confirmed what his friends referred to as his worst prejudices. Invoking the cheapest kind of missionary revivalism, the speaker enveloped his argument in emotional phrases which successfully drowned what little logic they possessed.

Surprisingly, Jones claimed that – his father apart – T. H. Huxley was the only man to influence his mental development. This seemed to eliminate at least half a dozen of his school or university teachers previously acknowledged as his partial mentors in different fields.

There were also – inevitably – many authors besides Huxley who left a deep impression. Kingdon Clifford's essays in ethics, edited by Leslie Stephen, he read and re-read. Ethics and religion led naturally into philosophy and he plunged into Comte, Herbert Spencer and Descartes with an excitement which as his reading developed was steadily dampened. Instead of illumining the nature of man and revealing insights which made the enigma of the universe clearer, the works of these philosophers seemed to Jones dazzling displays of intellectual ingenuity which helped to sustain the inflated reputation of a self perpetuating elite but left very little of substance worth grasping when the verbage had exhausted itself. When this first reaction seemed to him charged – not unexpectedly – with a mistaken hubris he hade another attempt to read Comte and Descartes with greater humility.

Perhaps it was his own intellectual limitations which failed to respond to such profound thinkers and given sufficient application the force of their arguments might reveal the cogency which was self-evident to the majority of philosophic students. All his perseverance proved in vain. Admitting his incapacity for the more extreme demands of abstract thinking, he still found one great philosopher after another disappointing. Passionately rejecting Descartes' parallelism of mind and body, he yet discovered a few passages which he was able to endorse but it seemed to him that there were occasions when the description – self-evident – fitted what some of these authors seemed to regard as highly original. For instance, Descartes' statement that: "The power of the will consists only in this that we so act that we are not conscious of being determined to a particular action by any external force." Later in life Jones became convinced that philosophers, like so many people, converted personal problems which had their source in the unconscious into intellectual problems, turning away from reality in search of substitute gratification. It was all of a piece with applied psycho-analytic doctrine and needs more detailed scrutiny, but for the moment psychology and its complexities played a lesser part in his development.

Current sociology and ethics fared no better in his studies since they lacked a basis in biology and psychology. They could, "for the most part be summed up as merely fumbling attempts to gather together descriptions of facts with little appreciation of their significance."

Sociology has always been martyred by the humanities. Jones was in the vanguard of the attacks but his criticism carried adolescent undertones and his understanding of sociological techniques remained limited. These attitudes were reflected in his lack of moral indignation about the widespread social injustices which he encountered. Indeed a certain insensitivity apparent in these early years, persisted into adult life and was crystallised in his own words: "What concerned me far more than the cruelty of mankind was its apparent irrationality." Only many years afterwards "was [he] able to perceive the relationship between the two." Whether from class conditioning or socio-economic factors, if Jones did not subscribe to the precept that people should know their place in society and keep it, he certainly took social and economic differences very much for granted.

When, in the next few years, socialist thinking began to influence him it was not because it promised a solution to social injustice but because it seemed a more efficient way of running society. In this period he read Comte and Saint-Simon whose plans for reshaping society appealed to him, but Fourier's diatribes against the existing order were less sympathetic. Long hours which should have been concentrated on medical studies were surrendered to the texts of Abbé Mably, Babeuf, Proudhon and Karl Marx leading into a close study of the anarchist Bakunin and a glancing acquaintance with the much more romantic Tolstoy.

A curious contradiction arose from these studies. A man who now complained that he had no faith in any single formula to explain the dissatisfactions of society was later persuaded to accept a single formula to explain the nature of psychological man.

Incursions into political and social literature were given as a reason for getting a second and not a first class in the Intermediate medical examination, but later in life he professed no regret. Widening his horizons was an essential part of formulating a Weltanschaung and "the experiences of those years made me find myself and discover the values that were to guide me through life." It cost him considerable mental strain. Nothing he read was accepted at face value and he was fond of quoting Croce's famous dictum: "A thinker who does not suffer his problem, who does not live his thought is not a thinker: he is a mere elocutionist repeating thoughts that have been thought by others."

Still a raw young man, destitute of any cultural refinement, he did not believe that he had any very great mental endowments with which to realise the ambitions now fermenting in his mind. These ambitions included a desire to reach a position in life where he could influence the lives of his fellow men, a desire dominated by a sense of duty which included becoming a benevolent influence. There was a certain ambivalence in this attitude. What he later referred to as the narcissistic components sustained a second aspect of his ambitions — "that he had it within him to achieve some lofty aim." A third conflicting element was a belief in the essential goodness of humanity and a refusal to accept evil as ineradicable. Painful disillusions were to follow, but the confidence he displayed to a number of friends at the time had one source which permeated his whole personality — resilience. Gradually he began to forge from the ferment of many conflicting sides of his nature a frame of thinking which insisted that all metaphysical conclusions without a biological basis should be subjected to scathing scrutiny. In short he was fast becoming a disciple of scientific methodology.

CHAPTER II

Medical Studies

THE LONDON to which he came to complete his medical studies at University College Hospital in 1898 was superficially the same as the city he had first encountered in 1897 but now he brought a different scrutiny to its teeming diversity. Beneath the surfaces he saw the divisions which had produced Disraeli's description of two nations and was newly aware of a great culture flowering beside inexcusable poverty. It was a city divided between one way of life in the east and another in the west, with big houses and handsome carriages distinguishing the west while ordinary people poured in and out of factories, working sixty hours a week for a pittance, in the east. It remained externally a romantic, gaslit city with fine public buildings, banks and museums, hansom cabs and garish music halls, with drink available at incredibly low prices and thousands of prostitutes openly roaming the West End streets. Property was venerated as a god, thinking in women sometimes regarded as unbalanced and Kipling's message still made London the jewel in the Crown of Empire, the centre of world dominion and commerce.

Leaving Wales for London meant that for the first time since his childhood Ernest had to rely financially on his father without contributing anything himself. He travelled to London with his old friend Jennings and they agreed to share "diggings" which they found in Lansdowne Place, overlooking the old Foundling Hospital in Bloomsbury. His first introduction to London's cosmopolitanism became apparent when he found a German waiter serving at table, and the waiter, looking out on the grounds of the Foundling Hospital where the pre-Territorial volunteers were drilling, remarked in "In Germany drill all day: in England drill after tea." The same waiter revealed the depths to which exploitation of foreigners could go when Jones discovered that he "worked for practically nothing" and slept in what was literally a dark cupboard under the stairs. Chatting to the "poor wretch" Jennings and Jones were taken to task by the landlady because if he learnt English too fast he would promptly leave her and no-one else would tolerate the conditions under which he worked.

Medically Jones seems to have spent more time exploring the facilities and teachers in other London hospitals than he did in University College, his friend Jennings setting the pace because he was studying at the famous St. Bartholomew's Hospital. There at Bart's he met a relic of a fast disappearing age in the person of Mr. Lockwood, a surgeon who still indulged in phrases like "huntin' and shootin' " and frequently threatened his students with the dire fate of becoming "mere doctor men." If anyone could have anticipated anti-Freudian attitudes it was Mr. Lockwood, who frequently delivered himself, in a voice that brooked no contradiction, of phrases like . . . "Patients don't break down – cabs break down."[24] Jones wandered with Jennings from hospital to hospital in search of illuminating lectures and they listened to Virchow, the doyen of pathologists, Hitzig, the man who led the way in cerebral localisation, and of course the great Huxley Memorial Lectures at Charing Cross Hospital.

The ten medical schools in London at that time did not easily interchange staff, and hospital loyalty assumed absurd proportions with Bart's as the oldest claiming first place in the hierarchy. It was one of Jones' new friends who had the audacity to tell a group of Bart's students that their chrono-logical precedence was matched by their outdated methods. A certain amount of smuggling between one hospital and another was regarded as a prerequisite of student pranks and all kinds of undergraduate conspiracies were concocted. Bertie Ward of Barts was another man who became a close friend in Jones' first year and on one occasion he smuggled Ward into the out-patient surgical clinic at University College, disguised in a white coat as a dresser. The intrusion was inspired by the presence of a pretty young actress due that day for a minor operation. Whether the surgeon in charge became equally absorbed by her prettiness, or whether such lesser minions as dressers never achieved much individuality, the surgeon did not appear to notice the stranger and everything went smoothly. "The following Sunday accoutred in silk hats and frock coats we most improperly paid a professional call" on the actress to dress the wound and see that "all was well." They all became friends and Jones learnt many details of a profession which fascinated half the young medical students for reasons far removed from medicine. Un-fortunately the patient herself died not long afterwards but there was no connection between the two events, the cause of death being given as pneumonia.

All his life Jones was very conscious and proud of his Welsh origins and for the next five or six years he kept in touch with the London Welsh and helped to organise an annual Welsh Medical Dinner Society of which he became secretary. Generalising about national characteristics is habitual to most people and on one occasion later in life Lord Horder quoted Burke at Jones – "I do not know the method of indicting a whole nation" to which Jones replied "Genes will out."

Certainly Jones' recognition of very special qualities in the Welsh – "their

24. Ibid, 71.

quickness in personal response, their ready reaction of friendliness and helpfulness'' – did not blind him to certain shortcomings even in these very early and sometimes indiscriminate days. ''The negative quality of the Welsh . . .'' he wrote was the ''remarkable parochial, or even petty nature of their interests.'' In certain spheres he regarded them as displaying ''vividness of imagination'' but as with the Swiss and Dutch he said ''the parochial, limitations quickly re-asserted themselves.''

All the available evidence supports the probability that Jones worked very hard in these early years but there were many relaxations. Pub crawls became a familiar indulgence and frequently ended up in noisy sing-songs. Economy set certain limits to the lighter side of life. Dining out was restricted to once a week and a complete four-course dinner could be eaten under pleasant circumstances at Roche's in Soho for one shilling (5p). Special occasions took them to Pinoli's (price eighteen pence) and on grand occasions they recklessly spent a whole half a crown at the Cafe Marguerite. These were the great days of music hall and musical comedy, ranging from The Geisha Girl and The Belle of New York to Gilbert and Sullivan. Jones took a certain pride in his detailed knowledge of music hall stars and knew the words of many a song sung by Albert Chevalier, Harry Tate, George Robey and Dan Leno. As for Gilbert and Sullivan, he positively patronised those who did not share his appreciation. ''I am merely sorry for, and cannot blame, the present generation that affects to despise such sources of beauty and merriment.''[25] Serious drama from Ibsen to Shaw also played a big part in leisure hours, yielding insights into ''dynamic psychology'' which were later to be assimilated into his life's work.

Immensely energetic, Jones and Ward would rise at six or seven, work through the day until six in the evening, dash off to make a foursome with two girls, eat a somewhat hurried dinner, arrive just as the curtain was rising on the Mikado, escort the girls home in a hansom cab and walk the six miles back to their Bloomsbury lodgings, arriving at two in the morning, ready to rise again at six once more.

On one occasion two gangs of students drawn from Barts and University College combined to occupy the whole gallery of Daly's Theatre for the play The Greek Slave and from the outset it was clear that they were heading for a ''Big occasion.'' Bit players whose parts were small and almost irrelevant met a crescendo of applause which refused to diminish until the bewildered actors had rendered an encore for the first time in their lives, and stars were received in scornful silence. Afterwards Ward and Jones swarmed up some pipes to the famous Green Room where a group of startled but unembarrassed actresses provided the gallants with pairs of tights. Back in the street they found the main body of students storming the Cafe de Paris and as they tried to join them a cry went up from the police ''Let's get their leaders!'' Jones found himself being frog marched towards Vine Street police station and a

25. Ibid, 76.

rescue attempt proved useless. One hour later an old school friend, Forsdike, arrived at Vine Street pleading that they must release "the little fellow" because his health was "very delicate." "Yes, bloody delicate" the police sergeant said. "It took three of us to hold him."

Escapades of this kind seldom interrupted a full day's hospital work from nine until six, followed by nine hours of intensive study. Curiously, Jones read the older classics of French medicine by men like Trousseau, Brouardel and Charcot in preference to the English textbooks, but Charcot carried none of the special significance then which was later to link Jones and Freud and the whole psycho-analytic movement.

Temperamentally Jones preferred medicine to surgery and sometimes, when "dressing" in the wards he would slip away to witness a particularly exciting medical demonstration in his favourite department – neurology. Freud, of course, was a considerable neurologist and those who believe in forces which the adult Jones abhorred may see the hand of fate deliberately guiding him in an inevitable direction. So strong did his neurological interests become that he managed to win a clinical assistantship at that ultimate citadel of neurological medicine the National Hospital in Queen's Square, a remarkable feat for a relatively raw young student.

Midwifery was learnt under dramatic circumstances which have long ago either vanished or changed out of all recognition. The student-doctor responded to a buzzer beside his bed and sallied out into the slums of London at all hours of the day and night to visit overcrowded rooms, basements and semi-basements where the birth was sometimes the central drama of a family group forced into the role of spectators by sheer lack of space. Sometimes the elder children would be peering with awed eyes at their naked mother in agony, dirt and blood, while between her groans she would vainly command them to avert their gaze and the lodger would from time to time interpose her person. Occasionally the only person available to act as a midwife and procure hot water would be a child of ten or twelve.[26] There were other occasions when the mother to be had nothing more than a bag of straw for a bed and the single room in which she and two children lived was entirely unheated. "Then the 'doctor' would have to turn to, buy wood and coal, light a fire and boil a kettle before proceeding to his professional duties!" When midwives were available, they caricatured the eighteenth century stereotype of a squalid shabby creature who sat by an open fire literally crooning or smoking a long pipe. Acid comment frequently broke into the crooning: "You've 'ad the sweets – now you must 'ave the bitters – it's no use complaining."

On one occasion a mother to be called out "Oh doctor, is it a black 'un" giving some indication of indiscriminate promiscuity. Predicting the sex of the child was sometimes thought to be part of the magic box of tricks which the doctor could invoke to divert his patient. Jones refused to descend to the

26. Ibid, 91.

stratagem of one colleague whereby he would announce that the baby was a boy but write "girl" on a slip of paper, and when the time came, if his prediction proved wrong he simply produced the forged document as evidence of the bad memory of the mother.

Three months before he qualified Jones began a year's clerking with Dr. C. E. Beevor, a man whose clinical mastery of the behaviour of nerves and muscles was remarkable. Jones witnessed his power to demonstrate a precise picture of the whole musculature by asking a patient to twist a limb into impossible positions and found it fascinating.

Nineteen months after entering the hospital he had no difficulty in passing all the qualifying examinations and — as he put it — "there he was at the age of 21 with the field of medicine open before him."

Jones considered himself more than fortunate to belong to University College whose history was thick on the ground with Fellows of The Royal Society. Dr. Sidney Ringer, the senior physician, was a man of many parts whose work on the potassium and sodium salts of the blood won him an F.R.S. in the eighties. Ringer still used the old wooden stethoscope and regarded it as superior to the new-fangled binaural types then coming into use because it gave "purer results." In his hands it certainly became a subtle diagnostic instrument and since he had acquired his skill from a man called Walsh, once a great heart specialist who in turn had once studied under none other than Laennec, the man who invented the instrument, there existed something equivalent to a line of apostolic succession. One phrase from Ringer remained in Ernest's memory all his life: "You young men like to be right; we old men don't like to be wrong." It was Ringer who convinced Jones that he had a special flair for clinical work and he now decided to concentrate on that aspect of medicine.

A break occurred in 1899 when his disciplinarian father actually conceded that his son might be working too hard and decided to take him abroad for a holiday. In fact his father had a double motive. Still hard at work, he wanted to buy for his company an iron ore concession in Portugal and they travelled together — *train de luxe* — from Paris to Lisbon, with brief glimpses of ancient cities like Salamanca en route. Ernest's relationship with his father had now entered a new phase. Jones senior still tended to treat him like a young son who needed to be tutored about cultural monuments and wordly wisdom and this quickly led to strained relations during the tour which followed. The strain mounted to the point where they constantly irritated one another, and suddenly one day Ernest rebuked his father for refusing to open the window in a small bedroom which they were sharing. Heated words were followed by a cold silence. It had at last dawned on Jones senior that Ernest was now a fully grown up, fast maturing young man in his own right, but his attempt to adjust psychologically to his new relationship — temporarily — failed. The following day he decided to "go straight home on his own," whether in a state of anger or as a "wise and generous gesture" is not clear.

A dramatic episode preceded that break, which may or may not have been closely connected. Years later, discussing the relationship between Havelock Ellis and his father with me, Jones remarked "I broke away from my own father in peculiar circumstances. We were away on holiday together during my student days. . . ."

The precise words he used after that preliminary I cannot recall but he proceeded to tell me of an episode which is repeated in *Free Associations* with different implications. They had spent a morning together surveying the ground from which the iron ore would eventually be extracted and in the afternoon Ernest wandered away from his father. Some time later, seeing a derelict castle in the distance he determined to make a detour and investigate it. Ten minutes later, climbing one of the towers, he was lolling, relaxed in the sunshine, glad to be free of humanity and especially business men in the guise of his father, when suddenly his "gaze encountered one of the most hideous apparitions [he had] ever seen."[27] The description which followed seemed deliberately exaggerated as if it carried undertones of something beyond the reality it described. "Below me was a huge creature, naked to the waist, whose dark swarthiness, hairiness and repulsive features made him look more like a gorilla than I thought a human being could. . . . His face was distorted with rage and I soon perceived that he was uttering menacing cries . . . which were reinforced by the waving of his club and the baying of his savage hound." This was, in fact, a man guarding the local territory. In *Free Associations* the story is told without any reference to his own father but when Jones spoke to me many years later he remarked "that apparition came back to me in my dreams and on one occasion I remember it had a distinct resemblance to my father."[28]

The real situation was resolved when Jones "somehow managed to convey to [the monster] that [his] intentions were not maleficient and his gutteral speech gradually subsided to a growl."

Whether the mature Jones, steeped by then in psycho-analytic doctrine, wanted – retrospectively – to demonstrate the oedipal complex at work in his relations with his father or whether he did, on occasion, actually regard his father in that light is unclear, but certainly the break with his father either closely followed or preceded the episode so vividly recalled.

Back once more from the holiday to the turmoil of London he plunged precipitately into the remainder of his medical studies with renewed zest and in January of the following year attained his majority. Six months later he took his medical degree and qualified to become a house physician.

27. Ibid, 93.
28. Interview, Ernest Jones, July 26, 1953.

CHAPTER III

Success and Failure

IN RECOLLECTION Ernest Jones saw the next three years as a period of glittering success which reinforced a certain "spoilt" quality in his nature, originally derived, he believed, from his mother's untiring devotion. No sooner had he planned a new step forward in his career than it was realised and the tangled jungle of medical ambition yielded to his "insistence on getting his own way" in a manner which generated respect and envy among his colleagues. His bounding confidence reached a pitch where he was impatient of failure among fellow students and assumed with the hubris of the young that given sufficient drive these casualties could have shaped their ends very differently.

Some aspects of these traits in his character were to persist all his life and to lead eventually into recrimination within the psycho-analytic movement, but for the moment he did not pause to consider the consequences of the single-minded drive which he was determined would convert him into "an ornament of the profession." All unaware that the fate which he had bent to his will was waiting, a few months away, to have its revenge, he plunged into the role of resident House Physician and in the beginning several fortunate features connived to develop his success. Images like Fate were so alien to Jones' thinking that he would have regarded such a description as offensively inaccurate. It was not some mysterious element called Fate deriving from another dimension, but rationally based accident and luck which were presently to play havoc with all his glittering success. For the moment luck became his pliant mistress.

In charge of the wards at University College in 1900 was a Dr. Rose Bradford who regarded Jones as a promising doctor with a high potential and when his house physician fell ill it was almost as if Jones had himself manipulated the situation. He knew that if he volunteered for the vacancy his chances were good and within a week he was duly appointed with certain reservations. Still not qualified, it was arranged that the Resident Medical Officer should sign death certificates or prescribe dangerous drugs for Jones, while he trod the wards coping with everyday routine and, within limits, emergencies. Recalling Ernest Jones as his first house physician, Bradford said some years later "I don't expect ever to have such a good one." Signs of three characteristics – devotion to duty, a conviction that he was right and a degree of tactlessness – now became evident according to the record left by some of his colleagues. Undoubtedly he kept the ward routines running smoothly and provided Bradford with very suitable patients for teaching purposes but he tended to exhaust the staff with his demands and was so absorbed in "the necessity for efficiency" that he seemed insufficiently sensitive to their protests. It took him a long time to realise that what he described as his "passion for the highest standards" of work was steadily building up resistance and unpopularity. By the time he came to write *Free Associations* he had sufficiently seen through himself to quality the words out of all recognition. "I should not cavil if someone couched it in harsher terms – using such words as opinionated, tactless, conceited or inconsiderate. At the time I was blissfully unaware of this growing danger and sailed ahead on my path with gusto and enjoyment."

It was to be a persistent paradox in Jones' life, as in the lives of so many others, that from time to time he turned and scrutinised himself with devastating honesty only to continue to give full play to the traits in his character which he condemned.

In the early years of the century the duties of a house physician were multiple and exhausting. There were no separate pathologists, medical registrars or casualty officers and the house physician somehow incorporated these activities into the daily routine of walking the wards. At the end of a preposterously long day he gave an hour's teaching to his four or five "clerk students," followed by two hours study for higher examinations and another round of the wards at midnight. There being no pathologists it was the house physician's duty to carry out post mortems and these yielded the material for Jones' first incursion into medical research. He came upon an unusual calcification of the pericardium and the Resident Medical Officer, Dr. Charles Bolton, "a capable and lovable man," suggested that he should swot up the literature and demonstrate his conclusions in a paper to be read before the Pathological Society of London. Illustrating his life long capacity to overwork without apparent strain Jones complicated his already heavy duties by writing and delivering the paper which "proved to be the first of my contributions that text books thought it worthwhile to incorporate."

Also in 1901 he made a tiny contribution to neurological knowledge with a case of hemiplegia where he found reproduced symptoms which corresponded to those discovered by Beevor and Horsley in their clinical experiments. They had detected a small spot in the frontal lobe which, when stimulated, produced a twisting movement in the tongue. Identical "tongue twisting" troubled Jones' hemiplegic patient. He recorded his results in *The Lancet*.[29]

Neurology now dominated all his other interests and he was quite undeterred by the general lack of results in treatment of diseases of the

29. *Lancet*, September 1901.

nervous system. Already he held the view that no satisfactory solution to human social and economic problems could be found unless it incorporated and satisfactorily deployed man's biological nature, and the cortex was the very core of that nature. For a while he believed that the ancient mind-brain problem would best be illuminated by a profound study of speech and language, "the only mental function where some counterpart can be localised in the cortex." In a sense this anticipated one aspect of modern linguistic research and was a very interesting shot in the dark. Ironically, despite all his success the only official position he ever achieved in the University of London was his later membership of the Board of Studies for Comparative Philosophy.

A permanent appointment on the hospital staff usually traced its ancestry through the Resident Medical Officer but since that gentleman had to supervise the hospital as a whole he needed wider knowledge than one resident post yielded. Jones decided that the next citadel he must assail was the heavily competitive House Surgeonship and especially that under the great Sir Victor Horsley. There were three other highly promising candidates and to the astonishment of the staff − an astonishment not shared by Jones − he was selected.

His appointment brought him into touch with Wilfred Trotter who was Surgical Registrar to Horsley and a man frequently left to tackle even the most extravagant operations without supervision. Trotter became, next to Freud, the second most important man in his life.

They now worked together − sometimes dramatically − as when a patient with both legs crushed led to a double amputation, with Trotter sawing through one leg while Jones simultaneously removed the other. The patient recovered but Jones anticipated a combined physical and psychological trauma when the patient awoke, the end result of which he hesitated to predict. We do not in fact know what happened to the man.

Seven years older than Jones, Trotter had been working as a student for higher surgical examinations when they first met in the late 1890s, but Jones only came to know him well in 1900. Trotter was, by that time, an "extreme and even bloodthirsty revolutionary" who wanted to sweep away the degenerate society in which they lived and entirely recast its economic, emotional, spiritual and medical organisation.

According to Jones, Trotter was a paragon in so many fields that his name should have become a household word in the history of England. He excelled in the "philosophic calm, with which he apprehended experience, however arresting," he was supreme in "sobriety of judgment," he had a "penetrating understanding of human nature," his grasp of the "scientific attitude and its significance for mankind" was profound; the sweep of English literature he encompassed with ease; stylistically his discrimination was subtle and he brought to bear in these fields an all embracing scepticism in which Jones at that stage regarded himself as somewhat deficient.

Mr. Allsop James who knew him much later in life reported to me that "he may when younger have combined all those talents but he must if he did, have also, been a priggish bore. When I knew him I regarded him as a reasonably talented surgeon and by then his encyclopaedic knowledge certainly failed him on many an occasion. As for English literature – which I teach – he had no more than an average acquaintance with it. If he knew somewhat more of the scientific method than I did that's not saying much."[30]

Jones proudly reproduces examples of Trotter's wit in *Free Associations* but few of them stand up to comparative evaluation. Undoubtedly a very humane and highly sensitive man, when confronted with a young boy who had died a gruesome death from carcinoma of the thigh he remarked: "If I ever get to heaven I should like to ask the Principal Person there what he has to say about this." A born iconoclast, he delighted to humble the high and mighty. Mr. Balfour became "that precious nincompoop" and H. G. Wells "a sensible little chap." One of his best witticisms he found it necessary to spell out to his audience. "Genius consists in an infinite capacity for enduring pain and inflicting it," he would say and add: "You will observe the sting of the remark is in its tail." Another effective sally occurred during an operation: "Mr. Anaesthetist, if the patient can keep awake, surely you can."

Jones was still working with Trotter as House Surgeon when he took the examination for a Batchelorship of Medicine, but he seemed to find no difficulty in keeping fully up to date in both fields. Following the pass papers, he took the honours ones and in medicine he won second place with a gold medal and came first in obstetric medicine with a university scholarship and gold medal. A certain sense of inevitability accompanied Jones' success in his own eyes and later, talking to Money-Kyrle he remarked: "My success seemed to me a foregone conclusion but as with many people the sweet smell of success became too intoxicating."[31] His greatest pleasure came in the reflected glow from his parents who were delighted that their clever son had unmistakeably and beyond any question "made it" with distinction. For the first time in years his father's reserve cracked as he struggled to express his appreciation.

Many people in the psycho-analytic movement regard Jones as a man quite incapable of self criticism but any careful reading of *Free Associations* shows that at the age of seventy-nine self scrutiny was sometimes severe. Of his success in all these examinations he wrote: "Presumably [they] catered to my omnipotence complex which was beginning to be stronger than was good for me."[32]

There followed this interesting and revealing passage. "Coming as it did after my earlier years of burning self criticism, with its sense of guilt in the spheres of religion and sex, it necessarily put a considerable strain on my

30. Interview, September 10, 1977.
31. Interview, Money–Kyrle, October 9, 1972.
32. Jones: *Free Associations,* 105.

mental balance and harmony by inducing a swing in the opposite direction.''

So far as I can trace there is little if any written evidence of sexuality between the years seven and twenty-four. It is a curious omission for a Freudian. The gap becomes more surprising because these years are so crucial in sexual development that expectations of a revealing account are high. No mention of struggles with his conscience; no account of sexual stirrings; only one recorded encounter with young women and that without sexual detail; and complete silence about a habit he later granted universality – masturbation. All we read is ''a sense of guilt in the spheres of religion and sex.'' The one young woman mentioned is dismissed as a seaside affair but it appears to have been more important than he suggests and he did in fact become engaged to her for a time.

Two new appointments now changed his way of life once more, one at Brompton Chest Hospital and another at the North Eastern Hospital for Children in Bethnal Green. It was at the Children's Hospital that the reversal of his long and glittering success really began, with a relatively trivial affair of a differential diagnosis. The physician in charge of a puzzling child patient whose condition deteriorated dangerously over a number of days, had firmly decided on his own diagnosis. From the child's general condition and a blood analysis Jones counter-diagnosed an abcess in the chest but the visiting physician insisted that ''it was a solid lung condition''. One Saturday morning at the beginning of the weekend, the abcess burst and the child began coughing up blood and pus. Since almost three days would elapse before the visiting physician again saw the child Jones had no choice but to operate at once to save the child's life. On the following Tuesday the physician made it clear that he suspected the whole procedure, resented Jones' ''interference'' and considered the operation premature. The records – not now available – must have shown the burst abcess but the physician behaved as if Jones had invented the emergency to justify his own diagnosis. Apart from his consultative capacity at the hospital the physician was a highly placed member of the National Hospital staff, a Mecca towards which Jones continuously aspired, and important consequences followed.

To compound his diagnostic felony, some months later Jones learnt that his erstwhile fiancee – the result of the seaside affair – was undergoing an emergency operation for appendicitis. Still emotionally involved with her, he suddenly wanted to see and reassure her, but she lived six hours away from London and it needed the imprimatur of a full hospital committee to permit a resident houseman to spend a night outside the hospital.

One of what were later to become Jones' famous flashes of ''omni-potence'' came to his aid and he swiftly converted the whole committee into the Senior Surgeon. The sheer impracticability of summoning the committee to meet such an emergency seemed to undermine the purpose it sought to serve but the senior surgeon was vague: perhaps it would be all right if Jones returned on the Monday morning. Carefully briefing the two remaining Residents, Jones summoned a taxi and departed.

When he duly returned on the following Monday he knew at once that trouble was brewing in the formidable person of the Matron, a woman whose long continuity of service enabled her to over-rule some of the decisions made by passing Resident doctors. It was a common complaint amongst Residents in those days, that these "splendidly arrayed creatures would come sailing into the wards and simply countermand instructions and even prescriptions given by the doctors." This particular woman would have delighted some modern feminists, since she not merely carried an air of natural authority but had a physical presence capable of intimidating anyone who dared to question that authority. Unfortunately she did not intimidate the relatively diminutive Jones. Here the story diverges. According to Jones – extraordinarily on such a small issue – the Matron was able to railroad the committee into asking Jones to resign. The hospital minutes reveal a different story.[33] In fact, on two other occasions a similar situation had arisen, and Jones had been forced to apologise for absenting himself from duty without permission. Now he wrote a letter to the Secretary asking them to reconsider his "enforced" resignation, but it was of no avail. The Matron argued her case with such power and authority – and Jones believed distortion – that he had to resign. His omnipotence had revealed serious shortcomings. Wilfred Trotter commented: "to a hospital committee it is the unessential that matters." Jones himself rode the episode with a light heart at the time. Convinced that he was the victim of a conspiracy between a tyrannical matron and a bureaucratic committee, Jones failed to see that his ambitions had for the first time received a check which might become serious. As, later in life, he easily rationalised the underlying fact that he had taken matters into his own hands and broken the rules with a senior surgeon as a lame alibi, but his devotion to the mysterious and un-named fiancee must have been considerable.

In reaction to the resignation he plunged fiercely into intensive study for the next M.D. examination, which combined in those days medicine and psychological medicine. Unaware at this stage that psychological medicine would become the dominant motif of his later career, he none-the-less came first in the examination with, as he interestingly put it – "a heavy gold medal then worth £20 and since much more." By the following month he had also taken his M.R.C.P. and thus reached the rank – if not the practice – of a consulting physician.

33. Hospital minutes.

CHAPTER IV

His Relationship with Maude Hill

WITH ALL THESE achievements and distinctions behind him, Jones was still only a mere twenty-five in 1904 and the first encounter with failure at the North Eastern Hospital for Children had not disturbed his bubbling self-confidence. Since it concerned hospital regulations rather than medical qualifications his abounding resilience quickly absorbed his enforced resignation and he now approached a major new step without any qualms. It was necessary to spend two years as a House Physician in the exclusive atmosphere of the National Hospital before returning to U.C.H. and the appointment not only seemed easily within his grasp but a foregone conclusion. He possessed the best academic qualifications, he had already had wide clinical experience in no less than five residential jobs, and he had actually served for two years in the National Hospital as a clinical assistant, thus declaring a special interest in neurology. Since Beevor and Horsley, his old chiefs, were already on the National Hospital staff Jones received an effusive welcome at the preliminary interviews and sailed through the clinical scrutiny with a relaxed, almost superior, ease. So sure was he of getting the appointment that interview nerves, which had troubled him once or twice before, evaporated and he responded to the closest interrogation with complete sang-froid.

The blow when it came was in proportion to his expectations. Someone else had been selected. It seemed even more incredible when he learnt the identity of the rival candidate, a man who, according to Jones, "possessed none of my qualifications." Indignation produced this obvious exaggeration. The candidate did in fact have some of his qualifications but taken as a whole Jones stood out pre-eminently as the man for the job. He literally staggered out into the sunshine of a perfect summer's day in Queen Square, his mind too numbed to try even to consider the origins of what seemed to him a major disaster which put his whole career in jeopardy.

Unravelling the facts behind a smoke screen of evasion and rumours, some days later he at last pinpointed the villain of the piece – none other than the doctor at the Children's Hospital whose wrong diagnosis he had so dramatically unmasked. Jones discovered that this doctor from the

Children's Hospital had given evidence to the selection board that in his experience Jones was a very difficult man to work with and claimed that the committee of his hospital had been forced to "send him away as an impossible person." Equally significant, it was the same man's nephew who had been given the job.

Now the interesting point about the evidence brought against him is Jones' comment when the episode was recollected in tranquility: "There was no doubt a modicum of truth in [the doctor's] account."[34]

Throughout the remainder of the narrative the reader will encounter other witnesses who claim that Jones was a difficult man to work with, but such words come easily to the lips of all those people whose prejudices are met and sometimes defeated by prejudices no less intransigeant. It is frequently difficult to disentangle the truth from the psycho-dynamics of group behaviour. Certainly for considerable stretches of his life Jones was to be engrossed – almost professionally – in prolonged and sometimes acrimonious debates which occasionally could not escape the charge of quarrelling.

Once again it is most important to remember that Jones in recollection subjected the episode and his own character to frank – if not savagely frank – psycho-analytic examination. Steeped as he was in psycho-analytic sophistication when he came to write *Free Associations* at the age of seventy-nine, he clearly saw that the roots of what he referred to as "my excessive reaction" were easily traceable to his life history. It is equally important, initially, to notice that an element of deliberately eating humble pie crept into his words. In fact his reaction to the lost job was not in the circumstances excessive; it might have overtaken the most "normal" human being. There is a psychological device – well known to analysts – whereby sackcloth and ashes are deliberately invoked to produce the impression of impartiality in order to mask a subject's belief in his own omnipotence. The theory is too complicated to analyse here but will be developed later.

Jones' case against himself began with his premature weaning when his mother was forced to subject him to the mercies of milk substitutes which produced serious malnutrition and ill health. The early insecurity which this bred was reinforced, he claimed, by "internal factors" which unfortunately he does not spell out. These could have been the product of his uneasy relationship with his father, his attempts at school to compensate for his size and the conflicts which inevitably emerge in climbing from one social class to another. A sense of inferiority might demand compensatory action which would be greater in proportion to his immense energy, life force, libido – call it what you will. When he was a small boy his mother asked him which of many qualities were top of his priorities. She hoped for the response – spiritual – but he uttered one word – energy.

In practical terms, three years of soaring success were suddenly brought

34. Jones: *Free Associations*, 115.

down to earth in a collapse which changed his whole attitude. He had discovered that neither the medical universe nor the events of everyday life were malleable to his will, and he later wrote: "However strongly one might wish for, deserve and expect a particular issue there was not the slightest guarantee that it would therefore come about."

Resident jobs yielded a small salary and accommodation with the result that, thrown on his own resources, he was now penniless if not homeless. As if to reassure himself he seems to have plunged into a series of part-time jobs and courses of study remarkable in their multiplicity. A quarter-time appointment with the Education Department of the London County Council was combined with a course in public health, a clinical assistantship at the Hospital for Sick Children and a similar job at Moorfields Eye Hospital. Within a short time he also launched at least two research projects and the results of one — to determine the relative frequency of various features accompanying a stroke — were once again incorporated in some medical text books. Already familiar with the statistical theory of probability, he was surprised to find how frequently medical papers ignored it, and now he gave a more sophisticated analysis of innumerable hemiplegic cases. As if all this were not enough he presently embarked on yet another undertaking which involved giving tutorial classes for a University Correspondence College which coached students for medical examinations by correspondence. In reaction against his dismissal he dispersed his retaliation over so many fields that no one could doubt his ability to tackle and master every branch of medical activity, but there remained in these activities a feverish quality as if he had to show himself that he was still an undefeated medical polymath.

According to *Free Associations*, he at last broke a prolonged chastity and experienced sex again in 1904, one year after all these events. The Freudian principle of sublimation would need application in its most extreme form to redirect his libido, over such diverse and totally exhausting fields.

There is no explicit evidence about the sexual side of his relationship with a woman called Maude Hill who seems to have come into his life between 1902 and 1903 and the dating has some ambiguity, but prolonged sexual abstinence certainly broke in one of the three years 1902 to 1904. Maude Hill, the daughter of the well-known Birmingham Hill family was "years older than myself" a phrase implying anything up to ten years with its easily divined psychological significance. A woman who placed security high on her list of marital priorities, she seems to have urged him from the outset to equip himself with a reliable practice in the country where they could settle down together. Such comfortable ideas were anathema to the mercurial Jones and her constant drive towards conventional satisfactions first made him question the desirability of his relationship with her. However, somewhere between the years 1902 and 1904 they became engaged.

The affair drifted on for a whole year becoming steadily more unsatis-factory until one day Jones discovered that in her eagerness to marry him she had actually called on one of his old medical chiefs, Dr. Bradford, explained their uncertain financial position and pleaded with him to give Ernest a hospital appointment. Jones hastily apologised to Dr. Bradford for what he called "unwelcomed petticoat influence" and his relations with Maude became even more strained. Shortly afterwards they parted company.

It was at this time that the first seeds were sown which were slowly to re-direct Jones' interests from neurology to psychopathology and later psycho-analysis. In fact the interval between his early interest in psychiatry and his first meeting with Freud was only four years. Direct contact with psychological medicine began when he went one day in 1902 to visit his friend Ward who had become a resident physician at an asylum outside London. Fascinated by two of the cases he saw on that first occasion, he decided to repeat the visit and soon it became a regular Sunday expedition. In the overwhelming tide of his activities even Sunday it seemed was not a day of rest. Through Ward, Jones came to know a number of other psychiatrists like Bernard Hart at the famous Long Grove adolescent unit, and Stoddart at Bart's Hospital in London. Psychiatry was then in a very primitive state with very little if any research in progress and a kind of theoretical paralysis remained impermeable to fresh ideas which were developing in Europe. A psychologist friend asked Jones one day whether alienists – as they were then called – "read papers on improved varieties of Chubb locks" and claimed that the satirical content of his question was not high. On another occasion a superintendent asked Jones on the telephone one day whether he knew anyone who could fill a vacancy at his asylum with the rider "I don't expect him to be interested in insanity but he must be able to play cricket with the patients." Contact with the staff of what were to become known as mental hospitals next led Jones into an intensive course of reading which included the French literature on hysteria, double personality and hypno-tism. He read such diverse authors as Binet, Durand de Gros, Mesmer, Schrenck-Notzing, Azam and Baréty. Thinking about hysteria in those days was elementary enough to trace its origin to "a wandering of the womb" and hence the received wisdom said that you must treat it with valerian, the odour of which was obnoxious to the womb. Jones claims that even at this very early stage of his career "something in me rebelled against these materialistic views and inclined me strongly towards a psychological explanation. It was an inner flair perhaps sympathy with suffering but strongly supported by what I was learning from my reading."

If there was no systematic research work to be found on insanity, at least some elementary attempts were made to investigate and relate symptoms to causes. Psychopathology was exclusively the prerogative of organic neuro-logists whose knowledge of "nerves" clearly qualified them as specialists in dealing with neurotic conditions generalised under that label. It was acknowledged that the nervous system contained more phosphorus than other organs and getting the phosphorus balance right became an accepted treatment in combination with prolonged holidays or change of scene. Basically the pathology of such conditions as obsessional neurosis was said to be a disorder of the cerebral cortex, a disorder given no specific definition and unresponsive to all but drugs and surgery. One patient who came to Jones at this time suffering from severe depressional neurosis had first been sent on a trip to the West Indies and when that failed on another trip to the East Indies. Finally an increased dose of the same medicine was clearly thought by a most distinguished neurologist to be an infallible last resort and a trip round the world ended with his obsessions undiminished. Later in life Jones was reminded of Noel Coward's story. "I was in the grip of a colossal neurosis and my doctor packed me off to the Bahamas to get rid of it. My neurosis followed on the next boat."

Conversion hysterias, paralyses and hysterical transference were, surprisingly, more common in those days than after the first World War and Jones frequently encountered cases in hospital. When a girl one day was overtaken with hysterical convulsions the all-wise Trotter once more came up with what Jones regarded as the appropriate remark: "One sees the blood trickling under the door but we know nothing of what tragedy is being enacted within." The image seemed somewhat extravagant beside the actual event, but it gave Jones pause to think and he deepened his reading in, for some reason, almost exclusively French psychopathological literature. Whether he read at this time the accounts of multiple personality given by Morton Prince and William James remains unclear.

CHAPTER V

His Affair with Loe Kann

ONE DAY towards the end of 1904 Trotter suggested to Jones that they should burn their traditional boats, abandon all compromise and audaciously appoint themselves members of the medical elite inhabiting Harley Street. There was nothing to stop any brand of charlatan from practising consultancy behind highly polished brass plates which to the unitiated converted ordinary doctors into medical gods. Consultants who held staff appointments in well-known hospitals were reckoned to be highly reputable – an evaluation open to sceptical qualification – but doctors without such distinctions were regarded as outsiders. Trotter at thirty-two was mature enough to play the consultant role but for Jones, still a mere stripling of twenty-five, with no immediate prospects whatever, it was the ultimate audacity. The whole scheme depended upon the purchase of the lease of No. 10 Harley Street and finally it was Jones' father who generously came forward with the money in 1905 which launched their experiment.

The move to Harley Street not only broke up Jones' relationship with Maude Hill: it led into a labyrinth of problems. Scaling the highest medical peaks without a penny to support him, seemed to Maude Hill's petit bourgeois values reckless, but intellectual as well as financial reasons led to the break. The evidence is thin but it seems most likely that Jones got bored with her suburban thinking, and turned in relief to practical problems. Although his father waived the payment of any rent for the Harley Street house there were rates and taxes to be met and the combined domestic inadequacy of Jones and Trotter produced chaos. Whereupon Jones' sister Elizabeth, a mere slip of a twenty-four-year-old girl, took over and did her best to cope with the semi-bohemian habits of her two "tenants." Ironically Trotter and Elizabeth exchanged very little conversation over these years and communication between them seemed to her brother limited but something must have drawn them together because in the end the unexpected happened.

For the moment the two young doctors struggled to fight their way into the rich preserve of patients waiting on the edge of the great mass of poor patients in a city as large and ruthless as London. *Free Associations* becomes confused at this point glossing over exactly what took place. Attempts to check with what few records remain are equally frustrating. The most optimistic estimate occurs in this sentence in Jones' autobiographical fragment: "It was useless to expect much consulting practice at my age though in fact there was more of it than I had thought likely."[35] Whatever the precise facts, Jones quickly set about finding alternative sources of income "in justification of [his] new pretensions" and it led him into a jungle of drudgery and humiliation which he never forgot. So persistent and scattered were his attempts to diversify his income that the time remaining for private patients must have been minimal. First he applied for a vacancy at Charing Cross Hospital only to see it given to a Dr. David Forsyth, a man who had come second to Jones in the M.D. examinations. Next he assailed the West End Hospital for Nervous Diseases, only to find himself in competition with a very senior neurologist of the highest standing. As his applications multiplied the quality of the jobs involved declined. A vicious circle developed. The more rejections he received the more he became known as an applicant who "in some way was undesirable."

After six months a success, which by its nature indicated failure, saw him accepted on the staff of a curious organisation midway between hospital and private practice called the Farringdon Dispensary. Professionally it was better not to mention any direct connection with such a dubious hybrid and Jones continued his search for something worthy of his talents. At the end of the year he was at last appointed assistant physician to the Dreadnought Seamen's Hospital at Greenwich, which for the first time brought him into close contact with tropical medicine in all its fascinating differences.

There followed once again a foray into such a multiplicity of activities as would dismay the average G.P. struggling to develop nothing more than his single practice. Recital of all the roles Jones played in every kind of medical and educational capacity becomes boring by its very complexity. Suffice it to say that it even included that worst of all money-making chores – giving evening lectures for the London County Council, and sometimes involved extensive coaching of medical examinees. Among these one day he met a man who was to change the course of his personal life. M. D. Eder had developed a small and somewhat odd practice in Soho among its largely foreign community and might have seemed a medically dubious entity to the more correct members of the profession. Jones quickly discovered that he was a man "of exceptional parts" but these parts never sufficiently cohered to carry him past the oral examinations which were a necessary corollary of his written work. Some perverse streak in his otherwise competent nature always produced the worst possible impressions when Eder faced an examining board.

These were the days when Jones – surprisingly to those who knew him later – had some commitment to socialism inherited from Trotter's revolutionary vision of a new world where he, Trotter, became its Saviour. Among

35. Ibid.

other qualities in Eder which appealed to Jones, was a devotion to a brand of socialism not far removed from his own, and it was Eder who introduced him to the Fabian Society where he met H. G. Wells, Bernard Shaw and Sidney Webb. A temporary diversion, almost an aberration from his normal thinking, Jones' socialism was far removed from Marxist revolution. As he later wrote: "the complex interrelationships of human society were such that no political or social revolution ever brought about the results expected by the agents of it."

It was the day that Eder casually introduced Jones to a young Dutch Jewish lady called Loe Kann which opened up a dimension of his life until then sacrificed almost entirely to professional aims. Before Loe appeared Trotter and Jones spent many evenings eating dinner together at Frascati's, walking in Hyde Park and talking "fast and furiously" about "everything under the sun" with special reference to the new world they – and particularly Trotter – were committed to creating. Since lack of patients made their splendid Harley Street consulting rooms relatively empty shells they shared a large study in which they had placed an enormous desk capable of accommodating both parties and their multitudinous literary projects. "There" he wrote "we did our work in the intervals of making plans for the world . . . but mostly we talked and talked."[36]

Loe Kann broke into this partnership and destroyed its exclusive nature with the result that Trotter found himself forced to accept new limitations which did not please him. According to Jones, Loe Kann's upbringing had been difficult and had converted her into a person capable of an adolescent defiance which persisted into adult life. Jones treasured a photograph of her as a young girl in which she stood with one foot triumphantly planted on a hatbox, symbolising a case which she had brought and won against a milliner who had failed to carry out to the letter the hat design she required. Jones in *Free Associations* neither fully names nor admits the extent of his relationship with Loe which went very deep at many levels. Equally his psychological skills were not exercised on Loe when he spoke of her peculiarly defiant character producing disruptions in family life instead of family disruptions themselves producing the defiance. Loe's passionate devotion to detailed thoroughness in everything she undertook and her obsession with tidiness and order, did not, he commented, make life easy for those near her and even fifty years later he still did not see her as a prime example of the anal erotic type so carefully delineated by Freud.

Nearly eighty years have passed since Jones began what became a full-blown affair with Loe Kann and very few reliable witnesses are available who remember her. Among them Anna Freud[37] recalls her as a delightful companion but she does not recall the manic depressive nature she was said to indulge in private. In company she talked vivaciously and could hold her own in many fields but there were tensions and difficulties between Loe and

36. Ibid, 127.
37. Interview, Anna Freud, October 14, 1980.

Ernest which no attempted camouflage could conceal. Jones put these characteristics quite differently: "Her peculiar kind of psychoneurotic constitution manifested itself mainly by developing various character traits in a much higher and also finer degree than is to be met with among the so-called normal."

Some of these traits he admitted were distressing, "such as an exquisite sensibility to suffering." Confronted with this phrase Dr. Moore who knew her commented: "exquisite paranoia would be a better description – her paranoid episodes were impossible to handle."[38] Jones' admiration in recollection knew no bounds: some of her finer traits were "ennobling, such as an indomitable courage, an invincible will, and a devotion to all that is fine and good in life." Dr. Moore simply smiled when I quoted this passage to him.[39]

A woman said to be relatively rich, she was born in Holland but her love of London drove her to take up residence there. She and Jones quickly fell into the habit of sharing her flat, a habit Trotter thought dangerous. "What if the affair should suddenly yawn like the grave." Neither in fact had any thought of marriage and from the outset Miss Kann's health was a disadvantage. Already she had more than once undergone operations for renal calculi and Trotter's prognosis was pessimistic. It also came as something of a shock to Jones to discover that she had begun taking morphia twice a day to cope with the pain and what he feared quickly developed. The sale of morphia was then unrestricted and she could easily buy and consume increasing quantities until she became a drug addict.

There is little doubt that Jones' sexual life with Loe Kann became intense and there is some evidence to show that sexual fixation reconciled him to her fluctuating moods which at their worst could be destructive. Anyone who has lived with a drug addict knows the appalling hazards involved, and it needed something more than a sexual fixation – totally obsessive though that could become – to maintain a relationship which lasted over seven long years. The obvious answer is – love – but nowhere in his account does Jones use the word. Anna Freud felt that their feeling for one another did not go beyond mutual affection and referred to "their capacity for companionship" as a very important factor.

Whatever the precise bond which held them together within a year of meeting they were representing themselves as man and wife and somehow carried off the charade with their respective families. It must have distressed Jones senior to discover that his clever son had selected a bride and married her without introducing her or inviting him to the marriage. The present Mrs. Ernest Jones recalls that Loe simply took Jones' name and they were referred to as Mr. and Mrs. Jones.[40] Visits to the parents in Holland seem to have gone off very satisfactorily and travelling abroad together was no problem because the elaborate apparatus of passports, identity cards and

38. Interview, Dr. Moore, May 15, 1965.
39. Ibid.
40. Interview, Mrs. Jones, September 16, 1977.

police checks on hotel registers simply did not exist in those days.

Jones had a certain facility for foreign languages and having maintained his school French by wide reading, acquired a working knowledge of Italian grammar and picked up a considerable smattering of Dutch from Loe Kann, both he and Trotter decided that the glaring hiatus was German. They hired a private German tutor two or three times a week and since the man was "a typical Berliner" picked up a Prussian accent which later produced bursts of mimicry among Jones' Viennese friends.

Two professional episodes stood out in Jones' memory at this period. One an encounter with the great economist Professor Karl Pearson at University College London was pleasant if frustrating. The other nearly brought his career to an abrupt conclusion. Jones had conceived the idea of working under Karl Pearson in order to apply higher mathematics to an investigation of what he referred to as mental heredity. Pearson was deeply in correspondence at the time with Havelock Ellis about similar issues and their relationship never recovered from the quarrel that ensued. Confusingly, Pearson quickly cut across his first conversation with Jones to point out that "his mathematical methods were so devised as to swamp all fallacies of observation and even to make superfluous any more exact knowledge about . . . inherited elements."

Jones felt that this sweeping assertion was a reaction to Karl Pearson's discovery of the Mendelian theory which was said to have undermined much of his work. The two men seemed to have differed on every point which arose in their conversations and Jones certainly challenged Pearson's proposition that the current commercial standards of worldly success had a universal applicability to human values.

The second episode was the forerunner of two similar occurrences which led some of Jones' enemies to draw malicious conclusions about his moral behaviour. It came as a terrible shock one morning to confront charges from a local schoolmistress at a school for mental defectives that he had behaved indecently with two small children during a speech test. A Dr. Kerr who acted as intermediary said that the complaint came from the children themselves but was completely believed by the schoolmistress. Jones carefully explained that it was not unusual for children to create these fantasies partly because they feared such interference and partly because there was a hidden desire to know what took place in sexual intercourse.[41] It was seen as a not very convincing attempt to exonerate himself. No decent schoolmistress in possession of her senses could contemplate the idea that innocent children wanted to know about sex.

Dr. Kerr found himself in a dilemma. His attempts to convince the schoolmistress that some children found a malicious delight in implicating adults in indecency were met with even more strenuous denials and accusations. In the face of her intransigence he had no alternative but to report the whole matter

41. Ibid.

to the Education Committee. They in turn were undecided how to react until the threat of newspaper exposure forced their hand, but instead of instituting an enquiry and cross-examining the girls they simply put the matter straight into the hands of the police.

Jones was horrified to learn that at any moment he might – even on the street – be arrested and find himself charged in open court with what the still Victorian values of England regarded as the most heinous of all crimes – sexual interference with children. Freud's discovery of infantile sexuality had not yet become common knowledge and the stereotype of childhood innocence unblemished by any hint of sexual fantasy remained intact. Confident that his friends, and especially Loe and Trotter would never have a moment's doubt of his innocence, apart from the devastation it must wreak in his career, Jones most recoiled from the reaction it would have on his ageing parents.

Dramatically, on the morning following the warning from the Education Committee, the parlourmaid announced, in some distress, that an aggressive policeman was demanding to see Dr. Jones. Steeling himself for the interview Jones confronted a shuffling, self-conscious, blue-eyed English bobby who very deferentially asked whether Dr. Jones would buy a ticket for a police charity raffle. At one o'clock that afternoon the maid once more announced "Two gentlemen to see you, sir" whispering under her breath "It's the police."[42] Immediately the inspector entered the room he said dramatically: "Doctor there are two ways out of this room – the door and the window – I hope you will choose the door." Jones' sister, Elizabeth, was very upset when they tried to march him straight down to the police station and he had to camouflage the true accusation in order not to distress her too much.[43] He also asked the inspector's permission to telephone his parents and to select something from his bookshelves to read. The inspector was deeply interested in his choice of reading matter, hoping perhaps for a clue to his debauchery. Jones chose Neitzsche's *Thus Spake Zathrustra*.

Still wearing the regalia of the Harley Street consultant – a top hat and morning coat – Jones was escorted to a cell in Vine Street and discovered for the first time what solitary confinement in a space 6 ft × 8 ft with a stone bench and no pillow meant to a middle class professional man on the brink of a brilliant career. He hardly slept at all. At first light of dawn he re-envisaged what the morning held for him and he became even more depressed. The press would certainly report every detail of the case, and already outside on the streets the newspapers carried headlines like "Harley Street Man – Sexual 'Offences.'"

Within an hour of his appearance in court the case was remanded, and he was released on bail but as he filed through the crowds on his way to the exit he heard one man say "He can cut his bloody throat, he can." It was not exactly reassuring.

42. Ibid.
43. Jones: *Free Associations*, 146.

Trotter at once recommended securing the services of a rising young barrister Archibald Bodkin (later to become Sir Archibald Bodkin) and Jones promptly plunged into argument with him. Preliminary stirrings of psychological insights he was later to apply with great penetration suggested to him that the children had really played out a sexual scene among themselves and wanted to project their guilt on to him. Bodkin sniffed at such an elliptical approach to something which he thought required straightforward treatment followed by a blunt plea of guilty or not guilty.

It now became clear to Jones that the law not only qualified on occasion as an ass, but disregarded the tormented anxieties of waiting litigants by following one remand with another until it seemed a Kafka-like perspective of delays stretched eternally ahead of him.

With all his professional activities suspended, as the weeks slipped away his anxieties multiplied and he found himself "developing a sort of shame-facedness as if [he] were in some way to blame for the whole thing." He spoke of the stirring of unconscious sources of guilt "probably of sexual origin" without specifically referring to the *unexpressed* sexual response many adults have to children at the *unconscious* level. That Jones was now a deeply sensual man with a very active sexual life was clear from many sources.[44] Indeed, as we know, these charges were three times preferred against him, but there is no shred of evidence to suggest that he was ever in any way guilty.

For two whole months Jones lived in a state of frequently sleepless suspense, aware that the evidence of one little girl corroborated by an ill-educated puritanical teacher was about to ruin not only his career, but probably his life as well, since such a smear produced widespread social as well as professional repercussions. When, at last, the case was called and the magistrate heard the actual evidence against him he weighed the calibre of the witnesses and in a very short time dismissed the case out of hand. Indeed he later wrote Jones a letter of sympathy, and the staff of University College Hospital organised a subscription to pay for his legal expenses, which were by then considerable.

There is little evidence of Jones' reaction. He did not, it seems, go out and celebrate, but his relief must have been immeasurable and only years of understatement could have produced this classically English comment from his pen: "I resumed my usual professional life."

Not that he felt himself released to move serenely towards the goals which he had for so long formulated. Some of his colleagues remained very suspicious of what had taken place and one at least went to some pains to keep rumour and counter-rumour alive. The B. M. J. came out powerfully on Jones' side. "Completely successful as was the result of the case it was not accomplished without considerable expense which fell entirely on Dr. Jones. Baseless charges of this kind are unfortunately only too well known to the

44. Interview, Mrs. Jones, September 16, 1977.

profession.''[45] In the light of what subsequently took place it is surprising that at the age of seventy-two Jones himself recorded: ''personal respectability would not be enough in future; only the most rigid medical orthodoxy would save me.'' Barely two years later he was once again in similar trouble.

45. *B.M.J.*, May 26, 1906.

CHAPTER VI

Psycho-Analytic Beginnings

BETWEEN THE YEARS 1906 and 1908 his interest in psychiatry became very active and he was constantly in argument with colleagues about such disreputable questions as the possible development of sexuality at a much earlier age than was commonly supposed.

It was part of a much wider and deeper interest in mental processes which was beginning to permeate his neurological thinking. The received wisdom said that symptoms like convulsions, hysterias, paralyses and anaesthesias bore superficial resemblances to equivalent disease of the brain and it followed that they, too, could be treated by physical means. It was all part of medicine's deep commitment to a form of materialism which permitted the body to influence "the mind" but not "the mind" the body. Hence disorders like epileptic-convulsions should be treated by putting the patient to bed and resting the mind while he or she was fed innumerable fish dishes, because fish were rich in the phosphorus which might be missing from the patient's central nervous system. Here a paradox un-mentioned by Jones in *Free Associations* arose. Confining a patient to bed and limiting his environment turned the patient in on his own thoughts with a consequent increase in mental distress but Jones, who remarked on this danger, did not draw the analogy that concentrating a patient in the closed world of his own problems by psychoanalysis might have a similar result.

Certainly, over a number of years, Jones had questioned the reductive materialism of biological medicine where "events" which appeared to have a strong mental content clearly appeared independently of any actual physiological disorders. Simultaneously he linked social with medical problems and believed that the injustices and irrationalities of our social organisation clearly had a root first in the nature of man himself but more specifically in what was loosely referred to as aberrations of mind. Both Trotter and Jones began their psychological explorations from similar socio-logical motives and cherished what eventually became one of Freud's funda-mental aims – a desire to comprehend psychology in terms of biology. They read and discussed the works of William James, Frederic Myers and Milne Bramwell, and Jones built up a library of French medical psychology which he read and re-read. Their reading in medical psychology continued to widen and the works of men like Morton Prince and Boris Sidis became closely familiar. As early as 1906 Jones had already contributed to Morton Prince's new *Journal of Abnormal Psychology*.

Inevitably their studies led them to the writings of Pierre Janet and these were closely connected with a remarkable case which Jones had encountered two years before. Nowhere in *Free Associations* does Jones admit that he was experimenting with the possibilities of treatment by hypnosis at this time but he does refer to one case, the case of Tom Ellen. Ellen suffered from a condition called allochiria which meant that he was paralysed on one side of the body as the result of a train accident and this led to the most severe symptoms including blindness, memory disturbance and a loss of the senses of taste and smell. The most remarkable symptom of all was bizarre. He felt that his body was "folded over on itself" which meant that, mentally, he regarded himself as a one-sided person.

Jones gives us no details of his hypnotic techniques but he did later discuss these with one witness and they seemed to follow a simple formula. He would get a patient to lie down and relax, limb by limb from the toes to the legs, from the arms to the eyes. These he allowed to remain closed for some minutes while he gently intoned some such words as "you are now relaxing more and more and will soon come to the point where you think of sleep, and when you think of sleep I want you to empty your mind of any idea other than that of sleep." He would then ask the patient to open his eyes, switch on a lamp and require him to stare straight into his own eyes. A gentle flow of language and concentration of his own personality frequently completed the desired effect.[46]

He applied this technique with Tom Ellen over several months and suddenly one day Ellen exclaimed that he was beginning to see again. Differential diagnosis could of course claim that as he recovered from the shock of the accident in the natural course of events he might slowly regain his sight but with one astonishing qualification of special psychological interest. The faces of human beings continued to look like blank sheets of white paper to Tom Ellen. This limitation also disappeared in the end but left yet another remarkable exception: his wife's face remained a blank.

Jones made very little play with this episode in his reminiscences but if we take it at its face value he was in fact practising something very similar to that famous feat with which Janet had so astonished Freud in Paris. Since Jones was by now familiar with Janet's work he could not claim to be a pioneer, but it remained remarkable that away in provincial England a young Welsh doctor should be employing similar techniques and having what appeared to be a similar success. It so happened for instance that after the train accident Tom Ellen underwent another in which a cartwheel passed over his foot which was on the side of his anaesthetised or non-existent body. The

46. Interview, Lancelot Whyte, June 14, 1953.

cartwheel left a very nasty bruise but at the time Ellen reported to Jones that he had felt absolutely nothing. Jones once more applied his hypnotic techniques and within a few minutes Ellen began to release the cries and groans which should have accompanied the accident at the time of its occurrence, reproducing in sound patterns what were recollected in word patterns with Pierre Janet's talking cure.

Jones may be right in underplaying this episode in *Free Associations* because he appears to have failed to make the connection between the two experiments. He also fails to spell out his hypnotic cases, but he did verbally enlarge on them to Lancelot Whyte who recalled him saying "You physicists might do better hypnotising a few atoms and post-hypnotically changing their behaviour patterns. I never went in for post-hypnotic suggestion but on at least two occasions I achieved remarkable results with hypnosis. The trouble was as Freud later found – the results didn't last."[47] However, in Tom Ellen's eyes, Jones' treatment was an unqualified success. An unpublished letter from Ellen himself reads:[48]

Dear Doctor,

Shall be glad to avail myself of the opportunity you so kindly afford me of once again hearing your dear old voice, which has in days gone by eased my pain; made the darkness seem light, brought tranquillity to a mind that had nearly lost all hope of human aid and restore unto me once through your own bravery, courage and indomitable will a hope that I might once again be as other men and so enjoy the life that now is. I never think of you without a feeling of deep love and intense gratitude for all the love, respect and brotherliness you have shown to me.

Sincerely yours,
Tom Ellen.

It was one of a number of such letters of gratitude written to Jones during his early years in Harley Street.

While he was treating Tom Ellen, Wilfred Trotter came to him one day and mentioned a review in *Brain* of a new book, *Studies in Hysteria,* by a man called Freud. In fact *Brain* – a well-known neurological journal – devoted a whole number to the subject of hysteria which included a detailed study of Freud's *Conception of Hysteria* by Bernard Hart, with 281 references to psycho-analytic literature. Jones had himself already published in *Brain* the results of his research into *The Onset of Hemiplegia*, the conclusions of which were subsequently incorporated into medical textbooks. Jones paid no more than passing attention to Trotter's remark but read the review with some interest, and then a second incident concentrated his attention on Freud. He came across Freud's Dora analysis in *Monatschrift fur Psychiatrie* and his account of what followed in *Free Associations* had certain ambiguities: "I came away with a deep impression

47. Ibid.
48. Letter, August 16, 1910.

of there being a man in Vienna who actually listened with attention to every word his patients said to him. *I was trying to do so myself but I had never heard* of anyone else doing it."[49]

These words carry the implication that he had been thinking along the same lines as Freud and place him among the pioneers of this approach.

It is difficult to disentangle the facts because there are so many gaps in what remains of written evidence but Jones claims in *Free Associations* that despite his admiration for Janet's "ingenious thinking" and his beautiful command of language he saw through his deceptive presentations. Janet's explanation of his famous "talking cure" at La Salpetriere in Paris was simply, according to Jones, "an ingenious trick." His thinking, Jones argued, really proceeded upon physiological lines but was subsequently clothed in psychological terminology, a device which Jones regarded as misleading. Of course, Janet did not anticipate Freud's discoveries but he certainly produced the evidence which inspired one of the most important principles in subsequent psycho-analytic techniques. The boundary between physiology and psychology in his work was blurred and he, personally, laid no claims to pioneering the latter but Jones wrote "It was very revealing to observe just where he had burked the problem." Unfortunately he did not spell out the details. In fact, Janet did not attempt to explain psychologically the phenomena uncovered in the talking cure. Jones made considerable play with this unmasking of Janet and related it to the discovery, years before, that his father was omniscient. In both cases his reaction was "compounded of triumph at the thought that I could know better than he did and of resentment − ostensibly against him but really against myself − at having been credulously misled."

Jones' reading of Freud's *Studies in Hysteria* and Dora analysis became seminal. Here was a man who used the casual utterances of patients as data for scientific analysis, applying techniques similar to those exclusively reserved for the hard sciences, physics, biology and chemistry. He treated thoughts as mental events capable of scrutiny like atoms or chemicals. Freud, in short, was a man who approached the mind scientifically, a method which had already occurred to Jones. The Dora paper generated an intellectual excitement in Jones which inspired him to set about improving his German and widening his reading. When, exactly, he read Freud's *Traumdeutung* is not clear and nowhere does he record what impact it made upon him, but he certainly saw it as one big step in his later mastery of written German. (His verbal command of the language was never perfect.) The nature and originality of Freud's ideas at this time normally produced strong resistances but Jones found himself already prepared for the shock of their most unorthodox components − sexuality and the unconscious. There were times, as he widened his reading, when he felt that things "could not be quite so simple as that" but by now the tremendous surge of Freud's ideas was

49. Jones: *Free Asociations,* 160.

beginning to carry him only too willingly towards an entirely new way of professional life.

It really began when he attended the International Congress of Neurology in Amsterdam in 1907, where he met a man, Carl Gustav Jung, destined to become a focal point in the next ten years of his life. They both read papers at the Congress and Jung found Jones' scepticism about the role of heredity in mental disorders so sympathetic that he offered his friendship. Jones was the first English psychiatrist Jung encountered and it surprised him to find that an Englishman was already familiar with the elements of psycho-analytic doctrine. In February of the same year Jung had met Freud in person and Jones was fascinated by the first hand account he now gave him of a man who already promised to dominate the psycho-analytic scene. "He had very much to tell Freud and to ask him and Jung with intense animation poured forth a spate for three whole hours. Then the patient absorbed listener Freud interrupted him with the suggestion that they conduct their discussion more systematically."[50]

In November of the same year, 1907, Jones attended a special post-graduate course in psychiatry at Kraepelin's Clinic in Munich. Organised with German thoroughness, the course included Plaut on serio-diagnostics, Alzheimer on cerebral histology and finally the great man Kraepelin himself in clinical diagnosis. Work began at eight in the morning in the middle of a very cold Bavarian winter and ran on through the greater part of the day. The course lasted a complete month and Jones emerged with widened perspectives and an ever-growing fascination for psychological medicine.

Now occurred an incident which remained vividly in his memory for the rest of his life. He had written to Jung in November suggesting a second meeting and Jung replied:

Dear Dr. Jones,
  I should be very glad to see you as soon as possible. If you arrive Sunday evening let me know it by telephone Monday morning at 9. I expect you for lunch at eleven. If you arrive Monday evening I will meet you in the Hotel Bauer au Lac between 11 and 12. I hope we will have many interesting talks.

                                        With best greetings,
                                        Yours very truly,
                                        Jung.[51]

In these first encounters Jones found Jung a person capable of great charm who quickly put him at ease, but Jung's commanding prescence and immense vitality, his flow of language and soldierly bearing combined to produce a formidable presence. Shortly after Jones' arrival they visited the Burgholzli, then directed by Professor Bleuler who had already made a number of important contributions to the study of schizophrenia. On the

50. Jones: *Freud, Life and Work,* Vol. II, 36.
51. Jung to Jones, November 23, 1907.

basis of his clinical research Bleuler had developed a new approach in contra-distinction to the purely *organicist* theories prevalent at the time. Bleuler assumed that schizophrenia derived from an unknown cause (perhaps from the action of toxic substances in the brain) in which heredity played an important part. In the chaos of the manifold symptoms of schizophrenia he distinguished primary or physiogenic symptoms and secondary or psycho-genic symptoms deriving from primary symptoms.

At the time they were working at the Burgholzli on Veraguth's psycho-galvanic phenomenon and also present was A. A. Brill, an American of Hungarian descent later to become a founder of the New York Psycho Analytic Society. Unaware of Jones' steadily growing psycho-analytic sophistication, Brill began to explain the psycho-galvanic phenomenon to Jones and Jung interrupted him with the words: "We didn't invite Dr. Jones here to teach him but to consult him."[52] At this stage, full of enthusiasm for the new Freud theories, Jung had created a small Freudian group in Zurich and among its members were Franz Riklin, a relative of Jung's, Professor Bleuler, and Alphonse Maeder, all to become recognised as distinguished pioneers.

The group met intermittently at the Burgholzli and while Jones was in Zurich he attended one gathering at which a guest member, the famous neurologist von Monakow, spoke. Jones gave me an account of the meeting: "It was interesting in the light of what followed to hear Jung defending psycho-analysis and risking Monakow's scorn, although it was difficult to know Monakow's precise reaction – he kept his face pretty masked during the proceedings."[53]

Certainly in these early days Jung found himself in the position of a defender of the faith who suffered personal attacks from Swiss doctors, lawyers and writers and refused to recant in the face of fierce pressures. No one doubted the horror in certain Swiss circles when sex – which many considered an unfortunate pre-requisite of reproduction – was put forward by fully qualified doctors as the underlying cause not only of mental disturbance but of much human behaviour in general. This was supping with the devil indeed.

Jones described Jung after several meetings as "A breezy pesonality" who had "a restlessly active and quick brain, was forceful, or even domineering in temperament and exuded vitality and laughter." In direct opposition to a view expressed thirty years later he added "He was certainly a very attractive person."

Already internationally known in psychiatry, Jung had published his *Studies in Association* from which the whole technique of free association may have developed, and in the same year as he met Jones, the *Psychology of Dementia Praecox*. No one doubted that following in the footsteps of Bleuler he was the coming man in psychiatry, second only to Sigmund Freud.

52. Jones: *Freud, Life and Work*, Vol. II, 43.
53. Interview, April 1951.

Two other men destined to become important in the psycho-analysis movement, Brill, the American and Abraham, were also associated with the Burgholzli at the time although Abraham had just left for Berlin and Jones personally re-encountered only Brill.

Following Jones' visit on November 30, 1907, Jung wrote to Freud "Dr. Jones, an extremely gifted and active young man, was with me for the last five days chiefly to talk with me about your researches. Because of his 'splendid isolation' in London he has not yet penetrated very deeply into your problems but is convinced of the theoretical necessity of your views. He will be a staunch supporter of our cause for besides his intellectual gifts he is full of enthusiasm.''[54]

According to Jung it was Jones "along with my friends in Budapest" who first mooted the idea of an international conference of Freudians to be held in Innsbruck or Salzburg in the following spring. The first small hint of difficulties between Jung and Jones which were to develop into a full-scale feud became apparent as they arranged the meeting. Jung wanted to designate the conference a Congress for Freudian Psychology and Jones felt this personalised what should remain objectively scientific. Jones told me that at the very outset of their relationship Jung "formulated his arguments very rigidly."[55]

Something personal now broke into Jones' London life to overshadow even this most important pioneer experience. Still a medical registrar at the West End Hospital for Nervous Diseases, Jones suddenly found himself confronted with a second charge of indecent behaviour. A colleague, astonished by the proposition that children experienced a sexual life of their own which could explain hysterical symptoms, had challenged Jones to investigate the case of a girl of ten suffering from a mysterious paralysis of the left arm with no apparent organic basis. Not unexpectedly, Jones approached the proposition warily since he did not want to risk the remotest chance of repeating his experience with the mentally defective child, but the precautions he took seemed totally inadequate. First he did not get the permission of the girl's doctor to talk to her and since Dr. Savill was regarded as an authority on the psycho-neuroses this seemed professionally inept. Second he did not arrange for a nurse to be present during his interview with the child but talked to her in the operating theatre with the door open while nurses occasionally passed to and fro.

Clinically he had the satisfaction of uncovering psychological roots for the paralysis which seemed irrefutable, but professionally. . . . The girl it transpired had been in the habit of going early to school to play with an older boy who one day tried to seduce her. Turning away from him, she attempted to ward off his embraces but suddenly one arm "went weak" and within seconds appeared paralysed. Jones regarded this as "a pretty example of a 'compromise formation' between the desire to be seduced and conventional

54. *Freud–Jung Letters*, 1979, 88.
55. Interview, Jones, April 1951.

horror at any such possibility.

The inevitable followed. The child began boasting in the ward that she had talked to the doctor about sex and when rumours reached her parents' ears the father exploded angrily. Complaining first to Dr. Savill and through him to the Hospital Committee he demanded an immediate investigation matched by suitable retribution. Jones appeared before the committee but his attempts to explain the relationship between his methodology and Freudian theory were received with incredulity. What decent minded man, demanded a clergyman member of the committee, could possibly think in such terms. Once again the inbuilt power struggle between matron and physician characteristic of so many hospitals expressed itself in a damning deposition from the hospital matron who stated that his frequent requests for chaperones while he examined hysterical out-patients were sometimes so urgent that the examination went ahead without one. This was tantamount to a lie, but the conclusion was foregone.[56] The committee asked Jones to resign.

Once again his whole career seemed on the verge of ruin and his auto-biographical fragment gives no indication of the weeks of disturbed sleep and anxiety which followed.[57] Clearly no neurological hospital would in future ever appoint a man with such a record, no matter how many extenuating circumstances were produced.

Convinced by now that psychological medicine if not psycho-analysis was the speciality which most attracted him, Jones felt doubly dismayed by the turn of events until one day a colleague mentioned to him that a Dr. C. K. Clarke, Professor of Psychiatry and Dean of the Medical Faculty in the University of Toronto wanted to found a psychiatric clinic in that city. Dr. Clarke was completing a tour of European clinics in search of a young and enthusiastic director. Jones now felt that his reputation in England was damaged for several years to come and he bitterly reflected that he must search for a new way of life far removed from London. Dr. Clarke presented an obvious way out of his difficulties, but how could he explain his resignation from the West End Hospital for Nervous Diseases to a man from a culture said to be more puritan even than its English equivalent.

Further complications arose because his mistress Loe Kann did not want to abandon what she regarded as cosmopolitan London, rich in European culture, for provincial Toronto with its North American functionalism. There were a number of quarrels, the precise nature of which we do not know, but Jones decided that such frictions were a gratuitous waste of time when he still had not won the Canadian appointment.[58] From what little evidence is available it appears that Ernest and Loe still occupied separate flats and found continuous confrontation in cohabitation a strain. If they went to Toronto, such were the sexual mores of Toronto that they would have either to marry or masquerade as husband and wife. According to

56. Interview, Mrs. Jones, September 16, 1977.
57. Ibid.
58. Ibid.

Anna Freud, Loe Kann "came from a wealthy Dutch family and as far as I know she helped Ernest a great deal during this time of . . . establishing himself.[59]

That a curiously contradictory tie had developed between them with a powerful sexual component is clear and now the crucial question arose — should he consider going to Toronto without her.

A lucky coincidence came to his aid. He had met, through medical colleagues, Sir William Osler, recently appointed Regius Professor of Medicine at Oxford and — more important perhaps — a Canadian. Jones decided to call on him and was delighted at the warmth of his reception. Whether his sense of integrity demanded at this stage that he reveal the cause of his resignation, or whether a defensible expediency demanded its suppression is not recorded. Suffice it to say that Sir William wrote recomending him to Dr. Clarke and with surprising ease and never a single hitch Dr. Jones found himself appointed Director of the Toronto Psychiatric Clinic of the University of Toronto.[60]

England had rejected him, Canada welcomed him, but in the six months before he took up his appointment several events confirmed the direction his career was to take.

59. Letter, Anna Freud, December 15, 1980.
60. Jones: *Free Associations*, 151.

CHAPTER VII

First Meetings with Freud

THE FIRST historic Congress of what became known as the International Psycho-Analytic Association took place at Salzburg on Sunday April 26, 1908. Jung, Brill and Jones travelled together to Salzburg and arrived at the Hotel Bristol on the same day as Freud. Ernest Jones told me "As you would expect, the air was full of expectancy and I felt distinctly nervous as a relative newcomer among so many people who already knew one another. . . . Especially of course I wanted to meet Freud and I kept scanning the lounge hopefully . . . until suddenly there he was."[61]

In *Free Associations* Jones wrote: "My first impression of Freud was that of an unaffected and unassuming man. He bowed and said 'Freud Wien' at which I smiled, for where else did I think he came from? . . . His first remark was to say that from my appearance I couldn't be English, was I not Welsh? This greatly surprised me . . . since I was getting accustomed to the total ignorance of my native land on the Continent. . . . We had a long talk together of how I had come across psycho-analysis."[62] Jones was very flattered when Freud suddenly said: "What we most need is a book on dreams in English: won't you write it?"

One impression Jones did not record in *Associations*. On a visit to his country house, The Plat, in Sussex, six years before he wrote that book, we were comparing Freud and Havelock Ellis and Jones said: "When I first met (Freud) the power of his presence gave the illusion of height to his person but he was barely five feet seven inches. In fact, like myself, a relatively short man. But his flashing eyes and fine moustache added a panache quite alien to a man like Ellis."[63]

Jones was, in fact, only five feet five inches, but like the Master, his vitality and flow of quick, precise talk, his very alive eyes and gestures, marked him out in most company. Now, with forty-three other distinguished doctors, neurologists and surgeons including the six key members who were to dominate the International Association – Jung, Rank, Abraham, Ferenczi, Stekel and Adler – they all gathered on the morning of the 27th to listen to the remarkable case history of the Rat Man given by Freud.

Freud "sat at the end of a long table along the sides of which we were

61. Interview, Jones, April 1951.
62. Jones: *Freud, Life and Work*, Vol. II, 47.
63. Interview, Jones, April 1951.

gathered and spoke in his usual low but distinct conversational tone. He began at the Continental hour of eight in the morning and we listened with rapt attention. At eleven he broke off suggesting we had had enough but we were so absorbed that we insisted on his continuing which he did until one o'clock."[64]

The case of the Rat Man, a well known Viennese lawyer, began when he came to Freud complaining of obsessions from which he had suffered since childhood and which had grown worse during the last four years. "The chief features of this disorder," Freud said, "were fears that something might happen to two people of whom he was very fond – his father and a lady whom he admired. Besides this he was aware of *compulsive impulses* – such an impulse for instance as to cut his throat with a razor; and further he produced *prohibitions* sometimes in connection with quite unimportant things."[65]

The experience which precipitated the Rat Man's treatment by Freud took place on army manoeuvres when a fellow officer with sadistic tendencies described to the patient a particularly horrible punishment inflicted on a soldier in the East: "A pot was turned upside down on his buttocks . . . some rats were put into it . . . and they . . . bored their way in."[66] Freud described the expression which came over the patient's face as he re-told this story: "I could only interpret it as one of *horror at pleasure of his own of which he himself was unaware.*" And "at this moment the idea flashed through the patient's mind that this was happening to a person who was very dear to (him)."[67]

The elements in the case which remained vividly in Jones' memory and figure largely in his recollections was the underlying idea of alternative love and hate in the same person, "the early separation of the two attitudes usually resulting in the repression of the hate." Equal expression of such polarised emotions led, Freud said, to a paralysis of thought clinically expressed as *folie de doute*. Obsessive tendencies, a main characteristic of this neurosis, signified "a violent effort to overcome the paralysis by the utmost resistence."

The patient was still in analysis at the time of the Congress but by then Freud had traced the obsessions back to infantile sexual experiences. Jones recorded at the end of the paper, that he had never been so oblivious of the passage of time.

Nine papers were read at this first Congress, four from Austria, two from Switzerland and one each from England, Germany and Hungary. Jones himself spoke on Rationalisation in Everyday Life, a paper he thought a poor one which did not justify inclusion in his two volumes of *Essays on Applied Analysis*. Superficially, relationships were harmonious enough at Salzburg, but under the surface the Viennese contingent grew suspicious of the special attention Freud paid to the non-Jewish German "upstart" Jung, from

64. Jones: *Freud, Life and Work,* Vol. II, 47.
65. Freud: *Collected Works,* 10, 158.
66. Ibid.
67. Ibid.

Switzerland, who had not been forced to face the pioneering difficulties of the Viennese group. Already they suspected Jung of the hidden anti-semitism allegations of which later plagued no small part of his career and even at this early stage Jones heard murmurs amongst them that Jung would not remain long in the psycho-analytic movement.

Following the Congress a small group came together and decided to launch a new periodical exclusively devoted to psycho-analysis under the typically portmanteau German title of *Jahrbuch für psychoanalystiche und psychopathologische Forschungen*. Fulfilling the worst fears of the Viennese, the paper was to be edited by Jung and directed by Bleuler and Freud. Jung's influence with Freud at this time seemed overwhelming and Jung certainly had no great respect for the group surrounding Freud in Vienna. He openly expressed his scorn to Jones and spoke of the "degenerate and bohemian crowd which did Freud little credit" but Jones saw them differently: "They were all practising physicians, for the most part very sober ones and if their cloaks were more flowing and their hats broader than what one saw in Zurich, London or Berlin . . . that was a general Viennese characteristic." Jones added with a touch of snobbishness: "they were decidedly middle class and lacked the social manners and distinction I had been accustomed to in London."

Jones' closest friend Trotter attended this historic conference but his behaviour sadly disappointed Jones. Explaining that his poor German could not cope with Freud's complicated statements, Trotter failed to attend the first meeting and when he sat next to the youthful Wittels at the banquet which followed, he found him irritatingly facetious. Wittels commented on the proneness of certain Greek goddesses to hysteria, coining a witty phrase which connected prone-ness with sexuality and Trotter, failing to follow the pun in German, turned to Jones and muttered sarcastically: "I console myself with the thought that I can cut a leg off, and no one else here can." Two days later Trotter decided that the company was uncongenial, packed his bags and abruptly returned to London.

The episode illustrated sharp differences between Jones and Trotter. Unlike Trotter, Jones at this time was an outgoing person who, when introduced to a group of relative strangers, quickly adjusted and made himself amenable. Having overcome his initial shyness he was already popular at the conference.

A triangular correspondence had developed between Jung, Freud and Abraham which steadily became more acrimonious. The trouble first arose when Freud expressed the opinion in personal talks with Jung that dementia praecox (schizophrenia) differed from any other neurosis merely in having a much earlier point of fixation. Jung could not accept this. He insisted that the disease "was an organic condition of the brain produced by a hypo-thetical 'psycho-toxin'". Abraham agreed with Freud and according to

Jones said that what was called "dementia" in this disease was due, not to any destruction of intellectual capacities, but to a massive blocking "of the feeling process."

Now, at the Congress, matters came to a head when Abraham, delivering his paper on dementia praecox, failed to mention either Jung or Bleuler's work which not unexpectedly annoyed Jung and left Bleuler sceptical of psycho-analytic integrity.

After these first encounters with Karl Abraham, Jones later came to respect him almost as much as Freud himself. Snatching a momentary break in the intense proceedings, Jones was walking swiftly one morning towards the Opera House when he encountered Abraham who asked him how far he thought that the touch of mysticism Jung brought to his thinking invalidated any genuine belief in the materialistic basis of psycho-analysis. Jones, at that time, thought highly of Jung, and replied that nothing Jung had said at the conference led him to any such conclusion. Abraham dropped his voice as they re-approached the hotel and said "Do you think Jung can escape the anti-semitism of a certain type of German?" It had never occurred to the young, eager and enthusiastic Jones that anything so scientific as psycho-analysis could admit the crudities of anti-semitism and he asked Abraham whether he was familiar with the words of Edmund Burke: "I do not know the method of indicting a whole nation." At that moment Jung came towards them and their conversation dwindled away.[68]

Many years later Jones told me "Jung (at that time) could change his mood like a chameleon. One moment the big, vibrant, charming chairman and the next a vociferous intervener who when confronted by opposition put his case with a vigour which some thought pretty rough. . . . He was forthright and at that stage neo-Freudian to the point where you wouldn't have known the difference. However there certainly was a difference all right. I could see he was very uncomfortable with the idea of monosexuality, not that that was a good description of Freud's position at that time. . . . Jung could not go along entirely with Freud. . . . I had the impression at the time that he was suffering from a good deal of stress – some conflicts I could only guess at which he did not bring into the open."[69]

In the long rally of letters between Freud, Jung and Abraham which followed immediately after the Congress Jones took no direct part but he became aware of what was happening by means of the psycho-analytic bush telegraph, then a fast-developing and already somewhat malicious mechanism. With remarkable prescience, from the outset he foresaw that Abraham would remain a shining star of their circle while Jung aroused suspicions.

Just what part Jones played in these early quarrels is unclear but he told Lancelot Whyte that when he went to visit Freud in Vienna after the Congress, Freud asked him to "use his good offices" as Jones put it, to

68. Interview, Lancelot Whyte, June 14, 1952.
69. Interview, Ernest Jones, May 10, 1955.

reconcile the adversaries, should opportunity occur.[70]

It was a very minor beginning of Jones' intervention in psycho-analytic politics which later was to develop into a full time professional activity.

After the Congress Abraham wrote to Freud, who replied on May 3, 1908[71]: "I recollect that your paper led to some conflict between you and Jung. . . . Now I consider some competition between you unavoidable and within certain limits quite harmless." Freud unhesitatingly believed that Jung was in the wrong due to his "oscillation" but he would not like, he said, any really bad feeling to come between them and he hoped that Jung might find his way back to [Freud's views] which Abraham so ably expressed.

Already the signs of a quarrel which was to explode volcanically were clear but so were Freud's attempts to reconcile the antagonists. Jones believed that since Abraham revealed himself as a faithful discipline, it was Freud's responsibility to write to Jung asking him to keep the peace. Instead, to Jones' surprise, he now pleaded with Abraham: "Thus you will actually be doing me a great personal favour if you inform (Jung) in advance of what you are going to write and ask him to discuss with you the objection that he then made." It would be an act of courtesy, Freud continued, which could simultaneously serve two if not three purposes. Dissension would be nipped in the bud and some small demonstration made that they themselves had drawn "practical benefit" from the practice of psycho-analysis. As for the third purpose, it was a simple and highly personal one: it would give Freud great pleasure. Already, it seemed, Jung's ascendancy in the developing history of psycho-analysis was rapidly growing and other members were expected to accommodate him in any dispute which arose. "Do not make too heavy going of the small sacrifice demanded" Freud said to Abraham, when in fact he was asking Abraham to consult him before he committed his thoughts to paper. Heavily camouflaged as an "act of courtesy" it could be read quite differently and, absurdly, it was Freud's undeviating disciple Abraham who had to make concessions to the Crown Prince Jung whose ideological loyalty was already showing signs of strain.

Abraham and Jones proved in the end to be more perceptive than Freud and now Abraham wrote a letter to Freud which presaged coming events with alarming clarity. The manuscript of the paper which Abraham had read on dementia praecox at Salzburg contained, he now revealed, an acknowledgment to Bleuler and Jung which would have satisfied them but on a sudden impulse he did not read it aloud. "I deceived myself momentarily with a cover motive, that of saving time, while the true reason lay in my animosity against Bleuler and Jung.[72] His animosity, in turn, resulted from a paper given by Bleuler in Berlin which omitted any reference to Freud.

After the Congress Brill and Jones decided to visit Vienna and in due course called upon Freud at his home at Bergasse 19. Talk first ranged around the development of psycho-analysis in America and Brill was able to

70. Interview, Lancelot Whyte, June 14, 1952.
71. Freud to Abraham, May 3, 1908.
72. *Letters, Sigmund Freud—Karl Abraham,* Ed. Hilda C. Abraham & Ernst L. Freud, 36.

predict an encouraging future with the result that Freud – unfortunately as it transpired – agreed to give Brill the right to translate his writings into English. Jones described Freud at this time as: "fifty one years old at the height of his powers and full of energy. He was most genial and friendly to us and was in a specially happy mood because of the dawning recognition of his work. . . ."[73]

Freud spoke a somewhat literary English in a voice which Jones found rather rough and unmusical but presently they were all too lost in finding English equivalents of technical German terms for that to matter. Unaware of the complications which were to arise about Brill's abilities as a translator, Freud suggested to him that perhaps the English word "repression" would be a useful equivalent of "Verdrängung." Jones later wrote: "Freud's manner was gracious and at times heartening . . . his eyes constantly twinkled with perception and often with humour of which he had a highly developed sense." But at the very outset Jones doubted Brill's translating abilities if he very much approved of him as a person.

Freud, at this time, was emerging from his Viennese isolation and medical ostracism into the beginnings of international recognition. Only a few months away Stanley Hall, President of Clark University, Worcester, Massachusetts, was to invite him to visit America and give a course of lectures in the "new science of psycho-analysis." Over the past ten years Freud's revolutionary theories had begun to soften some of the more extreme medical opposition and to permeate far and wide in psychological, and neurological circles. He spoke now with a confidence and vitality which continuous conflict had before dampened.

Jones nowhere records the touch of awe and reverence which overtook him on entering not merely the presence of the man who was to become the Master, but the famous consulting room and not least the Wednesday meetings with which the whole movement began. Lancelot Whyte bore witness to this.[74]

According to Wittels – the doctor who played an important part as a popular expositor of psycho-analysis – the Wednesday evenings were not carefully planned or organised. Members of the group would drift into Freud's waiting room after supper and range themselves round a long table. The door leading from the waiting room into the study was always left open and they could glimpse the collection of statuettes on Freud's desk, the famous couch with the armchair behind it and the walls lined with books.

According to Wittels Freud would enter the room briskly when the company had assembled and black coffee and cigars were served by Mrs. Freud. A hardened smoker, Freud sometimes consumed twenty cigars a day and he invariably smoked throughout the evening. According, once more, to Wittels Freud would "begin by ennunciating his main contentions categorically so that they were apt to repel."[75]

73. Jones: *Free Associations,* 168.
74. Interview, Lancelot Whyte, June 14, 1952.
75. Fritz Wittels: *Sigmund Freud,* 134.

Wittels believed that Freud's motives for organising the Wednesday circle were "to look into the kaleidoscope lined with mirrors which would multiply the images he introduced into it."

This, on Jones' testimony, was a gross travesty of the facts. Freud's motives, he believed, were mixed but a genuine desire to distil from discussion fresh insights into psycho-analysis and to pass propositions through the fire of argument, played an important part.

Jones' account of the Wednesday meetings differed widely from Wittels': "Freud took the chair and did not speak until the discussion was finished when he would bring together the salient points and add his own comments."

To these meetings came Wilhelm Stekel, a dashing young doctor with a pointed beard, bow tie and a curly-brimmed hat. He had read one day an article by Freud which referred to a paper of Stekel's on child seduction. It was the same romantic Stekel whom Jones now encountered with Brill at one of the Wednesday meetings. Also present were Adler, Rank, Sachs, Federn and Hitschmann. Perhaps predictably, because Stekel and Adler were destined to leave the circle with considerable acrimony, Jones later claimed that he did not like either. Jones tended, when writing his reminiscences, to inject retrospectively views which he only developed some years after the encounters he described. Of Adler, for instance, he wrote in *Free Associations* "He struck me as sulky and pathetically eager for recognition. I remember his writing to me not long afterwards thanking me for quoting him in an article."

As for the rest of the assembled company that evening, not many were spared the critical eye of Jones who said of Sadger that he was "a morose, pathetic figure very like a specially uncouth bear." Jones simply did not regard them as worthy disciples of the Master and remarked that if anyone had a reputation to lose it was still dangerous to associate with Freud which explained the mediocrity of those who took the risk. One other figure momentarily appeared on the scene that historic evening of his first encounter – a small, pretty young girl of eleven named Anna who was awakened by the talk downstairs and momentarily appeared in the doorway.[76] Later in life she had no recollection of seeing Ernest Jones and he indeed did not see her, being lost in his struggles to understand certain difficult German colloquialisms.

After Jones' visit Freud wrote to Jung on May 3, 1908: "Jones and Brill have been to see me twice. . . . Jones is undoubtedly a very interesting and worthy man but he gives me a feeling of I was almost going to say racial strangeness. . . ."[77]

He is, Freud continued, a fanatic who so deeply denies the hereditary that even he, Freud, became a reactionary in his, Jones', view. How, Freud wondered, would Jung – given his relatively liberal approach – get on with a man who accepted such rigid basic doctrines. Finally Freud complained that

76. Interview, Anna Freud, November 1979.
77. Freud/Jung Letters, May 3, 1908.

Jones did not eat enough and reminded him of lean and hungry Cassius. "Let me have men about me that are fat" he concluded. This letter contained so many paradoxes it seemed to upset the basic understanding of psycho-analytic history. Jones not Freud was the fanatic, Jung not Jones a relative liberal.

It seems highly unlikely that Loe Kann accompanied Jones on this European trip which lasted several months and took him from Vienna to Budapest and on again to Munich and Paris. She may, however, have made the trip financially possible. Jones seems to have had no source of income after he left the West End Hospital and whether any accumulated savings would cover such a trip is impossible to establish. Anna Freud recalls that Loe was a generous person and as we have seen she came from a rich family.

Brill accompanied Jones to Budapest where a warmly welcoming Ferenczi arranged a rota of friends to show them the sights of the city. Jones found a ready response with Hungarian people which had been lacking in the Londoners he had recently left. Paula Heimann told me that there was in fact a rumour deliberately spread by his enemies that he had been forced to fly the country, a rumour which she and Tom Main emphatically denied. There was a sparkling zest for living in Budapest which appealed to the Celt in Jones and left him wondering whether temperamentally he wasn't better suited to mid-European cultures. What he did not know was that within a few years he and Ferenczi were to be embroiled in one of those complicated priority claims which continuously beset the developing psycho-analytic movement and led to open quarrelling.

Presently Brill had to take ship back to America and he left Jones to journey on to Munich where he immediately sought out the great Professor Kraepelin whose studies had confirmed Freud's view that the nosological status of paranoia should be grouped together with the various forms of dementia praecox. Freud had warned Jones that he might find Kraepelin's "coarseness" off-putting and Jones certainly detected in his gruff manner a lack of consideration for his patients, characteristic of several German doctors he met at the time. Diametrically different in behaviour from the warm, ebullient Ferenczi, Kraepelin was none the less very open-minded and generous, giving Jones the free run of his already famous clinic. Jones quickly made friends with an Italian student, Assagioli from Florence, who once again found some special response to the outgoing, talking, gesticulative Jones. Together they proceeded to explore the city of Munich, first exhausting the opera, music, art galleries and museums and then retreating into the lower life of the beer halls and cafes, occasionally even setting foot in the dance halls.

Clearly at this stage in his development Jones had abandoned the austere sexual morals of his family background and exemplifying Marx's emanci-pated intellectual, escaped the conditions of his class to indulge affairs with no sense of sin. He was not, as Anna Freud told me, faithful to Loe Kann.[78] Jones' diaries give no enlightenment about his conduct in Munich but it was a city where every variety of night life produced a zest for superficial gaiety which pre-supposed a relaxed way of life behind its massive monumental architecture. As Jones wrote in *Free Associations*, "I began to understand why Germany was the land of youth, of romanticism, of wine, women and song." A few miles beyond Munich were the magnificent Bavarian Alps with their woods, romantic lakes and fantastic castles and Jones spent "longer and longer weekends" wandering this beautiful countryside "mostly in good company."

But Jones would not be Jones if he did not, with his puritan dedication, give top priority to his work in Kraepelin's clinic. Selecting what he regarded as his two most deficient areas he set to work to study critical histology under Alzheimer and experimental psychology under Lipps. His encounter with Lipps is particularly interesting because here was a man whose work anticipated more of Freud's hypotheses than Havelock Ellis, Hartman, Krafft-Ebbing and many other pioneers. Jones claimed that this was the only period in his life when work became subordinated to pleasure but there is a good deal of evidence to the contrary.

If Loe Kann accompanied him to Vienna it is unlikely that she was with him in Munich because one day in the Café Passage he showed Ludwig Klages – an intellectual then studying graphology – a letter from her and asked for a character reading. Klages gave an obviously not too flattering account of the writer and when Jones said "Between ourselves she is my sweetheart", Klages launched a fierce attack on the ruthless self control of the English which "so misled the innocent Germans."

The Café Passage yielded many colourful personalities and for a time, in the evenings, Jones' life approached the bohemian. Two other personalities remained vividly in his memory, one an English transvestite artist and the other the fascinating complex and already slightly mad Otto Gross. Gross was a drug-addicted analyst who had undergone some preliminary treatment from Freud, only to be passed on to Jung, an exchange-convenience frequently practised with difficult patients. The English artist – a man of virile build and personality – would take a handful of cronies from the cafe back to his apartment and almost immediately excuse himself, re-appearing in full feminine dress even down to high-heeled shoes which made walking difficult. Already familiar with homosexuality, it set Jones thinking about the infinite variety of the polymorphous perverse but there is no written record of his reactions.

An extraordinary ritual would sometimes occur with Otto Gross in the Café Passage. Someone (unnamed) would sit opposite him amidst the smoke, talk and music, while a select group, including Jones, watched what to all intents and purposes was an analytic session take place there in public.

78. Interview, Anna Freud, November 1979.

Examplifying the relaxed way of life in the Schwabing district of Munich, the Café Passage never closed, and the deeply disturbed Gross would sometimes spend twenty-four hours lost in the swirl of life which kept him in touch with some form of reality, simultaneously treating occasional patients. Jones wrote: "he was my first instructor in the technique of psycho-analysis" but Gross certainly perfected a distinctly unorthodox style. According to Jung he used the café for one-hour sessions with patients, taking payment in cash and frequently hurrying out to buy a new supply of drugs with the money.[79] When he passed into Jung's hands at the Burgholzli, Jung concluded that he was suffering from dementia praecox and wrote to Freud some weeks later: "I have let everything drop and have spent all my available time day and night on Gross pushing on with the analysis. Whenever I got stuck he analysed me. In this way my own health benefited."[80]

Opposition to the "filthy new science of psycho-analysis" was still mounting and Gross would have provided devastating ammunition for the enemies of Freud and Jung. A drug-addicted analyst discussing sexual neuroses openly in cafes, driven himself to be analysed and occasionally exchanging roles with his analyst − what better demonstration of the wildly uncontrolled technique called psycho-analysis could anyone desire.

In fact, as Jones later discovered, this first encounter with psycho-analytic practice was part of a tragedy in which a man he regarded as "the nearest approach to the romantic ideal of a genius" was finally driven to destroy himself. When Gross diagnosed his own condition as dementia praecox he committed suicide.

When Jones left Munich and made his way to Paris he found it, at first disappointing beside the rich life of Munich. He took rooms off the Boule' Mich in the heart of the Latin quarter but it was some time before he began to respond to the café life and picked up echoes of Verlaine and Maupassant. Already the interlocking network of studios and artists characteristic of the district were slowly filtering away to Montmartre, but the cafés were still crowded at two in the morning, prostitutes flaunted at every other street corner and the rue Bal Bullier, where he lived, seemed to vibrate with life for the greater part of twenty-four hours. On July 14 he went out into the streets and the spirit of "Parisian gaiety" at last took possession of him when the dancing began under the ancient windmill and a passing pair of girls invited him to dance.[81]

It is uncertain whether Loe Kann accompanied him on this trip and he makes no reference to her in *Free Associations* but comparing notes on the Parisian way of life with Michael Balint many years later he did refer to "the friend I was with who liked it more than I did." When Balint said with a smile "it must have been a woman" he replied "Yes it was."[82]

79. Jones: *Free Associations,* 173/4.
80. 25 May, 1908, Freud/Jung Letters Abridged, 115.
81. Interview, Mrs. Jones, November 18, 1980.
82. Interview, Michael Balint, December 1957.

The first few days of idle indulgence were followed by a burst of work, but when he tried to persuade Janet to allow him to work with him, Janet said he had no student assistants and preferred working alone. Jones then called on Professor Pierre Marie at the Bicêtre Hospital and the professor was so impressed with Jones' approach to hemiplegic problems that he made available his own "ample material." Jones worked solidly for the next month in the Bicêtre Hospital and claims that in the end he did more work in Paris in one month than he had done in Munich in several.

By July of that summer Freud, writing to Jung, commented about Jones: "I saw him as a fanatic who smiles at my faint-heartedness and is affectionately indulgent with you over your own vacillations. How true this picture is I don't know. But I tend to think he lies to the others, not to us . . . he is a Celt and consequently not quite accessible to us, the Teuton and Mediterranean man."[83]

It was a prophetic letter. There was a sense in which Jones quickly became more Freudian than Freud, his ruthless posivitism recoiling from Freud's occult speculations and unrepentant Lamarckianism. Freud's letter also exposed one very sensitive area. The troubles with Jung were already shown to be fermenting but the reference to Jones "lies" remained inexplicable. Lies about what? Jones certainly had not lied about his troubles with the West End Hospital Nervous Diseases. It would have been a contradiction in terms for him to conceal the true nature of his relationship with Loe Kann to a Viennese circle already committed to sex as the instinct from which all else sprang.

Jones returned to England briefly in September 1908 to visit his father and mother, before sailing in the Empress of Britain for Canada. He recorded, with characteristic coolness when talking about his family, "It was the last time I was to see my mother."

He made no reference to Loe Kann, but either she sailed with him on the Empress of Britain or followed him shortly afterwards.

83. Freud to Jung, July 18, 1908.

CHAPTER VIII

Canada and America

ARRIVING IN TORONTO in October 1908 Jones was received by the Professor of Psychiatry at the University, Dr. C. K. Clarke, a Canadian who combined a forceful outdoor personality with a genuine desire to establish psychiatric research in Canada on a level with that in the United States and Germany. A man who could live off the land in the wilds of Canada with the toughest trapper, he compensated for his lack of scientific subtlety by boldly primitive techniques which included having one of his patients, a madman, jump into the lake with him in order to see the effects of shock treatment. He responded to Jones' personality and quickly revealed the reactionary forces with which they were confronted. Politicians who had considerable power over the university, were prepared to hang any murderer no matter how mad he was, and madness itself they regarded as an intolerable interruption of an efficient society which had to be removed or segregated.

As pathologist to the Hospital and Director of the Clinic, Jones quickly found himself involved in multiple activities which led him to describe himself as The Lord High Everything Else. Clarke's extrovert heartiness and expansive goodwill were quickly shown to be partly motivated by a desire to shift the burden of his lectures, demonstrations and examinations to Jones. Moreover Clarke's initial display of relative openmindedness was soon heavily qualified. Almost at once, as a new government employee, Jones was expected to pay his respects to the Home Secretary and when he sallied forth wearing his Harley Street top hat the Canadians thought yet another English freak had come amongst them. Immaculately attired himself, Jones was astonished to confront a big beefy man known as the Provincial Secretary who received him in his shirt sleeves and proceeded to sit back in his chair with his feet on the table. Throughout the audience his feet remained on the table but his affability was in proportion to his informality.

Recollecting those first few Canadian weeks in *Free Associations,* Jones prefaced his remarks with the statement that "I had by now got into the habit of taking other people far more into account and had revived a capacity for tact . . . which had subsequently remained dormant." The facts do not bear this out. His usual honeymoon period in any new situation was soon overtaken by strife so destructive that he himself was forced out of the university.

For the moment he quickly discovered that Englishmen were not the most popular people in Canada and advertisements for jobs sometimes brazenly stated "no Englishman need apply." This was the result of an influx of colonially minded Englishmen who came close to sneering at the Canadian way of life and became known as broncos because they were always kicking the Canadians. Jones decided that sensitivity to criticism was inbuilt into the Canadian character and he must avoid such indulgences at all costs, simultaneously parading his Welsh, non-English, roots. However he could not accept the Canadian proposition that having escaped the obsolete ways of the Old World they proceeded to avoid the lawless brashness of America and automatically emerged as a superior civilisation. He described the Canadians in a letter to Freud[84] as "naive, childish and [holding] the simplest views of the problems of life. They care for nothing except money-making and sport, they chew gum instead of smoking or drinking and their public meetings are monuments of sentimental platitudes."

Two women helped to sustain him in his early days in Canada, his elder sister Elizabeth and his mistress Loe Kann. Elizabeth, who had run his Harley Street establishment with such efficiency, now revealed her courage when she agreed to risk an entirely alien way of life as his housekeeper in Toronto. Jones had rented a small house in the middle of Toronto before the two women arrived but when they saw the house they did not like it and immediately went house-hunting, eventually selecting one in Brunswick Avenue, then on the outskirts of Toronto.

Sir Robert Falconer, the President of the University, presently suggested that Jones should become a demonstrator in pathology and medicine and since he was already an Associate in Psychiatry that implied some upgrading. Nearly two years were to elapse before he at last became an Associate Professor and the long interval was open to several explanations. Higher education does nothing to dilute the feuds which characterise academic politics, and certainly Jones became embroiled in fierce departmental struggles and jealousies. Canadian colleagues resented an Englishman being brought in to direct the Clinic and they resisted his quick take-over of so many activities, but he himself did not sufficiently exercise his new-found tact.

Since Loe and Ernest represented themselves as man and wife and Elizabeth was clearly his sister, in the beginning this menage-a-trois did not trouble anyone in the University, until somehow messages trickled across from England that all was not what it seemed. A young doctor whose promotion had been overwhelmed by Dr. Jones' arrival set moving a whispering campaign and finally Dr. Clarke summoned Jones to his presence and asked for clarification. Jones frankly admitted his duplicity and Clarke agreed that

84. Jones to Freud, December 10, 1908.

some modus operandi was inevitable, given the austere sexual morality of the University governing body.[85]

Precisely how they resolved the situation remains obscure but Jones certainly rejected the suggestion that he should marry Loe Kann. By now differences had arisen between them and psychological problems were troubling Loe which eventually drove Ernest to recommend that she consult none other than Freud. But that was some years away.

In December 1908 Jones went to visit Morton Prince in his beautiful house in Beacon Street, Boston, and there met for the first time the charming, gentle, over-conscientious Putnam, a man to become a major influence in the development of psycho-analysis in America. Putnam, Jones recalled in *Free Associations,* behaved "with a deference quite absurd in the circumstances, and then, with his characteristic frankness, said he was disappointed in my appearance since he had expected to meet a tall man with a grey beard." Privately Putnam described Jones as "a brash 29 year old demonstrator. . . ." Nathan G. Hale Jr. who edited the Putnam–Jones letters commented "On the surface Jones might not have seemed qualified to dispel Putnam's doubts. He was a brilliant neurologist but endowed with an 'omnipotence complex' and a caustic tongue." The omnipotence accusation will be filtered through the facts as they unfold in following chapters.

In Boston, Jones held three colloquiums with sixteen people from American academic life, presenting an outline of Freud's new doctrines, and although New England was by no means unprepared to listen, "the only one with whom I had any real success was Putman".

Jones also renewed his acquaintance with the American A. A. Brill, who had abandoned his birthplace, Austria, at the age of fifteen and settled in the United States where he began his training as a psychiatrist early in the century.

Back in Canada, within a few months Jones wrote to Brill in New York proposing that they should begin making psycho-analytical contributions to Morton Prince's *American Journal of Abnormal Psychology* which could easily become an influential platform. When he heard about the plan Freud wrote to Jones: "I heartily agree with you and wish you had already done it. It might be the best way to introduce my teaching to your countrymen (sic). Perhaps much more efficacious than a translation of my papers."[86]

Jones now maintained a flow of letters to Freud, reporting on the American situation, but in December he commented[87]: "I am not very hopeful of the present wave of interest for the Americans are a peculiar nation with habits of their own. . . . Their attitude towards progress is deplorable. They want to hear of the 'latest' method of treatment with an eye on the Almighty Dollar and think only of the credit or 'kudos' as they call it, it will bring them. Many eulogistic articles have been written on Freud's psychotherapy of late but they are absurdly superficial and I am afraid they will

85. Interview, Jones, May 10, 1956.
86. *James Jackson Putnam and Psycho Analysis,* Ed. N. G. Hale.
87. Jones to Freud, December 10, 1908.

strongly condemn it as soon as they hear of its sexual basis. . . . I published my Salzburg paper in Prince's journal in August and from the letters I received about it it seems to have found favour. . . . I am very eager to keep our movement scientific for that will greatly increase its 'respectability' and power of obtaining a hearing.''

By February 1909 Jones reported that he had spoken to the American Therapeutic Congress in New Haven, Connecticut, where the reception was unsympathetic and "a shiver . . . went through the audience when I said that Freud had sometimes treated a patient daily for as long as three years." Morton Prince next arranged another meeting in Boston at which Jones spoke and the audience was more responsive. Reporting to Freud, Jones wrote that the main problems for psycho-analysis in the United States "are peculiar to the Anglo-Saxon race and one must know nicely the kinds of currents and prejudices in order to combat them most successfully. I am sure it is important to aim first at the recognised people and not to popularize too soon. There is so much exploitation and vulgarisation here. . . .''[88] Then came this: "A man who writes always on the same subject is apt to be regarded here as a crank . . . and if the subject is sexual he is simply tabooed as a sexual neurasthenic. Hence I shall dilute my sex articles with articles on other subjects."

In February of 1909 Freud was complaining to Jones that he had mis-understood Morton Prince who "proclaims that my views are mostly taken from Janet and in fact identical with them."[89] Prince had also, Freud said, rejected Brill's papers for his journal on grounds — completely inadmissable to psycho-analysis — that they concentrated too much on sexuality. Freud was angry and even went so far as to suggest that Jones should break off relations with such a hyprocrite as Prince. Jones, in reply, insisted that Prince was not a hypocrite but a thorough-going gentleman whose fears about Brill's abstracts were only too well founded. The exchanges between the three men presently became fierce with Freud describing Prince as "having no talent at all" — "Something of a schemer" — and "really arrogant." One moment Jones' criticism of Prince was moderate and the next Prince bitterly resented what he considered Jones' attempt to "discredit" his work. Prince claimed that Jones was a psycho-analytic "fanatic" and found one of Jones' letters "not only bitter but offensive, not to say insolent." Jones, he concluded "was a nervous, high-strung self-centred young fellow and takes everything one says as personal to him-self."[90]

To add to the confusion, in March of 1909 Jung was writing to Freud: "I still can't figure out the news about Jones. In any case he is a canny fellow I' don't understand him too well. . . . He displays a great affection not only for me but for my family. To be sure he is nervous about the emphasis placed on

88. Ibid, February 7, 1909.
89. Freud to Jones, February 22, 1909.
90. *James Jackson Putnam and Psycho-Analysis,* Ed. N. G. Hale, 328/9.

sexuality in our propaganda a point that plays a big part in our relations with Brill.''

This put in ironic perspective Jones' subsequent criticism of Jung for trying to eradicate sexual etiology from the Freudian model. Against the received wisdom it was Jones, not Jung who, in the early pioneering days, was apprehensive of too much sexual emphasis.

However, Jones in Toronto and Putman in Boston first spread the Freudian gospel — albeit with certain modifications — and attempted to practise his techniques in relative isolation. It was this lack of supporting groups which drove Putnam to develop a considerable correspondence with Jones. Their letters ''record the apprenticeship of a distinguished physician in a new historic profession,''[91] but on the 13th January 1911 Jones wrote to Putman: ''You will be grieved to learn that this week very serious personal trouble has arisen here: to put it quite shortly a woman whom I saw four times last September (medically) has accused me of having had sexual intercourse with her . . . has gone to the President of the University to denounce me, is threatening legal proceedings and has attempted to shoot me. At present I am being guarded by an armed detective. She is an hysterical woman who has been divorced for adultery and whose main complaints on coming to me were (1) being haunted by erotic thoughts concerning a certain women with whom she used to sleep (she is pronouncedly homosexual) and (2) general mental confusion and tension arising from fear that she might satisfy her desires by appealing to some man in the street. I did not treat her by [psycho-analysis] but got her to talk, tried to calm her etc. Unfortunately she had an acute fit of Übertragang [transference] (she was a stranger here and I was the first man she had spoken to for months) and made unmistakeable overtures.''[92]

A number of people proceeded to ''cook up rumours about my 'lax' views and harmful treatment . . . and a regular incubation of delusions took place all round.''

Then came this astonishing statement in the letter: ''I foolishly paid the woman $500 blackmail to prevent a scandal which would be almost equally harmful either way. . . . You may imagine I am very worried indeed and dreadfully tired.''

That a man already the victim of two similar accusations should have implicated himself in the crime of which this third person complained by paying her blackmail money, is beyond comprehension.

Ten days later Jones wrote to Putnam again: ''I would of course have felt happier about the support of the medical profession here had I not known of the rancorous hostility towards and misunderstanding of my views as regards the sexual aspects of neurosis. Indeed I have just heard that a chief instigator of this very woman was one of the three Professors of Medicine in the University. Fortunately it looks at present as if the trouble will subside. I

91. Ibid.
92. Jones to Putnam, January 13, 1911.

am to see tomorrow the President of the University whose attitude towards the matter has been very sensible. . . . My legal adviser is considering the question of writing a warning letter to the woman doctor who is responsible for the bother. He is a very reliable and shrewd man and I feel safe in his hands. I am obliged for my wife's sake to keep detectives here and it is that uncertainty that is one of the most trying aspects of the matter.''

Jones re-told the story in a letter to Freud which named the woman (Dr. Gordon) and revealed that she was secretary of the local Purity League. Now, he said, he was accused of sending young men to prostitutes and recommending free love to young women. "Two of the latter became pregnant – there were three last May – but one seems to have disappeared.''

According to Anna Freud, Jones did not remain faithful to Loe Kann but that he should put at risk his whole career by seducing a patient does not make sense. Despite his male chauvinism he was a man who attracted women and did not need to exploit professional privilege. Clearly he was once again the victim of an hysterical patient whose overtures were rebuffed and took her revenge in a familiar manner.

The context in which this episode occurred made it all the more dangerous. As Jones again wrote to Freud "the attitude in Canada towards sexual topics has I should think hardly been equalled in the world's history: slime, loathing and disgust are the only terms to express it.''

These attitudes crystallised in the reaction of the Provincial Minister to a paper Jones published of a case of hypomania where sexual details were, in his view, essential. When the Minister's attention was drawn to the paper he called Dr. Clarke to his office and exploded in a stormy scene, saying that he would have prevented such "filthy stuff" going through the mails if he had been pre-warned. He also threatened to have the matter exposed in the Canadian House of Commons but this threat was never carried out.[93]

Another letter went to Putnam early in February: "My troubles seem to be slowly settling provided that no fresh explosion takes place. The woman doctor again called on the President and urged him to save the youth of Toronto by dismissing me but he told me he was convinced the whole story was nonsense and flatly advised her to keep her mouth shut otherwise she would find herself involved in serious legal action. I had a most satisfactory interview with him.''

Two unfortunate sentences followed in the letter. It was one thing to retaliate when attacked, but quite another to "hope to get her deported as an undesirable alien. She is certainly very psychopathic, is a morphimaniac, has attempted suicide and quarrelled with her employers.''

It is easy to select a number of Jones' early patients in Canada whose relatives persecuted him and create a false atmosphere of continuous feuding. He was reasonably successful with most of his patients but two more did result in indirect persecution. As a result of her analysis with Jones,

93. *James Jackson Putnam and Psycho-Analysis,* Ed. N. G. Hale.

one woman, the wife of a Dr. Joseph Collins, determined to divorce her husband and Collins proceeded to persecute Jones by every means in his power. Another irate husband decided that he would attend some of Dr. Jones' meetings and create rowdy scenes because the doctor's treatment of his wife had not only been unsuccessful but had "led him into great difficulties."

Loe Kann, Jones' mistress, was now finding the strain of threatened lawsuits, private detectives and persecution too much for her. Jones wrote to Freud: "Fortunately an end is in sight for I have had to come to a definite decision. My wife said she could not stand the anxiety and suspense of the situation here, and that if I stayed on she would leave me for good. There was also reason to think that that would soon mean suicide, though she did not say so. She is very pessimistic, and suffers greatly from complicated abdominal trouble (kidney stone, etc.). I decided to accompany her, and our plan at present is as follows: I go to Europe in September and if I get my Professorship before I go, I will come back for one session only to lecture and then leave; if I do not get it I shan't come back. In the meantime I will try to get a position in the States. If I do not get one to my liking I will go to England. In any case I shall find a way to go on with the work.

"I have not been able to do any work in the past two months or more, but I now feel I can settle down to it again."

Another letter to Freud in July said[94]: "But as you know the whole question has been complicated by my wife's feelings. She is a chronic invalid, from calculous pyleo-nephritis and other complications, and suffers from severe and almost constant pain for which she has had to take huge doses of morphia, which has considerably affected her both bodily and mentally. Her life here is miserable and apart from me very lonely, for she is away from her friends and relatives, and cordially detests the Canadian people, as I do myself. She has made big sacrifices for me in the past in many ways, although she does not believe in my work and is very fearful about the dangers of it to my reputation. She has done her utmost to stand the strain here and was willing to try to stand another year of it for the sake of my getting the professor's title. As it is, however, it would be inhuman of me to ask her to stay longer, and, I expect, fruitless. My only option, therefore, is to return with her to London or to separate, which is unthinkable. I have thus decided to leave here for good in the middle of next September. The future is of course uncertain. I have very little chance of getting much of a position in London, but I believe that there should be enough demand for my services to keep me busy in psycho-analytic work."

By August Jones was writing[95]: "When it became known that I was leaving, various university authorities, particularly the Chancellor, whose daughter I had successfully treated, became surprisingly active in their efforts to retain me; Adolf Meyer and others also wrote strong letters about

94. Jones to Freud, July 13, 1911.
95. Ibid, August 31, 1911.

it. The result was that they have given me the professorship (in psychiatry) as well as a special department in neurology. On the strength of that I have, after considerable difficulty, persuaded my wife to stay a little longer, until next April. After then we shall settle in London, but I hope to be able to retain the position and cross over every year for four months (to Toronto) for the work of the session."

By now Jones was devoting all his energies to mastering psycho-analytic theory and technique and presenting it to others in lucid papers which revealed great gifts of exposition. At least six papers were written between the years 1907 and 1909 but his culminating essay on Hamlet was still in process of fermentation. He now wrote a very revealing letter to Freud: "Your encouragement is especially valuable to me for many reasons: first the obvious one of pupil and master, then the fact that I am more responsive than initiative by nature and only work under an external personal stimulus, then further that in my work I am very isolated, for all my friends and relatives have used their strongest influence to dissuade me from undertaking 'such dangerous work' (sexual). It was a big break with them all for me to continue it alone, for at that time I had no personal help from you and the school, having various internal troubes, and only my intense conviction that your work was profoundly true and important carried me through. Fortunately things are now in smoother water, chiefly owing to you personally, so you see I am both grateful to and dependent on you."[96] In the same letter came the revelation that Freud did not know what he meant by the word orgasm — irony could go no further. "Brill tells me you didn't understand what I meant by 'orgasm.' Well, I don't know what other word to use. The patient, who of course did not touch me, would close her eyes, get flushed cheeks, breathe rapidly, make movements of coitus (she was on her back in bed), and come to a climax just as in an orgasm. It was curious, wasn't it? She did not use her hands for masturbation in it." By June of the same year he once more delineated his professional potential in derogatory terms: "The originality-complex is not strong in me; my ambition is rather to know, to be 'behind the scenes,' and 'in the know,' rather than *to find out*. I realise that I have very little talent for originality; any talent I may have lies rather in the direction of being able to see perhaps quickly what others point out: no doubt that also has its use in the world."[97]

Inspired by Freud and Ferenczi, on September 10 Jones wrote to Putnam suggesting that they should send a circular to G. Stanley Hall, August Hoch, C. Macfie Campbell and four other interested men proposing the formulation of an American psycho-analytic organisation. It launched a bitter controversy about the precise nature of Freud's discoveries and techniques with Morton Prince imploring Putnam not to get "so far involved with Jones and his crowd as to unconsciously slide into his attitude." Prince observed, with obvious disdain, that Freud's followers were "styling themselves

96. Jones to Freud August 6, 1911.
97. Jones to Freud, June 1910.

psycho-analysts'' which he believed characterised a cult of "believing," and he did not want to become involved with what was tantamount to a religious sect.

Although Jones met more opposition to Freud's theories in Canada than he and Putnam encountered in Boston, when Putnam suggested Jones as an ideal man to work in Harvard's Psychological Laboratory, Hugo Münsterberg, head of the laboratory, said he knew of no more suitable candidate but would the emphasis Jones put on sexual matters be suitable for a course not intended for medical students.

Nothing was more calculated to arouse Jones' energies than resistance. In the next few months he busied himself between the two countries, interviewing, lecturing, discussing, and slowly the movement showed signs of organisational structures within the fiercely contending parties. Brill, who was a good organiser, founded the New York Psycho Analytic Society early in 1911 and Jones, still in Toronto, countered by forming the American Psycho Analytic Society in May 1911, an organisation intended to embrace all analysts living outside New York.

One of the more distinguished and most sympathetic Americans was Stanley Hall, then president of Clark University in Worcester, Massachusetts, who had as early as 1904 risked academic damnation by giving a series of lectures based on sex. He had also written a book, *Adolescence,* in which he mentioned Freud a number of times and predicted that his theories would become important to the psychology of art and religion. Thus the ground was prepared for a major event in Freud's life: his visit to America in 1909.

At first sight Stanley Hall's invitation to Freud to lecture at Clark University underlined spectacularly the spread of Freud's doctrines, but Freud's initial enthusiasm for the trip was quickly qualified by a mysterious reluctance. At the outset sheer money matters made him hesitate. He did not regard himself as financially secure enough to surrender three weeks' earnings from his practice in Vienna and when he discussed the matter with his wife she was equally reluctant to see him setting out on "such a vast journey" without guaranteed fees.

All these difficulties were overcome and Freud set sail from Bremen with Jung and Ferenczi on the George Washington on August 21, 1909, and in Bremen a remarkable incident occurred.

Two very different accounts of this episode are available. When Jones wrote the first he did not have at his disposal Jung's personal testimony given to Aniela Jaffé in his eightieth year.

According to Jung the three men met in Bremen, where Freud was host at a luncheon party and Jung turned the conversation to the so-called peat bogs in certain districts of Northern Germany. He mentioned the bodies of prehistoric men who either drowned in the marshes or were buried there. Jung, fascinated by the legend, talked interminably about it until Freud began to interrupt with phrases like "why are you so interested in these corpses?"

In Jung's own words Freud "was inordinately vexed by the whole thing and . . . suddenly he fainted." According to Jung "when he came round again Freud was convinced that all this chatter about corpses meant that I had a death wish against him. I was more than surprised by this interpretation."[98]

Jones gave a very different version of an incident which clearly revealed the difficulties already developing between Jung and Freud. According to Jones, Freud was in high spirits at the luncheon, "doubtless elated at winning Jung round again,"[99] but Jung made no reference to the fact. This victory, according to Jones, consisted in breaking Jung's fanatical anti-alcohol tradition and persuading him to drink wine during luncheon.

Freud himself later analysed the occurrence, turning his own techniques on himself, but the explanation did not satisfy Jung. Freud said that as a boy he had often wished his baby brother Julius dead and when, at the age of one year and seven months, the boy did die, it left a terrible sense of guilt. Jones commented in his biography of Freud: "It would therefore seem that Freud was himself a mild case of the type he described as those wrecked by success, in this case the success of defeating his opponent — the earliest example of which was his death wish against his little brother Julius."

Freud, Jung and Ferenczi arrived in New York on Sunday evening September 27 to be received by Dr. A. A. Brill who quickly organised a lightning tour of New York, which carried them first to Central Park West and then into Harlem and the Chinese quarter. Jones joined the party on the third day to eat dinner on Hammerstein's roof garden and then the American sense of fun insisted on their going to see one of those early films in which one comic chase followed another. Jones recorded "Ferenczi in his boyish way was very excited . . . but Freud was only quietly amused."[100]

Freud, as we know, did not like America. He said the food gave him indigestion and the lavatories were inaccessible but Jones said he had a good digestion and dyspepsia was merely a disguise for other reactions. Apart from his difficulties with the language Freud disliked the idea that commercial success dominated the scale of values in the United States, as if it did not permeate most late industrial capitalist societies. Grudgingly admitting some American achievements to Jones, Freud said "America is gigantic — yes — but a gigantic mistake."

Later all four men took the elevated from 42nd Street to the piers and boarded an old-fashioned steamer with beautiful white decks, proceeding up the East River under the Manhattan and Brooklyn bridges until they reached Long Island. When they at last arrived at Worcester, they stopped at the Standish Hotel on the American plan with board, and at six o'clock in the evening had their first meeting with Professor Stanley Hall. He was a man

98. Jung: *Memories, Dreams and Reflections.*
99. Jones: *Freud Life and Work* Vol. 2, 165.
100. Brome: *Freud and His Early Circle,* 104.

close on seventy, refined, distinguished and endowed with a wife who cooked wonderful meals. A pioneer in American experimental psychology Stanley Hall had written several books which Freud and Jones regarded sympathetically. Already a great admirer of Freud's theories, he was to become a foundation member of the American Psycho-Analytic Society.

On the first day at Clark University, Freud took Jones aside and discussed with him the lectures he was about to give. He explained that he would have preferred to devote the whole course to dreams but thought that practically-minded Americans might find it all too transcendental. Instead, he gave a straightforward introductory course on the whole subject of psycho-analysis. Following the third lecture a woman waylaid Jones outside the lecture theatre and expressed her grave disappointment that Freud had not dealt with the kernel of the whole matter – sexuality. This, of course, was not true, but Freud did tactfully avoid being too explicit about a subject which he felt might build up unnecessary resistances. Indeed, after all his protestations to Prince, Brill and Jones it converted him into something of a hypocrite and the answer Freud finally gave to the lady was ambivalent: "I do not let myself be moved either to or away from the theme of sexuality."

It was significant that in the lectures which followed Jung alone among the visitors gave two complete talks on his own work mentioning Freud in the third lecture only. Jones and Ferenczi kept strictly within Freudian precincts and paid tribute to the Master throughout. Jung spoke on dementia praecox, Jones on Rationalisation in Everyday Life, and Adler Sadism in Life and in Neurosis.

On September 8 Jung wrote to his wife that Freud had delivered his lecture the previous day and received great applause. "We are gaining ground here and our following is growing slowly but surely. I was greatly surprised since I had prepared myself for opposition."[101]

Jones makes no reference in his account of the American trip to the generous way in which Jung responded to the overwhelming response given to Freud: "Freud is in his seventh heaven" he wrote "and I am glad with all my heart to see him so."[102]

Another member of the assembled company was that great psychological pioneer William James who had arrived at a belief in the unconscious through his exploration of a case of dual personality. Jones and James responded warmly to one another and one day, walking together, James put his arm across Jones' shoulders and said "Yours is the psychology of the future." There was a dramatic moment when walking with Freud, James stopped, suddenly handed Freud his bag and asked him to walk on "saying that he would catch me up as soon as he had got through an attack of angina pectoris."[103]

Astonishingly, in view of the letters he had written to Jung, on the sixth day of their visit Freud had a small brush with Jones. It seemed impossible

101. Jung to Emma Jung, September 8, 1909.
102. Ibid.
103. Freud: *An Autobiographical Study,* 95.

that anyone could question Jones' total devotion to Freudian theory but for reasons which later emerged Freud formed at Worcester an exaggerated idea of Jones' independence. "He feared" Jones wrote "that I might not become a close adherent." Jones understates in his autobiography his early resistance to the sexual basis of neurosis. It was this which troubled Freud.

Clearly Jones must have been an attractive person to Freud who went to considerable lengths to re-affirm their relationship, and when Jones had to hurry back to Toronto University it was Freud who personally saw him off from the station. Before the train left he repeated his strong desire that they should "keep together." His final words were "You will find it worth while."[104]

One other episode needs emphasising in view of what followed. Before he left, Jones had a brief talk with Jung and was surprised to hear him say "he found it necessary to go into unsavoury topics with his patients." It was disagreeable, he said, when one met them at dinner socially. Such matters should be hinted at and the patients would understand without plain language being used. Later Jung gave the American visit as the date of his first dissensions from Freud's sexual doctrines and the Oedipal complex. Somewhat disingenuously Jones recorded this exchange with Jung without acknowledging that at this stage he, too, had his sexual reservations. Indeed, on his return to Vienna, Freud told Jung that he had received "a nice contrite" letter from Jones. Yet in the *Bulletin of the Ontario Hospital for the Insane* for November 1909 Jones published an address on Psycho-Analysis in Psycho-Therapy which made no reference to the sexual nature of unconscious wishes in the neurotic personality.

By the beginning of 1910 Freud wrote to Jung: "The other day I had a letter from Jones more contrite than necessary. His resistance seems to have been broken down for good." And by the Spring of 1910 Jones was writing to Freud: "About six or eight months ago I determined not only to further the cause by all means in my power which I had always decided on, but also to further it by whatever means you personally decided on and to follow your recommendations as exactly as possible."[105]

A few weeks later another explanation of the Worcester contradictions became apparent in a further letter to Freud. "My resistances have sprung not from any objections to your theories but partly from an absurd jealous egotism and partly from the influence of a strong Father complex. You are right in surmising that I had at one time hoped to play a more important part in the movement in England and America than I now see is possible: it should and must be directed by you and I am content to be of any service in my power along the lines you advise."

Did Jones hope to lead the British and American Analytical Societies independently from Freud? That meaning is implicit in his letter. Freud could easily have read such an ambition as another break away attempt

104. Brome: *Freud and His Early Circle,* 108.
105. Jones to Freud, October 17, 1909.

comparable with that which eventually followed in the case of Jung. Hence his concern at Worcester.

The letters he addressed to Jones continued to reflect other small anxieties. In November of 1909 he wrote:

My dear Jones,

". . . your critical remarks on Stekel's book are obviously true: you have hit the mark. He is weak in theory and thought but he has a good flair for the meaning of the hidden and unconscious. . . ."

Then followed this sentence: "It is interesting for me that you prefer the broader aspects of the theory, the normal, psychological and cultural relations to the pathological."[106]

Contradicting the view of some of his colleagues at the time Freud wrote in another letter: ". . . As for your diplomacy I know you are excellently fitted for it and will do it masterly."[107]

By March 1910 Freud was writing to say that he had received and read Jones' revised *Hamlet* article "which is excellent." Having read the original draft while they were at Worcester together he now found it so much improved that he scarcely recognised it.[108]

As everyone knows, in *The Interpretation of Dreams* Freud had maintained that Shakespeare's play was "built up on Hamlet's hesitations over fulfilling the task of revenge that is assigned to him: but the text offers no reasons or motives for these hesitations."[109]

The Oediptal complex Freud believed had driven Hamlet to desire to sleep with his mother, and when he was called upon to slay the man who had murdered his father and taken his place, Hamlet found himself crippled because he too had once contemplated such a transformation and, possibly such a murder. Jones had taken this seminal idea and worked it up into a complex and scholarly paper with a wealth of literary and historical reference reinforcing step by step Freud's interpretation. Modern Shakespearean critics scorn Freud's approach and point out that it is a matter of opinion whether Hamlet's hesitation constitutes the kernel of the play, but this is only the beginning of a subtle argument which will be examined in greater detail later. The extraordinary point about the Hamlet essay is that it was one of no less than forty such papers Jones wrote while in Canada, and certainly the most distinguished.

Jones' prolific literary output was partly due to the fact that his personal life had fallen into disarray. As we have seen, Loe Kann found it much more difficult adjusting to the Canadian way of life than Jones, and their mutual homesickness for Europe was magnified in her case by physical ill health which activated her latent neurosis. This led to fits of depression, quarrelling and a constant plea to return to London, Vienna, Paris, anywhere except this bland functional society where the failure to integrate a national identity led to so many forms of misunderstanding.

106. Freud to Jones, November 20, 1909.
107. Ibid February 2, 1909.
108. Freud to Jones, March 10, 1910.
109. Freud: *Interpretation of Dreams,* 264.

The second International Psycho-Analytic Congress took place at Nuremberg on March 30, 1910 but Jones was so concerned about Loe and enmeshed in psychiatric work, that he could not leave Toronto. It was a great disappointment. By now the direction of his career was not only clear; he was deeply committed.

Freud joined the 1910 conference early on the very first day in a mood which can be judged from a letter he wrote to Abraham: "I no longer get any pleasure from the Viennese. I have a heavy cross to bear with the older generation, Stekel, Adler, Sadger. They will soon be feeling that I am an obstacle and will treat me as such."[110]

Jones later gave a detailed account of the conference but there were several interpretations of what took place. According to Jones in his *Life and Work of Freud* "Because of certain administrative proposals . . . the second Congress passed off in a less friendly atmosphere than had the first." It was a masterpiece of understatement.

No less than fifty or sixty analysts came together at Nuremberg and several interesting scientific papers were given, among them one by Freud on *The Future of Psycho-Analysis* which made "valuable suggestions concerning both its internal development and its external influence." Freud had, of course, already initiated the idea of "bringing together analysts in closer bond" and now Ferenczi, regarded by Freud as a person of great importance, was nominated by Freud to put the proposition to Congress. He seems to have gone out of his way to indicate that the Viennese analysts were of a decidedly inferior order to those of Zurich and concluded that future administration should be left in the hands of the men from Zurich. This in itself deeply disturbed Adler and Stekel, and Adler intervened to demand a hearing. Ferenczi elaborated his proposal, and now came an even more startling proposition. "I was surprised", Stekel wrote in his Autobiography "when Ferenczi (induced by Freud) proposed that Jung should be elected lifetime President of the International Society . . . [with] the right (among other things) to examine all papers submitted and to decide which he should publish." This meant in effect that no analytical paper would be published without his consent.[111]

Even Jones, in his biography of Freud, was driven at this point to admit that this last proposition caused "a storm of protest."

No verbatim account of the ensuing discussion has survived but so heated did it become that the chairman was forced to suspend the sittings until the following day.

Jones lays the blame for what followed on Ferenczi but Ferenczi was merely the willing instrument of Freud and there were some present at the Congress who believed that Freud had deliberately chosen a "stooge" to present his revolutionary proposition, knowing how inflammatory it would be.

110. Brome: *Freud and His Early Circle,* 41.
111. Ibid.

Stekel takes up the story once more in his autobiography but it must be remembered that the Freudians regarded Stekel as an unreliable witness. "According to Stekel he now arranged what he described as a 'secret meeting" of his Viennese colleagues, nearly twenty in number, carefully excluding all their rivals from Zurich, and made a rousing political speech which drew applause from everyone. For years, he said, they, the Viennese, had overcome opposition, defended Freud and fought for his reputation and now this astonishing little man Ferenczi had the audacity to suggest that the leadership should pass to a newcomer like Jung who knew nothing of the hardships of pioneering. It was outrageous. "Suddenly the door opened" Stekel wrote "and there was Freud. He was greatly excited and tried to persuade us to accept Ferenczi's motion: he predicted hard times and a strong opposition by official science. He grasped his coat and cried 'They begrudge me the coat I am wearing: I don't know whether in the future I will earn my daily bread.' Tears were streaming down his cheeks. 'An official psychiatrist and a gentile must be the leaders of the movement' he said."[112]

The whole account reads somewhat melodramatically and the picture of Freud in tears is difficult to reconcile with the realist we know him to have been; yet even Ernest Jones, who was the last man to emphasise weaknesses in Freud had him declaiming: "My enemies would be willing to see me starve; they would tear my coat off my back."

Much more to the point was Jones' comment in his autobiography: Freud was too mistrustful of the average mind to adopt the democratic attitude customary in scientific societies so he wished there to be a prominent leader "who should guide the doings of branch societies and their members: moreover he wanted the leader to be in a permanent position."[113]

Once again divergent accounts are given of what followed. Jones says that Freud announced his retirement as President of the Viennese Society and agreed that Adler should take his place. He also agreed that, partly to counterbalance Jung's editorship of the *Jahrbuch,* a new periodical be founded, the monthly *Zentralblatt für Psychoanalyse* which would be edited jointly by Adler and Stekel.[114]

Freud later carried out a post mortem on the Nuremberg Congress in a letter to Ferenczi which said that they were both somewhat to blame for not anticipating the effect of their announcement on the Viennese.

Jones, in the account he later wrote, gave it as his view that Freud was no Menschenkenner — or judge of individual men. Hence all these troubles.

*   *   *

Back in Canada, Jones received reports of the Congress with some uneasiness and wondered whether he "wasn't wasting his time in the wilds instead of returning to the psychoanalytic centre."

112. Stekel: *Autobiography.*
113. Jones: *Free Associations,* 214.
114. Jones: *Freud, Life & Works,* Vol. II, 77.

In June of 1910 Jones helped to arrange a special "symposium of psycho-neuroses" and marshalled his forces effectively. Two of the four major speakers were by now Freudians – J. J. Putnam and Dr. August Hoch, a New York psychiatrist who had studied with Jung. Only Dr. W. H. Hattie, superintendent of the Nova Scotia Hospital, found himself "not sufficiently convinced" to commit himself entirely to Freud's theories. Jones' paper, *A Modern Conception of the Psycho-Neuroses* complemented Putnam's more general paper.

One man he failed to win over was crucial to his future in Canada – Dr. C. K. Clarke, Jones' boss at the Toronto Hospital for the Insane. After reading Freud's Clark University lectures he informed Jones that "any ordinary reader would gather Freud advocates Free Love, removal of all restraints and a relapse into savagery" – as wildly inaccurate an account of the lectures as unbridled prejudice could produce.

The impermeability of Canada to the rapidly growing new approach to psychological medicine, sex and morality, which had begun far back in the 1880s with the work of Krafft–Ebing and Havelock Ellis, was remarkable.

It was not surprising that Jones' inclination to abandon Canada remained strong and even America as an alternative did not attract him. By June 1911 Adolf Meyer was writing to Jones: "Mrs. Jones must feel very isolated in this country. But I thought you would give New York or Boston a chance. Putnam and I [would] feel your going away most keenly because we were a working force in this country to counteract the tendency to easy-going opportunism of the rank and file."[115]

Jones' mother had died recently from a cerebral haemorrhage which caused him what he coolly described as "normal grief." At the time Jones' two sisters were both on the American side of the Atlantic and he deputised them to attend the funeral only to find neither of them anxious to return to the life of an unattractive and remote country village. All three were examples of people who had broken out of their cultural background, with one sister oscillating lightheartedly between art and medicine, and Elizabeth thoroughly enjoying the company of her brother and his mistress in Toronto. In the end Jones said "it was decided that my younger sister should go" and Elizabeth remain.

As for Elizabeth, she continued as housekeeper-companion for another eighteen months and then decided to take what was said to be a holiday trip home which became in fact a romantic adventure. Already corresponding with someone she regarded as "an eligible suitor," Jones imagined that she intended to scrutinise the man at close quarters, but his old friend Trotter got wind of her movements and dramatically appeared at the railway terminus when she arrived in London with a proposal of marriage. They had never corresponded, Jones doubted whether they had ever been alone together and unless an operation for thyroid which Trotter had performed on her throat

115. Meyer to Jones, June 10, 1911.

qualified as intimacy, they were, in the modern sense of the word, strangers, but Elizabeth seems to have accepted him on the spot, and Jones cautiously called the marriage which followed "as successful a marriage as I have known."

Certainly by now he had encountered enough alienation, friction, open quarrelling and hatred among his married patients to reinforce his belief that "trial marriages" were a necessity before committing oneself to what Trotter had once described as that "emotional trauma."

On one excuse or another Jones succeeded in making at least one trip a year back to his beloved Europe and it was these excursions which complicated his already tormented relationship with Loe. The cultural atmosphere in Europe was for her so different that she literally felt she was breathing a new and liberating air whenever she returned to London, Paris or Vienna. Nothing could be more unsettling to such a sensitive person and she returned to Canada with greater reluctance on every occasion.

Jones never missed a chance to meet his old friend Trotter on his European trips but they were pulling apart emotionally and intellectually. Trotter now wrote in an undated letter: "As to Freud, I think you write greatly about this business and I have read and re-read your letter with much joy. . . . As regards the facts as far as I know them I don't think I'm restive. The actual state of affairs is, isn't it, that I do not get the sense of illumination, the sense of splendour that you do."

Despite all his protests, breaking away from the security of his university job was a daunting prospect to Jones and now he envisaged compromise whereby he spent part of each year in Canada and the remainder in England. "The university work itself could easily be got through in four or five months."

In the event that proved unworkable. Slowly, Jones' problems with Loe intensified. The Weimar Conference which intervened in the year 1911 took Jones away from Loe for a brief period and while in Weimar he consulted Freud about her. Eventually, Freud was to take her into treatment but the details of the Weimar Congress need examination first.

CHAPTER IX

Loe Kann, Jones and Freud

JONES described the Weimar Congress of 1911 as "in many ways the pleasantest and most successful of any." The Congress took place in September but three months before Jones had been instrumental in drawing Freud's attention to developing deviation in Jung's thinking.

In May 1911 Jung had written to Freud indicating that he could no longer accept a strictly sexual interpretation of the word libido and now regarded it as almost synonymous with general psychic energy. Both discussed their respective definitions in the correspondence which followed, and surprisingly, Frau Emma Jung intervened in the correspondence to warn Freud that he would not like what her husband was about to say in print.

It was Ernest Jones who next read the second part of Jung's two-part paper *Symbols of the Libido* in proof and immediately wrote to Freud outlining the essay and repeating Emma Jung's warning. This drove Freud to send for a copy of the *Jahrbuch* and after he had read the paper he wrote to Jones pinpointing the precise page where Jung had, in his view, gone astray.

Despite this, the Weimar Congress did recover the friendly atmosphere which had distinguished the first, Salzburg, Congress with no hostility from the Viennese to disrupt the proceedings. It also widened once again the international character of the whole psycho-analytic movement with Bleuler and the Reverends Keller and Pfister from Switzerland, Magnus Hirschfeld from Berlin, van Emden from Holland, Putnam, Brill, Ames and Hinkle from America and of course Jones from England. Jones wrote: "The papers were of a high order. Among them were several classics of psycho-analytic literature, notably papers by Bleuler on autism and by Jung on the symbolism in the psychoses and mythology."

It was remarkable that Jones should have written so casually of *Wandlungen und Symbole der Libido,* the paper delivered by Jung, because it contained the seeds of the tremendous upheaval in the movement which was shortly to follow. The year 1911 would go down as the first year in which a major figure in analytic circles, Adler, broke away from Freud and set moving reberberating shocks which were to topple Stekel and finally even Jung himself. For the moment all moved serenely. Jones found himself thoroughly enjoying the Congress and the sympathetic environment of Weimar, charged as it was with memories of Goethe.

It was the American, Putnam, who became the highlight of the conference when he delivered a very unorthodox paper on *The Importance of Philosophy for the Further Development of Psycho-Analysis,* a plea for the assimilation of his own Hegelian brand of philosophy into Freudian doctrine. [116] As we know, Putnam with Jones, had conducted a "noble" campaign to convert America to the psycho-analytic cause and now Putnam's distinguished personality and modesty combined to give his paper a hearing which normally would have been anything but sympathetic. Jones commented "Most of us did not see the necessity of adopting any particular system. Freud was, of course, very polite on the matter but he remarked to me afterwards: 'Putnam's philosophy reminds me of a decorative centrepiece; everyone admires it but no one touches it.' "

Although Jung clearly dominated some aspects of the Congress, Jones, whose retrospective hostility towards Jung in all his writings was strong, chose Bleuler from the Swiss contingent to put first in his list of commendations.

Jones also stressed – quite rightly – the importance of Freud's paper, *A Postscript to the Schreber Case,* in which he made his first reference to myth-making tendencies of mankind and suggested that the unconscious contained "not only the infantile material but also relics from primitive man." No attempt was made by Jones to relate it to Jung's paper *Symbolism, the Psychoses and Mythology* which dealt dealt with closely related matters, and invited comparison. Unfortunately Jung's paper has disappeared except in the form of an abstract by Rank, but Freud in his own *A Postscript to the Schreber Case* said "these remarks may serve to show that Jung had excellent grounds for his assertion that the mythopoeic forces of mankind are not extinct but that to this very day they give rise in the neuroses to the same physical products as in the remotest past ages." Jones frequently invoked this paragraph in later arguments to show that Freud was fully familiar with the "raw material" of the collective unconscious and its structures without finding it necessary to differentiate between the collective and "personal" unconscious.

Freud was at the top of his form, reading his elegant paper with a panache which made it almost a virtuoso performance. The audience particularly liked his reference to the myth that the eagle always forced its young to look at the sun without blinking, and rejected those who failed. "When Schreber boasts that he can look into the sun unscathed and undazzled he has redis-covered the mythological method of expressing his filial relation to the sun and has confirmed us once again in our view that the sun is a symbol of the father." Replying to the paper, Stekel reminded them that "Freud had left in Vienna an eagle who dared to look at the sun."

116. Jones: *Freud, Life and Work,* Vol. 2, 96.

There is little evidence of Jones' part in the Weimar conference and his autobiography passes over it in two paragraphs. By general agreement Jung and Riklin were re-elected President and Secretary of the International Association and it was decided that the *Corespondenzblatt* or Bulletin, of which six issues had been published in Zurich, should be incorporated into the *Zentralblatt*. According to Jones, Freud and Jung were on the best of terms throughout the Congress and when someone almost within earshot of Jung ventured to say that Jung's jokes were rather coarse, Freud immediately rejoined "It's a healthy coarseness."

*   *   *

As we have seen Jones had a private talk with Freud at the Weimar Conference about his troubles with Loe Kann and – somewhat reluctantly – Freud agreed to take her into analysis. Freud's reluctance was matched by Loe's. When Jones returned to Toronto he found her moods fluctuating, sometimes responsive, sometimes depressed, but she was apprehensive of committing herself to Freud's hands.

By October of 1911 Jones was writing to Freud: ". . . Adolf Meyer had done her much good by talking to her very reasonably about my work. I broached the subject of treatment to her, and in the joyful mood at my return she was surprisingly optimistic. Your opinion that there was a chance for her to get better carried very great weight, for she could hardly help living with me and not thinking highly of you. She said she would do anything, except so long as she wasn't expected to believe things she couldn't believe, (i.e. have ideas forced on her against her will). Rather to my surprise she was very definite on the point that she would rather be treated by you than anyone else, but I told her that it was very unlikely that would be possible but that you would judge best.

"I shall never forget the kind way you talked to me in Weimar, and am more grateful than I can say. I went away that night overjoyed at the thought that she might get better. To be honest, however, I must say that on the following day I had a disagreeable dream, which after a difficult analysis showed the wish that she might die instead of getting better. I felt greatly relieved after having it out with myself, and ever since have been freer and happier than for years.

"I have no other special news. This year I have much less routine work than before (hospital, etc.) and can devote myself to practice and writing. I have just started with five new patients, an alcoholic, two pseudo-epilepsies, a conversion hysteria and an anxiety-hysteria."[117]

By March 15, 1912 Jones was writing: "First let me talk a little about my wife. I am glad to sasy that she has been better in every way, except of course that the morphia is the same as before. We have been happier this winter than

117. Jones to Freud, October 17, 1911.

ever before, and have been very near together. She is also more hopeful about herself, and her attitude towards psycho-analysis seems to have changed to some extent, though of course one cannot be sure that this latter is deep; the resistances must still be there. Only recently she wistfully wondered whether a time would come when she might again be interested in my work and help me in it, as she used to in the days that I did only neurology. One thing I am sure of, and that is that she has a more sincere desire to get well than ever before. She has been for some time trying to overcome her inhibition about writing, so that she might write a letter to you; I do not know what it will be about, but it will probably give you a better idea of her state of mind than I can." [118]

Freud now finally agreed to "take her on" and in the summer of 1912, Ernest travelled with her to Vienna where they took a small flat and Loe finally placed herself in Freud's hands.

Anna Freud, who met her at this time, described her as "good looking, rather tall" and "very lively looking'. [119] "There is no question that my father liked her and appreciated her quite unusual personality."

Anna Freud's letter contradicts the date on which Loe's treatment began. "She came to [Freud] *after* her association with Ernest Jones ended." [120] (My italics.)

Whatever the precise date, Jones himself spent two or three evenings a week tête à tête with Freud and now there was no shred of ambivalence in their relationship. According to Jones, Freud had "taken a liking to me" and wanted to "open his heart to someone not of his own milieu." Freud, of course, was a magnificent talker and they ranged over philosophy, literature, sociology and "above all psychology." "More than once I had to reproach myself for allowing him to continue until three o'clock in the morning when I knew his first patient was due at eight o'clock." Jones now gave his evaluation of Freud's character, describing his "fearlessness of thought, his absolute integrity of mind and character and his personal lovableness." [121]

In a relationship destined to last thirty-three years, this was the honeymoon period which later underwent many fluctuations but now nothing could qualify Jones' admiration for Freud.

It came as a surprise to Jones that when Freud began his analysis of Loe, he quickly expressed the opinion that it would be wiser if Jones did not remain in Vienna. The relaxed schedules of Toronto University did not require Jones' presence until January and he now took a prolonged holiday in Italy, travelling from Rome to Venice and on to Florence, searching for aesthetic as much as psychological enrichment. Having many of the characteristics of the anal-erotic type — punctuality, tidiness, compulsiveness — he planned his day with great skill to avoid any unnecessary waste of time. He bought and studied modern critical guide-books and armed with these frequently arrived at the museums and churches as they were opening.

118. Ibid, March 15, 1912.
119. Anna Freud to Author, December 23, 1980.
120. Ibid.
121. Jones: *Free Associations,* 197.

Not in any sense an artistic man, Jones claimed that his aesthetic taste was "of the acquired variety" and he spent every evening reading authors like Ruskin, Vasari and Berenson on aesthetic principles or Italian painting. The overwhelming artistic richness of Italy left "an ineffaceable impression" and by December of that year he had exchanged his cultural allegiances with Germany for those of Italy, a transformation to be heavily underlined by the outbreak of the First World War, now only two years away.

Meanwhile, in Vienna, Loe's analysis with Freud produced two dramatically different accounts, one from Freud and another from Loe herself. Freud wrote to Jones[122] in October 1912 stating that Loe was in much better shape and that her daily dose of morphia had been halved. She was a "precocious creature of the highest value" and allowed him to read Ernest's letters from Italy which gave him great pleasure. By November he wrote to Jones[123] "Analysis progressing very satisfactorily. I could draw the outlines of her very interesting story." The transference was complete and she understood its meaning. One disturbing factor was the lack of resistance, and when an unexpected attack of pain arose he "wondered whether it was organic, exacerbated by neurosis" in which case he would have to revise his "diagnosis of the facts."

There now occurred in the correspondence the name of a girl acting as nurse or companion to Loe, but Lina's relatively menial role was to change over the next few years. Lina found blood in Loe's urine and Freud's attempts to have it analysed were foiled when Loe accidentally spilt the specimen. New specimens, Freud wrote, were to be obtained and further diagnosis would depend on the results.

In a letter from Florence[124] Jones gave a very different account of the analysis derived from Loe's letters to him. "I want to thank you very deeply for the details about my wife, which were just the kind I wanted to know. It was a great relief to read them. I agree that the gain of treatment would be almost as great even if an organic element remained, but what you called her 'fanatical' character makes her wish for 'all or nothing'; she finds it difficult to reconcile herself to half results in anything. You gave me good news about the progress, but today I got a letter from her, written two days after yours, which gives the reverse side of the medal – no doubt provoked by her attack and other things. She complains bitterly about you, that you do not trust her, do not believe her statements, and twist everything until she is quite confused in her mind. I suppose the resistance had previously been concealed in a woman's deceptive way, by her pretending to agree to conclusions that in her heart she did not accept. At all events, you probably have as much resistance to deal with now as will more than make up for its previous absence. She is beginning to feel the treatment as an attack on her personality; she repeats that if she were allowed to conduct it herself, at her own speed, etc., she would be good and do her best (evidently anal-complex) but to be 'forced,

122. Freud to Jones, November 8, 1912.
123. Ibid, November 8, 1912.
124. Jones to Freud, November 13, 1912.

bullied and teased' against her will makes her feel broken and hopeless with no heart to give herself to the treatment. And her chief cry is your want of faith in her, your doubt, disbelief and suspicion of what she says. (Personally I have always found her invariably trustworthy in her statements, though of course she deceives herself as we all do.)'' The letter concluded that he had frequently found blood and pus in her urine.

Freud replied at once to reassure Jones[125] on November 14, 1912. Loe's hysterical attack he said had expended its force in her letter to Jones — "that last famous letter" — and she was once again her charming self. The letter, Freud said, must have told Jones all that she had so far not dared to tell him and if this first burst of abreaction had disappeared they would "get more profit" from the next one. As for the urine, a new sample revealed only a small trace of pus.

By November 15, Freud was writing that the only justification for Loe's claim that he mistrusted her statements was the doubt he expressed about the origins of her troubles: whether in fact they were "from the kidney or from the soul.'"[126] She had now disclosed that as a child she had developed a habit of constantly lying. Perhaps, after the first abreaction, it would have been more profitable to exclude the organic diagnosis and on the next occasion he would certainly do so.

Jones had written the day before he received this letter: "I got a letter from my wife of a very different tone, full of sunniness and life and you can imagine how much it cheered me.'"[127]

On the 17th he wrote again from Florence: "From your hard work you spare time to soothe my anxiousness. I have seen many such attacks, and they are terrible to live with. From no patient have I received a more vivid impression of the terrific forces pent up in the unconscious than I have from my wife. It is as though a horrible abyss of unutterably black despair and hopelessness suddenly yawned in front of one, and one stands paralysed and helpless before an awful *Abgrund*. Then it closes again, and a smiling surface appears to help one forget what one would willingly forget. I trust that you will get a look inside this volcano of emotion, and teach her how to make a better use of its fires." It now became clear in the correspondence that Loe had been suffering from "sexual anaesthesia" or in other words no longer slept with Jones.[128]

By December 26 Freud was telling Jones that he, Jones, failed to appreciate how much Loe had improved and how well she was although she had been unable to write to him. More accurately, she had forced herself to write and then by some "unconscious error" sent it to the wrong address.[129] As if to reassure himself Freud spoke of having done much good to Loe which should in large part remain permanent.

In the event this proved a pious hope. Over the next few months the story fluctuated, bouts of deep depression alternating with Loe's remissions.

125. Freud to Jones, November 14, 1912.
126. Ibid, November 15, 1912.
127. Jones to Freud, November 14, 1912.
128. Freud to Jones, December 8, 1912.
129. Ibid, December 26, 1912.

To compound the complexities of the situation Jones was now writing from Budapest, where he himself was undergoing a short, intense analysis from Ferenczi which must have brought him to the centre of a whirlpool of contradictions. He wrote to Freud: "I am doing my best in the analysis and think it is going on satisfactorily. Ferenczi discovers in me very strong aggressive tendencies which I have reacted to by too much suppression and submissiveness and which revenge themselves in various impulsive tendencies. It is to be hoped in the future all this will be better balanced."[130]

According to Jones he spent one hour "twice a day with Ferenczi during that summer and autumn" but the analysis was in fact short and sharp, occupying only two months, a period which, for ordinary patients, would have been regarded as unsatisfactory.

Before he died I had a long talk with Michael Balint, Ferenczi's closest friend, who possessed many of his papers. He told me that Ferenczi concentrated in the last sessions with Jones on his mother's insistence that he should be placed on quack milk substitutes which led to rickets and other serious side effects. In order to cope with the rejecting breast, his small stature, and lower class origins Ferenczi claimed that Jones had at the beginning of his career developed an omnipotent complex. At the time of his analysis he was slowly adjusting to that complex, becoming less forceful and more tactful.

In Jones' words his analysis "led to a much greater inner harmony with myself and gave me an irreplaceable insight of the most direct kind into the ways of the unconscious mind which it was highly constructive to compare with more intellectual knowledge."[131]

In the middle of his analysis Jones suddenly decided that he would pay a visit to Vienna to see Loe but Freud warned him that she might be eager to renew sexual relations only to find that she was still anaesthetised. Jones replied[132]: "I feel that next month is an unfavourable occasion to test the anaesthesia matter, partly because it is unlikely to be overcome in such a short stay (don't you find that it often takes much time and practice?) and partly because it would not be wise to expose her to the risks of pregnancy when she has so much in front of her, while she finds all kinds of precautionary measures very distasteful. On these grounds I do not think I will make any overtures myself, but will be guided entirely by her feelings; I anticipate she will desire intercourse."

It now emerged in the correspondence with Freud that Loe had once conceived a child which miscarried and that this had deeply disturbed Ernest and herself. More dramatically Jones, in a state of total sexual frustration and at the very point where Freud thought Loe was making progress, committed adultery with the nurse-cum-maid-companion Lina.

Full of pain and penitence Jones wrote[133]: *"The relation with Lina was an old affair (which explains the identification behind her hysterical attacks) and in Italy I was fully determined to break it off. But some devil of desire*

130. Jones to Freud, June 17, 1913.
131. Ernest Jones: *Free Associations,* 199.
132. Jones to Freud, January 1, 1913.
133. Jones to Freud, January 30, 1913.

made me yield to the temptation. I do not feel very guilty about my relation to her, nor did it indicate any abnormality in myself, but something tells me from within that the continuation of it in Wien was dictated by a repressed spirit of hostility against my dear wife, and you can imagine what heart-rending remorse that is causing me. That is the secret of an otherwise inexplicable inconsiderateness and *Leichtfertigkeit*. That I should have done something to wound her, whom I love so passionately and for whom I would do anything to save her, is almost beyond my endurance to bear.''

In his reply Freud said that Jones unfaithfulness had come as a tremendous shock to Loe and her old pains had returned with renewed power. She immediately converted psycho-analysis, Freud and Jones into a single compressed image from which she had to fly, and it was only with the greatest effort that Freud maintained some thread of the analysis between them. Freud completely failed to understand why Jones chose this most inappropriate moment to be unfaithful but it certainly had not damaged his respect for Jones. Moreover, he was able to develop the thread of contact remaining between Loe and himself, with the result that the pains and the morphia were both diminished and elements of normality were returning to her behaviour. Thus, Freud said, psycho-analysis can turn such episodes to profit and he had to thank Jones for what was none the less a dangerous experiment.

This implied that Jones had deliberately used unfaithfulness to break open a stalemate in analysis and reactivate the treatment but the evidence does not support the theory.

As for the young, innocent Lina . . . her reactions crystallised another aspect of Freud's theories when she was suddenly hit by two severe attacks of pain in the pelvic region, precisely the region where it normally attacked Loe. Freud said that it was the nicest case of *Übertragung* (transference) he had ever seen.[134] As for Loe's inability to write to Ernest for the time being, that was either resistance to further treatment or hatred of Jones (the reversal of the glorious medal of love).

Much more important, Loe now regarded herself as free of any obligation to Ernest and in effect she had ''left him'' both psychologically and emotionally.[135] Jones, Freud said, must have been prepared for this possibility when he sent her to Vienna, and he himself had to treat the case in vacuo, aiming at the best conclusion for the patient without taking too much account of his friendship with Jones.

By March, Jones said that he was in complete agreement with Freud and added ''I must take my chance of her coming back to me spontaneously and I believe she will do so though this may be merely narcissism on my part.''

Freud now wrote what must have been a very painful and difficult letter, dated April 9. It was supremely difficult, he said, to play the analyst between

134. Freud to Jones, January 1, 1913.
135. Ibid.

two such close friends and unfortunately he had no power to bring them back together again.

*   *   *

Loe next proceeded not only to fall in love with another man but that man's name was Jones and in future correspondence Jones referred to his successor ironically as Jones the Second.

Simultaneously he developed a desperate desire to see Loe again in the hope that perhaps some remnant of their old relationship could be recovered. Finally the urge became too strong and he decided to set out for Vienna.

On March 26 he wrote again to Freud saying that he would reach Vienna on about the 27th and wondered "what sort of reception [he would] get."

By June he was writing a much more detailed letter to Freud. The key passages said[136]: "The idea of losing my wife has not yet penetrated fully into my mind. I have difficulty in 'taking it in.' She has meant so much to me for years, and I held so fast unconsciously on to the *Bedingungslosigkeit* of her love, that it will cost me pretty severe depression before getting over the blow of seeing her love given to another, especially her *full* love, which I had always dreamed of winning. It is, of course, worse for me that I know how much I have contributed to the present situation. I only hope that happiness for her will be at last a gain amidst the surrounding loss. For me the next year or two will be especially critical, in many ways, so that the help of this analysis comes just at the right time.

"One thing that helps to reconcile me to the parting is that her hostility to me seems to have increased, or at all events to have become more manifest. I tried my best in Vienna, in spite of the suddenness of the blow, to behave in the best possible way to her and also to Jones, but it was quite without success. Every remark I would make she would at once snap up, contradict, or else twist it into another meaning, and then dispute with the greatest affect. On Saturday night I made a final attempt to get into good relations with her, and succeeded a little by means of agreeing with her (which was not at all true) that our friction that week was due to my 'irritability.' Later we had a good talk, and she brought this to the subject of our child. She insisted with the greatest vehemence (and quite unnecessarily, for I did not contradict her) that she had never resented its loss, or reproached me in any way about it, and that she had quite convinced you of this. I have never told her of the tooth scene where she repeated in French the Paris operation, and I don't suppose she remembers this, as it was under chloroform that it happened."

From Budapest in the same month came yet another letter giving his reaction to Ferenczi's attempts to analyse him[137]: "You were of course right about an unconscious personal resistance in regard to yourself, and Ferenczi had, in the first few days, analysed the psychical side of my Coblenz tired-

136. Jones to Freud, June 3, 1913.
137. Ibid, June 11, 1913.

ness. As you no doubt suspect, my unconscious, with the logic peculiar to itself, had been blaming you for the loss first of my greatest friend (Trotter), then of my wife, i.e. the man and woman who were dearest to me. With such a great loss it is little wonder that I mechanically sought for someone to blame, especially when I had so much self-blame that needed projecting. However there isn't any doubt but that this will be only a passing pheno-menon, even in the unconscious, for consciously my attitude is quite the opposite, and has been all through. There is no question about appreciating your attitude, for the delicate correctness of this is sky-clear, and I am only sorry that you should have been placed in such a painful situation.

By June 17[138]: "Yes wounds are rapidly healing now, though, and I am coming to realise that this break is the best thing not only for Loe, but also for myself. It is doubtful if we could ever have made a satisfactory life of it, even apart from Jones' existence. We have both worked off our infantile sensuality at the expense of the other and must now both face a more adult form of life. The future is at present dark for both of us, but wide open for possibilities of happiness or at least satisfactoriness. Now that I love her less, I can afford to feel more friendly and kindly towards her, and I will do all in my power to further her happiness."

Magnanimity could go no further. It would be absurd to blame Freud for the loss of two such important persons but he did have his contributory share and especially with Loe Kann.

Meanwhile, Ferenczi's analysis of Jones continued and he now said that it was giving him "more self dependence and freedom by diminishing further what was left of [his] father complex. . . . I think you will welcome that as much as I do. . . . It is better to have a therefore permanent attitude of respect and admiration than a kind of veneration which brings with it the dangers of ambivalency. . . ."[139]

If Jones was desperately missing Loe, she too, felt a kind of desolation without him and presently she, in her turn, could not resist visiting him in Vienna where they came to an accommodation and resumed friendly relations. The third phase in their long drawn out relationship had come to a close but a fourth was to follow.

Jones returned to Toronto in January 1913 without Loe, and now that Elizabeth was about to marry, he found himself in a state of considerable emotional and domestic turmoil. The house on Brunswick Avenue was empty, cold, without Loe, and Canada an increasingly alien place.

Beyond these disturbances there were other influences which make no appearance in *Free Associations*. As Jones's commitment to psycho-analysis deepened, the necessity to stress sexual factors in neurosis became imperative and it was met, in many quarters, by steadily increasing hostility, but this may not have been the root cause of his final resignation from the University.

138. Ibid, June 17, 1913.
139. Ibid, June 25, 1913.

CHAPTER X

Canadian and American Troubles

PHOTOGRAPHS of Jones taken when he was twenty-seven reveal a relatively innocent young doctor with a round, unblemished face and an eager challenging look. Now, at thirty-five, the innocence had gone, the face was tense and lined and his letters revealed an embattled state of mind. He had by March of 1913 finally decided to leave Canada, return to London and attempt to set up private practice once more.

As Professor Greenland wrote in the *Canadian Psychiatric Journal,*[140] "Ernest Jones (in Canada) was not always . . . the most tactful of men. For example as co-editor of the *Bulletin* of the Ontario Hospital for the Insane it might have been prudent of him not to monopolize its pages. We find however that *Bulletin No. 3,* March 1909, Vol. II[141] contains three articles: the one by Jones on *The Cerebro-Spinal Fluid in Relation to the Diagnosis of Meta-syhilis of the Nervous System* occupies 24 of the available 50 pages. No. 4, March 1909, Vol. III seven out of ten articles are by Jones. *Bulletin No. 1,* October 1910 Vol. IV unlike earlier editions does not include the names of the editors but carries ten articles three of them by Jones. . . .

Professor Greenland anticipates one obvious comment: "Conceding that all his articles were of undoubted value and their reprinting fully justified, it is clear that Jones' virtual monopoly and extravagant output would hardly have endeared him to his colleagues, contributors and subscribers." Moreover, sheer quantity did not explain the occasion when the Provincial Minister had called the Dean to his office, complained of the "filthy stuff" printed by Jones in the *Bulletin,* and insisted that he be removed from the co-editorship.

The cause of this uproar was a paper, *Psycho-Analytic Notes on a Case of Hypomania* which, according to Greenland, departed from Jones' usually high standard of scientific objectivity.

It is worth quoting from the paper in some detail since Jones might have been sacked without further quibble if the Provincial Minister's view had prevailed.

"A woman of passionate temperament and strong religious training had at the age of 16 been seduced and at the age of 19 had married another man by

140. *Canadian Psychiatric Association Journal,* Vol. 6, No. 3, June 1961.
141. *Bulletin of the Ontario Hospitals for the Insane,* No. 3, March 1909.

whom she was already pregnant. After bearing one child she had a miscarriage which she attributed to a gonorrhoea contracted from her husband, and underwent a number of gynaecological operations and other treatment for the relief of subsequent pelvic complications: her ovaries were removed at the age of 23. As the years went by her desire to have more children was strong and her sexual inclinations increased in intensity."[142]

No one could raise objections to such a resume but now Jones revealed that her seduction, by her music teacher, at the age of 16, had frequently taken the form of having sexual intercourse with her a dozen times in one night. "After marriage her sexual demands reached nymphomanic proportions far exceeding her husband's capacity to satisfy them," and in her frustration she turned to the Church for gratification. Appeals from the pulpit to forsake her evil ways she misread as indications that she had indulged sexual gratification incorrectly, and one Minister in fact indicated − in veiled language − that true intercourse involved admitting the male organ to her mouth and not her vagina. "The seed," Jones wrote "was in this way to enter into the body − had not Christ said 'Take and drink' − where it would peform its function of creating and nourishing a child."

Clearly the patient was either simple minded or highly imaginative, and it is just possible that Jones' Freudian beliefs gave him a streak of gullibility, for what followed seemed extravagant indeed.

"When speaking of religious observances particularly of Holy Communion the patient broke off, and slowly and reverently went through a perfect pantomime of the whole ceremony. This culminated in her taking a glass of water which she placed on a Bible and gradually raising it to her lips where she beatifically sucked the rim slowly revolving the glass as she did so. During the latter part of the performance a complete and exhausting orgasm took place."

"Exhausting" seems a gratuitous detail in a scientific paper. "I pointed to the glass and asked her if it was the Communion cup: she answered 'Do you call it a cup. It has another name' and later remarked: 'This is the way, the birth, the life.'"[143]

Among the cognoscenti − as Professor Greenland remarks − such sexual analogies may have been acceptable, but the medical profession in Ontario in 1910 was scandalised by their publication in the *Bulletin*. Jones' paper had originally been published in *The American Journal of Insanity* and a less determined man than Jones might have been satisfied with such a technically limited audience. However, this overlooked his passionate proseletysing on behalf of Freud who viewed all forms of sex with complete calm. It is unlikely that Jones regarded *épater le bourgeois* as part of his propaganda technique but his paper certainly shocked. Professor Greenland asks − "was his judgment impaired by an excessive enthusiasm for psycho-analysis?" Well, Jones agreed with Westermarck: "The only indecorum known to science is

142. Ibid.
143. Ibid.

the concealment of truth."

The precise reasons why Jones was eventually asked to resign are still not quite clear. A letter from Jones at his new address, 321 Jarvis Street, written in the summer of 1913[144] to Dr. Clarke, Dean of the University, recalls that Jones had been given permission by Clarke to stay in London with his wife until February 9 of that year. Without notifying Jones the authorities changed the curriculum and Jones' course began on an earlier date with the result that Clarke had to step in and give his lectures. When, in consequence, a cut was made in Jones' salary, Jones wrote again to Clarke asking him to intercede on his behalf with Falconer, the University President.

Another letter from Jones to Falconer in the autumn[145] requests permission to spend as much time as possible in London with his still ailing wife. Falconer's final letter to Jones says that Clarke and the Board of Governors have decided that Jones cannot spend so much time away from the University and they therefore have no alternative but to ask him to resign. Jones' reply regretted that his case had been presented to the Board in prejudiced terms. "I have always been willing to be in Toronto at any time of the year that the head of my department may desire."[146]

This seemed somewhat disingenuous and could not in the end save him. Professor Cyril Greenland, in a letter to me stated "I also have in my files letters from the Hon. Dr. Herbert A. Bruce, deceased, describing in a florid style why Jones resigned. This letter was written to me in strict confidence and I am unable to disclose its contents at this time."[147] The resignation is further complicated by an unpublished letter from the Dean's Office, Faculty of Medicine, in November of 1913, signed by G. K. Clarke[148]:

"I have your letter of November 7th and feel very badly to think that affairs have ended as they have done. However there was no other way open. You know what my personal feelings have been towards you and how much I have valued your friendship because I regarded you as the one bright spot in the whole Psychiatric situation. Why you should have become the centre of so much unpleasantness was always a mystery to me and the only reason I could find was that of very picayune personal jealousy.

"There are several men in Toronto who have very little brains themselves and are exceedingly jealous of any one who disturbs their imaginary greatness. Unfortunately they have what is called 'pull' in certain directions and make a good deal of trouble.

"In my own affairs I have been able to avoid them quite successfully and to a certain extent in yours, but not altogether. Possibly I have fought far more battles for you than you have ever known and certainly have, sometimes, felt very much hurt at the things said and done by those who should have known better.

"However this may be, you know my opinion of you has not altered in any shape or form and while I think you have not always known how to manage

144. Jones to Clarke, May 1, 1913.
145. Jones to Falconer, October 22, 1913.
146. Ibid, November 15, 1913.
147. Professor Cyril Greenland to the Author, December 3, 1980.
148. Dr. Clarke to Jones, November 17, 1913.

the men who were unfriendly towards you, yet that very weakness in your armour made me feel more like defending you than ever. . . ."

One hard fact emerges from the confusion. By the summer of 1913 Jones was back in London busily trying to re-establish a private practice and continuing to spread what had now become equivalent to the Freudian gospel. His reception in London varied from open hostility to armed neutrality. Few received him with unqualified enthusiasm. His devotion to psycho-analytic practice was now common knowledge, and even in London it seemed to those who spoke with the expertise of ignorance that he must be obsessed with sex.

Jones believed that the world had lived through three periods of organised prejudice during which persecution became the natural weapon of irrational dogmas. The first period he called odium theologicum, when religious intolerance made life hazardous for thousands of people, the second replaced that with odium sexicum when sex became the new devil to be hounded and tormented, and the third was odium politicum when deviation from the party line represented ultimate corruption. Freud and his small band of followers had lived for some time under the shadow of odium sexicum.

In public this had already made itself felt, sometimes obliquely but often with a vicious frankness which employed street corner vituperation. Freud had been publicly cut in the streets of Vienna, and once a man came up to him and said "Are you Dr. Freud." Freud admitted his identity. "Then let me tell you what a dirty-minded filthy old man you are."[149]

When Sandor Ferenczi read a paper before the Medical Society of Budapest one of the audience stood up and denounced Freud's work as pure pornography.[149] The personal abuse of Freud occasionally achieved the characteristics of a vendetta and during a Neurological Congress in Berlin a famous neurologist, Professor Oppenheim, rose and proposed in a voice charged with emotion that they should boycott any institution where Freud's views were accepted.

In London, Jones confronted more subtle methods of English disapproval whereby former friends received him "with politeness but without intimacy." Only one amongst them, Harry Campbell, came out and bluntly stated that he would be "ostracised if he stayed in London," but innuendos were rife and quite clearly any chance of orthodox medical advancement remote. Jones regarded Campbell's comment as a preparation for the affronts which awaited him in organisations like the Royal Society of Medicine but presently he learnt that Campbell himself was spreading disreputable stories about him. "I was beginning to learn", Jones wrote, "that proximity to sexual ideas has the power of evoking the worst in man as well as the best."

Equally worrying to Jones was the resistance to psycho-analytic thinking which became apparent when he met his oldest friend Wilfred Trotter, who

149. Ferenczi to Freud, February 16, 1911.

could, at least, be said to be reasonably well informed. Trotter responded with cordiality and a readiness to listen but the old sense of sympathetic intimacy had gone and somehow Trotter managed to convey the barrier which "had grown up between us." Jones received no invitation to visit Trotter, and that marked a new and clearly understood demarcation in their relationship. The old revolutionary Trotter had disappeared and in his place was a man who opted for security in life, orthodox surgery and a distinguished place on the staff of University College Hospital.

In recollection Jones displayed that streak of magnanimity which – buried as it was under so many other characteristics – could emerge and transform him into a most understanding person. Where other people might have regarded Trotter's behaviour as treachery, Jones now saw it as a repudiation of the romantic revolutionary which Trotter could no longer, in maturity, accommodate. There was one other quite different explanation transparently apparent to Jones. A man who still regarded himself as the witty dispenser of penetrating philosophic comment, Trotter could open "his heart only to those he considered his disciples." In short, he was jealous of what had by now become Jones' obsession with psycho-analysis and his devotion to Freud.

Certainly Jones remained in close touch with the Viennese Circle. By 1912 new difficulties had arisen between Freud and Jung and Jung once more crossed the Atlantic to lecture to the Jesuit Fordham University in New York. He wrote a long letter to Freud in which he claimed that by omitting sexual themes he had made psycho-analysis much more acceptable to many American intellectuals. Freud brusquely replied that it needed no great brilliance to carry out such a feat and that if he omitted more the opposition would dwindle even further. Indeed by not mentioning it at all, perhaps all opposition would vanish. In his key lecture Jung more or less rejected the crucial ingredients of the Oedipus complex and seriously qualified the tendency towards incest as an absolutely concrete sexual desire.

Putnam wrote a disturbed letter to Jones from Boston:[150]

"I made two attempts to meet Dr. Jung in New York and the last one was in so far successful that I heard his address . . . What Dr. Jung said in effect was that while he still held to the importance of the psycho-analytic technique he had come to rate the infantile fixations as of far less importance than formerly . . . as an etiological factor and indeed as I understood him as an almost negligible factor in most cases – though I hardly think he could really maintain this if he were pushed for a positive opinion. At any rate the point on which he seems now inclined to lay emphasis is the difficulty of meeting new problems and environmental conditions which arise at the time of the actual onset of the neurosis. It seems to me that we all recognise the importance of these influences and I cannot as yet feel that anything is won through minimising the significance of the other factor."

150. Putnam to Jones, October 14, 1912.

In May of the same year (1912) the now famous Kreuzlingen incident took place, adding fresh and as it transpired unnecessary frictions. Jones' account of this incident has since been qualified by Ronald Clark in his biography of Freud and it is worth pausing to examine the details. The young Swiss psychiatrist Binswanger, an old friend of Freud's, was forced to undergo a serious operation for the removal of a tumour in March 1912. Freud expressed a wish to visit him in his home at Kreuzlingen at the northern end of Lake Constance and suggested Whitsun. On 18th or 23rd – according to Jones – he wrote to Jung pointing out that he would be in Kreuzlingen for the coming weekend, and since Kreuzlingen was only forty miles from Jung's home in Kusnacht he apparently assumed – without making it explicit – that Jung would visit him. When Jung failed to appear Freud read a meaning into his absence. It was another detail of Jung's increasing hostility. Jung later maintained that Freud's letter had not arrived until Monday 27th, the day on which Freud was due to leave Kreuzlingen, but Binswanger disclosed that Freud's letter to him had been written on May 16th which made it highly unlikely that it would be delivered as late as the 27th. As Clark comments: "While Jones was insistent that Freud had expected Jung to come to Kreuzlingen, Binswanger's story is that Jung reproached Freud for not having met him in Zurich. Whatever the truth about the contretemps it seems that it could readily have been removed by either man picking up the telephone. Whether the result of a simple mis-understanding or of an unconscious wish to avoid the meeting, the Kreuzlingen incident further exacerbated relations between the two men."

Jung deliberately postponed the 1912 Congress to accommodate his lecture tour in America and Jones now felt that he was prepared to put his own career before the interests of the Society, a view which Freud was beginning to share.

Relations between Freud and Jung seemed to go from bad to worse but as late as September 1912 Freud said that if their personal feeling could be restored there was no danger of a real break. A meeting which followed in Munich in November seemed superficially to reconcile them. This was not a congress but a meeting called by Jung – at Freud's behest – to transfer the editorship of the *Zentralblatt* to Stekel while a new *Zeitschrift* was founded to take its place.

Jones recorded a confusion over the arrangements whereby he almost failed to arrive on time. Fully aware that Jones had gone to Florence at the time, Jung wrote a letter giving the conference details, but he not only sent the letter to Jones' home in Wales; he gave Jones the wrong date, sub-stituting November 25 for November 24. It is more than possible that Jung did not want Jones to be present because Jones was clearly an unquestioning disciple of Freud and liable to be less tactful in expressing his views about Jung's "deviations" in America. When Jones told Freud what had happened, Freud remarked "A gentleman should not do such things even if he is unconscious." Jones did, in fact, discover the correct date by accident from Loe Kann who was in Vienna at the time, and duly arrived with his unfailing punctuality at the precise time on the correct day.

The meeting began at nine o'clock in the morning, when Jung proposed that the change over of journals be accepted without further discussion. "I was in favour" Jones wrote "of taking further steps to make Stekel vacate his position . . . but Freud, ever averse to anything savouring of a fight, preferred to start a new periodical instead, the *Zeitschrift* and of course we supported him." Everyone – and especially Jung – sympathised with Freud, his proposals were accepted and the meeting ended just after eleven o'clock. There is a photograph of Jones preserved from this meeting which shows him with an elegant walking stick, a panama hat and immaculate jacket standing – gaily – beside Freud, a young man in the full flower of self confidence. After the meeting, Jung and Freud set off on a long walk together during which they cleared up a number of "misunderstandings," with Freud, according to Jones, letting off steam and giving Jung a fatherly lecture. One such misunderstanding was the Kreuzlingen incident. According to Jones, Freud expressed astonishment that Jung had not received his letter about his visit to Binswanger until the Monday and now, suddenly, Jung recalled that he had in fact been away for two days at that weekend. This new explanation given in Jones' biography becomes irrelevant of course if – as seems likely – Freud wrote both letters on the 16th instead of the 23rd. However it is clear from Jones that whatever Freud's conscious mind accepted, his unconscious still harboured many suspicions.

Jones' account of what followed in his biography of Freud has been variously interpreted. Luncheon was served when Freud and Jung returned from their walk and Freud was in high spirits, believing that once more all their troubles were over and the Crown Prince had abandoned any idea of abdication.

Towards the end of luncheon Freud suddenly turned to the two Swiss analysts Jung and Riklin and asked them why, in recent articles on psycho-analysis, they had failed to mention his name. Jung rationalised the omission by oblique flattery. It was too well known that Freud had founded psycho-analysis he said to need continuous repetition in periodical literature; mentioning Freud's name in historical recapitulations had become super-fluous. This, of course, sounded disingenuous to Freud who suddenly wondered once more whether his attempts at rapprochement with Jung were as successful as he had imagined.

On the point of replying to Jung, Freud suddenly slid to the floor in a "dead faint" as remarkable an illustration of hysterical transference as any in the literature. To Freud's later embarrassment it was the very powerful Jung who picked him up with ease and carried him into the anteroom. As

Freud revived he was heard to mutter "How sweet it must be to die."
Discussing this episode with Michael Balint, Jones said that so intense was
Freud's relationship with Jung that he could not face the possibility that
Jung was still a traitor and registered Jung's hidden desire to break away
from him as a death wish against him which became so strong that he did
momentarily undergo a kind of death. [151] Beyond this explanation lay many
other complexities one of which Freud later elaborated to Jones. "I cannot
forget that . . . years ago I suffered from very similar though not such intense
symptoms in the same room of the Park Hotel." He had first seen Munich
when he visited Fliess there and the town "acquired a strong connection with
my relations to that man."

In his Freud biography Jones categorically stated that there was ample
evidence to show that Freud "suffered from a very considerable psycho-
neurosis." He also claimed that during the years when the neurosis became
fierce Freud did his most original work. What, throughout Jones' autobiography remains consistent, is the denial that Jones himself suffered from
anything more than an occasional neurotic lapse. The picture implicit in this
work of a balanced, rational human being capable of practising objectivity
with considerable skill and untroubled by such elemental conditions as
jealousy, is set in a series of events which sometimes contradict that picture.
As we now know from his analysis with Ferenczi, many neurotic symptoms
troubled him, along with the rest of mankind.

When the five men including Jones dispersed from the Munich Conference
they were superficially reconciled to Freud's leadership but if Ferenczi
remained optimistic about the future, Jones was pessimistic. "I felt we had
all gone through the motions of reconciliation without any of the corresponding reality."

By April of the following year Jones was writing to Freud: "I am deeply
impressed by the success of Jung's campaign for he appeals to formidable
prejudices. It is my opinion the most critical period that psycho-analysis will
ever go through. . . . I have written a strong protest to Jung at his treatment of
me but in such a form that it need not lead to an open rupture which I am not
eager to provoke. . . . Still I do not expect he will answer me for his recent
conduct in America makes me think more than [ever] that he does not react
like a normal man and that he is mentally deranged to a serious extent: he
produced quite a paranoic impression on some of the psycho-analytic
psychiatrists on Ward's Island." [152]

From this point onwards psycho-analytic historians have accused Jones
and his Viennese colleagues of projecting mental derangement on to any
opponent who refused to accept the received wisdom within which committed psycho-analysts were expected to work.

Undismayed by the multiplication of deviations, Jones ended his letter on
a crusading note: "It is a grand time to be alive in; better than any other

151. Interview, Balint, December 1957.
152. Jones to Freud, April 25, 1913.

period of history because it is fuller of fight on which so much depends. . . .
Yours enthusiastically.''

Freud and Jung approached the last Congress of the International
Psycho-Analytic Association at Munich on September 7, 1913, with the
expectation that there would be ''no open break'' between its members.

From America, England, Germany, Austria and Hungary, eighty-seven
members and guests of the still rapidly growing psycho-analytic movement
converged on the Bayerischer Hotel on September 7. They quickly fell into
different groups with different sympathies and many small sub-meetings
discussed the latest details of the possible schism with Jung which simmered
under the surface.

Jung was still reigning President and confrontation seemed imminent
when he and his supporters sat at a separate table facing Freud's as the conference began. Jones did not have at his disposal when he wrote his biography
of Freud the testimony of Lou Andreas Salome in her diaries. She wrote ''It
is not so much that Jung diverges from Freud as that he does it in such a way
as if he had taken it on himself to rescue Freud and his cause by these divergencies. . . . Five years ago Jung's booming laughter gave voice to a kind of
robust gaiety and exuberant vitality but now his earnestness is composed of
pure aggression, ambition and intellectual brutality.''[153] It has to be
remembered that Adler had already abandoned Freud and in the midst of
what threatened to become total disintegration, Jones claimed that either he
or Ferenczi conceived the idea of a central committee whose loyal members
would be more or less sworn to Freudian faithfulness.

One interpretation of the part played by Jones in the genesis of this idea
can be followed in his letter to Freud in August 1912[154]: ''The idea of a
united small body designed, like the Paladins of Charlemagne to guard the
kingdom and policy of their master was a product of my own romanticism
and I did not venture to speak about it to the others until I had broached it to
you.'' In fact he had already discussed the idea with Rank and Ferenczi. His
letter of July 30, 1912 to Freud had said: ''I get a little pessimistic at times
when I look around at the men who must lead for the next 30 years. Jung
abdicates from his throne, Stekel is obviously impossible, even Rank may be
hindered by material considerations. . . . Ferenczi, Rank and I had a little
talk on these general matters in Vienna. . . . One of them, I think it was
Ferenczi, expressed the wish that a small group of men could be thoroughly
analysed by you . . . and thus build an unofficial inner circle.''[155] But this
again needs qualifying. Freud replied to Jones' letter by return of post
welcoming the idea which had taken hold of his imagination, but Jones in his
biography omitted two sentences in the letter which indicated that Freud
himself ''might'' have originated the idea.

153. Lou Andreas-Salomé, September 7/8, 1913, Ed. Stanley A. Leavy, *The Freud Journal of
    Lou Andreas-Salomé.*
154. Jones to Freud, August 7, 1912.
155. Ibid, July 30, 1912.

According to Jones the level of the scientific papers at the Munich Congress was mediocre but he allowed two undeviating Freudians, Abraham and Ferenczi, the distinction of delivering "two interesting ones." One Swiss paper, overwhelmed with statistics, became so prolonged and tedious that Freud remarked "All sorts of criticism have been brought against psychoanalysis but this is the first time anyone could have called it boring."

Jung's heretical work *The Psychology of the Unconscious* had by now been published and it committed Jung to the view that vestigial imprints of collective myths and/or experience of the race as a whole were part of the minds and/or brains of all human beings. These imprints took the form of archetypes which if re-activated in the correct manner could invest the individual with a new and revitalised way of life. Any condensation violates the complexity of Jung's thinking and it is necessary to read the book to appreciate his real meaning.

Freud had already spoken of archaic material in the mind which must be taken into any account of the psyche but he remained tentative about its potential whereas Jung regarded it as a fact of human existence which could be harnessed for our enlightenment. Both men were contradicting modern genetics which states that acquired characteristics cannot be inherited. Kline put their differences very succinctly: "In short for the Freudian theory which is hard enough to test but has some degree of support Jung had substituted an untestable system which flies in the face of current genetics."[156]

Whether these differences were analysed in detail at the Munich Congress we do not know, but Lou Andreas Salome recorded the behaviour of the Zurich members in her diary: "It is not so much that Jung diverges from Freud as that he does it in such a way as if he had taken it on himself to rescue Freud and his cause by these divergencies. If Freud takes up the lance to defend himself it is misconstrued to mean that he cannot show scientific tolerance, is dogmatic and so forth. . . ."

Jones bluntly stated that Jung "now conducted the meetings in such a fashion that it was felt some gesture of protest should be made." Freud called the proceedings "fatiguing and unedifying" and said that they were "conducted by Jung in a disagreeable and incorrect manner; the speakers were restricted in time and the discussions overwhelmed the papers."[157]

In the presidential election which followed Jung accepted re-election for two years with 52 votes against 22 but this was not the result of a free vote. Abraham had suggested that those who disapproved should abstain from voting and Jones among many others did so. Afterwards Jung came up to Jones and said "I thought you were a Christian." According to Jones, Jung meant by this that he was not a Jew but colloquial English allows the more common interpretation that he was not a tolerant person. Jones wondered, at the time, just how far what he called Jung's anti-semitism conditioned this

156. Kline, 324.
157. Freud: *Short History of Psycho-Analysis,* 45.

remark and his whole attitude to Freud, but my own investigations[158] tend to undermine the whole anti-semitic myth.

The Munich Congress concluded with Jung still in the Presidency but Freud wrote "We dispersed without any desire to meet again."

158. Brome: *Freud and His Early Circle*.

CHAPTER XI

The War Years

BEFORE THE First World War Britain was a country where the State hardly intervened in the life of law-abiding citizens. Jones later recalled that anyone could leave the country without a passport, foreigners could spend a lifetime among the British without reporting to the police or holding a permit of any kind, military service was not required from young citizens, income tax stood at 2s. 6d. in the £1 and drinking took place at any hour of the day and night which suited the premises serving it. But this was a surface situation, full of deception. Only those over seventy received a tawdry few shillings to sustain them through their old age, the gap between the rich and the poor was sometimes appalling, unemployment when it materialised occasionally threatened starvation, and in 1911 the first crude attempts at sickness and unemployment benefits were — in Jones' view — hopelessly inadequate.

Although Queen Victoria had disappeared in the mists of immortality as far back as 1901, King George V in 1913 still seemed to enjoy a power almost equal to hers and not far removed in some respects from that wielded by Henry VIII. Now, at 3.0 p.m. on August 4, 1914, His Imperial Majesty received in audience a solitary Minister of the Crown and these two men, supported by the graces of two court officials whose knowledge of foreign affairs did not extend beyond Buckingham Palace, committed to a prolonged and devastating war, not merely the forty-five million citizens of Great Britain, the Dominions overseas including Canada, Australia and New Zealand but fifty million Africans and two hundred million Indians.

As Jones reflected at the time — "No one consulted any of those peoples and none was less consulted than Ernest Jones."

Such was his evaluation of the importance of psycho-analysis that when war did break out, as a free and unattached person he considered reserving himself for the high office of Defender of the Faith instead of volunteering for military service. It came as a considerable relief when the Medical Board advised him "not to press [his] claim to be enlisted." He had for years suffered from a distressing form of rheumatoid arthritis and when actual conscription reached his age group he was re-examined twice "but was each time judged unfit for active service.''

The Royal Army Medical Corps in those days was a solid body of men with down-to-earth ideas of ready-made medicine. They were largely incapable of assimilating new thinking in psychiatry and recoiled from anything so outre as psycho-analysis. Chaotically, gynaecologists were sometimes put in charge of opthalmic wards, and Sir Victor Horsley, whose investigation of head and nerve injuries would seem indispensable in wartime "was sent to Mesapotamia where he died of sunstroke.''

Pressing on with his private practice Jones abandoned the idea of returning to Harley Street and rented a modest flat in Great Portland Street. There the majority of men who rang his bell were officers suffering from one or another form of war neurosis. It will be possible to deal with one very important case history in due course, but for the moment there were many other interesting patients.

Jones found himself confronted with the revolutionary task of applying his new psycho-analytic knowledge to war neuroses some of which were distressing even to his hardened susceptibilities. In many cases it was a matter of using insights without therapy because Army Medical Boards refused to give patients sufficient leave to indulge the luxury of psycho-analysis. They either ignored or openly denied the existence of war neuroses and equivalent symptoms were regularly attributed to concussion of the brain or malingering.

To say that psychoanalysis triumphed in the end would be gross exaggeration, but its slow penetration of medical defences was due in no small part to Jones work and influence. As his son Mervyn put it: "The acceptance of the idea that breakdowns were psycho-neurotic, by parts of the Medical and even the Military Establishment (c.f. the experience of Siegfried Sassoon) was a big breakthrough. Ernest Jones always said that the progress of psycho-analysis in the 1920's would have been impossible but for the way it got on the map during the war.''

A naval officer of forty consulted Jones in the very first days of the war and slowly revealed that he could not take up his new appointment as captain of a battleship because — he had a crick in his neck. [159] What seemed a trivial excuse Jones knew to be the outward symptom of a deeper conflict but on the two occasions when he saw the man he knew that prolonged treatment was required and that the Navy would never cooperate. In the few hours he spent with him Jones discovered that he moved his neck obsessively, trying to discover whether the crick was still there and this simple preoccupation made it impossible for him to concentrate on anything resembling naval commands. If Napoleon lost his Russian campaign because of piles, then this man was likely to lose a battleship because of a crick in the neck. The R.A.M.C. remained completely unmoved by such a wildly unorthodox diagnosis. Unfortunately we have no further details of the case.

Equally bizarre was the man who said that his resolve to abandon his

159. Jones: *Free Associations*, 246.

reserve job and volunteer for the Army had been completely undermined by his big toe! Trench warfare, bombardment, even wounds he could face but if, he confided to Jones, another soldier squeezed past him in a trench and trod on his big toe – the whole world would explode in agony.[160] It perfectly illustrated Freud's distinction between anxiety phobias and real fear. Jones commented: "There could be no doubt which of the two is the more dreadful." Once again no documentary evidence of the case or its outcome remains but since the chances of a big toe escaping the attention of floundering feet in the middle of a war were small, it seems likely that the patient remained in his civilian job.

More tragic was the case of a brilliant officer in the Intelligence Service who suffered from a crushing sense of inferiority which created fits of profound depression.[161] Jones treated him for six months and recorded – very simply – that "I restored him to health." As a result the man married and for a time all went well. Then, suddenly, some extravagance in his behaviour brought him up before a medical board and they decided that he should be incarcerated in Palace Green Mental Hospital. Two months later "deprived of all treatment and of all hope of consolidating his cure," he escaped one night. The man's wife called on Jones the following day and lodged her husband's revolver with him fearing that his next step would be suicide. The wife returned home reassured, but the following morning the man threw himself in front of an express train.

Another person who underwent what might be called a swift treatment by Jones was Frieda Lawrence, the wife of D. H. Lawrence. Social life for Jones was always subjugated to work but he did occasionally dine with families whose bohemian friends included more distinguished people like D. H. Lawrence. Abandoning the precise language of the clinician for literary flourishes Jones wrote of Mr. and Mrs. Lawrence that they were "impelled by mischievous demons to goad each other to frenzy." These outbursts, he wrote, culminated in sadistic orgies, sometimes followed by peace, but late one night a panic-stricken Frieda Lawrence burst into Jones' flat and begged for refuge since her husband was about to murder her. To her complete surprise Jones snapped at her "From the way you treat him I wonder he has not done so long ago." Jones then delivered himself of a short sharp analytic homily intended to enlighten her about the dark forces at work in the complicated forest of her psyche. Lawrence scholars have made some inspired guesses about the nature of this homilly but there is no documentary evidence.

Throughout the war years a paradox appeared in Jones' life whereby he constantly fell ill from one cause or another and always ignored psychological origins. The rheumatoid arthritis which had exluded him from the army developed into a serious affliction, attacking his spine, nerves, joints and muscles. Whether its exacerbation was due to stress is unclear but so

160. Ibid, 247.
161. Ibid.

acute did the pain become that it was impossible for him to use a pen or hold a telephone receiver "for six months at a time." He tried vaccines made from his own germs and other people's, he had an operation on the septum of the nose and he had removed in the following order teeth, tonsils and appendix. This splendid array of surgical interference nowhere gave a hint of psycho-analytic investigation. Yet Jones was now in the midst of such storms and stresses as would put to the test the most cast iron ego. Still partly ostracised by London society, as yet not integrated into the war effort, he appears to have taken back into his home none other than Loe Kann, simultaneously remaining involved with Lina. He wrote to Freud in August 1913 "Loe is well but much perturbed. The Jones's [alias Jones 2 and Loe] family is in London and she spends every afternoon with Herbert in great apprehension of being discovered by the father . . . Loe's tension and irritability are discharged on me in the most disagreeable way. . . . My father has been seriously ill and I must go down to Wales soon."[162]

Another letter from 13, Princes Street, Cavendish Square, said that Loe had generously offered to pay his expenses for the first three years until he was once more re-established. Herbert Jones, he wrote, "is more desperately in love with [Loe] than ever. . . . I take up the benevolent attitude of blessing two happy lovers. At the same time I rejoice to think we are parting, for with all her magnificent character and many charms she has, as well, a devouring and all absorbing personality so that life with her is at best a strenuous performance and at worst, when she does not love, a painfully disagreeable and racking experience."[163] He hoped, he concluded, to settle arrangements about taking a new flat in a few days.

Until this date it is not clear in the correspondence whether Loe was once more living with him but he wrote early in September "Loe is very much better and is throwing herself rigorously into the work of furnishing. . . . She brought home a stray kitten when I was away."[164]

It becomes clear from his letter of October 27 that Loe was about to go back into analysis with Freud but kept delaying it "partly because of her desire to plague me." There were two other "resistances" at work: her fear of re-entering analysis and hatred of Lina. Whether Lina was also living with them at this time is not clear but it became a reasonable proposition in the light of what followed.

By November Loe had, at last, left for Vienna and once more gone into analysis with Freud. He found her in a deplorable condition which he described pessimistically to Jones. She had withdrawn deeply into herself, he said, and become almost inaccessible. By February of the following year Freud reported that her case was at last clear and diagnosed her medically as suffering from a left-side pyelitis. Psychologically, he wrote, the case was very interesting but the details would only become explicable in terms of Loe's relation to her mother which he had not yet unravelled.[165] Some weeks

162. Jones to Freud, August 8, 1913.
163. Jones to Freud, August 18, 1913.
164. Ibid, September 13, 1913.
165. Freud to Jones, February 8, 1914.

later there followed a much more detailed letter which at last justified the insights of psycho-analysis. As a child, Freud wrote, Loe had desired to give her father a child and developed acute constipation as a pseudo pregnancy. When her mother forced her to cure this condition with daily enemas she interpreted it as a miscarriage and raged with fury. In adult life she had "married" a husband-father in Jones and did herself literally miscarry. As a result of a remarkable metamorphosis had taken place. She had, in fact, become her mother and Loe and her mother imago were still in the throes of struggling for her soul which frequently tore Loe if not the imago apart.

The climax to the whole long story appeared in Freud's letter of June 2.[166] He went to Budapest to attend the marriage of Loe to Jones the second and remarked how hard it was for both Jones the first and himself to face the situation. Not only had the extraordinary chain of events led to the analyst attending the marriage of his best friend's "wife" to another man, but his relationship with Jones had somehow survived the strain of such an unexpected conclusion.

While this long, tortured story was running its course Jones remained hard at work developing psycho-analysis in England by every means in his power. He read many papers to a variety of learned and medical bodies including the British Medical Association, the Royal Society of Medicine, the British Association for the Advancement of Science and the British Psychological Society. "They were miniature congresses where one had satisfactory opportunities of meeting people of standing and discussing in a personal and informal way matters that in public debate [led] only to blind opposition."[167]

Early in November of 1913 Jones had eight patients applying for treatment and was feeling personally "much happier in every way." By November 24 his practice had rapidly developed and was "already paying all living expenses."[168] Simultaneously he reported to Freud that "Dr. Eder and I have arranged to found a London group and expect to have perhaps a dozen members. . . . In order not to leave selection of new members to a committee we will arrange that all names must first be passed by a committee consisting of the President, Secretary and Vice President." This seemed a highly specious arrangement: to avoid involvement in committees they were to have another committee consisting mainly of Jones and Eder. It became standard practice in due course for members to be personally vetted by the two "leading officers" of the Society and that was to create considerable criticism of Jones.

On November 29 — a classic day in English psycho-analytic history — Jones wrote to Freud[169]: "The London Psycho Analytic Society was duly constituted last Thursday with a membership of nine." Then followed this statement, remarkable in view of Jones' rigorously expressed hatred of Jung and his theories. "I have written to Jung applying for admittance to the Vereinningung."

166. Ibid, June 2, 1914.
167. Jones: *Free Associations,* 242.
168. Jones to Freud, November 29, 1913.
169. Ibid, November 29, 1913.

Freud replied that Jung's position was strong but with luck he would ruin himself and Jones would have to fight hard to overcome his influence in England and America.[170] Writing to Abraham, Freud said "the question now is the extent to which Jones will be able to steer the new London group into our channel: all further political steps depend on that."

By January of 1914 Jones told Freud jubilantly: "Practice exceeds all expectations. I have eight patients daily and had to send another one away to Eder.... If things go on this way I shall be able to marry."[171] By January 16 Freud was advising Jones not to make marriage the next step in his life in case he repeated the story of Jeptha's daughter.[172]

Jones' manipulations behind the scenes now became more powerful and his interventions more frequent as the success of his private practice and freedom from love's torments re-created his old confidence. By January of 1914 he was writing to Freud[173]:

"Dear Professor Freud,
   Abraham tells me that Jung has enquired about the place of the next congress, and I wonder if this is not the last moment to suggest a dissolution of the association. If Berlin, Budapest and Vienna (London is not yet an official group, and we have not heard from Jung) combine in this request, Jung may simply get defiant and hold the congress willy-nilly, hoping we will stay away from it. That would leave him in full possession of the field, which would never do at all. Don't you think you personally could write to him proposing either a dissolution or at least a postponement of the congress for this year, there being no one else with any authority or moral right approaching yours? Then the matter might be submitted to a referendum of all the groups, with individual voting and this would give us a good chance of winning, for many undecided men, like Eder, would vote for this rather than have the painful farce of last September repeated."

In March 1914 Jones fell ill with a severe cellulitis starting at the back of his neck and involving all the glands on both sides, but it did not stop him working on his Madonna paper with comic results.[174] "I have completely re-written my Madonna essay for the *Jahrbuch* adding both some valuable material and what I think is an important deepening of the theory (relating afflatus to castration); the last part of it was sent to Sachs a fortnight ago. Towards the end an amazing episode occurred. The crocodile part all depended on the fact that these animals, like frogs, have no external genitals. On reading Wallis Budge's book on Osiris, which by the way is very good, I was horrified to read that the Egyptian performed certain rites with the *penis* of the crocodile. I telephoned in a panic to various professors of zoology, none of whom could tell me what I wanted, and the next day went to the Zoological Gardens to investigate the point. None of the keepers knew, so

170. Freud to Jones, November 22 or 29, 1913.
171. Jones to Freud, January 9, 1914.
172. Freud to Jones, January 16, 1914.
173. Jones to Freud, January 9, 1914.
174. Ibid, March 13, 1914.

the only thing to do was to turn over an undoubted male crocodile on to his back by means of poles, etc. This proved to be an appallingly difficult task, and created an exciting scene. I found, also later from textbooks, that the animals penis is *entirely* concealed within the cloaca, so that the psycho analytic assumption that it must be invisible from outside proved correct. What a dull life the ordinary doctor leads in comparison with that of a psycho-analyst! . . ."

Meanwhile psycho-analysis continued to develop apace in London. "I am very pleased with the work done by the Society here and hope in another year to have four reliable trained men. Not much but such men are rare enough in our work. . . ."[175]

Freud revealed to Lou Andreas Salome that he had been hard at work on a history of the psycho-analytic movement for the *Jarhbuch*. "This will put an end to all compromises [with Jung and the Swiss school] and bring about the desired rupture." He sent the draft to Jones who objected to one phrase which until now has remained unknown. Here it is with Jones' comment[176]:

> "*S.44. jene Charakterzüge von Jung . . . seine Neigung zum rücksichtslosen Beiseitedrängen eines unbequemen Andern.* [This characteristic in Jung – his inclination ruthlessly to push aside someone who stands in his way.] This is of course absolutely true, and in principle I am in favour of no mercy being shown in such an important war, but none the less I find this rather strong personally and fear it would weaken, by its personal note, the general effect of the essay rather than strengthen it. One does not want to put weapons in the hands of the enemy. Sachs asks me to add that he is quite of my opinion."

In the summer of 1914 Jung was in London addressing the British Medical Association on *The Importance of the Unconscious in Psychopathology*. Without directly mentioning psycho-analysis he thanked Freud for having called his attention to the importance of dreams and in the following discussion won a sympathetic hearing. He also gave other lectures and Jones reported to Freud that – unfortunately – he was a great success. Thus, by the summer, the nucleus of three schools – Freudian, Adlerian and Jungian – were competing in London.

Both Freudians and Jungians had been in touch with Deutsche, the publisher of the *Jahrbuch,* making independent offers for continuing to edit that journal, and Freud had read into Jung's approach a desire "to gain sole control of it after my withdrawal." Now Abraham read the worst possible motives into Jung's manoeuvres and suddenly his mood changed and he was in favour of taking extreme measures against Jung.

Jones seemed to recant his earlier view and made it clear that he thought "Ferenczi's plan" for the Vienna, Berlin and Budapest groups to join forces and request Jung to wind up the International Association, was too full of

175. Ibid, April 22, 1914.
176. Ibid, May 18, 1914.

hazards. Ferenczi expected Jones to persuade the British and American societies to take similar action but Jung had not yet recognised the British society and the Americans, who had seen more of Jung than any other psycho-analytic leader, were unlikely, with the exception of Brill, to agree. Jung had visited America on two recent occasions and received a warm and sympathetic reception. Like Abraham, Jones clearly saw that "if Jung refused to dissolve we should have to resign and he would be left in possession." When Jones put these doubts to Freud he at once telegraphed "Letter received. Excellent. Will have moderating effect and will be sent to our friends at once."

The advice of Jones and Abraham prevailed. The impetuous Ferenczi agreed to abandon his plan and proceed with greater caution. From the letters which followed it looked very much as though the Freudians were about to deliver a series of attacks on Jung's next book and certainly a number of critical reviews appeared in *Zeitschrift,* but by now the bigger bombshell was ready – Freud's short account of the history of psycho-analysis. It duly appeared on June 25 and Freud wrote to Lou Andreas Salome: ". . . I intentionally [have] given everyone a good clobbering."[177] And later to Abraham: "So the bombshell has now burst. . . . I think we should allow the victims two or three weeks . . . to collect themselves and react."

Jung had already resigned his editorship of the *Jahrbuch,* ostensibly because he had heard that Freud doubted his bona fides. Moreover he had written a scathing letter to Freud which would have shattered any normal friendship at once. "You go round sniffing out all the symptomatic actions in your vicinity thus reducing everyone to the level of sons and daughters who blushingly admit the existence of their faults. Meanwhile you remain on top as the father, sitting pretty. For sheer obsequiousness nobody dares to pluck the prophet by the beard and inquire for once what you would say to a patient with a tendency to analyse the analyst instead of himself. You would certainly ask him 'Who's got the neurosis.' "[178]

And then at last came news that Jung had already resigned the presidency and it was unanimously decided that Abraham should become acting president until the next Congress. Finally Jung announced his withdrawal from the International Association and let it be known that no Swiss analyst from Zurich would attend the next Congress.

Freud himself made a last comment which struck an entirely new and ruthless note: "So we are at last rid of them" he wrote to Abraham, "the brutal sanctimonious Jung and his disciples."[179]

*   *   *

As we have seen it was Jones and Ferenczi – inspired by Freud – who first conceived the idea of an Old Guard surrounding Freud which would only

177. Freud to Lou Andreas Salome, June 25, 1914.
178. Jung to Freud, December 18, 1912.
179. Freud to Abraham, July 25, 1914.

deviate from an understood set of psycho-analytic principles under certain carefully controlled conditions. "If anyone wished to depart from any of the fundamental tenets of psycho-analytic theory . . . he would promise not to do so publicly before first discussing his views with the rest."

To see the whole struggle in perspective it is necessary to stress the ever widening resistance to the "science" of psycho-analysis. In Britain not only its suspicious German character but the dark nature of its investigations troubled the newspapers, the Church and some medical circles. Charlatans took full advantage of the widespread publicity and every kind of exploitation for commercial purposes was brazenly explored. The bogus English Psycho-Analytical Publishing Company put an advertisement in the *Evening Standard* which read "Would you like to make £1,000 a year as a psycho analyst? . . . Take eight postal lessons from us at four guineas a course." A whole correspondence sprang to life in *The Times,* beginning with a little masterpiece by Archdeacon J. Malet Lambert who wrote deploring an alleged move to introduce psycho-analysis into schools. A *Times* leader proceeded to deplore Freud's teachings because it dethroned the will and made men creatures who had little control over instinct. The *Daily Graphic* launched a wholesale enquiry into the "true nature of psychoanalysis" revealing many cases of "victimisation."

Since Jones, in his excellent biography of Freud, has spelt out the history of the formation of the Committee there is no need to repeat the details but there was one aspect which came as a surprise in a man of Freud's stature. He insisted that the Committee would have to be *"strictly secret"* and the italics were his. As the plan developed its secret society characteristics multiplied. It was reasonable enough to nominate men like Jones, Ferenczi, Rank, Sachs, Abraham and Eitingon for the inner council but when on May 25, 1913 Freud issued special insignias to everyone, the Committee acquired the characteristics of blood brotherhood. Freud presented to each member an antique Greek intaglio which all six men mounted in gold rings and they became the seven rings of an almost mystic circle with direct roots in a tradition reaching back to King Arthur and his knights, a world more suited to Jung than Freud.

Jones had no idea that while negotiations were still proceeding with Ferenczi and Otto Rank, Ferenczi had already become suspicious of his own and Rank's loyalty. He wrote to Freud: "It has seldom been so clear to me as now what a psychological advantage it signifies to be born a Jew . . . . you must keep Jones constantly under your eye and cut off his line of retreat." Never a man to remain consistent, within two months Ferenczi had changed his mind and Jones had suddenly become "unflinchingly steadfast" but it presaged further difficulties which were waiting in the wings.

I talked to Jones about the early days of the Committee[180] "Don't be misled," he said, "by the boyish business of the rings. They didn't amount to

180. Interview, Ernest Jones; Brome: *Freud and His Early Circle,* 140.

anything and at least two members of the Committee were embarrassed to wear them. Indeed I once caught Eitingon without his ring and when I remarked on it he said 'I must have left it in the bathroom' but he looked embarrassed for some reason I could only guess at . . . . The combination of external hostility and internal dissension drove us to somewhat picturesque methods and − alas − even those in the long run didn't save us.'' This approach was certainly borne out by the final fate of Jones' ring. It was stolen from a box in the boot of his car, a demeaning repository for a symbol of such significance.[181]

Jones went on to explain that one of the primary functions of the Committee − to reassure Freud in the midst of the many savage attacks made on him − was accomplished without difficulty. Similarly a unified policy made it much easier to cope with the complicated problems which arose. If the main object of the Committee was to reassure Freud in the jungle of feuding it certainly succeeded. Given a unified set of beliefs within a carefully defined model, any new ideas could be matched to the model and ranked as deviationist or developmental. Before I left Jones on that second occasion he reminded me of a letter he had received from Freud just before the war which was a supreme example of psycho-analytic parapraxis.

Freud it seemed had referred back in his letter to his troubles with Jung and instead of writing ''Jung's gospel'' had written ''Jones' gospel''. In a follow-up letter to Jones he wrote ''Now my interesting Verschreiben may have aroused your suspicions. But you remember I did not try to conceal it but even called your attention to it.''[182]

Then followed a rationalisation of the slip. ''It is a common trick of my unconscious to supplant a person disliked by a better one.'' Thus substituting Jones for Jung did not reveal his hidden hostility to Jones but ''a veiled tenderness'' towards him. Much more convincing, logically, was another explanation. The hidden thought really said ''Why can Jung not be like Jones.'' This explanation gathered greater substance when Freud recalled that ''after the Munich Congress I could never utter the name 'Jung' but had to replace it by 'Jones'.''

181. Ibid.
182. Freud to Jones, March 25, 1914.

CHAPTER XII

First Marriage

BY NOW Jones' emotional life had entered a new phase and Lina, the companion of Loe, appears to have taken her place. That Lina was overwhelmingly in love with Ernest is clear from her unpublished correspondence but it is also clear that she could not satisfy him intellectually.

Loe so dominates the emotional scene that it comes as a surprise in 1917 to learn that Lina had been living with him for three years. Among a number of Lina's letters one was particularly moving:[183]

My dearest Ernest

I have just received your letter and was very sad to read such a distressed letter from you. I had hoped very much for the change of being quite away from me would improve you very much and therefore I have not written to you as often as I otherwise would have . . . .

Yes our last month was a failure wasn't it. But was partly due to my run done *(sic)* state of health and also the under bitterness that surged up in my soul from time to time of your sending me away from you and I have felt so very bitter sometimes when thinking of you insisting on me going done *(sic)* to the cottage with your father for I felt in my heart that he would not approve of our relations, no father would. But you assured me so firmly that it would be quite alright and I have felt that this caused the final break and oh! how my heart bleeds at the thought of it.

But words are useless now and I fully realise that I am not an angel to get along with owing to my jealousy and sensitiveness. Oh but I have loved you my dearest Ernest in spite of the unhappiness I have caused you and but for that love that is still so deep for you my life would certainly end with the parting. Perhaps if I had not loved you so much we could have been happier together but in my heart I wanted you and only you and all of you. I see my mistake and you have really been a loving sweetheart to me . . . . But I am sure our last week together will be a happy one at any rate. I intend to put my full strength into trying to make it so . . . .

I hope you get this in time and that you are feeling very much happier. I am looking forward so much to seeing you again and I have missed you so very very much . . . .

183. Lina to Jones, December 28, 1916.

With fondest and deepest love and best wishes for a happier New Year.
With all my kisses

From Lina

Just how long his relationship with Lina lasted is difficult to determine but by January 1917 he was writing to Freud:[184] "I have recently parted with Lina, and set her up in a little flat and found work for her. She has been with me for over three years, which is long enough time to spend with such a character. It has been very difficult lately and altogether I feel I have paid heavily for my sin against her and Loe. I now have a housekeeper of 50 who shines with respectability. Loe telephoned to me this week. The morphia had gone up again to 15 gr. and she is now making a final and determined effort to abolish it, in three stages. The circumstances are favourable, as Herbert is well, and they are happily settled."

Jones was now successful enough to think of buying a small country cottage to satisfy his yearning for "fresh air and natural life." After weeks of searching, late in 1916 he hit upon an isolated cottage in the heart of the Sussex countryside which he quickly nicknamed The Plat. Many years later he wrote: "a home needs a mistress and I was, in the mood to find one."

In co-operation with Eric Hiller, he had by now founded an embryonic press to promote psycho-analytical literature and it was Hiller who one day introduced him to a musician Morfydd Owen, a Welsh woman twelve years younger than Jones. After three brief meetings, with an impetuosity which preceded at least four of his emotional commitments, he proposed to Morfydd Owen. Since he was not primarily a musical man, there were other facets of her personality which attracted him, not least her extraordinarily soulful face with its withdrawn beauty. Essentially a practical scientific man himself, he found complementary artistic elements in her personality. She had graduated at the University of Wales and swept up a number of scholarships to enter the Royal Academy of Music where she became an Associate Professor at the very early age of twenty-four. Pianist, singer and composer, people spoke extravagantly of her as the most gifted musician Wales had ever produced, but however overwhelming his love for her, Jones was not deceived, and simply remarked that she stood out among the musicians of her generation.

That any two such different personalities could quickly find a modus vivendi was not to be expected, and the main conflict quickly developed around religion. Morfydd experienced great difficulty in disentangling herself from her father fixation in order to marry Jones and the painful break seemed to intensify her religious preoccupations. Her beliefs were of the simplest and whereas Jones' incipient pantheism drove him to spend week ends "worshipping" the country, she went obsessively to one religious service after another and even maintained her Sunday school attendance. That he deliberately set out to modify her religious convictions is clear but he

184. Jones to Freud, January 1914.

crystallised the essence of his personality at this time in the phrase: "As may be imagined my notion of adjustment in such matters consisted in persuading the other person to approach my view of them and that is what gradually and painlessly happened."[185]

Beyond these details hard facts about the marriage are scarce but a slow adjustment to one another did take place. Given time the marriage might have developed deep and mutual satisfactions but accident tragically intervened.

In the summer of 1918 they were on their way to pay a belated visit to Jones' father when Jones suddenly decided to buy her a box of chocolates which she declined. That such a triviality could have saved her life seemed absurd but a series of circumstances combined to confirm Jones' belief that we were all at the daily mercy of such "frivolities". No sooner had they arrived at his father's house than Morfydd fell ill but it took the local doctor, with Jones' cooperation, two days to diagnose appendicitis which by then was forming an abcess. When Jones at last reached Trotter by telephone, Trotter advised him to rely on the local surgeon rather than wait for his arrival. What seemed a simple straightforward operation quickly led to a high temperature and delirium. It seemed like blood poisoning but Trotter, when he arrived, quickly identified chloroform poisoning. In those days such a condition was likely to occur in a young person suffering from suppuration who had — and here the chocolates became relevant — been deprived of sugar by wartime rationing. Trotter and Jones fought hard to save her life but it was all of no avail.

Morfydd's death came as a terrible shock to Jones and his grief was profound. For weeks he found himself unable to work, suffered from persistent insomnia and wandered from one friend to the next in London, staying two or three days with each. In Jones' philosophy there was no divine being to curse for this misplaced tragedy but his own experience appeared mild compared to that of Morfydd's father who lost his wife, two sons and daughter all in the space of one year and came to regard the God he once worshipped as malevolent. But Jones now underwent such shattering grief that one person found it extravagant.

It is at this stage in the story that an entirely unknown element and person intervenes. Whether during the years 1916/18 Jones had become enamoured of another woman and was once more struggling to control his torn loyalties, or whether it was simply that a patient fell hopelessly in love with him during psycho-analytic transference and persuaded herself that Jones reciprocated that love, can only be determined by a close reading of her letters. They were written by Joan Riviere, a cultured woman who had become interested in psycho-analysis and later became a member of the inner circle of the London Society.

Mrs Riviere's daughter Diana, describes her mother as a "handsome

185. Jones: *Free Associations*, 254.

woman with a superb carriage and a strong personality . . . . It seems possible that at certain times in her life she suffered from the idea that people either did not appreciate or disliked her." Whether Jones discovered that she was jealous of her brother and sister and haunted by the idea that people were doing their best to put her down, is uncertain. Nowhere in their correspondence did this come through but it seems unlikely that such elementary traits would escape his attention. She married a distinguished barrister at the age of 23 and her only child was Miss Diana Riviere. Aware that his wife had undertaken analysis there is no means of knowing whether Mr. Riviere knew the emotional turmoil into which it had thrown her. At the time her daughter was too young — eight years old — to be her confidante and it is highly likely that she had to keep the situation bottled up inside her which led to the outpourings in her letters.

The first letter, dated October 1918 written shortly after Morfydd's death,[186] reveals that she had for some time been in analysis with Jones.

Dear Dr. Jones,

I was surprised and cheered to see your letter for you are never long out of my thoughts and I am always painfully wondering how you are in mind and body. But it's very hard for me to write to you — I have been through the hardest time of my life over all this — the final stage of the long tragedy of my relations with you. It nearly broke me but a recognition of the truth has saved me — a realization so infinitely sad that you would call it cynicism . . . ."

A brief paragraph next stated that she had put aside any possibility of resuming her analysis, and then came this:

"It has been in my mind to tell you the plain truth, that it can never be done but they were hard words for me to write . . . . You yourself see now the impossibility of objectivity on your part and on my part the impossibility is just as great. I who love and understand and ought to help you am the one person who can I suppose do nothing for you . . . . No wonder you were afraid of me and I knew you would be. You know me well enough to know the impossibility of continuing in any relationship on an assumption which I know to be false . . . . So I cannot speak without hurting you . . . . I see your grief as to you completely *selbstverständlich* but perhaps you do realise a little that it is too extravagant . . . "I can't tell you how terrible it is to me to know you in this broken and pitiful state . . . .

"In all the pain of the last month or two of my final separation as it seemed to me, I have often been consoled by the thought that at last you have reached the greatness that I always knew was in you."

His "hardness" towards her, she continued, was really a symptom of feeling and psycho-analysis was familiar with this inversion.

186. Joan Riviere to Jones, October 25, 1918.

"But that torture .... that turning back of love – that's what I can't go through again." You must, she said "ask yourself why your suffering is now so great ...

"You have failed me so often over easier things than this and yet my faith in you is never destroyed ....

"For the millionth time I say to myself what a madman you are and how wonderful you can be. Which will you end as."

This letter is open to many interpretations. By implication Jones had known Joan Riviere before he took her into analysis and developed some sort of relationship with her, or she had fallen so desperately in love with him during analysis that she projected her own love on to him and received it back in fantasy. Alternatively, Jones had become in analysis some figure in her life whose love she desperately needed and he – consciously or unconsciously – played out the role in counter transference. As we shall see from letters he later wrote to Freud this interpretation is probably the true one. True or not the whole correspondence is an intimate revelation of one of his major case histories, but it can only be read accurately in the analytic transference. Some of Joan Riviere's criticism of Jones is passionate to the point of invective but it is characteristic of the kind of abuse to which Jones was accustomed when positive transference became negative.

Five days after her first letter she wrote another twelve-page one recapitulating their situation and attempting an analysis of Jones' character which rationalised his failure to respond to her love.[187]

"You have asked me to do the hardest thing I ever had to do in my life – and one which I would not dream of doing if there were not a possibility that it might be some help to you. It rouses in me every kind of inhibition and I can hardly bring myself to set about it ....

"You have evidently always been a person liable to states of mind in which you see things temporarily in an unreal and totally subjective light. This is what the two or three people I have met who know you and admire you have all separately and independently without suggestion from me, characterized as your being 'so extraordinary'. The first notable instance of it that I saw was of course the marriage episode though I had seen puzzling indications of it before and its what I to myself have always called the 'mad' side of you – it is liable to affect your judgement even in small things where your feelings are much concerned for instance, in matters connected with your health. The state of mind into which you were thrown on your wife's death would be to the most casual observer unnatural and abnormal and it is clearly of this 'extraordinary' character. However well founded such a grief may be, it would not itself produce a state of mind which is certainly a little 'mad', to say nothing of having all the characteristics of a 'neurosis' – sleeplessness, irritability etc. So far I feel there

187. Ibid, October 30, 1918.

can be no question whatever, but the interpretation of your 'neurosis' is far from obvious, and I can only put before you what occurs to me as possible and probable and leave you to deal with it yourself. In 'hinting' what I did in my last letter I didn't mean any more than to point out to you, what you may have realized to some extent, that your need for self analysis was urgent and extreme. If you now want me to attempt some such analysis for you, I will do the best I can. . . .

"I regard it as absoloutely unquestionable that your wife was to you a substitute for me, in the beginning perhaps even to some extent deliberately and consciously so, though I now have some doubt about this – but at the time it was so obvious ('the exact opposite' etc.) that I imagined you saw it quite clearly. It added very much to my pain that you should imagine there could be any substitute for me, much less my exact opposite, but I need not go into that. When under all the very painful circumstances you married and I left London, I had no idea what your feelings for your wife were, and I remained in total ignorance of your relations with her until after I got back, but it had been quite clear that you *expected* to be happy in your marriage, and I with great difficulty constrained myself to resuming the analysis (because it was my only means to a knowledge of psycho-analysis which I felt was bound up with my interest in life) under the expectation that your feeling for me in the future would be simply one of friendly indifference. What was my astonishment when I got back after 6 months to find, not this, but a formality and impersonality in you that amounted to 'hardness' quite brutal in *my* then 'quivering' and 'wounded' state; in the discussion in regard to your marriage which shortly resulted, a refusal on your part to admit anything more than a 'blundering' in your treatment of me. . . .

"Your treatment of me over your marriage *had* been utterly inexcusable and mad, (how often I have wished to put the circumstances before an impartial third party and for you to hear their verdict.) At the moment, in spite of evident good intentions, your treatment of me *was* forgetful and hard, and to crown all, you had not even succeeded in your marriage – you seemed to me completely without capacity for feeling and I was inordinately sorry for your wife. With this view of things, I left London in July and returned in the autumn, determined now not to allow your deficiencies to interfere with my analysis and to pursue it at all costs. Throughout the winter your hardness to me persisted, (no doubt to a great extent because of the contempt and hardness I was feeling towards you) – and I may say here that throughout my relations with you I have been much struck by the repeated and bitter opposition with which you have disputed my accusations against you of love or of 'hardness' *towards me* but not other accusations, only willing to admit the love after I had begun to accuse you of the opposite. . . .

"At this time I began to suspect that things were going better with your wife. In April on the occasion of your attack of illness your situation roused all my love and longing to help you, regardless of *what* you were. . . .

"To complete this acount I may as well say, that you seemed to me at the time to depend on me a good deal for intellectual sympathy and interest, though perhaps you only did it out of kindness, but I got the impression that possibly your wife did not fulfill all requirements. . . .

"When I got the telegram of her death my own feelings were as far as I can judge quite normal and natural − mixed of course − and did not, I think, affect my judgement. But I almost instantly saw that any satisfaction I might feel at her death would come to nothing in reality, because of *your* attitude to me, and I also felt an instinctive certainty that you would again become 'mad'. . . .

"Finally I had your letter in which you told me of the great love and happiness which had existed between you for some time − which you had (mistakenly I think) taken pains to keep from me. . . .

"Your sorrow at her death is inordinate − why? Is it some form of a resistance to a satisfaction at her death?. . . .

"When you married and I left London you discovered that as a substitute she would not work, in fact that she was *not* me. . . .

"While I was away you could still love me and idealize me. . . .

". . . . and when consequently you found *me* changed, no longer loving, wise and docile, but hard, contemptuous and bitter, you could no longer want me then. Your love for me was then really repressed, not by your conscious efforts only, but by the nature of the situation. *Then* − you managed to achieve what had failed before, the substitution of her for me − most successfully − most gloriously − making such an effort as to break down all resistance, sweep away all her faults and carry you both into a perfect union. . . .

By November 5 matters had become desperate for Joan Riviere:[188] "I had the most appalling time last night struggling with an overwhelming longing to take 60 grams of veronal. I am sure if the letter in this had been posted I would have. I simply could not walk and go out with it. I tried but I couldn't stand. . . . At 5 o'clock I made a compromise and took 16 grams. I had it once before you know − 8 years ago − but then I was younger I had more hope − it wasn't quite so bad − it was connected with two men. . . . What a pity I made that 'costly effort' and wrote those letters − they haven't helped you and they've done me harm − it was only to help you I wrote them. . . .

"*Now* you're telling me about your happiness with her and her death − and the middle *(sic)* time you stopped the conflict by telling me you wished you hadn't married her. . . . I don't know if I shall come and see you again. . . ."

188. Ibid, November 5, 1918.

By November 6 she wrote:[189]

Dear Dr. Jones

After the events of the last week I feel I ought in decency not to bother you any more. I feel too despairing after such bad luck again to hope anything from troubling you again. . . . I would give anything in the world to help you, only to have set you more against me by what I did so unnecessarily and so unwillingly. Before that I was still hoping one day to be a friend of yours. . . ."

She was, she continued, undergoing frightful conversion symptoms and "I am so frightened. I could fly to anyone for help. I feel I am going to have another breakdown like 8 years ago. I could not go through that again."

November 11 brought a letter which contained the sentence "You did literally save my life for a time at least," but "since your mariage I have noted changes in regard to your attitude to marriage and free love. . . . I don't know whether you are aware that there has been a notable change in your attitude to homosexuality in men towards which you have for some time shown a tone of contempt regrettable in an analyst."[190]

Obviously there were breaks in Riviere's analysis from time to time but the letters continued to flow. After one of these breaks in December she wrote that in the first few minutes of meeting her again Jones told her that he had not been able to read her last letter – yet! . . . "You who spend hours every day analysing other people – hadn't even read my letter enough to know what I had said: . . . I was stunned into horror. . . . It destroys me. I don't know how to endure it. . . . After you have taken away my belief in myself what can you give me now. . . . I know you thought I didn't love you really. I didn't know you saw my heart as quite empty and black. I have a sort of feeling you have destroyed yourself to me. . . . I haven't been so inhuman to you as you think. . . . I believe in narcissism i.e. sadism and masochism as well as object love. . . . It hurts me to find how much I have hurt you. . . ."

By January of 1919 she was in despair again:[191] "I have no desire to live or recover. But I must keep my resolve. I will not fail myself though I fail you. It is unspeakable. . . ."

Another letter followed on January 15:[192] "It will not fail us though we shall fail it. I'm not blind to what it means – I know I've got to go through horror, mud and slime and deep water and drag you too – the worst part – but I shall go I shall not be drowned I will not drown you. Here *is* my omnipotence – but in endurance you see I have none. That's where I have failed . . . yes, horridly but I'm not cured – that's why I disappoint you.

"You did it though unwilling, so nobly and generously. That was really great of you . . . a real proof of your greatness."

By February she was writing:[193] "I do feel that it is pretty hopeless going

189. Ibid, November 6, 1918.
190. Ibid, November 11, 1918.
191. Ibid, January 7, 1919.
192. Ibid, January 15, 1919.
193. Ibid, February 18, 1919.

on [with the analysis]. It's not all resistance because even in the days when I endowed you with so many virtues I never thought you sympathetic about the analysis. I suppose you really are like Arthur and people who can't help others. . . . I certainly shant care to live if I am not to be cured and if I did not die I should have to kill myself. I couldn't face a neurotic old age.''

In April came another passionate outpouring which ended with the words: "Do you think I really care about the analysis. I do when I can. I try to keep an interest in it and work at it, for both our sakes because if I didn't I should have no right to be seeing you.''

By October of the same year it became apparent that Joan Riviere was undergoing a *training* analysis and at this stage had begun to develop an analytical practice of her own:[194] "I realized that your grief was inordinate and in its way a madness. You seemed to me this year so much sobered and ennobled and dignified by it, at last grown up. Since July though I have realized that the old you is still there, the Celtic quality, as I call it the unreliability. . . . I don't condemn you – my judgement is this – one can't take you seriously.

"I have five patients now. I don't know how I am going on for I am horribly ill. I am frightened of what will happen of illness and exposure of every kind. . . . My last hope of cure has gone. . . .

"You ask what you can do. I must see you as soon as you get back. Chiefly I think for appearances – so many people know I know you well. I am afraid of being publicly thought to be in any way cut off from you by this. I must see and hear news of you as a friend. . . . That I must manage to go through. I dread it horribly. . . . God bless you and give you happiness my darling loved one – my dear foolish one – my terrible one. . . . Weddings and funerals and weddings . . . how many times will you kill me Bluebeard, I shall always love you. I want you to be happy, yes, with *her*.''

By April of the following year she wrote:[195] "I know I have hurt you in small things – small compared to what I have endured at your hands – and indeed I am sorry – but you have your other love – I have no-one. Good-bye. . . .''

Certainly by now Jones did have another love. Before examining the head-long romance into which Jones had once more launched himself Joan Riviere's case has to be placed in the perspective of other more successful cases. Lancelot Whyte once asked Jones what percentage of his cases he regarded as successful and Jones replied "I don't like talking of success – it's too big a word. . . .'' Roughly sixty per cent he said were benefitted by treatment, twenty per cent were failures, ten per cent broke off treatment and among the remaining ten per cent "there were some cases where it changed their way of life dramatically.''

Janet Rowlandson was once such a case. She came to Jones in 1919 shortly after she had married a man recently "demobbed'' from the armed forces. A

194. Ibid, October 12, 1919.
195. Ibid, April 1920.

powerfully built, handsome man, as a Major in the army Rowlandson had a distinguished war record and went into his new marriage with romantic gusto only to find that his wife was hopelessly frigid. Within a few months he was in despair. A tremendous conflict between his hopeless love for his beautiful young wife and his overpowering sensuality which could not countenance a way of life without physical satisfactions made him miserable. One day Janet read in a newspaper a letter from Jones defending psycho-analysis and without consulting her husband, went to see him.

The analysis which followed began dramatically. She had no sooner entered his consulting room than she went into "one of those theatrical swoons characteristic of Queen Victoria's day." Jones quickly revived her and almost at once she began talking as if she had been in mid sentence when she became "unconscious".

Three main facts emerged in the first four sessions. She was convinced that she had some physical deformity, she had never slept with a man before her husband and somewhere in the background of her mind lurked a demon figure who slowly revealed itself to be her father.

After three months' treatment Jones found that her father had performed cunnilingus with her at the age of twelve and on one occasion was almost discovered in the act by her mother. The father, in panic, had leapt up, taken Janet in his arms and pretended to console her, but the mother had realised that some thing "wrong was going on". She grilled her daughter, discovered the truth and instead of attacking her husband beat Janet severely. Jones considered that the mother's jealousy of her daughter overwhelmed her sense of moral outrage and demanded personal retribution. She was also, it transpired, frightened of physical violence from her husband.

"The source of Janet's trouble was obvious", Jones wrote, "but it took another three months before something like abreaction really began to work."[196] Six months later he received a letter full of gratitude signed by Janet and her husband which said that they were very happy and they owed it all to Jones.

He received a number of such grateful letters but very few survive among his papers.

It remains to say of Joan Riviere that she too, in the last analysis has to be regarded as "successful" because she finally became a respected psycho-analyst and a distinguished member of Freud's inner circle.

196. Jones to Balint, July 14, 1935.

CHAPTER XIII

Re-union with Freud

IMMEDIATELY after the war, Jones began haunting the Ministries of War, Health and Trade in search of "permission to leave" England only to be met by bureaucratic evasions which worked on the assumption that Germany might rise from her ashes and renew her attack at any moment.

He was desperately anxious to meet all his old European colleagues once more and especially of course, Freud. While he battled with bureaucracy he began to organise the London Psycho-Analytical Society.[197] As we have seen, in 1913 he had set up the London Psycho-Analytical Society, but only four of the original fifteen members actually practised psycho-analysis. Among them was Dr. David Eder, an early pupil of Jones who was commissioned into the R.A.M.C. during the war and put in charge of the psycho neurological department in Malta, writing a seminal book *War Shock, The Psycho Neuroses in War Psychology and Treatment*. In only six of a hundred cases was he able to use psycho-analytic therapy but he claimed that in all six cases "the form of the typical Oedipus myth [was] brought out."

Apointed by Jones as Secretary of the London Psycho-Analytical Society, Dr. Eder slowly changed his view of the oedipal complex and came to regard it in a different light from Freud. "Though, in the phantasies or dreams of the adult, one gets evidence of this love toward the mother and rivalry toward the father this is rather to be viewed as symbolic of a desire to return to the infantile dependence upon the mother and the undisputed claim to her whole care and tenderness, the rivalry towards the father symbolising the resentment at the interference with this relationship."

Such words were heresy to Jones who spent many long hours arguing with Eder only to find that instead of surrendering to his irrefutable logic Eder was becoming infected with even more virulent heresies from none other than the arch enemy Jung. Reasoned argument sometimes collapsed into angry exchanges and in the end Jones claimed that Eder remained constitutionally incapable of distinguishing Freudian and Jungian doctrine. Thus by 1919 Jones felt that he had no alternative but to dissolve the London Psycho-Analytical Society and immediately reconstitute it as the British

197. Jones: *Freud, Life and Work*, Vol. III, 2.

Psycho-Analytical Society with a somewhat different membership and different secretary.

Anxious to avoid the problems which had bedevilled the old group, Jones decided that all new members must be proposed by someone who knew them and nominated by the Council before being balloted among the members. As the procedure worked out new members attended meetings as visitors and were asked to read a paper during the first year of their Associate Membership, no organised training being available at the time. The Council agreed that each Associate Member should be re-elected annually in order to separate out those patently unsuitable to psycho-analytic work. As a result a considerable turnover took place but slowly a sympathetic and enthusiastic group gathered around Jones to develop the teaching and practice of psycho-analysis in Britain. By late 1919 there were thirty Members and Associate Members and within three or four years they had been joined by names destined to become part of psycho-analytic history. . . . Professor J. C. Flugel, Dr. Douglas Bryan, Professor Cyril Burt, Dr. Stoddart, Dr. Riggall, Dr. John Rickman, Dr. James Glover, Miss Ella Sharpe, Mr. and Mrs. James Strachey and perhaps not unexpectedly the unrelenting and ubiquitous Mrs. Joan Riviere.

If the British society was to deepen its roots in the International Society certain correlative operations became imperative. Facilities for translating and publishing psycho-analytic literature were a prerequisite and some training organisation must be launched. In the first place Jones founded in 1920 the *International Journal of Psycho-Analytisis*.

*   *   *

It was not until March 1919 that Jones at last received permission to leave the country and reached Berne on the 15th, where he met Otto Rank and Hanns Sachs. "I was very much astonished at the remarkable change the war had wrought in Rank. I had last seen him a weedy youth, timid and deferential, much given to clicking of heels and bowing. Now in stalked a wiry tough man with a masterful air whose first act was to deposit on the table a huge revolver."[198] When Jones enquired why he needed a revolver he replied "Für alle Falle" [for any eventuality]. Asked how he had managed to smuggle such a "colossal weapon" through the frontier checks he explained that when the official pointed to his bulging pocket Rank calmly assured him "Bread." According to Jones, Rank's Viennese friends attributed his changed character to his recent marriage, but Jones believed it to be the result of "hypomanic reaction to the three severe attacks of melancholia he had suffered while in Cracow."

All attempts to reach Austria from Switzerland proved useless and it was not until his second visit to Switzerland in August of 1919 that Jones at last made his historic reunion with Freud. The English Board of Trade was very

198. Ibid, 13.

suspicious of a man who wanted to go abroad twice in the same year and it was only Jones' connection with the psycho-analytic press which produced a permit in the role of publisher for himself and Eric Hiller. Once again he met Sachs in Basle and they went off together to spend "a well earned holiday at Locarno." Freud, at the time, was on holiday in Garmisch, Germany, and Jones' first attempts to reach him were once more frustrated. Jones next engineered a meeting with the Austrian Ambassador in Berne who "in his nonchalant, aristocratic manner . . . expressed surprise that anyone should wish to go to such an unhappy and dismal place as Vienna." Reluctantly he agreed to have visas issued and Jones and Hiller set out three days later.

The first foreign civilians to reach Vienna, they were enthusiastically welcomed at the Hotel Regina, the famous visiting centre for psycho-analysts. En route they discovered just what hardships had overtaken the Austrians when they met the ragged officials and noticed the "vain efforts of emaciated dogs to stagger to the food" which they threw to them.

Jones found Freud "somewhat greyer and a good deal thinner than before the war; he never regained his former plump figure. But his mind had lost nothing of its alertness.[199]

Cheerful, friendly and full of talk he greeted Jones warmly and "it was hard to think" that they "had not seen each other for nearly six years." Suddenly Ferenczi burst into the room and to Jones' "astonishment" kissed both men on the cheeks. "We all had endless news to exchange about what had been happening to us in those years and this was the first of many talks."

It was a great pleasure to Jones to be able to invite the Freud family with Rank and his wife to lunch at the beautiful Hotel Cobenzl outside Vienna. Watching their joy at experiencing a proper meal for the first time in years, Jones found himself moved. A great part of the rest of his week in Vienna was occupied with manifold details of new publishing plans in Vienna and London which mainly involved Rank, with Freud holding a watching brief.

One big question remained – should Ferenczi who had been voted Acting President at the Budapest Congress of 1918 – be re-affirmed as President or should someone else take his place? The severance of Hungary from Austria after the war had so deeply disrupted communications between Vienna and Budapest that it was almost as difficult to reach Vienna from Budapest as from London. Freud therefore felt that it would be expedient to shift the "centre of gravity of psycho-analysis" westward.

As a result Freud proposed that Ferenczi should transfer the Acting Presidency of the International Association to Jones and Ferenczi agreed with good grace. Freud remarked "It is to be hoped that we have found the right man this time." Jones commented: "In years to come it was a source of keen regret to Ferenczi that he was never called upon to function as President and I had good reason later for thinking that he bore me an irrational grudge for having had to supplant him."

199. Ibid, 17.

CHAPTER XIV

Second Marriage

JONES' PERSONAL LIFE had almost simultaneously undergone a complete metamorphosis. He had wooed, won and married, with his old impetuosity, Katharine Jokl, a Viennese woman who combined voluptuous good looks with the intellectual ability to master the intricacies of a Ph.D.

It all began when he wrote inviting her to become his secretary, her fluency in German providing the perfect liaison for his analytic work with Freud.[200] Difficulties arose about the appointment and in July he wrote again[201]:

> Dear Dr. Kitty, your letter was a great blow to me as I had greatly counted on and looked forward to your coming. But of course I must accept your decision. . . . The other objections seem secondary and might even be overcome (for instance I might pay you more to help your mother) but I see that the physical bond at the moment is not to be broken. We are familiar with that in psycho-analysis . . . .
> I shall be in Basel on August 25 . . . and I shall certainly call on you. . . . I feel we know each other already. . . ."

It was on his second trip to Switzerland in August that Jones first met his wife to be. As we have seen, waiting in Switzerland was Sachs, in the middle of a cure for his tuberculosis, paid for by Ernest Jones. Mrs. Jones in the course of a series of interviews frequently stressed to me a neglected aspect of Jones' character – his financial generosity.[202] Sachs, who knew Katharine Jokl, arranged a rendezvous at what Katharine described as "one of those charming garden cafes." Jones arrived wearing an all-white suit and came striding up to her in a very un-English manner with outstretched hand. "We talked, had dinner with a large company that night and arranged to meet again the next day. I had a big basket of flowers on that day – they were sweet peas, an English flower – as the attached card said."[203]

Jones telephoned later the same day and suggested a walk in the woods. On the following day "in the Dolder Woods he asked me whether there was a part of Switzerland I didn't know and wanted to see. 'Oh, the South Lugano, I long to go there' I said. He then asked me whether I would come with him and added – almost casually – 'I mean as my wife of course.' "[204]

200. Jones to Katharine Jokl, May 22, 1919.
201. Ibid, July 31, 1919.
202. Interview, Mrs. Jones, September 14, 1977.
203. Ibid, January 4, 1981.
204. *International Journal of Psycho-Analysis,* Vol. 60, Part 3, 1979.

It was typical of Jones the secular rationalist who had been through the fire of several romances that his proposal to the woman destined to share the rest of his life should have been made in such functional terms, but the relationship which followed was anything but functional.

Difficulties arose at the outset: In September he wrote to her from the Hotel Regina[205]:

"My Kitty,

... But my heart was troubled because I am sorry to have to tell you that quite possibly there may have to be a delay in our wedding which would be very trying to both of us and would cause me serious difficulty in England. Rank's brother Dr. Rosenfeld has been three times to the authorities ... and has not been able to get your marriage certificate. I can understand their being loath to part with such a charming citizen but the grounds they give are too stupid for words. The marriage must be valid in Austria. To begin with it is impossible if only one party is a Christian. Fortunately my parents were wise enough never to baptise me, so I have never been."

Katherine Jones wrote from Zurich[206]:

"My Ernest,

"It is only ten o'clock in the morning and tho I wanted to wait for your news my wish to speak is so great that I must sit down and write. . . . I wish it were already October and the eleventh. As you don't tell me where to address my letters I write to Rank. Have a nice time in Vienna. . . . I am always wishing good morning and good night to you by kissing my chain. Do you feel it? Goodbye my sweetheart *my* Ernest.

"Yrs. Kitty."

On the same day Jones was writing from Vienna[207]:

"My very own sweetheart Kitty,

"The first letter to you since you have belonged to me! and so much to say. I am wondering if there is anyone else besides me in Switzerland in Europe who is quite completely happy.

"I shall never forget the wonderful way in which you came straight to me to my heart in such complete confidence and faith and love knowing at once that your heart had at last found its true resting place. . . . How can I grasp this overpowering fact that you *want* me and that you ask me to fill you with happiness.

"Your very own Ernest."

This was the beginning of a long series of love letters which never faltered in endearments which appeared to remain genuine for twenty-five years. For a man seasoned by many affairs who had passed through one marriage and vicariously experienced the fire of many others it seemed almost absurd that

205. Jones to Katharine Jokl, September 26, 1919.
206. Katharine Jokl to Jones, September 19, 1919.
207. Jones to Katharine Jokl, September 19, 1919.

he should be gathered up in such romantic clouds and delivered over to
occasional extravagances. Perhaps he emerged from his *a trois* situation with
Loe and Lina to pass through the tragedy of his first wife's death with one
dominating need in the shifting uncertainties of his life: the need for a stable
base which would take the stress from life, and now he seized it with an
almost exaggerated romanticism[208]:

"My darling sweetheart, Kitty,
    "I find this distance and separation unendurable as I surmise you do
too. Thank God it will soon be over.
    "Borrowed money from Rank. Don't get expensive Viennese clothes.
Wait till London.
    "It is hard to tear myself away from writing to you but I am late already.
. . . I will write once again and after that it will be telegrams and after that it
will be. . . .
    "Your own *real* devoted lover for always,
                                                    Ernest."

Katharine herself was equally lost in romantic clouds[209]:

"My dear dear Ernest,
    "The third day that you are far from me and my thoughts have never
ceased to seek you. The time is indeed our enemy because it has lead on her
feet and must go on. . . . Yesterday my heart was so heavy I did not know
what to do the patience and joy for all work was gone. I am very busy but
work is the only help when one is unhappy. . . . If people are astonished
that we engaged after such a short time I only remember it is really so. You
are so deep in my heart in my life that I cannot remember the time when
you were not. Did I live before I knew you?"

On the following day Jones wrote[210]:

"My darling Kitty,
    "If you get more letters than we bargained for at our parting I am sure
you will forgive me for I simply have to have a few words with you before
going to bed. . . .
    "What have I done to deserve such a great happiness I keep asking
myself.
    "And so to bed and thoughts of Kitty, my Kitty, my wonderful lovely
loving Kitty whom I love and adore so far above the rest of the world.
    "Your own sweetheart,
                                                    Ernest."

    On October 11, 1919 Jones duly married Katharine Jokl in a Zurich
Registry Office with no great ceremony marking the occasion. From thence
on their life was divided between his London home at Portland Court where

208. Ibid, September 29, 1919.
209. Katharine Jokl to Jones, September 21, 1919.
210. Jones to Katharine Jokl, September 22, 1919.

he remained what his wife described as "a terrific worker" and his country home, The Plat, where they relaxed at week ends.

However, patients, after the war, did not come flooding back and he wrote to his wife who was staying at The Plat [211]: "Cable came from 'New York World' asking for my views on love. It seems strange to think that one's views are supposed to be worth flashing along deep sea cables. I wish appreciation took a more worldly form at present in the way of patients: I have a revival at the moment of the wish to retire to [the Plat] .... Not really pessimistic darling only ups and downs of moods."

Roughly one year before Jones settled down to married life, the Hungarian, von Freund, made a magnificent donation of £100,000 towards founding a private publishing house which would be exclusively psycho-analytic. Such were the currency controls that it was only possible to transfer less than a quarter of the money – half a million crowns – to Vienna and of this it was decided to transfer half to London.

Jones conspired with Eric Hiller to smuggle the money across the Austrian frontier but he knew that customs officials stripped naked any suspect and made random checks on those they did not suspect. The stripping took place first, and then their suitcases were searched, one independently of the other. Whether by luck or cunning, Jones' suitcase was searched first – and "I then calmly fetched the roll of notes from Hiller's case and placed it in my own which had now passed through customs." On the surface the manoeuvre seemed so simplistic it would not have deceived a child, but Jones gave no further details. However a fresh customs scrutiny was to be carried out on the following day when the train left for Switzerland.

Jones' resourcefulness revealed its full flower when he later rescued Freud from the hands of the Nazis, and now at a lower level he simply "hired a car the next morning and drove over the Rhine bridge separating the two countries." Once they reached the further boundary, according to Jones "they could justly claim that [their] luggage had already been examined," which implied a casualness among Austrian customs officials he had previously denied. Whatever forces combined to get them safely across the frontier it was all of no avail. Within a year, raging inflation rendered the money hardly worth the paper on which it was printed.

Elaborate efforts were made to transfer sums from the main body of the fund to Vienna but even with Freud's powerful intervention, anti-semitic and anti psycho-analytic forces were too strong and nearly three years passed before a small part of the money was rescued. Over-optimistic, the *International Psychoanalytischer Verlag* had long before committed itself to extensive undertakings and it was only the intervention of Eitingon, who induced a sympathetic brother-in-law to donate 5,000 dollars, that avoided serious complications.

Some months before, Rank and Jones had already decided to launch a

211. Ibid, April 10, 1922.

branch of the Verlag in London which would publish a periodical and translations of Viennese books. By printing these publications in the new Czechoslovakia "where paper and labour costs were many times cheaper" than in England, they hoped to fulfil the capitalist's dream of "producing in a cheap currency and selling in a dear one." They certainly succeeded in providing English speaking audiences with valuable literature but fell short of their aim of supporting the Verlag.

"Ex-enemies" could not open offices in London at the time, which forced Jones into the role of publisher of what he called The International Psycho Analytical Press. Eric Hiller, Jones young assistant, became manager of a bookshop which the Press opened in Weymouth Street, London, with the express purpose of selling German books unobtainable elsewhere.

The shop survived for less than a year when they were forced to close the premises and sell the stock for £100. Their second new enterprise, the International Psycho-Analytical Library Series launched its first volumes in 1921, seven of which were, as planned, printed abroad. "After that" Jones wrote "The London Institute came to a satisfactory arrangement with the Hogarth Press and their joint publication has continued ever since."

It was Jones, once more who, as Chairman of the Board of the Institute, assisted by John Rickman with Flugel as secretary, led the discussion which eventually formulated the Institute's policy: "To stand aside from scientific discussions and to confine itself to publishing activities, the organisation of a Clinic and the fostering of the science of psychoanalysis through the establishment of educational facilities and lecture courses."

The leviathan task of translating Freud's works, preoccupied the early days of the press and led into multiple correspondence with Freud who patiently cooperated on every detail.

The other big undertaking, the *International Journal of Psycho-Analysis,* called for support for Jones as editor and he nominated Bryan and Flugel in England. Finding an America editor proved more difficult. When Freud and Jones wrote to Brill asking for his advice he failed to reply and only much later did they discover that his silence was due to some "jealous, hurt sensibility." He had in fact become convinced that Freud was displeased with him because of the continuous flow of criticism about his translations. The candidates put forward by New York seemed highly undesirable to Freud and Jones and the final choice fell on Brill, Frink and Oberndorf.

Jones as co-editor of *Internationale Zeitschrift für Psychoanalyse* now made arrangements whereby they could freely exchange material with the *International Journal,* but it was "the difficulties arising in connection with the Journal that loosened the publishing bonds between London and Vienna."

When Brill at last responded to Jones' outline of their plan he said he would give it his "cordial support." Simultaneously he added another convolution to the backstage conspiracies which continued to bedevil psycho-analysis, and suggested to Jones that they should form an Anglo American Psycho-Analytical Association in − would it be rivalry − with the International Association? Jones commented in his Freud biography "Being among other things a good European as well as being always internationally minded I frowned on the suggestion and heard nothing further of it."

CHAPTER XV

Conflict with Freud

SHORTLY AFTER the war Jones had been anxious to arrange an early if not immediate Congress only to receive a reprimand from Freud who said that Jones "knew nothing of the conditions" in which they lived and had learned nothing from the newspapers. Considerable wrangling among members of the International Association followed but in 1920 they settled for The Hague as the Congress centre and in September of that year Jones was one of the first sixty-two members to arrive. The British sent fifteen members, the Germans eleven, the United States two and the resident Dutch contingent numbered sixteen, the remainder being drawn from Hungarians, Austrians, Poles and Swiss, the seven Swiss representatives coming from the newly-formed pro-Freudian Swiss Psycho-Analytical Society.

"It is still pleasant to remember" Freud later wrote "how kind our Dutch colleagues were to us starving shabby Central Europeans."[212] Freud addressed the Congress on *Supplements to the Theory of Dreams,* qualifying his earlier position that all dreams represented wish fulfilments. Groddeck enlivened the proceedings by introducing himself as a wild analyst who believed that actual organic disease could be treated psycho-analytically. He illustrated his thesis by claiming that myopia and retinal bleeding were "efforts to defend against forbidden wishes. . . ."

The tone of Jones' circular letter to all members which followed, was more in sorrow than in anger[213]: "Ps-A has so many attractions for the popular entertainer that it seems to me better that we official representatives should lay stress on the dignified and scientific aspects, just those which our opponents deny in our work."

The Hague Congress was a relative success and several others followed in Berlin, Salzburg, Bad Homburg, Innsbruck, Oxford, Lucerne, Wiesbaden, Marienbad and Paris. Freud attended only the Berlin Congress but he continued to exercise control behind the scenes with Jones as one of his main lieutenants. It quickly became a matter of dispute whether Jones was in fact his chief lieutenant.

Shortly after the war Ferenczi and Rank became involved in quarrels with Jones and the air grew thick with accusation and counter-accusation all over

212. Freud to Arnold Zweig, July 15, 1934.
213. Jones to Members of Committee, February 11, 1921.

again. In his biography of Freud Jones states that "the first sign of anything going wrong was a gradual mounting tension between Rank and myself over the business of publication." He does not say that he simultanously tried to cope with a three-cornered battle between himself, Mrs. Riviere and Freud.

Joan Riviere's extraordinary relationship with Jones had by this time reached a new climax. She had become integrated into the London Psycho-Analytic Society and was trying to reconcile the roles of lover, analyst and political manipulator. Against the peace of his new marriage Jones found her mounting presence too much for him and he recommended that she should go to Vienna to consult Freud. Then came a letter to Freud which gave his inner views of the whole situation[214]:

"I thought it might interest you if I told you a few words about your new patient Mrs. Riviere, who is going to Vienna next week, as she plays a considerable part in the society here. It is a case of typical hysteria, almost the only symptoms being sexual anaesthesia and unorganised Angst, with a few inhibitions of a general nature. Most of her neurosis goes into marked character reactions, which is one reason why I was not able to cure her. I am specially interested in the case, for as it is the worst failure I have ever had I have naturally learnt very much from her analysis. She came to me in 1916 and was with me till last June, with about a year's interruptions from tuberculosis and other causes. Seeing that she was unusually intelligent I hoped to win her for the cause, a mistake I shall never repeat. I underestimated the uncontrollability of her emotional reactions and in the first year made the serious error of lending her my country cottage for a week when I was not there, she having nowhere to go for a holiday. This led to a declaration of love and to the broken-hearted cry that she had never been rejected before. From that time on she devoted herself to torturing me without any intermission and with considerable success and ingenuity . . . . : my two marriages gave her considerable opportunity for this which she exploited to the full. The treatment finally broke down over my inability to master this negative transference, though I tried by all means in my power. The situation was complicated by her position in the society, which gave her a certain personal contact with me. . . . Her symptoms are much better (she can talk fluently at a meeting where she was once dumb from Angst) and she has a far-reaching insight, but the main complexes are only intellectually resolved. She has a most colossal narcissism imaginable, to a great extent secondary to the refusal of her father to give her a baby and her subsequent masculine identification with him. Naturally she comes to you with a strong positive transference ready, and my only fear is lest there be not time enough to provoke and work through the necessary negative aspect of this. In that case we should lose a valuable translator and member of the society, for I think she understands

214. Jones to Freud, January 21, 1921.

psa better than any other member except perhaps Flugel. Incidentally she has a strong complex about being a well-born lady (county family) and despises all the rest of us, especially the women."

Mrs. Riviere's arrival in Vienna in April 1922 did not entirely free him from her influence. From London he wrote to his wife who was staying at The Plat[215]:

"I have been specially wanting you today because there came a very worrying letter from Professor. I do wish he were *not* so womanish in being easily influenced by Rank and Mrs. Riviere being the villains this time. I had a strong tendency to react but thought hard of you when writing and will show you the letters. Rank wants to make me responsible for all the delay in the Press which is too absurd."

The early stages of Rank's dispute with Jones drew from Jones an admission of one his weaknesses. He had he wrote "a rather obsessive insistence on doing things in what [he] conceived to be the best way with an impatience of sloppiness and a risk of provoking the sensibilities of other people concerned."

In the intricate exchanges which followed between Freud, Jones, Rank, Ferenczi and Mrs. Riviere that mild criticism was sharpened by Freud into trenchant denunciation on occasion and there were moments when Jones' automatic reverence for the Master was put under intolerable strain.

Late in 1921 he wrote a very revealing letter to Freud which began with a reference to the Hague Conference[216]:

"The day I joined you all (at the Congress) I was thoroughly well and active, but that evening my cold in the head began. Partly for toxic reasons and partly from my intolerance of naso-pharyngeal irritation (erogene zone, I suppose), this trouble always affects me physically, in the direction of a slightly hypochrondrical withdrawal. . . . Also I knew that within four days of my return I would have to provide a large sum of money for the house I was buying and was not sure whether I could borrow it from a certain friend (the bank had refused to lend me anything, being under Government orders on the matter, and my savings were unsaleable – having shrunk to *one fifth* of their value in the past six months, owing to the cessation of trade in England). I am glad to say that this difficulty has been overcome for the moment and we are now enjoying the pleasure of arranging our delightful new home. We have at last accommodation to invite you to stay in on your long-expected visit to England."

Jones' new house was No. 42 York Terrace, Regents Park, a house "well organised from the point of view of work", which had a large garden overlooking the park and was only ten minutes walk away from 81 Harley Street to which august address he had now transferred his consulting room. For the following ten years he lived, worked and took a major part in the still

215. Jones to Katharine Jokl, April 10, 1922.
216. Jones to Freud, October 11, 1921.

developing psycho-analytic movement from one or other of these two addresses.

For various reasons Freud abandoned an intended trip to England to meet Jones and his nephew, then living in Manchester, but by correspondence he now kept in touch with Jones and became very outspoken.

In my first book on Freud's early circle I wrote: "One has to sympathise with Jones. He became the centre of a series of hostile communications, lawyers' letters, complaints and fierce exchanges quite apart from his troubles with Rank, and Freud, but a new development suddenly brought the Rank quarrel to the fore."

Rank first launched an attack on some of the American papers published in the Journal and then overstepped his powers by actively intervening in the actual editing of the journal. This took the form of simply not printing papers from the Americans which he described as "rubbish" and thus contributing to an American-European conflict which simmered on for fifteen years. Jones himself would invite a contribution from the President of the New York Psycho-Analytical Society and when it turned out to be mediocre, have to face the embarrassing consequences. Jones proceeded on the principle that since every third paper had the possibility of being a good one he should print the others in the interests of Anglo-American amity."[217] This did not placate the Viennese who still believed that the Americans were "Rootless intellectuals dabbling in matters which required a European tradition."

Further complications arose over the English translation of Freud's works which Freud had first regarded sceptically. Jones' grandiose vision of a whole oeuvre beautifully reproduced for the English speaking world, slowly aroused his enthusiasm, and as a man who frequently saw death looking over his shoulder Freud began to press for more speed in producing the Collected Papers. This created new frictions between Rank and Jones. Conflict over what precisely should be included led to editorial changes, with Rank arbitrarily issuing final instructions to the printer "which Jones point-blank refused to accept."

Freud's cavalier attitude to copyright further compounded a highly charged situation when he granted the English rights to Jones only to allow his nephew Edward Bernays to negotiate their sale in the United States.

Meanwhile Rank in Vienna claimed that he was fighting against over-whelming odds because Jones insisted on doing things "the correct way" which according to Rank meant his, Jones', way. Rank wrote strong letters to Jones, the tone of which Jones considered "overbearing and hectoring". Matters steadily worsened as Rank persisted in his new habit of over-ruling Jones' instructions and Jones commented "What had aroused this harsh dictatorial and hitherto unseen vein in Rank's nature I could not guess."

Freud wrote in December of 1921 saying that for him, life was still "rich in

217. Brome: *Freud and His Early Circle*, 173.

hardships'' and in order to survive he had to work nine hours a day.[218] Jones replied: ''The only way to deal with a press of patients is for you to raise your fees still further. Many analysts here . . . even unqualified ones get two to three guineas and you have surely the right to ask five from those who can afford it.''[219] It was in the same letter of December 9 that Freud complained forcefully of the quality of the contributions to the *Journal* for which Jones as editor was responsible. Rickman and Strachey had already criticised certain articles in the *Journal* and their remarks were reinforced by Anna Freud and Hugo Hella. Such a combination of perceptive and well-informed people Freud wrote was not likely to be ''altogether wrong''.

He concluded: ''Now I lay this matter before you as you are the only one responsible for the level of the Journal and I hope you will reduce the reproaches to their true size and try to remedy for what remains.''[220]

Jones replied with an analysis of one issue of the journal which explained the origins of the articles and their translators. He then referred to his two assistants saying that one, Bryan, was relatively uneducated and the other, Flugel, clever but with two weaknesses. ''He is rather selfish and only likes doing his own work.'' Moreover ''he has not overcome a strong reaction to a sadistic complex. . . .''[221] ''I cannot do everything alone so use my time and powers for whatever I consider the most important. . . . You may at all events be sure I do not underestimate the importance of the linguistic factor. . . . Perhaps I am to blame in accepting Varendonck's article. I was influenced by your high opinion of him, my own being, I must confess, much lower.''

This displaced responsibility for the low quality article on to Freud and made Rickman and Heller partly responsible for bad translations. Worse was to follow. By now a number of rifts, quarrels and dissensions were beginning to tear at the very fabric of the Committee itself and threaten the purpose for which it was established.

In the long and tortured story which followed it became clear — as in the past — that when one member of the Committee quarrelled with another he would explain away his opponent's behaviour as ''a sudden neurotic outbreak''. Similar convenient occurrences of mental illness were used by various members of the circle to explain away new defections from Freud as they developed. No-one ever went into the wilderness because he rationally or sanely differed from Freud. Thus with Rank, Jones now said: ''It took a couple of years before it became plain that a manic phase of his cyclothymia was gradually intensifying.''

In a determined effort to preserve Freud's peace of mind Jones went to great trouble to conceal his quarrel with Rank, but Rank, living in Vienna, took every opportunity to pour into Freud's ears a long account of what he regarded as Jones' impossible behaviour. All Jones' attempts to reassure Freud were received at first with suspicion, later with coldness and finally

218. Freud to Jones, December 9, 1921.
219. Jones to Freud, December 15, 1921.
220. Freud to Jones, December 9, 1921.
221. Jones to Freud, December 15, 1921.

anger. "This last year brought a disappointment not easy to bear. I had to find out that you had less control of your moods and passions, were less consistent, sincere and reliable than I had a right to expect of you and than was required by your conspicuous position." Since Jones himself, Freud said, had proposed the idea of the Committee he did not understand why he should then proceed to endanger it by an exaggerated and unjust sensitivity. He was prepared to run the risk of telling him this home truth, but hoped that the year 1923 would restore their faith and friendship.

A remarkable displacement of the quarrel now took place in Jones' mind. The reference to "his passions" completely bewildered him until he associated it with Mrs. Joan Riviere, his ex-patient. Explaining the situation to Freud, Jones said that she had made "a declaration of love [to him] and a friend had misunderstood this as a declaration of love by Jones."

It was Mrs. Riviere who once more figured large in Jones' unceasing correspondence with Freud. The capacity of these two men to maintain a multiple corespondence with many people in the midst of eleven patients a day, routine publishing complications, family life and international manipulations of the psycho-analytic scene belong to an age of letters which has passed.

On April 1 Jones wrote:[222]

> "A day or two ago I received a handsome offer from Mrs. Riviere to take over the revision of translations for the journal. There is no one who could do it as well and there is no work that I would more gladly be relieved of. . . . The delicate problem arises however about Rickman whom I should like to see as assistant editor. He is far easier to work with . . . [but] owing doubtless to some remaining infantilism he makes extraordinary mistakes in spelling and even grammar. . . ."

He concluded that Mrs. Riviere would logically have the better claim but he did not want to "give a slap in the face to the Americans by putting another lay person on the staff of the journal."

Jones then tried to clear up any remaining misunderstanding of his past relationship with Mrs. Riviere:

> "I was surprised at your suspecting any sexual relations between [us] and I think it must have been a Verlesen of the expression 'declaration of love', which was of course on her side only. She is not the type that attracts me erotically though I certainly have the admiration for her intelligence that I would have with a man. But, speaking generally, you need never have any fear about me in such respects. It is over twelve years since I experienced any temptations in such ways, and then in special circumstances; even should it arise in the future, which is very unlikely now, I have no doubt at all of my capacity to deal with it."

222. Jones to Freud, April 1, 1922.

Freud replied that since Rank, editor of both their periodicals, was a layman he did not see why the Americans should object to Mrs. Riviere.[223] Moreover Jones owed Mrs. Riviere some compensation for having complicated her analysis by "inconsequent behaviour" which he had now confessed. In fact Jones had confessed to nothing of the kind and staunchly maintained a completely opposite version of events.

As for the machinery of publication "another wheel . . . seems to be wrong" Freud wrote "and I imagine it is your position . . . in the middle of it and the ceremonial that prescribes your personal interference at every step. . . ."

No less than five men, Freud said, seemed to read the proofs before the final copy went back to him and at this rate he would hardly live to see the appearance of "two poor pamphlets". "I don't see why you want to do it all alone and suffer yourself to be crushed by the common drudgery of the routine work." The whole process, Freud said, could be accelerated enormously if only Jones would not insist on supervising every minute detail.

Jones at this stage had not accepted Mrs. Riviere as a translating editor but Freud assumed the opposite and said he would inform Mrs. Riviere accordingly. His letter concluded with a remark which evoked in Jones what he described as "a mirthless laugh". Freud said "Pardon my meddling with your affairs but they are ours and mine too and Rank is too meek to oppose you in these quarters."

Matters now went from bad to worse with Mrs. Riviere. Jones wrote on May 22nd that "her story of my unkindness" was a "pure myth. . . ." "She is known in the Society as my favourite" but "even Heller who has more capacity than I for getting on with hectoring women writes that he has almost reached breaking point."[224]

By May 26 Jones was saying that unless their publication problems were grasped with a firm hand they would "drift into a condition of anarchy. . . ." "It is plain that the only satisfactory way of working is to institute one definite head to be responsible for . . . editing and publishing. . . . I had assumed this role would fall to my part both as editor of the Press and because I am probably in the best position to form an all out judgment."[225] Jones was dismayed, he continued, to find that Mrs. Riviere was "under the impression that she [would] replace [him] in this position. If you wish this then of course I will agree but I cannot pretend that it will be with indifference. I should not be able to work under her orders because of the impossible tone in which she issues them."

In a marathon reply of nine pages[226] Freud proceeded to take Jones apart on practically every issue and complained that his idea that Mrs. Riviere might replace him was purely imaginery. Mrs. Riviere had not, as Jones implied, deliberately set out to woo Freud to her point of view and convert him into a puppet in her hands. Jones must face up to the possibility that he

223. Freud to Jones, April 4, 1922.
224. Jones to Freud, May 22, 1922.
225. Ibid, May 26, 1922.
226. Freud to Jones, June 4, 1922.

was completely incapable of organising "people and work" and if left to his own resources might reproduce a situation only a few months old.

As for Mrs. Riviere's character: she was not the self-conscious intriguer implied in Jones' letters but she no longer behaved sweetly and had become "harsh, unpleasant and critical even of me." Apparently unaware that these last phrases accurately reproduced Jones' view of Mrs. Riviere, Freud developed his analysis of her character. She could not, he said, take praise any better than blame, success any better than failure.

It all pointed towards a conflict between the Ego and the Ideal and it seemed that the "formation of a high and severe ideal took place at a very early age" but this ideal became . . . "repressed" "with the onset of maturity and ever since [had] worked in the dark."

Secondary analysis of Mrs. Riviere forced Freud to analyse Jones himself and he found in him a lack of "accuracy and plainess" in his dealings accompanied by a whole armoury of memory lapses, subtle distortions and evasions, until, time and again he, Freud, was driven to accept Mrs. Riviere's version of events.

Jones was taken aback by this letter. That anyone could draw such conclusions from his relationship with one "overbearing and supercilious woman" astonished him when "he had enjoyed such great success with other co-workers." Bluntly he conveyed this astonishment to Freud. What Jones did not know was that Mrs. Riviere had become one of a number of women including Lou Andreas Salome and Ruth Brunswick who attracted Freud for more than purely analytic reasons. She was handsome, clever and devoted to the cause, and Freud had no illusions about her attractions.

None of this appears to have appeased the various contestants and as late as November of the same year Freud was writing that Heller complained bitterly of Jones' treatment[227] of him and said he was sorry there remained so much disagreement.

According to Freud, for two years Jones seems to have blundered from one false step to the next, but the evidence is conflicting. All the English evidence indicated that Jones in the area of publications had put up a wonderful performance which was qualified by his inability to delegate work and responsibility.

All these difficulties coincided with a desperate shortage of patients for Jones and he wrote on November 19:[228] "Please forgive me if this letter is not written in to happy a vein; you will not find that surprising if you reflect for a moment on the complexities of my position as it appears to me: health, friends, the future of the Journal, work, even practice (my solitary consultation since July has remained solitary and I have several vacant hours)."

Very disturbed by the prolonged wrangling he continued: "As to your own repeated disapproval of me I need not tell you how grievous I find that,

227. Freud to Jones, November 6, 1922.
228. Jones to Freud, November 19, 1922.

for you must know what part you play in my life and feelings. I can only wait till I receive some criticism which is concrete enough for me to put to the test and which also corresponds to the facts as they are known to me, but such criticism is rare." His letter concluded: "But I will end on a brighter note — my domestic happiness is all that a man could wish it to be."

Relations with Freud now passed through a series of fluctuations to improve on the whole but Rank, possibly because Freud remonstrated with him, turned an even more bitter eye on Jones. Whatever scepticism one brings to bear on Jones' account of the whole affair there is no questioning the fact that Hiller resigned from the job and left Vienna in March 1923. The psychoanalytic press was then separated off from Vienna and began an independent existence in London, backed by the Institute of Psycho Analysis.

In the midst of all these exchanges neither Freud nor his colleagues made sufficient allowance for the fact that Jones had doggedly pushed on speaking to medical societies, writing papers, and preparing the ground for the foundation of the Institute of Psycho-Analysis (1924). He was President of the British Society from 1920, took the chair at scientific meetings and committees and founded the Society's Training Commission. His collected *Papers on Psycho-Analysis* had first appeared in 1912 and now in 1923 a third reprint was issued and in terms of technical publishing sold well. (The whole body of his theoretical contributions to psycho-analysis which runs into over two hundred papers and books is analysed at length in Appendix One).

Nowhere in his writings does Jones refer to yet another battle which he conducted simultaneously in 1923 with Sandor Ferenczi. The trouble began when Ferenczi put forward the proposition that in hypnosis one of the most important elements was the auto-suggestive ideas of the patient which in his view were libidinal and infantile in origin. Jones claimed that Ferenczi's basic proposition was a truism and not unexpectedly such an attack on what Ferenczi regarded as his "originality" did not please him. Whereupon Jones said that he could produce a long list of authors who stressed the importance of internal initiatives in such cases and to call it a truism was no exaggeration. Letters became heated until Jones wrote a long placatory note which had little effect, but this was a storm in a teacup compared to further troubles waiting in the background.[229]

A network of inner relationships had developed within the Committee with Rank and Ferenczi cooperating closely, Freud sharing something of their intimacy and Jones away in London largely condemned to rely on correspondence. Rank and Ferenczi had been co-operating on a new book for two years, each exchanging confidences with the other about Jones, and one day Rank remarked to Ferenczi "He [Jones] doesn't really belong to us. He sits there in London writing instructions to everyone about the Press as if

229. Jones to Ferenczi, December 1923.

we were children.''[230] In July 1923 Rank and Ferenczi were away in the Tyrol still collaborating on their book and devising new strategies for coping with Jones. By now they were considering proposing a motion that Jones be expelled from the Committee, and then in August, Rank learnt, in the highest confidence, that Freud had cancer, and he approached the last meeting of the Committee at San Cristoforo towards the end of August in a mood of growing independence.[231] Largely dependent on the patients sent to him by Freud, Rank realised that his death might threaten his whole way of life.

Anxious to avoid the brunt of the coming battle at San Cristoforo Freud remained aloof at Lavorone on the grounds of bad health, waiting hopefully for news of a rapprochement. When Jones pressed him to join them he said it would be better if he did not personally intervene and Jones, unaware of the explosion which was to follow, went to the meeting with hopes of achieving reconciliation.[232]

The atmosphere as the meeting opened was tense and Rank put his case forcefully but when Jones apologised for any unintentional pain he had caused, Rank refused to accept the apology and dramatically demanded that Jones be expelled from the Committee. The majority voted against expulsion and Rank stormed out of the room in a fury, with Ernest Jones holding himself back in what he described as "puzzled silence," a marvellous euphemism for his true feelings. Jones summed up the situation in a letter to his wife:

August 26, St. Christoforo.

"The chief news is that Freud has a real cancer slowly growing and may last years. He doesn't know it and it is a most deadly secret. Eitingon is here too. . . . We have spent the whole day thrashing out the Rank–Jones affair. Very painful but I hope our relations will now be better and believe so, but on the other hand expect Ferenczi will hardly speak to me for Brill has just been there and told him I had said Rank was a swindling Jew (stark übertreiben).

Brill of course has gone back to the U.S. without seeing me."[233]

As Jones later wrote in his autobiography "after San Cristoforo Freud agreed to receive us and I shall never forget the kindly forbearance with which he made every effort to bring about some degree of reconciliation." Some degree of reconciliation there was, but the majority of the Committee went their separate ways full of disillusionment.

230. Interview, Dr. Clara Thompson.
231. Brome: *Freud and His Early Circle,* 176.
232. Ibid.
233. Jones to Katharine Jokl, August 26, 1922.

CHAPTER XVI

Private Life

IN TOTAL CONTRAST to all this guerilla warfare Jones' personal life flourished. His marriage was a complete success, his wife a beautiful woman who gave him total devotion and all deviations had ceased. From now on — domestically — there stretched ahead a number of years which gave him an understanding and immensely tolerant base to which he could return to pour out his woes, confidences and not least, love.

Against all the torture he endured in other areas this remained a love match and when Katharine was at The Plat and Jones in London they continued to exchange romantically extravagant love letters.

She wrote on June 18 "Since then (our wedding) our love has become deeper but not less passionate. And it will be four years next October. Quite a respectable time. . . .

"Many congratulations on your titled patient. I hope he will be the first of a series and I hope he pays well. . . . I hope Rank is coming round: it is high time."[234]

There were those amongst the pioneers of psycho-analysis Mrs. Jones did not favour and she frankly expressed her views[235]:

"My darling Ernest,
"I am rather against inviting Barbara [Low] to come here. When? Just when you came back after a long absence and want to tell me a lot without any witness. It is not the custom that the guest fixes the date of the invitation. If she could not come when invited the worse for her. . . . But I don't like to be forced and I am getting to see through her little ways."

Clearly Mrs. Jones was the repository of many outright opinions, the facts of which we may never know.

A daughter, Gwenith, had been born in 1920 and remained "the apple of [Jones'] eye." And then on February 27, 1922, Jones wrote to Freud[236] "You asked me to let you know at once of the son's arrival. It took place this afternoon in 1½ hours. He weighs K. 4.20, is an unmistakably male child, lusty and hearty . . . but with blond hair and blue eyes. He seems to adapt himself rapidly to his changed life and behaved masterfully at his first meal.

234. Mrs. Katharine Jones to Ernest Jones, June 18, 1923.
235. Ibid, September 4, 1920.
236. Jones to Freud, February 27, 1922.

My wife went through the ordeal splendidly, glowing with health and pride and feels very well. The name will probably be Merfyn (pronounced Merrvin).''

By March he wrote[237]: "I am glad to say that both [children] are progressing perfectly. . . . The boy resembles myself and my father much more than his mother facially, the reverse of the little girl. The contrast between them is remarkable. . . . Always gratefully yours, Ernest Jones.''

They were now living in the seven roomed house in York Terrace which remained their home for many years and Jones followed a punishing routine. As we have seen Mrs. Jones described him as a "terrific worker." He used, she said "to see the first patient at home because he was not allowed to start so early in Harley Street. That meant seeing the patient before breakfast. Then he rang the gong and breakfast was served. After that he went to Harley Street. The advantage of having a house so near was that he came home for all meals which meant that he could see the children who had their meals with us. That must seem to you to go without saying but these were the days of Nannies and their reign. It was never so in our house. I chose my Nanny very carefully and she submitted to his ruling.''[238]

"On his busiest days I remember him having eleven patients a day. He used then to take his tea in a thermos to Harley Street. After lunch he saw his secretary for his very extensive correspondence. Over dinner he read the evening paper and then once again it was work on a paper or reading a paper submitted to him as Editor of the *International Journal of Psycho-Analysis*. Then there were the Society meetings at which he presided. The training analysts met in our house. There was a large dining room in which the meetings took place. The other large downstairs room with steps into the garden was his library. The garden was used every year for a garden party.''[239]

Much later in life, when Mrs. Jones was 88, she said to me, with a touch of sadness, "There were really no evenings. He had this huge desk you know, and after dinner we frequently sat at opposite sides, he writing a paper or part of a book and I reading something or other.''[240]

Work might run on until ten or eleven o'clock and then followed another hour's reading with bed regularly around midnight. Perhaps half of the last hour of the day was given over to non-professional reading, including history and an occasional novel recommended by his wife.

"There was no more reading in bed for me as I used to do in my girlhood" his wife recorded. "He said – 'go to bed to sleep.' Ernest was a good sleeper and always had to be wakened.'' Thus at six or seven o'clock in the morning the prolonged daily routine burst into life again and sometimes a bustling figure greeted his wife and children with that indomitable vitality which was the wellspring of his incredibly full life. There were two other concessions to the frailties of relaxation, ice skating, at which he became expert – eventually

237. Ibid, March 2, 1922.
238. *International Journal of Psycho-Analysis,* Vol. 60, Part 3, 1979.
239. Ibid.
240. Interview, Mrs. Jones, December 14, 1980. The desk is now preserved in the Institute of Psycho Analysis.

writing a good book on the subject — and chess where he could outwit most of his opponents. Once a month he and Katherine sailed forth in their finery for a visit to the theatre which evoked the excitement of indulging a luxury.

Financial pressures still troubled the Jones family in the early twenties and Ernest wrote to Katharine: "We have £128 in the bank and unless Varley pays, nothing coming in till November with rents at the end of this month but there will probably be some small dividends."

By 1922 he was writing[241]: "Kittinks Darling, Gas bill is just under £20 for quarter and stern letter just come from King George saying we must paint outside of house and railings in August no delay being permitted now war is over! Cheerio! On the other hand many of our shares are going up and I am telling Gethin to sell the G.W.R. ones which must be about their top." Romantic asides continued to enliven his practical letters: "I know just what my sweetheart does at every hour — so can picture her. Au revoir my heart of hearts." From Harley Street he wrote when the family was at The Plat "Here I am deserted by all my harem, no daughter, nurse, secretary and worst of all no wife."[242]

The private man, for his wife, was very different from the public figure, a warm, kindly if somewhat authoritarian person who reciprocated his wife's devotion in almost idyllic terms. He wrote to Freud in May of 1922 "My wife's beauty grows daily radiant Muttergluck and her charms and devotion are unsurpassable. I am wise enough to know how to profit from my luck and so am exceedingly happy. The boy is singularly amiable for his age and Gwenith has her mother's charm . . . ."[243]

However the long drawn out saga of Mrs. Riviere was by no means exhausted and in the Freud–Jones correspondence of 1922 her name continued to sparkle as a centre of argument. Performing a dramatic volte face Freud changed his view of their publishing difficulties and said that he had to take back his original suspicion that Jones was at fault for delays in the press. In conference with Rickman, Strachey, Hiller and Mrs. Riviere he had discovered that it was all due to the *Kinderkrankheiten* of the Verlag, lack of space and types and no deadlines with the printers.

As for Mrs. Riviere she might be concentrated acid in some situations but once diluted she could be very useful to psycho-analysis. Jones' protestation that he would die happy if he could engineer the publication of a satisfactory English edition of Freud's work rang splendidly in Freud's ears but he, Jones, Freud said, must consider his own future.

Jones' whole tone changed in his letter of May 22, the reverence giving place to open criticism[244]: "It is too bad that you should be troubled over all these business matters, but you would plunge into them instead of entrusting them to me. You are eager to relieve me, and I you, it seems. But you have work enough otherwise to be able to leave such matters to your representatives, and I should like to take you at your word as you put it in your letter

241. Jones to Mrs. Jones, 1922 (n.d.).
242. Ibid, April 23, 1923.
243. Jones to Freud, May 22, 1922.
244. Ibid, May 22, 1922.

that you are willing to drop the matter of the Press."

Jones' letter of April 10 appeared to round off at last the interminable story of Mrs. Riviere.[245] "I see that you agree with me that Mrs. R certainly deserves a title if she desires it, and there can be no objection to the proposal she makes. As she makes so many claims that can't be granted it is a pleasure and relief to be able to find some that can. She is, as I told you, a most valuable and capable person (it is this undeniable fact that complicates the situation), but whether she will work as easily for me as she doubtless would for you remains for time to prove; it will depend largely on the result of her analysis."

It was indeed a tribute to the joint Jones–Freud analysis that Mrs. Riviere not only emerged as a tower of strength in the Press but eventually became a central and influential figure in the history of psycho-analysis.

There remained the problems with Rank: "Unfortunately Rank and I have not found it easy to be business collaborators. . . . You claim the right to say exactly what you think to friends. . . . Rank has also exercised it freely towards me. . . . But may I not claim also a little of the same right?"[246] Jones admitted that his Celtic blood gave him quick reactions and over-sensitivity on some issues but when Freud said he was insincere and not to be trusted. . . .

From a close reading of the correspondence it was a relief to come to this protest. The sincerity of Jones' devotion to the cause should never have been in question.

Patients had come and gone too easily towards the end of 1922 but by February 1923 "My practice has once more improved: one has only to wait in bad times. . . . Chance has brought me an unusual opportunity from which I hope to learn much. An actively homosexual girl came to be analysed in December. . . . Now her feminine partner who lives with her has also come. They are both well-educated and highly intelligent persons . . . so you may imagine that the analytic work is especially interesting."[247]

Jones said that the British Society was steadily improving in quality and "we now have large meetings with good discussions. Bryan is not moving forward very well and I should judge James Glover to be our best member. Rickman is of course invaluable on the business side. . . . Mrs. Riviere has broadened much."

Jones enquired how Money-Kyrle — destined to become an important member of the inner circle — was progressing in analysis and Freud replied that he had at last learned to listen but deeper recollection was inhibited by reason. Then followed the first ominous comment on the leukoplastic growth in his jaw which had been removed. Everyone assured him that it was benign but now. . . .

Illness haunted Jones in 1923 beginning in May with a severe abdominal operation, developing into a bout of influenza lasting twelve days, and inter- laced with bursts of his old enemy rheumatism. There are those alive today

245. Ibid, April 10, 1922.
246. Ibid, April 14, 1922.
247. Ibid, February 15, 1923.

who accuse him of being a confirmed hypochondriac but illness never for long interrupted his work and while convalescing in Wales he wrote to say it would "be interesting for us to meet in August without your presence, but I trust that you will not regard it as a precedent."

Mrs. Riviere had by now returned to London to undergo an operation and Jones commented: "I am glad to say she has made a recovery. . . . After an initial difficulty on her first return which did not last long she has proved a most valuable and loyal co-operator . . . and is on the best of terms with myself. . . . The Stracheys are harder people to get close to. . . ."

A new operation on Freud's jaw was foreshadowed in his letter of September 24[248] and he now clearly understood that he had cancer, with all the implications for life and work which flowed from that knowledge.

The name Ian Suttie occurred in Jones' correspondence at this time, a name destined to create a challenge to Freud's theories only dimly fore-shadowed in 1923. Suttie wrote a long, technical letter to Jones submitting an article for publication in the *International Journal*.[249] Suttie found it theoretically impossible to speak of the infant's love for an external object — the mother — from the earliest moments of life. "I thus regard love as social rather than sexual in its biological function as derived from the self preservative instincts not the genital appetite and as seeking *any state* of responsiveness with others as its goal. Sociability I consider as a need for love rather than as aim-inhibited sexuality while culture interest is derived from love as a supplementary mode of companionship (to love) and not as a cryptic form of sexual gratification." Suttie provided a systematic account of man as a social animal whose object seeking behaviour was discernible from birth. It replaced Freud's dual instinct theory with a full object relations theory.

These were revolutionary sentiments and Jones found himself in a quandary. Critical material was one thing: revolutionary principles quite another. His letter of June 14 found a way out of the dilemma[250]: "Dear Dr. Suttie, I have never given more anxious consideration to any paper than to yours. After my correspondence with you I submitted it to four of our colleagues, one of whom is a very distinguished biologist. I am sorry to say they advise me not to publish it in its present form — the two main reasons being that your presentation is too difficult for non-biological readers, and that the biological case against the old fashioned recapitulation theory is not constituted as clearly and strongly as it might be. As you know, I have been eager to have a criticism of this sort published in the Journal and still hope it may be possible. I should be very glad indeed of some opportunity to explain our difficulties more clearly than by correspondence."

Suttie died in 1935 at the age of 46 and his book was not published until 1936, but it left a deep impression on many thinkers in the field.

Rank, for so long the most trusted man in the inner circle around Freud,

248. Freud to Jones, September 24, 1923.
249. Ian Suttie to Jones, April 15, 1923.
250. Jones to Ian Suttie, June 14, 1923.

also performed at this time an act of theoretical treachery which Freud at first assimilated without too much disturbance: he published two books – *The Development Aims of Psycho-Analysis* and *The Trauma of Birth*. The second book maintained that patients spent no small part of their lives adjusting to the trauma caused by the shock of the birth processes. According to Rank psycho-analytic treatment should set out to repeat the birth process experience in the transference situation and free the patient from the angst which had haunted him since that first trauma. The heresy was clear. If Rank claimed that the original nexus of psychological complications began with the birth process and not the Oedipal complex then the kernel of psycho-analytic dogma was replaced in a revolutionary manner.

In the beginning Freud rejected this interpretation of the book. He surprised Jones by claiming that it was imperative to "guard against condemning any such undertaking as a priori heretical." He then set out to show that what others regarded as heretical could be reconciled with Freudian theory. There remained a crucial difficulty in Rank's belief that the desire to return to the womb was due to fear of a direct repetition of the horror of birth, whereas Freud believed that the incest barrier defeated such desires. "Neurotic regression was brought to an abrupt halt in one case by the repulsion of the birth trauma and in the other by the fear of incest."

Abraham wrote to Freud in February 1924[251]: "After a very careful study I cannot help but see in the Developmental Aims as well as in the Trauma of Birth manifestations of a regression in the scientific field, the symptoms of which agree on every small detail with those of Jung's secession from psycho-analysis." Three dangers were likely to ensure from these publications. First, two of their best members threatened to "stray away from psycho-analysis," second this was symptomatic of the falling apart within the Committee and third the books would damage the image of psycho-analysis. Jones entirely agreed with Abraham. "To me this [is] reminiscent of the charge I . . . brought against Jung at the Munich Congress of 1913."

Freud was now a sick man and he knew that he would never be able to sit through the coming Salzburg Congress listening to no less than fifteen threatened papers. The slowly developing cancer had sapped his reserves of strength with one operation following another, and by April 3 he had definitely decided not to attend.

The mounting tension suddenly broke into the open because Freud, in what was clearly an unguarded or very tactless moment, revealed to Rank the analogy which Abraham had drawn between Rank's book and Jung's defection. Rank promptly communicated the facts to Ferenczi and Jones recorded in his biography of Freud: "It was hard to say which of the two became angrier. Ferenczi wrote denouncing the "limitless ambition and jealousy that lay behind Abraham's 'mask of politeness' and declared that by his action he had sealed the fate of the Committee."[252]

251. Abraham to Freud, February 26, 1924; Freud–Abraham Letters.
252. Jones: *Freud, Life and Work*, Vol. III, 68.

Many years later Erich Fromm stated that Freud saw no sign of serious neurosis in Ferenczi but at this stage of the quarrel when half the members of the Committee were accusing and counter-accursing one another Freud "reproved Ferenczi about [the] re-emergence of his 'brother complex.' "[253]

Throughout the whole of this tangled web of increasing bitterness Freud remained admirably calm in his circular letters and constantly resisted pressure to take drastic action, but by the middle of March Freud wrote a sadly conciliatory letter to Ferenczi which said that perhaps it would come to pass that just when ill health had reduced him to his lowest ebb he would be "left in the lurch."[254] Then followed a statement which shook the whole Committee. It was useless trying to inspire Ferenczi to rescue the crumbling Committee — that was now inevitably lost.

Jones wrote on April 9[255]: "It was a great shock for me to hear from you about the dissolution of the Committee and as I have heard no other intimation in this direction I am quite in the dark about the meaning of it all. I only know I shall still make every effort to re-establish better conditions when we all meet in Salzburg."

Jones — the indomitable fighter as Freud once called him — was not prepared to suffer defeat easily, despite a circular letter sent ten days before the Salzburg Congress, signed by Freud, Rank and Ferenczi, which announced the Committee's dissolution. The Congress opened in a strained atmosphere but several members remained ignorant of what was going on and it was not until the second day that Jones and Abrahams collaborated to tackle Ferenczi directly. Choosing his words very carefully to avoid further exacerbation Abraham said that the path Ferenczi had chosen "would take him altogether away from psycho-analysis." Abraham's diplomacy was so successful that momentarily the three men, with Sachs as an observer, were brought back to a degree of harmony which had proved impossible in correspondence.

Rank was quite another matter. Pleased by their success with Ferenczi, Jones and Abraham turned their attention to Rank and were immediately confronted with defence mechanisms which threatened to remain inpenetrable. Especially Abraham concentrated all his diplomatic charm to break through Rank's implacable resistance, but after one concentrated hour of argument he abandoned the attempt. Jones did discuss with Rank the sale of a collection of Freud's papers in America[256] but on the following day Rank left hurriedly for that country. Finally, at least six members of the Committee achieved a reconciliation which made it possible for them to work together again and "the Congress broke up in a quietly satisfied mood" except for the already departed Rank.

Richard Ames, now President of the New York Society, had invited Rank to lecture for six months but instead of propagating the general cause Rank, to Jones' dismay, concentrated on his own theories. Moreover he had met

253. Ibid.
254. Freud to Ferenczi, March 20, 1924.
255. Jones to Freud, April 9, 1921.
256. Ibid, June 24, 1924.

the impetuosity of the American way of life by devising a foreshortened psycho-analytic treatment lasting only six months and Jones became worried that its meretricious appeal would overwhelm Freud's three year method.

Richard Ames received this innovation with enthusiasm and it came as a relief to many younger disciples, but Brill remained sceptical. He did not believe anyone could unlock the secrets of the unconscious in six months. When Freud heard the news from Jones he bluntly said the Americans were only useful to bring in money and his attempt to provide them with a suitable President in the person of Frink had failed so completely that it was his last attempt to save their soul. [257]

Jones' view that Freud was no judge of men received re-affirmation in his selection of Frink who according to Jones came a "bad cropper." [258] "After his discharge from the Psychiatric Clinic he has gone to Texas where he again behaved badly: it is more than doubtful whether he will ever return to New York. His wife is applying for a divorce. He has alienated the New York members not so much by his psychosis as by many dishonourable acts and his name on the journal can do us no good in America. What do you think about removing it?" [259] He understood Freud's attitude to the Americans but "in fifty years they will be the arbiters of the world so that it is impossible for us to ignore them. At all events I shall persevere in my endeavours to strengthen the slight foothold we have there."

"What" Jones continued "shall I say about Rank" and proceeded to say a very great deal invoking the technique now familiar to most members of the circle called "hunting the neurosis." "Rank's manifest neurosis of 1913 which disappeared in the war, has gradually returned in the form of a neurotic character, and is running its normal course – denial of the Oedipus complex. . . . As there is no one he would allow to analyse him . . . he is suffering from . . . a regression of hostility from the brother (myself) . . . to the father presumably Freud."

Since Jones' biography of Freud we have had a statement quoted by Eric Fromm from Dr. Harry Bones, a New York psychoanalyst in frequent contact with Rank over many years: "In all the numerous times and all the quite various situations in which I had the opportunity to see him in action and in repose I sensed no indication of psychosis or any mental abnormality whatsoever."

Jones wrote to Freud: "How much trouble Rank will give me in America . . . is another question; I have trouble enough as it is with the numerous malcontents there and am placing all my faith in Brill." [260]

Freud now received an "extremely unpleasant" letter from Rank and Freud wrote to Ferenczi in bewilderment. "Which is the real Rank, the one I have known for fifteen years, or the one Jones has been showing me in the past years." [261]

Jones' tendency in his biography of Freud to overplay his hand against

257. Freud to Jones, September 25, 1924.
258. Jones to Freud, September 29, 1924.
259. Ibid.
260. Ibid, November 11, 1924.
261. Freud to Ferenczi, August 24, 1924.

Rank led Fromm to claim that "... in the end Jones was to win out over his rivals." Rank himself felt that Jones could not bear any serious rivals to his role as Crown Prince and Fromm wrote: "If what Jones writes was true it was indeed a most amazing oversight on Freud's part that not until the moment of manifest conflict did he see the psychotic development in two of his closest pupils and friends. Jones makes no attempt to give objective proof for his statement about Rank's alleged manic-depressive psychosis — we have only Jones' statement that is, only the statement of a man who had been intriguing against Rank and suspecting him of disloyalty for many years in this fight with the court around Dr. Freud."[262]

When Rank attempted a reconciliation with Freud, Jones at once saw it as an indication of the depths of Rank's psychosis. "He discussed the whole matter with Freud" Jones wrote "as if *in a confessional*. . . . Freud was deeply moved by it and overjoyed at finding again his old friend and adherent." [My italics.]

The reconciliation did not last. Rank crossed the Atlantic once more in January 1925 but quickly returned in a very depressed state. Another visit to America at Christmas brought him back in a cold aloof mood once more and he completely ignored Freud. A last visit to Freud in April 1926 dashed Freud's hopes of yet another rapproachement and when Freud realised that this was the final break he saw no reason "for expressing any special tenderness. I was honest and hard. But we had certainly lost him for good."[263]

262. Eric Fromm: *The Dogma of Christ*, 93/4.
263. Freud to Ferenczi, April 23, 1926.

CHAPTER XVII

The Arrival of Melanie Klein

JONES WAS NOW forty-four and photographs show a tight-lipped man with taut lines running from the nostrils to the mouth in a face marked by the kind of strength which has a touch of ruthlessness. He had driven himself very hard over the years and accumulated experiences – harsh, loving, didactic, tragic – had left their inevitable mark. His character was even more complex. Discipline frequently checked his ebullience, self control his quick temper, logic his verbal explosions but the canalisation of the seething energy which permeated all these characteristics gave his personality what one person described as an electric quality.

Paul Roazen in his book *Freud and His Followers* saw him very differently: "Jones was a fiery little man with a staccato, military manner and at his worst he could be spiteful, jealous and querulous. His face was said by one psychiatrist to have been pale but pungent – like a salad dressing; his eyes were sharp and his tone imperious. At the same time Jones' view of himself stressed his 'tactfulness;' Freud was to say laughingly that my diplomatic abilities might lead to my being taken over by the League of Nations?"[264] It was Roazen's view that a capacity to "strike up acquaintances" easily was matched by an inability to make friends and among many people Roazen interviewed he was "much hated."

Certainly Jones had long revealed a considerable aptitude for tactlessness but this was usually evoked by what he regarded as some flagrant violation of analytic truth. It led, occasionally, to the mutilation of an opponents paper or opinion. Very much later Pearl King was to remark that the reverse of this failing produced a reconciliation between many rival points of view during one of the most crucial schisms in the movement, the Kleinian split.

As with most human beings it depended on his mood and the occasion, but contradictions multiplied. The loving father could be severely authoritarian, the omniscient analyst impatient of stupidity, the diplomat a hectoring lobbyist, and the guilty party supremely skilled at rationalising his own guilt.

Jones' analytic technique was tough and highly ritualised. Believing that psycho-analytic insight could be derived from mental suffering, he did not object to the analysand "suffering a bit." He considered that dream analysis

264. Paul Roazen: *Freud and His Followers,* 345.

was at the centre of practical therapeutic work and put tremendous emphasis on the power of analytic prophylaxis to prevent mild cases from becoming serious. Roazen believed that it was typical of the temperamental differences between Jones and Freud "that whereas the former feared religion's anti-naturalism, the latter was more aware of the dangers of medicine's scientific materialism."

Jones had the illusion in the 1920s that he "differed completely from Freud in many matters" but most of the differences were minor until Melanie Klein appeared. Whether medical training was necessary became a centre of contention in this period but Jones' claim that Freud dissuaded intending candidates from studying medicine was open to qualification. Jones placed himself in "a mid-way position" allowing each candidate to decide the issue individually. Whereas orthodox analysis in England now had a high percentage of lay analysts − 40% of the British Society were non-medical − in America the majority were doctors.

Three cases with dramatic characteristics occurred between 1922 and 1925. One man of fifty, a solicitor's clerk, who had passed the initial screening to which Jones subjected all patients, arrived for his third, session, took out a sheath knife, placed it equi-distant in the middle of Jones' desk and asked as casually as if remarking on the weather − "which of us do you think will need to use that?"[265]

Quick as ever Jones instantly replied "Neither" but the man persisted, saying "Oh no − one of us has to use it."

Whatever his shortcomings, Jones was among many other positive qualities a highly intelligent, widely read and above all brave man. It needed great moral courage to outrage some of his colleagues when he knew that his convictions would create real hatred, but physical courage also came naturally to him. Now − with the knife between them − there was a tense silence while Jones weighed the situation, and at last he said "All right − but suppose we just leave it there in between us for the moment and talk."

Quickly reminding the man of a dream he had repeated at the previous session, Jones asked for further details and the man swiftly lost himself in recounting them. Ten minutes later, his eye, swivelling round the room, suddenly fixed on the knife and he said "My God − how did that get there?" Whereupon he grabbed it up, thrust it into his pocket and was about to hurry away when Jones checked him.

It was at this point that courage seemed to become foolhardiness but Jones was so confident of re-gaining control that he quietly asked the man whether he had ever quarrelled with his father. It released a flood of recollection laced with eloquent vituperation.

Initially the man had come to Jones complaining that he had an uncontrollable impulse to attack certain elderly clients of the solicitor and now the explanation seemed elementary but Jones quickly discovered that behind

265. Interview, Edward Glover, June 6, 1965.

the surface explanation was a composite figure of brother-son-solicitor involving a labyrinth of interlocking motives.

Unfortunately Jones notes of the case are missing and its resolution unknown.

The second case concerned a young newly married actor whose wife desperately desired a child which he was determined not to give her and in the course of the analysis Jones remembered Rank's theory of the birth trauma.[266]

The thirty-two-year-old man suffered from fits of serious depression but when he came out of them he was hypomanic to such a degree that he would arrive wearing a big black hat accompanied by a silver-knobbed stick and play out the role of a Russian count capable of issuing orders to such canaille as Jones represented. Never at a loss to enter into the transference − sometimes as we have seen he overdid it − Jones found himself to his surprise experiencing a counter transference in which the man issuing the orders was finally unmasked as Professor Sigmund Freud.

Quickly controlling the interchange Jones came to the conclusion that his treatment was not developing on the right lines because he himself could not successfully break free from Freud's interfering image. He then passed the actor on to another unnamed analyst only to have him return within a week and demand to be taken back again. When Jones refused, the actor became icily angry and drawing himself up to his full six feet converted himself once more into the Russian count demanding to be re-accepted as Jones' patient. Jones quietly explained why a different analyst would be better for him but the by now imperious actor said that he was the best judge of such matters and repeated his demand for reinstatement. Still Jones refused and then began what became a persecution, with the actor ringing Jones at all hours of the night and day, arriving unbidden at his Harley Street consulting room, and involving the receptionist in argument.

When Jones decided to take him back into analysis again, such was the actor's euphoria that he quickly "abreacted in all directions." He now remembered some "awful black howling night" far back before he was born which had been reinforced by the birth of his younger brother, but this, the patient said, was secondary to something else; something he couldn't reach or express. In the end he associated his mother's birth pangs with his father's attacks upon her. The mother, it transpired, had taken a lover and whenever she returned in suspicious circumstances the father had beaten her. In the end Jones concluded that the whole tangled web had created a horror of fathering a child. What was almost a denouement happened one morning when the actor rang up in a madly manic state to say − "My wife − she's pregnant!" and promptly put back the receiver. Whether Jones' instructions about making love during the fertile period or his analysis had led to the

266. Interview, Jones, May 10, 1955.

wife's impregnation he could not decide but for once everyone emerged relatively happy.

There were, of course, several cases in which violence threatened to erupt but Jones acquired a technique for coping with them. As we have seen, far back in his Canadian days he treated a case of conversion hysteria which led to the patient divorcing her husband, a well-known neurologist, on the grounds of cruelty. The neurologist developed the unnerving habit of following Jones from one medical meeting to another "in order to exercise his very considerable powers of vituperation."

Professor Cyril Greenland has recorded that "the intrepid Jones was responsible for treating the wife of another New York neurologist. She in turn summoned up enough courage to leave her husband . . . thus . . . when Jones presented a paper to the Canadian Medical Association the meeting in Toronto – it was attended by two irate neurologists who had come all the way from New York to heckle him."[267] However Dr. James Putnam who had travelled thousands of miles was also there to support Dr. Jones. "Their attack was certainly virulent enough" wrote Jones "but it did not disconcert me and I felt that Putnam and I got the better of them."

Impotence was a not infrequent complaint brought to Jones and on at least one occasion he achieved the reserection with the minimum of trouble.[268]

Towards the middle of 1923 Jones ran into fresh trouble with Sandor Ferenczi which was to presage a long and tortured exchange leading in the end to Ferenczi's defection, but not until December of 1923 did Jones write a long letter trying to placate him.[269] Jones seems to have achieved his end because within eighteen months Ferenczi visited London, gave a number of papers and was a great success.

The years 1922 to 1925 saw Jones in the middle of a maelstrom of activities from a long correspondence with Allen & Unwin about pirated editions of Freud's works to negotiations with Leonard Woolf to take over publishing rights; from battles with the Americans to reconciliation with Ferenczi; from the setting up of a London Clinic to the creation of education committees; from widespread correspondence with what remained of the Old Guard in Vienna to struggles with the dwindling finances of psycho-analytic journals.

Dominating everything, it was in 1925 that he invited Melanie Klein to visit London and give a series of lectures, all unaware of the prolonged reverberations that innocent-sounding move was to create. The invitation was the result of a report which Alix Strachey – then in Berlin – sent to the British Society about Melanie Klein's work with children. Jones' diary records that he saw Melanie Klein on five consecutive days. A letter to Freud in July revealed that Melanie Klein "had just given a course of six lectures in English before our society."[270] "She made an extraordinarily deep impression on all of us and won the highest praise for both her personality and work." Jones

267. *Canadian Psychiatric Journal*, Vol. II, No. 6, December 1966.
268. Interview, Dr. Moore, May 15, 1965.
269. Jones to Ferenczi, December 15, 1923.
270. Jones to Freud, July 18, 1925.

supported her views about early analysis, he said, and although he had no direct experience of play therapy he regarded her development of the technique as "exceedingly valuable."

Freud replied that Melanie Klein's work had met with considerable opposition in Vienna and Berlin, but Jones, unaware that this was the first rumbling of something much bigger, happily answered: "I regard [this] as indicating nothing but resistance against accepting the reality of conclusions concerning infantile life. Psycho-analytic child analysis seems to me to be the logical outcome of her work."

The whole issue was crystallised in the erasure of the word – her – and the substitution in the margin of the word – your. Perfectly illustrating Freud's teaching it anticipated divided loyalties.

In 1925 the Institute received a gift of ten thousand dollars from Mr. Pryns Hopkinson in America and led by Jones, the London Society agreed to set up a clinic. Plunging in somewhat recklessly they purchased a lease of 96 Gloucester Place on Freud's 70th birthday, May 6, 1926 and John Rickman took the first patient there on September 24, 1926. Jones became honorary Director. Within a month everything promised well, with eleven patients under analysis, but progress quickly slowed.

The Hamburg Conference in the same year met without Freud whose health had deteriorated, and events began moving towards a further clash of views between Europe and America when five European societies and the New York Psycho-Analytic Society were admitted to the International Training Committee. Inspired by Jones, the Hamburg Conference decided that all component societies should organise education committees consisting of seven members and in October of that year the first British Training Committee was elected. Inevitably Jones became chairman. They met again in March 1926 and actual details of training were formulated and submitted to the International Training Commission.

The very difficult position of lay analysts in the medical world preoccupied Jones among his other multiple worries. The issue was particularly threatening in America and the following year came to a head when New York State made lay analysis illegal. Simultaneously Theodore Reik, then a member of the Vienna Psycho-Analytical Society, was accused of treating a patient while having no medical degree.

Freud immediately intervened with a sympathetic government official but all his pleas, backed by elaborate clinical evidence, were of no avail. In the event the prosecution's case collapsed for lack of evidence but Freud promptly sat down and wrote his famous paper *The Question of Lay Analysis,* a 25,000 word exposition eloquently addressed to an imaginary objector.

The Clinic quickly ran into financial troubles and Edward Glover, one of the early London pioneers, finally wrote a letter to Jones in 1926 which analysed their reduced revenue and advised the Committee to suspend its activities. "We decided to sublet the buildings for substantial premiums and doubled rent which in itself ought to provide both relief of our present financial embarrassment and an accumulation for the future."[271] Glover was divided about lay analysis at this time and his discussions with Jones prefigured deeper difficulties which were to develop between them.

In July of 1927 Jones returned to lay analysis in America in a letter to Freud[272]: "Our difference about lay analysis does not arise from one of aim, for we both want the best *medical and lay* material for our analysts, but of method in reaching this. You find lay analysts need defending, while I think they are safe except in America (and there only temporarily). On the other hand I believe that the plan of telling candidates they need not study medicine could only end in psycho-analysis being lay, and separated from medicine altogether – to the disadvantage of both. My reasons for this are given in my essay in the Journal, which I should like to think you have read. . . .

"I urged Eitingon to accept the Presidency at the Congress and hope you approve of this. He is universally acceptable, whereas – especially at present – Ferenczi might not bring the harmony we need. I hope we shall find a place for Anna in the Executive Council – certainly if Ferenczi goes to Budapest, for then we must have a Viennese – but I suggested that Ophuijsen as Secretary and Anna as Treasurer would work better than the reverse. I wonder if Federn has sent you the latest New York explosion. I deplore their action just before the Congress discussion, and had sent Brill last week a strong letter urging compromise (that they should admit lay members, but in small numbers)."

Jones' pocket diaries show that he was meeting Melanie almost daily and within a year, being nothing if not an English empiricist, he had arranged for her to analyse his children. Disingenuously, since Freud disagreed with her innovations, Jones now wrote to Freud saying that he owed him yet another debt for introducing him to Melanie Klein who, since September of 1926, had been analysing his children: "Though we had brought them up as wisely as we knew how, neither child escaped a neurosis, which analysis showed, as usual, to be much more serious than appeared. The symptoms of moodiness, difficulties with food, fears, outbursts, and extensive inhibitions seemed to make it worth while, and now I am extremely glad."

He expected the analysis to last another three months but the changes already achieved were so striking and important "as to fill me with thankfulness towards the one who made them possible namely yourself."

Implicitly this involved Freud in an agreement with Melanie's doctrines and made him responsible for clinical proof of views with which he totally disagreed. Then followed this analysis of the results: "The girl proved to have a severe castration complex, intense guilt and a definite obsessional neurosis. The boy was very introverted, lived in a babyish dream world, and

271. Glover to Jones, 1924.
272. Jones to Freud, July 17, 1927.

had an almost complete sexual inversion. They have responded excellently to treatment, are in every way freer, and are constantly gay and happy. It is plain that they were helplessly struggling with infantile conflicts that otherwise could only have ended in an unsatisfactory compromise, at considerable cost to the personality. These and several other experiences have convinced me that early child analysis is the logical conclusion of psycho-analysis in general. Just as prophylaxis is in general better than cure, both easier and more effective, so in regard to the neuroses it is surely more sensible to deal with them when they are being formed, still in a plastic state, than after the mind has become set and organized on an unhealthy basis and at great cost. I do not know what exactly you think about it, but there are no doubts at all in my own mind."

It is clear that Anna Freud agreed with her father and had already published a book rejecting Kleinian reasoning but Jones would have none of this: "It is a plain to me that I cannot agree with *some* of the tendencies in Anna's book, and I cannot help thinking that they must be due to some imperfectly analysed resistances; in fact I think it is possible to prove this in detail. It is a pity she published the book so soon – her first lectures, but I hope she may prove as amenable as her father to further experience. This hope is strengthened by my admiration for all her other qualities – also analytic ones."

Freud immediately replied that he found Melanie Klein's views of the super ego quite incompatible with his own and strongly resisted the tone of Jones' letter. Jones was trying to have it both ways, by joining the rebel and claiming that Freud belonged to her ranks. Jones pondered for a few days and replied: . . . "The only difference I was aware of is that she [Klein] dates both the Oedipus conflict and the genesis of the super-ego a year or two earlier than you have. As one of your chief discoveries has been the fact that young children are much more mature than had been generally supposed sexually and morally, I had regarded the conclusions reached from Frau Klein's experience as being simply a direct continuation of your own tendencies. May I therefore ask you to help me clear up the point?"

Jones' claim that Melanie Klein successfully analysed his children is not confirmed by his son Mervyn Jones. "I am at a disadvantage because I cannot remember a single thing about the analysis."[273] He does remember Melanie Klein as a strong, forceful personality – "Someone you didn't contradict"

Mervyn Jones once asked his father why so many analysts were neurotic and received the answer: "Ten hours a day living among neurotic people is certainly going to rub off on you and many of the people who went into the profession did so in order to overcome their own neurosis."[274]

"He thought of himself," Mervyn Jones said, "as a statesman who could either produce a compromise between people or knock their heads together

273. Interview, Mervyn Jones, November 10, 1980.
274. Ibid.

and get a different kind of agreement. Somewhere underneath all this I had the impression that he always felt that his view was the right view."[275]

Such delusions are not uncommon among professional people and especially those whose psychological competence underpins their views – Freud for instance.

He now wrote an unusually severe letter to Jones reprimanding him for campaigning against his daughter and launching illegitimate criticisms of her book on child analysis. "You are building up a campaign against Anna . . . claiming that she has not been deeply enough analysed. I have to call your attention to the fact that this kind of criticism is dangerous and [either 'illegitimate' or 'not allowed']. Who can be analysed enough. I can re-assure you that Anna has been analysed much longer and deeper than you."[276] The whole question was really between Mrs. Klein and Anna, he said and Anna wanted to know what "sort of things" should she analyse in a child if not the Oedipus complex? Anna had, in any case, arrived at her views independently, from her own clinical experience, and the fact that Freud shared them did not in any way affect their validity. Freud failed to mention in his letter that he had himself analysed Anna, a fact which must have been known to Jones.

He now asked – haughtily – for a full account of what he described as "this tempest in a tea-cup." Jones answered with a letter which rambled over ten pages but effectively dealt with point after point in the argument. This letter had to be seen against the background of what Jones regarded as a number of viragos who spread the rumour that his "quarrelsomeness" was concentrated on women. This he said, was partly the result of his early demands on his mother when his baby sister was born; but Anna was neither a virago nor a sister, and simple power manipulation within the inner Freudian circle an equally convincing motive.

Whatever the real explanation, Jones now claimed that the problem of child analysis had received more concentrated attention in London than elsewhere and especially among a wide variety of women analysts: Miss Low, Miss Searl, Miss Chadwick, Miss Sharpe, Mrs. Isaacs etc. Significantly Mrs. Riviere was missing from this list. Three years before, Jones said, a thorough discussion of how far back analytic method could be pushed was undertaken and they decided that "only experience could prove whether the young child's ego was capable of enduring repressed material like the adult."[277] Mrs. Klein then arrived in London and gave the impression of a "sane well balanced and thoroughly analysed person" whose lectures reflected that personality. The result was that they came to regard her extension of psycho-analysis into the first year of life as opening a most promising new avenue to investigate the earliest and deepest problems.

Such was the pre-history of the situation he claimed which in no way involved Anna or her views. "Anna's unexpected attack on Mrs. Klein could

275. Ibid.
276. Freud to Jones, September 22, 1927.
277. Jones to Freud, September 30, 1927.

therefore only evoke a reaction of regret here. Mrs. Klein's new method which seemed so valuable to us was repudiated as untrustworthy. Early analysis i.e. below the latency period was condemned and an extremely conservative attitude recommended throughout.''

Anna had, in fact, offered her book on child analysis to Jones for the International Psycho-Analytic Library and – lèse majesté – he had rejected a work by the daughter of the Master. Anna's attack was not only understandable in these terms but inevitable. Jones, in his letter, made no reference to this vital and preceding incident. Instead he went on:[278] ''A book issued by the Verlag and bearing the name it does could not fail to carry exceptional weight, in spite of the fact, which I well recognise, of Anna's personal independence from yourself: and that it has this weight is shown by the extent to which Mrs. Klein's work is thought on the Continent to have been discredited by it. My own reaction, which I did not hesitate to communicate to you at once, was simply one of regret that Anna had been so hasty as to publish her first lectures in such an uncompromising form and on such a slender basis of experience. I felt she might regret it later and that taking so decided a step would make it harder to adopt later on a more advanced proposition.''

Jones letter continued:[279] ''You may well imagine that it never once occurred to me that Anna would claim immunity from criticism of her writings, still less that you would expect any such immunity for her. Extremely important scientific issues were at stake and an open discussion on all sides seemed the obvious course . . . so the matter stood when in the natural course of things a review of Anna's book was read before the society by Miss Low. It was an excellent and comprehensive review – almost a translation. The discussion that followed had to be continued to the next meeting, but was not in any way organised or influenced. I did not myself partake in the discussion on either evening (my own contribution was written afterwards as a sort of summing up) and I exchanged very few words with anyone on the subject.''

In the second section of his marathon letter Jones dealt with the crisis which had arisen in the American situation:[280] ''You ask me'' he wrote to Freud ''what my aim is. . . . It is nothing at all else than to restore as much harmony as possible between us by trying to diminish the factors that have reduced that harmony. Everything I have said and done has no other meaning than that, even though you may, of course, not agree with the particular *means* I advocate. I should regret their secession much more than you apparently would, but for no other reason than that it would, in my opinion, impair the extension of psycho-analysis in America; consequently I am prepared to make some effort to understand their grievances. A secession is certainly possible, but I do not think it at all likely, and I am sure we could easily prevent it with some goodwill if we think it worth while to do so.

278. Ibid.
279. Ibid.
280. Ibid.

"All this naturally does not mean that I am blind to the faults of the Americans and I have made myself pretty unpopular with them by telling them what I think of their attitude.

"It is plain that if I consulted for a moment my personal interests I should have refrained from lifting a finger in the matter. But I had no hesitation in risking this when I felt that two sets of people were drifting apart in mutual misunderstanding and that I was in a peculiar position of being able to appreciate the points of view of both."

CHAPTER XVIII

The American Scene

ACCORDING TO Paul Roazen in his book *Freud and his Followers* the British Society in the early 1920s was substantially "non-medical" and the main motives for introducing Melanie Klein to London was "to overcome the members feeling of inferiority".

If Jones demonstrated inferiority it was a remarkable feat because a quick survey of power manipulations throughout England, Europe and America place him high in the power competing structure. By the 1920s the British Society had extended its ties and influence into many different fields and such highly respected intellectual circles as the Bloomsbury Group were deeply infiltrated with James Strachey (Lytton's brother) his wife Alix, Lionel Penrose, John Rickman, Karin Stephen (Clive Bell's sister-in-law) and Adrian Stephen (brother of Virginia Woolf) all becoming analysts. Not that Virginia herself became one of the faithful. On the contrary: Writing to Molly McCarthy (wife of Desmond McCarthy) she said: "... we are publishing all Dr. Freud and I glance at a proof and read how a Mr. A.B. threw a bottle of red ink onto the sheets of his marriage bed to excuse his impotence to the housemaid but threw it in the wrong place which unhinged his wife's mind — and to this day she pours claret on the dinner table. We could all go on like that for hours; and yet these Germans think it proves something — beside their own gull-like imbecility."[281]

The negotiations between Jones, Freud and Woolf for the publication of Freud's collected papers revealed that "Freud had sold outright to the London Psycho-Analytic Institute for £50 each the rights to the first volumes". However when Woolf had recovered his money from sales he wrote to Freud and offered him a more straightforward publishing contract with a normal royalty arrangement of ten per cent. Everywhere in the whole elaborate web of theoretical, political, propaganda and publishing activities Jones' influence was evident, and his battles with pirating publishers in America, his struggles with Allen & Unwin and scrutiny of psycho-analytic journals, would have constituted a full time job for any lesser man.

Undoubtedly Jones was a minor master, and by now his contemporaries were busy casting him in the role of villain or hero but any black and white

---

281. Virginia Woolf: *A Change of Perspective, The Letters of Virginia Woolf,* Vol. III, 1923/28, 134; Edited by Nigel Nicolson.

picture travestied the complexity of his nature. Amongst the welter of contradictory elements which produced a psyche seething with neurotic potential the sheer multiplicity of his activities marked him out as a master at that particular blend of power-intrigue-devotion which creates the Grey Eminence hovering behind the Master's throne. But Jones was no grey eminence. Sometimes he could he found sitting prominently on the throne next to the Master. Jones was frequently in correspondence with A. A. Brill, Oberndorf and Freud before and after Horace Frink, the first leader of the American Society, had suffered a severe breakdown in which he confessed that "I have no awareness of my body – only my lips". Brill, who took over from Frink, was a good organiser but – as we have seen – a doubtful translator who simply substituted his own examples of dreams or slips of the tongue in place of Freud's. Certainly Freud had recklessly given translators the right to make such changes but when the perfectionist Jones sent agonised letters to Freud he simply read them as jealousy of Brill.

Brill's leadership of the New York Society was insecure enough to make Rank – still Freud's favourite in Vienna – imagine that when he arrived in New York in the middle nineteen twenties he could easily reorganise the American analysts under his own leadership. Jones acknowledged that Brill had "rendered far more service to psycho-analysis" in America than anyone else,[282] but was very ambivalent in his three-way corespondence with Brill and Freud. Brill had visited Jones in London early in 1925 and their discussions about the American situation were intense. On his return Brill wrote a revealing letter to Jones:[283] "I did not write to you for a long time because I was in the midst of the greatest muddle that you have ever been in."

Originally, the President of the New York Society had invited Rank to lecture there for six months and Rank had taken advantage of this to disseminate his new psychological theories, one of which – the substitution of short-term for long term analysis – was especially revolutionary.

Brill in America and Jones in London received the fore-shortening with the greatest scepticism but it came as a relief to many younger disciples who quailed when confronted with the idea of treating one patient week in, week out for at least three years. Freud at first viewed Rank's American trip with tolerance and restraint, apparently unaware of the close similarity to Jung's behaviour before he finally defected.

Brill then wrote to Freud describing Rank's widening heresies in America which presently included serious qualification of sexual etiology, removing the necessity to analyse dreams and limiting interpretation to the birth trauma.

Brill's letter to Jones said that he had attacked some of the deviationists "tooth and nail" and in the process created "money complexes" among those who had been analysed by Rank. They felt, Brill wrote, that Rank's fees were far too high and the results negligible. They had all urged Brill to

282. Hale, Ed.; *James Jackson Putnam: & Psycho-Analysis,* 110.
283. A. A. Brill to Jones, February 17, 1925.

become President until Rank produced a letter from Freud which threw the situation into confusion and it devolved upon Brill to try to "bring about a rapprochement between Rank and his erstwhile followers." A battle royal followed with powerful resistance building up to the point where those erstwhile followers refused to meet Rank. Exercising great diplomacy – a characteristic not marked among the group – Brill managed to overcome the crisis and bring them all together again "in his home" where they successfully "straightened things out." Rank was permitted to get out of a difficult situation "as gracefully as possible."

Some of Rank's students insisted on continuing to follow his theories Brill's letter said, and Rank himself still believed that only the future would prove whose view was correct. Simultaneously, Rank insisted that his loyalty to Freud remained undiminished. Brill emerged from the discussion reasonably satisfied that harmony had been restored but Jones was unconvinced.

Doubtful of establishing peace between the Americans and Vienna, Jones wrote to Freud: "I shall certainly look forward to your attempts to convince me about the Americans." Then followed one of his classic claims to objectivity: "At present I am under the impression of being one of the few people with an open mind on the subject."[284]

Within two months he wrote again:[285] "I am hopeful about the future, though I recognise that Brill will have a hard fight in New York and that we must not be disappointed if his success is not immediate. I am sure, from various indications, that we cannot rely on Oberndorf in the matter, but I should judge that his influence is very limited. . . .

". . . My pessimism arose from the alternative ignoring and berating of the Americans, giving them so much reason to complain. Once I induced Eitingon and the others to treat them more humanely. . . . I was entirely hopeful that we should succeed. I kept writing the strongest letters to Brill in particular, for he is always easy to manage when one can get him face to face. This time he behaved really splendidly in every way and he deserves every praise."

As Roazen has put it "Freud's distrust of the American response to his ideas was buttressed by the American failure to welcome lay analysis", and Jones found himself a pawn between the two contending parties. Freud's fundamental aim was for an entirely new profession consisting of lay analysts, a proposition not shared by Jones whose reasons for disliking the medical profession were based upon persecution no less severe than Freud's. Under pressure from Jones and Freud the Americans did allow older analysts to operate without medical qualifications. It drove Freud to say "I feel hurt by the behaviour of American analysts in the matter of lay analysis. They it seems are not very fond of me."[286] Much later Freud remarked "I am by no means happy to see that analysis has become the handmaiden of psychiatry in America and nothing else."[287]

284. Jones to Freud, June 7, 1929.
285. Ibid, August 20, 1929.
286. Quoted Paul Roazen: *Freud and His Followers*, 386/7.
287. Freud to Jacques Schneir, July 15, 1938.

The Americans regarded their treatment by the Viennese as cavalier and the continued resistance to non-medical members reached an intensity which could easily have led to secession but for Jones' intervention. No less than twenty-eight papers were published in the *Journal* and *Zeitschrift* on the subject and the whole matter was debated – unsuccessfully – at the Innsbruck Congress of 1927.

The 1929 Oxford Congress followed at which Anna Freud represented her father with the relationship between herself and Jones remaining somewhat strained. She found the college accommodation "more tradition than comfort" and drew from her father the comment "You know that the English have created the notion of comfort then refused to have anything more to do with it."

Two compromises inspired by Jones were successfully accomplished. First the Europeans agreed that only those candidates – whether medical or lay – would be accepted for training who had first been approved by their own psycho-analytical societies. Second diagnosis must in future be separated from treatment which meant that no lay analyst could accept a consultation from a patient or see any patient, except one referred to him by a medical analyst.

*   *   *

Jones' personal life at this time was suddenly broken into by a quite unexpected tragedy. For years the relationship between himself and his wife had suffered nothing more than the mild frictions inevitable to daily confrontation. Jones divided his time between London and The Plat in Sussex and this broke the iron clasp of conventional marriage but he remained faithful to Katharine Jokl and took no advantage of his freedom in London.

After six years of marriage they wrote love letters to each other with the same authentic ring.[288] Jones kept his wife informed of his practice with brief letters from Harley Street. "Father's birthday today. He would have been just 70. . . . Berkeley Hill sending me another patient, a rich jeweller. . . . Someone telephoned for April 16 for a lady just sailing from New York. . . ."[289]

Three weeks later he wrote: "Mrs. Burnet has broken off and so I hear has gone to Hart. Schiller finishes tomorrow. Jeffreys has left and it looks as if Henrietta may go in a fortnight. So my latest vacancies at which you laugh will become distinctly manifest both in time and income. Still I don't suppose it will last long."[290]

In August of the following year his wife wrote: "Barbara [Low] gets more impossible and never learns from experience."[291] And three weeks later: "Mervyn said to me 'Oh I am going to run off with you: poor Ernest had better look out.'"[292]

288. Katharine to Ernest Jones, June 18, 1926.
289. Jones to Mrs. Katharine Jones, April 5, 1923.
290. Ibid, April 25, 1923.
291. Mrs. Katharine Jones to Ernest, August 6, 1924.
292. Ibid, September 12, 1924.

These letters continued over the years and then in December 1925 came news from Freud of Karl Abraham's death. Jones wrote to Freud[293]: "What is to be said about today's frightful news? You know that I share your feelings to the full. It seems as if very little is to be spared you in the way of suffering – and I too know what suffering means. There is no way of meeting this blow: it cannot be dealt with, for nothing can ever cure it – not even time. Karl was my best friend, and his wife one of my wife's best friends. We all understood each other completely. The loss is quite irreplaceable, both personally and to the movement. Nothing could have better illustrated the senselessness and meaninglessness of the universe, its awful blindness. And yet I am equally oppressed with the appearance the whole course of events gives of diabolical deliberate aim – from the trivial start to the terrible end, the selection of the best and most valuable man we know, even the choice of Christmas day, the rejoicings of which will increase his wife's poignancy to the end of her life."

Jones assumed that the funeral would be within a few days and he wired Mrs. Abraham and Sachs that he would be there. In fact he arrived on the day following his letter and later wrote to his wife ". . . the funeral was terrible. . . . Freud was rather formal perhaps from excessive control. Sachs was exceedingly moving, a great speech and many including myself broke down. . . . Kitty goodnight and fond kisses. . . ."[294]

Jones went to enormous trouble to soften the blow to Mrs. Abraham, launching an appeal fund for money, offering her accommodation in London and writing several letters which, because they were infused with his own feeling for Abraham, shared her grief intimately.

In 1927 he was plagued with various illnesses including a bout of influenza with bronchitic complications which lasted three weeks, but he told Freud that he had missed only two days' work. And then in 1928 came a blow from which he only recovered after three years of suffering and never forgot. In January or February of 1928 his beloved daughter Gwenith fell ill and quickly developed double broncho-pneumonia with a "barking diaphragmatic cough which quickly wore her out. For ten days she had no sleep, an active and most distressing insomnia that no drugs could influence. We had seven doctors and on three occasions they gave her only a few hours to live but her vitality survived crisis after crisis. Transfusion of blood was tried twice and venesection when her heart began to fail. At the end she was unconscious for two hours and the respiratory centre gave out. I cannot picture to you the agonies of alternating fear, despair and painful hope we experienced but it left us little able to bear the final blow."[295]

Freud's initial reaction to Jones' loss was to suggest a piece of Shakespeare research in the hope of distracting Jones' attention from the tragedy, but in February of that year Jones wrote[296]: "Your very kind telegram moved me greatly. Although I know that, to my deep regret, I have not found much

293. Jones to Freud, December 25, 1925.
294. Jones to Katharine Jones, December 26, 1925.
295. Jones to Freud, February 1928.
296. Ibid, February 7, 1928.

favour in your eyes of late years, it showed that you retained some affection for me.

"When you lost Sophie you wrote to me that you wished you could die too. At the time I only partly understood this, but now I do so fully. I am finding it hard, and as yet impossible, to discover enough motive to go on living and to endure the present and future suffering that this blow has brought. My dear wife feels this even more so. Our boy is happy and sunny and certainly does not need us. It is strange how little consolation he is in spite of our love for him. The politics and personalities of psycho-analytic work have brought more pain than pleasure in the last years, and what else is there?"

Despite the mental paralysis which overtook Jones, he forced himself to attend the committee set up by the British Medical Association to investigate the nature of psycho-analysis and the validity of its therapeutic claims. The enquiry continued for over three years and the outcome was interesting but for the moment he did not ancitipate the labyrinth of argument into which it led.

Early in April 1928 Edward Glover had taken over the management of the London Society and if Jones' grief was little diminished, his wife's condition had become serious[297]: "My main problem is my wife. While the catastrophe affected me as deeply and as painfully as her, it has had a more disintegrating effect on her. It is not only the loss of something ineffably precious and wonderful, but of something that for complicated psychological reasons was vitally *necessary* to her existence, or at least mental stability. Grateful as I was for the warmth and thoughtfulness displayed in your letter, I missed something in it, some expression of 'liefe lebensweisheit' which no one can utter so well as you. It was as though all my efforts had failed to convey to you our desperate need for some such support."

By June he recorded that they were finding their way, day by day, but the pain was very bitter to bear and Freud must not expect much creative activity from him. He had decided to send his wife to Vienna for a holiday to escape the small familiarities of The Plat which were inextricably bound up with the dead child. A few days later she wrote from Vienna: "My darling husband. What a wonderful letter you wrote to me. It moved me very deeply. I wish I could muster as much resignation as you. . . . My longing for her is overwhelming. Let me be silent of that. I am going to Freud's one day. I heard news of your business with a sinking heart."[298]

Another letter quickly followed the first: "That will be the great problem of my future life: how to make you happy when I am no longer happy myself. Well I had not seen Freud after his operation and I confess I had a dreadful shock. I found him dreadfully aged . . . he seems smaller and different. But he is still as alert as ever." She had, she concluded, found herself conversing with her dead child.[299]

297. Jones to Freud, April 29, 1928.
298. Katharine Jones to Ernest, June 25, 1928.
299. Ibid, Undated.

Despite the distress which comes through Jones letters there remains, somewhere deep buried but still active, a rationality which first recorded in close detail the full medical evidence of his daughter's illness and then began to speculate about the relationship of grief to the unconscious:[300] "I have lost by death my father and mother, three out of my closest friends, a wife and an only daughter. Of course the last two were in a quite different category from all the others. There cannot be much I do not know about grief on the conscious side, the variety, quality and conditions of its pain, and so on; but the connections with the unconscious are a more obscure matter. Of this too I know more than I can write in a letter, but I will mention one point. You have often raised the question of the libido of the extraordinary intensity of the pain in the *Trauerarbeit*, which you describe as a withdrawal. But this withdrawal is not necessarily in itself painful, in for instance simply ceasing to be in love with someone. Here the fact that it is sharply against one's will is evidently important and must re-activate castration fears. It seems to me that the Unconscious cannot conceive of another person's death except in terms of murder, so that when it is demanded of one to 'accept' the terrible fait accompli, this to the Unconscious means being asked to consent to the murder of the loved one. We know in this connection the guilt that often follows death, the searchings of heart, self-reproach and other more indirect consequences of guilt. Perhaps I have been better able to see this now just because my attitude towards my daughter was a purer non-ambivalent love than in any of my other experiences. The two features I have mentioned, castration (thwarting) and murder-guilt are obviously connected in more ways than one."

By September 1930 Jones' spirits were definitely recovering but his grief — which amounted in his case to a not inconsiderable illness — had obviously interferred with his practice. He wrote to Katharine, now back at the Plat from 42 York Terrace: "My darling, Today I am in much better spirits and it has also helped that the bank was mistaken about our finances last month. So far from my having underestimated I had done the reverse so we are well provided for and you will not have to go without a wedding present next month."

A week later however he "could not relax from the strain" and "get really close to you. It was as though something else quite unknown had to be dealt with first. No doubt it is so difficult to get rid of Father. Isn't it absolutely horrid being neurotic against one's will. It does make one hate and loathe oneself so much. Oh Kittinka I love you so. Would that I could express it more freely."[301]

Then on April 5, 1930 came the news which seemed to seal off the dead child at last and release paralysed areas of personality to explore the future. Jones revealed to Freud that his wife was expecting "a baby towards the end of the month." It was a girl child and they named it Nesta May.

300. Jones to Freud, October 20, 1928.
301. Jones to Mrs. Jones, September 8, 1930.

CHAPTER XIX

The Break with Ferenczi

THE GENERALLY accepted view that the British Medical Association's enquiry into Psycho-Analysis drew very favourable conclusions is not borne out by a careful reading of the report. The meetings began in March 1927 and ran on until May 1929 with twenty distinguished physicians listening to evidence and in the early stages Jones worked hard with Edward Glover preparing evidence and documents. In all he attended twenty-four of the twenty-eight meetings but after the death of Gwenith he had to drive himself to take a taxi to B.M.A. House and there were many times when his grief interfered with his concentration.

The report isued by the B.M.A. is not precise about who gave what evidence but Jones' hand appears at many points in the evidence.

"Though based on relatively simple principles the technique (psycho-analysis) is exceedingly complex, so that no short description of it can be given. It cannot be used to elucidate any single symptom directly but on the contrary has as its aim the laying bare of the unconscious material of the mind − that is the material in which, according to Freud's view, all such symptoms have their manifold and interesting roots. It is not strictly an active intervention but rather the providing of a favourable opportunity for a certain process to develop itself spontaneously."[302]

The conclusion of the Committee was summarised in these words:

"From the nature of the case the Committee has had no opportunity of testing psycho-analysis as a therapeutic method. It is therefore not in a position to press any collective opinion either in favour of the practice or in opposition to it. The claims of its advocates and the criticisms of those who oppose it must as in other disputed issues, be tested by time, by experience and by discussion."

That there were practitioners of repute in the field of psychology and psychopathology was not in doubt, and. . . .

"The Committee finds that even among many of those most hostile to psycho-analysis there is a disposition to accept the existence of the unconscious mind as a reasonable hypothesis."[303]

The use of the word "mind" interested Jones. When asked, in the body-

---

302. British Medical Association: *Report of the Psycho-Analytic Committee,* July 1929: 7.
303. Ibid, 22/23.

mind controversy, whether he accepted the correlative, identical or parallel schools, he opted for identity with the proviso that posivitism was nothing more than a working hypothesis.

Another not altogether satisfactory meeting occurred at the Lyceum Club in 1928 when its all-lady membership discussed psycho-analysis. In keeping with his rigorous exclusion of certain "pseudo-analytic types" Jones accepted the invitation on the understanding that "no guests should be invited except with my approval."[304] It seemed extraordinarily high-handed but by now Jones was determined to lay down boundaries within which informed discussion of psycho-analysis could take place and he had perfected a whole armoury of searing phrases to describe the ill-informed, the charlatan and fraudulent. "It could not be expected that a bunch of psychologically illiterate nincompoops would cope adequately with a subject of which they knew about as much as a peasant ploughing his furrow."

Reporting to Freud on the meeting Jones wrote: "Actually they had invited a number of objectionable people who had the posts of honour to the detriment of many of our members. Barbara Low, Flugel and I spoke — I believe all well with a good impression — after dinner and then the hostess, who throughout had behaved discourteously, announced that this was a controversial subject . . . [and] the debate would be opened by William Brown." The precise identity of this gentleman was not disclosed but obviously he qualified for Jones' hall of hate because "there were nine members of our society there and we all left the Club at this point, with the exception of Flugel, who with his usual cowardice could not bring himself to behave 'impolitely'. I sent a formal protest to the Club Committee afterwards and the matter is still in discussion."[305]

The report of the B.M.A. did little to dispel the widespread hostility to psycho-analysis, discussion of which at the non-technical level continued to concentrate on its alleged preoccupation with sex. Jones sailed in and out of many a discussion with aggressive eloquence and where reason did not prevail he was not above invoking pure invective.

"The imbecility of discussing technical matters with ill-informed pseudo professors of psychology is too self evident from their own wild ramblings about psycho-analysis."

In a mild exchange with William McDougall he wrote "You complain that Freud and perhaps others of us have unduly neglected to take into account your contributions to psychology. Well I find that the exact inversion of the situation as I see it."[306]

Between 1920 and 1929 Jones' corespondence with Freud ranged over psycho-analytic politics, telepathy, publishing, angst, lay analysis, family matters and fresh trouble with Mrs. Riviere.

Some letters were reverential: "You are doubtless right as usual when you say that . . . ." And . . . . "I am engaged on . . . . the arrangements for

304. Jones to Freud (n.d.).
305. Ibid.
306. Jones to William MacDougall, May 11, 1925.

carrying out your kind offer that your latest book should appear in the official International Psycho-Analytic Library. How proud I should be if all your works were in it.''[307]

The same letter finally resolved the controversial issue of admitting lay members: ''We are busy here revolutionising the relation between the Society, Institute and Clinic. Everything goes smoothly exept for Rickman who, being in the middle of his analysis with Ferenczi, is naturally in a difficult and very ambivalent mood. We have, at all events, succeeded in passing rules admitting all lay members to work at the Clinic whether on the permanent staff (in the case of full members of the Society) or as assistants (candidates etc.). There is no doubt that this signifies an important step in the consolidation of the new profession of psycho-analysis.''[308]

Despite his unflagging devotion as high priest of the cause, Jones had by now asserted a growing number of areas where he disagreed, sometimes tacitly, sometimes openly with Freud. The Melanie Klein deviation continued to rumble through the correspondence, but Jones was preparing his way for qualification of the death wish, for futher resistance to Lamarck, for fresh exposures of telepathy and an insistence that Angst arose from a source directly opposite to that given by Freud.

The last question brought this objection in one letter: ''I have never been able to feel satisfied with your formulations and so long ago as 1910 when I wrote my exposé of the pathology of morbid anxiety I felt bound to take the opposite view and maintain that Angst was generated from the ego in response to the dangers brought about by libidinal demands.''[309]

As for telepathy, Jones felt that Freud was ''lucky to live in a country where Christian Science, all forms of psychic research, mingled with hocus-pocus and palmistry does not prevail as they do here to heighten opposition to all psychology. Two books were written here trying to discredit psycho-analysis on this ground alone.''[310]

And Mrs. Riviere . . . . Jones had apparently arrived at yet another impasse about the contents of an article of hers with which he disagreed. Freud had written complaining that he ''neglected his part as leader in respect of Mrs. Riviere'' which continued to create unnecessary frictions.[311] Replying to Freud Jones wrote: ''To begin with, I did not find her views untrue in themselves, though they are presented in a one-sided and therefore misleading way. This I certainly endeavoured to influence to the best of my ability, but you know that she is a person of considerable determination and in any case there was no question of refusing to publish them. She gave way to the extent of modifying or omitting a great number of her expressions, but she could not agree with me that to present one side of the matter emphatically would have a misleading effect on the reader.''[312]

It looked very much as if Jones was once more pursuing his role of editor with too much zeal.

307. Jones to Freud, October 14, 1929.
308. Ibid.
309. Ibid, March 6, 1926.
310. Ibid, February 25, 1926.
311. Freud to Jones, October 1927.
312. Jones to Freud, October 18, 1927.

By February Freud disclosed that Jung was to give a public lecture in Vienna but he decided to miss the opportunity "of hearing about the Soul from a first rate source."[313] As for the possibility of Freud winning the Nobel Prize which Jones had brought up in his last letter, he knew nothing about it and wanted to know "who is fool enough to meddle in this affair."

A long letter from Jones in December contrasted youth with age and said "On the first of next month I shall be 50 years old. I suppose that seems young to you but it is old enough when I think how much work I still wish to accomplish."[314] Freud paid Jones a qualified tribute on that birthday. "I have always looked on you as a member of my intimate family circle and will continue to do so which points (beyond all disagreements that are rarely absent with a family and also have not been lacking between us) towards a fount of affection from which one can always draw again."[315]

Jones told Freud that his son had finished his analysis with Melanie Klein and it seemed appropriate that he should be the first young child to be analysed in England with results that "exceeded even my expectations". This meant that Mervyn was analysed in his fifth and sixth year along strictly Kleinian lines but as an adult, he could not assess the results because recollection failed him. Such amnesia could be open to several interpretations but it is not for me to speculate.

In the same letter Jones revealed that Groddeck had been lecturing in London and failed to make a good impression on the sober English with his extravagent ideas about psycho-somatic relationships. "He has very little knowledge of psycho-analysis and it is a pity he was admitted to the movement, for he certainly does it more harm than good. It is plain that his philosophical id is little else than an introjected God."[316]

With some regularity Jones underwent at least two bouts of illness a year and the year 1929 began inauspiciously: "I have been ill and sleepless from pain but am beginning to recover; since Christmas I have not been able to walk farther than the front door. But it will soon be a thing of the past."[317]

All these exchanges were a relatively trivial prelude to one of the most controversial episodes in psycho-analytic history – Freud's final break with Ferenczi. Twenty-one years Freud's junior, Ferenczi, unlike Abraham, had not enjoyed one steadily rising curve of success. Analysts, Balint said, admired Ferenczi for his "freshness and originality and fertility" but they rarely understood him.[318] He was "seldom studied thoroughly, seldom quoted correctly, often criticised, more often than not erroneously.[319]

Ferenczi's final difficulties with Freud began in 1930, a year which saw the beginning of the slump which swept America, England, Austria and Germany, bringing every kind of national and personal disaster. Jones wrote in November 1931: "My wife and I had hoped to take a short holiday in January in Vienna and Semmering but the economic crisis which reverses the old relation of the two shillings has made such plans uncertain."[320]

313. Freud to Jones, February 18, 1928.
314. Jones to Freud, December 12, 1928.
315. *Sigmund Freud Letters,* Edited Ernst L. Freud, 385.
316. Jones to Freud, December 12, 1928.
317. Ibid, January 21, 1929.
318. Interview, Dr. Balint, December 1957.
319. *International Journal of Psycho-Analysis,* Vol. XXX, Part 4, 1949.
320. Jones to Freud, November 15, 1931.

The Viennese attempt to overcome economic troubles with Creditanstalt failed, unemployment in Austria and Germany reached fatal proportions and the appalling situation of a loaf of bread costing as much as a suit of clothes rendered the exchange of money a meaningless farce. Depression hit the analysts no less than the ordinary worker and patients either broke off treatment or found themselves unable to pay.

After much discussion − since some analysts would be unable to afford the fare to Congress − it was finally cancelled for the year 1931. Thus the troubles with Ferenczi were never aired at the 1931 Congress but continued to appear and re-appear in correspondence.

Ferenczi's disagreement with Freud sprang fundamentally from the different emphasis each put on theory and treatment. From the earliest days Freud had regarded psycho-analysis as a means of investigating how the human mind works, whereas Ferenczi slowly became preoccupied with the need to cure and to help. No-one could accuse Freud of indifference to neurotic suffering, but the driving force at the centre of his approach was intellectual curiosity matched by imaginative insights unequalled in his field. For Ferenczi what happened to the patient as a result of treatment was of paramount importance whereas Freud still maintained a touch of Olympian detachment. Ernest Jones believed that the best analysis achieved a balance between these two aspects and the secret of success lay in changing the balance according to the nature of the patient.

It was in May 1931 that Ferenczi sent Freud a copy of a paper in which he "claimed to have a second function of dreams − dealing with traumatic experiences." Freud replied that years before he himself had pointed out that this was their first as well as their second function.

Ferenczi received this letter with some hostility and brooded over it for three months during which he constantly thought of writing Freud a new and elaborate exposition which would defeat any argument against his originality, but the letter remained unwritten.

In this interval Jones recorded that "a wealth of new ideas had introduced a bewildered confusion" into Ferenczi's methods, and Ferenczi at last wrote to Freud explaining the nature of this new upsurge. Freud replied "There is no doubt that . . . you are becoming more distant from me. I do not say more estranged and I hope not. . . ."

There was a touch of jealousy in Jones about the temperamental sympathies between Ferenczi and Freud. Freud regarded Ferenczi as a warm, lovable person with great charm and imagination. Ferenczi, Jones wrote, made a great appeal to Freud with his often child-like nature, his internal difficulties and soaring phantasies: "He was in many ways a man after his own heart."[321] Freud, always eager to rectify the periodic rifts in their relationship, now invited Ferenczi to visit him and after taking a brief holiday in Capri, Ferenczi duly arrived in Vienna. According to Jones they talked far into the night and Freud felt that personal contact had achieved what correspondence so often complicated. It was during such talks as these that Freud could seldom resist Ferenczi's unchecked flights of imagination "and the two men" according to Jones "must have had enjoyable times together when there was no criticising audience."[322]

"It was a side of his nature," Jones said, "which he displayed to me at times in the hours after midnight when we were relaxing after . . . more sedate discussions." Unlike the ebullient Ferenczi Jones added: "It sometimes shocked me slightly as it doubtless would have Abraham, since we were people always close to realities." Perhaps in that remark lies the clue to the fact that Freud never took Jones "completely to his heart."

Whatever midnight revels led to closer understanding the reconciliation did not last and on December 5 Ferenczi wrote a letter to Freud which revealed him as still deeply embroiled in his heresies.[323]

Freud's concern over Ferenczi sprang as much from some startling details of his new therapeutic methods as it did from the broad differences of their approach. "Ferenczi had come to the conclusion that when a patient during the course of analysis regressed to an infantile stage, the best way to treat him or her was to play the part of the loving parent thus breaking into the classic detachment which maintained a certain distance between patient and analyst."[324]

I was fortunate enough to have long talks with Dr. Balint, Ferenczi's close friend, before he died and he carefully distinguished between benign and malignant regression, arguing that Freud's final quarrel with Ferenczi crystallised around this distinction.[325] Jones put the matter somewhat differently: "In connection with his recent ideas about the central importance of infantile traumas, particularly parental unkindness, Ferenczi had been changing his technique by acting the part of a loving parent so as to neutralise the early unhappiness of his patients."[326]

This counter transference was not only brought to a special pitch of intensity but converted Ferenczi into the mother, not the father as practised by orthodox analysts, with the result that a much more intimate physical contact was required to replace the love and care of which the patient had been deprived. In order to achieve the maximum identity with the loving parent Ferenczi then took the dangerous if not fatal step of allowing the patients to kiss and caress him and even returned these attentions when it became desirable to establish the closest possible relationship.

Dr. Balint was later to state that "Psycho-analytic thinking is now beginning to re-examine Ferenczi's idea about the paramount importance of the adult's actual libidinous behaviour towards children in the pre-oedipal times."[327] and that came to the crux of the matter which Jones was to pinpoint at the Wiesbaden Congress of 1932':

322. Ibid.
323. Ferenczi to Freud, December 5, 1931.
324. Brome: *Freud and His Early Circle,* 198.
325. Interview, Michael Balint, October 10, 1963.
326. Jones: *Freud, Life and Work,* Vol. III, 174.
327. *International Journal of Psycho-Analysis,* Vol. XXX, Part 4, 1949.

Anticipating serious trouble Freud wrote to Ferenczi in December 1931 "You have not made a secret of the fact that you kiss your patients and let them kiss you: I had also heard that from a patient of my own."[328] Ferenczi, Freud said, would be faced with a choice at the Wiesbaden Congress: either he suppressed his theories and practice which would be a considerable loss of integrity or he read his paper openly proclaiming what must have very unfortunate results.

Not a person to be disturbed by vicarious indulgence of superficial sexuality, Freud knew that in the new Russia sexual liberation had reached a point where such exchanges were socially acceptable. "Unfortunately" he wrote "they were not living in Russia": they were working in psychoanalysis. What answer would they give to the critic who said "why stop at kissing. Soon we shall have accepted . . . the whole repertoire of demi viergerie and petting parties." The popularity of psycho-analysis would increase inordinately and younger colleagues might find themselves in a position where such clinical freedom opened up a considerable perspective of new temptations. Freud continued: "God the father Ferenczi gazing at the lively scene he [had] created [would] perhaps, say to himself: maybe I should have halted my techniques before the kiss." This should have read of course God the Mother Ferenczi, but even Freud's atheism shied at converting the Divinity into a woman.

The morass of dangers opened up by Ferenczi's bold new methods were self evident and there was no need to elucidate the calumnies which their widespread dissemination would bring down on the head of psycho-analysis. It would indeed be a "wanton act to provoke them." Freud's letter concluded pessimistically "I do not expect to make any impression on you. The necessary basis for that is absent in our relations." Then came this: "The need for definite independence seems to me to be stronger in you than you recognise."

Freud did not keep Jones fully informed of this new heresy but Jones' keen ear picked up echoes and as the Wiesbaden Congress approached he remarked in a letter to Joan Riviere "We shall have our hands full with Ferenczi at Wiesbaden."[329]

Many years after this correspondence Balint had access to Ferenczi's papers and spelt out this new deviation in considerable detail. Freud defined the theory of regression as a pathogenic factor and a mechanism of defence distinguishing three aspects: the topographical, temporal and formal.[330] Later papers dispensed with formal regression and replaced it with regression as part of the actual transference. The duality of regression became apparent when its adult form was an "ally of analytic treatment", but its infantile form invoked serious hazards.

Freud recommended two reactions to this: first sympathetic interpretation and second deliberately subjecting the patient to privation.

328. Freud to Ferenczi, December 13, 1931.
329. Jones to Riviere, February 3, 1932.
330. Sigmund Freud: *A Metapsychological Supplement to the Theory of Dreams*, 1915, 227.

Ferenczi's new methods were the very negation of Freud's but they had an autobiographical basis. Shortly after his own analysis, Ferenczi began experiments with regression and in the early days received approval – if not admiration – from Freud. First he developed a substitute for modern E.C.T. which Balint said proved very successful. This consisted in choosing a moment when "the patient was either deliberately led into or asked to expose himself to recollections which would increase the tension of and come as something of a shock to him."[331] When, as frequently happened, a period of stalemate occurred between analyst and analysed, the analyst carefully assessed the patient's "sensitivity" and chose a precise moment to give the required shock in the hope that it would set the current flowing once more. More important, the shock could easily produce "a break-through into consciousness of a hitherto repressed and instinctual urge changing an unpleasurable symptom into a pleasurable satisfaction.[332]

Thus a patient suffering from agoraphobia might suddenly be exposed to that very experience, or the threat of an abrupt termination of the treatment in fact re-animate it.

Freud had disclosed as far back as the Budapest Congress of 1918 that such innovations originated – as usual – in himself, but he also found that the break-throughs created did not have sufficient "momentum" to make them effective. Thus he tried to talk Ferenczi out of what he privately "regarded as the small madnesses inherent in the worst extremities" of Ferenczi's technique.

Jones, who was fully conversant with many details of these exchanges, took – as he frequently did – a middle of the road view. There were patients temperamentally suited to psychic shock treatment under certain special circumstances, but they were few in number and the method fraught with too many dangers. When Ferenczi began to develop shock treatment into active intervention he immediately raised objections. At first he was unaware to what extremities Ferenczi pushed his new techniques but as they became clear he registered strong disapproval.

Ferenczi claimed that when "the infantile pathogenic traumas were reactivated" they revealed what he called a bi-phasic structure. According to the first phase over or under stimulation had been given by the parents and according to the second, "the parents' conscious or unconscious guilt rendered it difficult for them to respond to the child's efforts to get reparation or understanding."

This led into the fully developed technique when he deliberately replaced the mother in counter transference and in that role responded to the child's need to give or receive affection. Such affection could, if necessary, be expressed as caresses and even kisses. Put more precisely, the analysts role fell into three parts: "(1) to help the patient regress to the traumatic situation. (2) To watch carefully what degree of tension the patient would be able to

331. Brome: *Freud and His Early Circle,* 201.
332. Sandor Rado Lecture, Michael Balint, May 24/25, 1963.

bear in this state. (3) To see to it that the tension remained at about that level by responding positively to the regressed patient's longing, cravings or needs."[333]

Whether, in 1931, Freud wrote Ferenczi a strong letter of disagreement because he believed that Ferenczi had gone scientifically astray, or whether he sensed a serious new deviation in one of his most trusted colleagues, is uncertain. Jones, like Freud, had come to the conclusion that Ferenczi failed to understand the problems raised by his new technique but Ferenczi's notes and papers published after his death show close insight into many of those problems. Jones was particularly concerned with the analyst's inability to set the patient free on his own feet again after such intimate and committed treatment. On this point Ferenczi did seem either blind or anxious to repress his own fears in order to preserve Freud's goodwill.

Stretching his tolerance to breaking point, Freud still could not endorse something which might easily throw psycho-analysis into widespread disrepute and after a long silence from Ferenczi he wrote in April of the following year to Eitingon:[334] "Isn't Ferenczi a tribulation? Again there is no news from him for months. He is offended because one is not delighted to hear how he plays mother and child with his female patients."

Suppressing an irritation which bordered on anger Freud now announced that he favoured Ferenczi's nomination as President of the Society in succession to Eitingon, perhaps as a sop which might persuade Ferenczi to abandon the more extreme aspects of his new technique.

Later biographies imply that Jones deliberately read pathological elements into Ferenczi's character at this time, but it is clear from the correspondence that Freud himself inspired this view and believed that Ferenczi's becoming President might act "as a forcible cure". Ferenczi did not immediately accept the offer of the Presidency and Freud again read mixed motives into his hesitation.

As the date of the Wiesbaden Congress drew near Ferenczi wrote to Freud protesting strongly that there was nothing pathological in his reaction.[335] The exigencies of a full blown practice with multiplying patients, forced on him his hesitation about the Presidency, but there were elements in the correspondence indicating that he desired to maintain his distance from Freud.[336]

By August he found himself forced into the open and admitted that his own views were now so much in conflict with classic psycho-analytical principles that it would be dangerous for him to accept the Presidency.[337]

Freud now wrote to Jones outlining Ferenczi's "evasions" and revealed that things were not going well in his own life.[338] Economic problems threatened everybody and the slump had seriously eroded the number of his patients. The repeated operations, the pain caused by the clumsy prosthesis, a steadily diminishing practice and a heavy sense that old age was daily

333. Ibid.
334. Freud to Eitingon, April 18, 1932.
335. Ferenczi to Freud, May 1, 1932.
336. Ibid, May 19, 1932.
337. Ibid, August 21, 1932.
338. Freud to Jones, August 26, 1932.

extending its grip, made further political complications in the movement and especially those arising from pioneer members like Ferenczi, very disturbing. He wrote to Marie Bonaparte saying that his four patients would be reduced to three in the following month and there was absolutely no indication of new patients from England. Jones had for years been sending a steady stream of patients from London to Vienna but London, too, was in the grip of the economic slump and analysis an easily expendable luxury. Referring to the lack of new patients Freud said to Marie Bonaparte: "They are of course quite right: I am too old and working with me is too precarious."[339]

Jones claimed that in the labyrinthine complexities of their three-cornered correspondence he felt that Ferenczi doubted Freud's sincerity in wanting him to become President. Simultaneously Ferenczi protested that it was not his intention to found a new school and this Jones was inclined to believe.

Meanwhile Jones heard from the American analyst Brill, that Ferenczi had telegraphed Eitingon asking him to suspend negotiations for the Presidency until he had visited Freud and discussed the whole situation.

Brill next set off for Vienna where he found Ferenczi bristling with suspicion and Jone heard that in the course of their talk Ferenczi had burst out that Freud possessed "no more insight than a small boy."[340]

Eitingon had by now concluded that Ferenczi with all his fluctuations of mood was unsuitable as a candidate for the Presidency and he wrote to Jones asking him whether he would stand.[341] According to Eitingon, Jones wrote "I was too healthy minded for there to be any danger of my starting a different direction."[342]

Healthy minded? Psycho-analytically it was a high claim but certainly there were, in many of the feuds which continued to dog the movement, powerful rational elements which had not characterised Jones' behaviour in some of the earlier troubles.

That rivalry existed for the Presidency between himself and Ferenczi is indisputable and his protestation that he "could not well refuse" Eitingon was genuine enough. "I had hoped," he wrote, "I should not have to assume such a burden again for some time until I could more easily delegate a few of my posts in London."[343]

A student friend of Ferenczi, Mrs. Izette de Forest, called on him before his final visit to Freud. According to Eric Fromm, Ferenczi told Mrs. Izette de Forest how sad and hurt he had felt at the harsh and hostile way Freud treated him.[344]

Jones described Ferenczi's last meeting with Freud in the third volume of his biography: "Without a word of greeting Ferenczi announced on entering the room: 'I want you to read my Congress paper.' Half way through Brill came in and since Ferenczi and he had recently talked over the theme Freud let him stay though he took no part in the talk."[345]

Still anxious to avoid a break Freud, in tolerant mood once more,

339. Freud to Marie Bonaparte, April 14, 1932.
340. Jones: *Freud, Life and Work,* Vol. III, 184.
341. Eitingon to Jones, August 30, 1932.
342. Jones: *Freud, Life and Work,* Vol. III, 184.
343. Ibid.
344. Eric Fromm: *The Dogma of Christ,* 97.
345. Ferenczi to Jones, October 2, 1932.

attempted to smooth over their difficulties but it was of no avail. "A month later Ferenczi wrote to Freud accusing him of having smuggled Brill into the interview to act as judge and also expressed anger at having been asked not to publish his paper for a year."[346]

Every kind of manoeuvreing went on behind the scenes at the Wiesbaden Congress in 1932 with Eitingon forbidding Ferenczi to read his paper, Jones regarding its contents as too vague to do any real harm and Freud feeling that it would do Ferenczi's reputation no good.

Jones dashed off a letter to his wife in the middle of the proceedings. "Here a great crisis. Not to my surprise at all but as a bombshell Eitingon and Brill announced this week (to Anna) that (Ferenczi's) new ideas (consisting chiefly of negations e.g. of the Oedipus Complex) were so incompatible with psycho-analysis that Eitingon thought he should not be President. . . . He has not communicated with Freud for two years . . . his wife – just like Mrs. Jung and Mrs. Rank – is in tears. Women have the insight. They all (including Ferenczi) insist I must take the Presidency but I am in favour of . . . . It is to be decided this evening."[347]

In the midst of the argument Ferenczi suddenly decided to read his paper which was received without open hostility, and to Jones' astonishment Ferenczi responded to him personally with some warmth.

There followed the now familiar accusation that Jones, by accepting the nomination for the Presidency in place of Ferenczi, was really manoeuvreing to bring the Viennese group under the aegis of the Anglo-Americans with himself as President. He did now become President but after long talks with Jones, Dr. Balint and others it is easy to rebut the charge that he had deliberately manoeuvred himself into that high office. Jones had given a large part of his working life to disseminating the gospel and had unsparingly applied himself to its problems for twenty-five years, which made the Presidency a natural reward at the age of fifty three. Moreover his claim that he was already overwhelmed by other work carried enough conviction to make his expressed reluctance genuine.

Later that year Jones discovered that Ferenczi had developed pernicious anaemia and he came to the conclusion that his wildly fluctuating moods could be explained by this disease which exaggerated psychotic trends.

Dr. Clara Thompson, who visited Ferenczi several times during the crucial year 1932, denied that he suffered from psychotic trends. Dr. Thompson said that "except for the symptoms of his physical illness there was nothing psychotic in his reactions which I observed. I visited him regularly and talked with him and there was not a single incident aside from memory difficulties which would substantiate Jones' picture of Ferenczi's psychosis or homicidal moods."[348]

"Aside from memory difficulties." If Ferenczi failed to recall previous conversations with Freud or letters from Jones that in itself could confuse

346. Ferenczi to Freud, September 27, 1932.
347. Jones to Mrs. Katharine Jones, 1932.
348. Eric Fromm: *The Dogma of Christ,* 99.

the situation. Jones in a later letter to Freud said: "Brill tells me that the American woman who was the evil genius in Ferenczi's later days was Clara Thompson."[349]

Balint also saw Ferenczi several times towards the end of his life. "He was paralyzed but there was no sign of mental disturbance." Dr. Balint treasured a large collection of letters from Ferenczi to Freud and he told me that the exchange ends on a note which could only be described as bloody-minded.[350]

After Wiesbaden, Ferenczi and Freud continued to correspond with some warmth but they carefully avoided references to past conflicts. As late as 1933, within a few months of Ferenczi's death he wrote, simultaneously with Hitler coming to full power, that Freud must get out of Austria before the Nazi persecution engulfed him. Jones is said to have commented that there might be "some method in Ferenczi's madness."

Writing to Marie Bonaparte about the resolution of their conflict, Freud said "Ferenczi is a bitter drop in the cup. His wife has told me I should think of him as a sick child . . . . You are right: psychical and intellectual decay is far worse than the unavoidable bodily one."[351]

Freud's last letter to Ferenczi was alive with warmth and sympathy for a very old friend, and deliberately avoided once more any reference to theoretical differences.[352] Freud had prefaced his letter "Lieber Freund" but Ferenczi in his reply began "Dear Professor." The letter itself was reasonably warm and said that the date of Freud's birthday was continually in his mind. The last phrase even managed a degree of optimism: "Let us hope that this next year will not bring forth such unpleasant events as the last has done."[353]

Ferenczi wrote a final letter of birthday greetings to Freud and three weeks later his condition rapidly deteriorated and he died. Jones telephoned Freud in Vienna — a rare occurrence — and they discussed Ferenczi's illness and death.[354] Later Jones recorded that "towards the end came violent paranoic and even homicidal outbursts" which statement Roazen regarded sceptically. However pernicious anaemia does produce brain damage with some patients and can even result in symptoms similar to those described by Jones. Roazen insists that "Jones' account of Ferenczi is widely acknowledged as a travesty of the truth"[355] and as one who interviewed scores of people connected with the Vienna incident he has to be given a hearing.

When Balint came to write a letter to the *International Journal of Psycho Analysis* disputing the theory of Ferenczi's psychosis, astonishingly Jones managed to persuade him to strike from his letter any reference to the fact that Ferenczi had analysed both of them.[356]

As for Jones, he was moved to re-emphasise Ferenczi's mental imbalance in unusually colourful language: "The lurking demons within, against whom Ferenczi had for years struggled with great distress, conquered him in the end. . . ."

349. Jones to Freud, September 18, 1933.
350. Interview, Michael Balint, December 1957.
351. Freud to Marie Bonaparte, September 11, 1932.
352. Freud to Ferenczi, April 2, 1933.
353. Ferenczi to Freud, May 3, 1933.
354. Jones to Anna Freud, June 1, 1933.
355. Paul Roazen: *Freud and His Followers*, 371.
356. *International Journal of Psycho-Analysis*, Vol. XXXIV, (1958), 68.

Without exception everyone rose above the feuds and recriminations to regret the death of a distinguished colleague who — whatever his personal shortcomings — had worked for half a lifetime in an arduous and embattled field and made many distinguished contributions.

Thus there was no spectacular final break with Ferenczi — he and Freud simply drifted apart — but with his death the Old Guard seemed on the point of disintegration. One by one Jung, Adler, Stekel, Rank, Ferenczi had defected, deviated or violently broken away but persistent erosion on such a scale which should have left a profound effect on Freud and Jones simply brought out their toughness and they adapted to a new era with remarkable facility.

Jones . . . yes . . . now he was the leading survivor of the blood brotherhood symbolised by the Order of the Rings and he emerged as the figure who, next to Freud, was to dominate the remainder of psycho-analytic history.

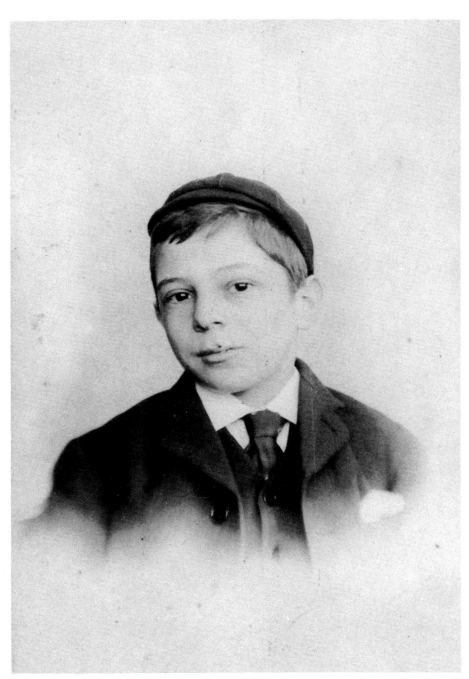

1. The Schoolboy

2. As a boy with his two sisters Elizabeth and Sybil

3. The Medical Student

4. The Young Doctor

5. Loe Kann who lived with him for seven years

6. The Harley Street Consultant

7. With his daughter Gwenith, son Mervyn and his wife, on holiday

8.   With his wife, son Mervyn and daughter Nesta

9. Mervyn, Katherine and Ernest playing chess

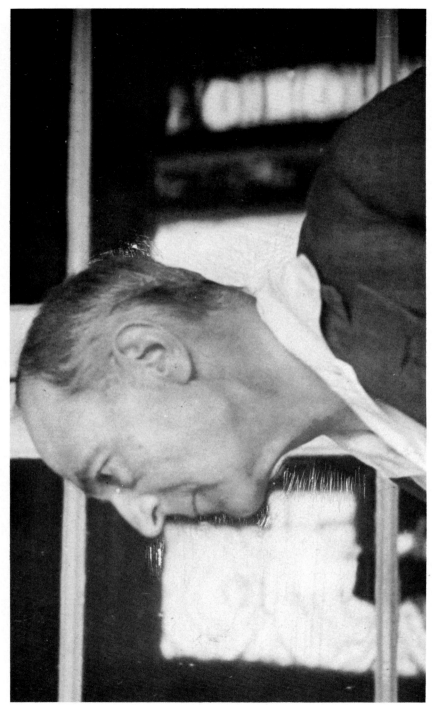

10. In combative mood

11.   With Anna Freud in London

12. Giving the Freud Centenary Address at Hampstead

13.   Late in life

14.   The gay cavalier in retirement

15.   With his wife in full maturity.

16.   In his garden at the Plat

CHAPTER XX

Family Life

IN THE BACKGROUND of this major upheaval a whole plethora of relatively trivial matters exercised Jones' considerable polemical skills with that kind of obsessional interest which indicated either a need to win every battle into which he entered or a dedicated sense of justifying his position. On most main issues his views still coincided with those of the Master but he had long abandoned unalloyed reverence.

Such was Jones' temperament that despite the success of his marriage many small eruptions of mood and event troubled family life. It would falsify events to suggest that there were not many stretches when relaxing in his beautiful garden at The Plat he enjoyed periods of serenity in which silent communion with his wife offered a solace not even the urgencies of psychoanalytical commitment could break, but family life had the usual built-in difficulties.

A letter from Harley Street to his wife in August 1932 said, "I was so pleased to hear you were happy again in our dear old Plat. It makes me sad to think that you might find it intolerable to live there. I also don't particularly want to in the winter but I like to think we could make a go of it if we had to."[357]

I remember, on my first visit to The Plat, thinking how wonderfully isolated it was and wondering what it would be like in winter. "If we had to. . . ." Did that indicate financial problems? In the same letter he said that patients were only − "so-so" and proceeded to enumerate a number of unpaid fees.

Another letter was more explicit. A patient had written a long letter pleading with him to reduce his fees because of the straitened circumstances which had been forced on him by the slump. Jones replied: "I had always hoped to be able to provide for a lodging for myself in my old age and lay aside the wherewithal for the education of my young family. As with other people this hope has receded into the invisible future. My small savings, a great part of which were in Chilean bonds, have been reduced to a quarter and I see myself compelled to buckle to once again in the few years of active

357. Jones to Mrs. Katharine Jones, August 4, 1932.

work remaining to me. . . . I do not feel justified in reducing my fees to a still lower level."[358]

These were the days following the Wall Street crash when capitalism had revealed its frailties, unemployment was unacceptably high, hunger marches arrived from the North in the capital city and retrenchment and bankruptcy went hand in hand to hit not only their accustomed target – the ordinary working man – but the professional classes as well.

Jones' mood was equally troubled in a third letter simply dated Tuesday: "It is plain I can no longer cope efficiently with all the responsibilities I have undertaken. My forgetfulness, a new symptom in recent years, is interfering with my work. But I must carry on as well as I can and try to be always brave, hoping I shall not be judged too harshly at all events by those I love."[359]

This letter, written before he became President for the second time, late in 1932, justifies his claim that he was a reluctant candidate. Stressing the over-crowded nature of his working day is unnecessary but his son Mervyn recalls: "Even as a child I was aware of the prodigious amount of work my father got through."[360]

Since analysis was by now regarded as a useful method of self discovery and did not require neurotic justification it would be easy to conclude that all ran smoothly with the children, but as we have seen Jones first sent Mervyn to Melanie Klein for specific complications. These began between the years three to five and now, coming up for his 'teens', fresh difficulties inevitably arose as he entered adolesence.

That Mr. and Mrs. Jones knew long stretches of happiness together is undisputed: that they were mutually supportive in the inescapable difficulties of life equally true, and invariably on his return from tormented battles in Vienna it was the relaxed, balanced Mrs. Jones who listened to his out-pourings. However it goes without saying that they did not agree on every-thing.

As Mrs. Jones put it in her eighty-sixth year: "His ideas of educating or perhaps I should say of bringing up our children were much more old fashioned than mine. I made him promise, and he kept the promise, never to beat the children. He also believed in the public school system. If I had been not so new to this country and older in years I should have objected. But I was convinced he knew better."[361]

The children's teenage problems added further complications but in 1932 he and his wife became preoccupied with a residential change. They decided to make London their main family base. "Be sure" he wrote to Katharine "that you won't mind being back in London."[362]

He now, in fact, had three residences, one in Sussex, one in London and another a small cottage in Wales. It was called Ty Gwyn and situated on the outskirts of the village of Llanmadoc. He sometimes spent the whole month of August in Ty Gwyn and it became important to him as a means of

358. Jones to a Patient, January 2, 1932.
359. Ibid, Dated "Tuesday".
360. Interview, Mervyn Jones, November 14, 1980.
361. *International Journal of Psycho-Analysis,* Vol. VI, Part 3 (1979).
362. Jones to Katharine Jones, September 1933.

periodically returning to his roots.

Letters between him and his wife were still prefixed "Dearest Katherine" and "Darling Ernest" but money troubles continued to recur. In September of 1933 he was worried about his bank balance which seemed to be down to £4. 0s. 8d. but he finally wrote to her with relief: "In fact it was £417 5s. 0d. They had confused me with the other Ernest Jones."[363] In August 1933 he spent a holiday apart from Katharine with the two children and wrote from Bridge of Allan, Stirlingshire: "Mervyn has not been quite so satisfactory. He is distrait and forgetful at times with all its consequences."[364]

Another letter followed later in the month: "My pain has returned (I suppose from having no hot baths). . . . Mervyn is growing up visibly and is really of a different generation."

There are very few references to dreams in his papers but now a nightmare occurred on two occasions which brought him awake with the words "Never! Never! Never!" It happened not in The Plat or Vienna but in Stirlingshire.[365]

The dream first took the form of an immense flock of sheep, all circling round something hidden in their centre, and Jones on the margin tried to fight his way through to discover their secret. The currents and eddies sucked him in and he was jostled and pushed towards the centre, but now, apprehension at what he might find, drove him to try to retreat. Inexorably the pressure of the sheep pushed him towards their centre and in one momentary glimpse he saw a bearded man surrounded by a group of children playing innocently in the middle of the maelstrom. Flashing in and out of the seething mass of sheep Jones saw the black form of an immense wolf. Closer and closer the wolf came, circling first the bearded man and then Jones himself with a stench from its body increasing until Jones felt he was about to be sick. And then the wolf's path and purpose changed. He charged in direct line straight at the children and Jones summoned all his courage to meet the attack as he came awake.

The artistry of the unconscious sometimes struck him as being too simplistic, as if anxious to defeat Freud's elaborate mechanisms of displacement, secondary elaboration and condensation. Certainly this nightmare spelt out in black and white a message painfully familiar to him. Had his concentration on professional life exposed his children to the wolf not merely of neurosis. . . . Just how much time Jones spent with his children is not clear but there were long stretches when he was away travelling, or busy in London, or lost in writing one paper after another. That he did take a deep interest in their education and future is indisputable and part of the reason for making London their main base may have been to see more of the family.

Mervyn remembers his father at this time as full of paradoxes. Believing himself to be a radical who frequently shocked other people, he was in fact conventional in dress, habits, educational beliefs and almost everything

363. Ibid, September 1933.
364. Ibid, August 11, 1933.
365. Interview, Dr. Moore, May 15, 1965.

except religion. Even his sexual views had undergone severe modification. Once a believer in free love, he was now committed in his own life to total faithfulness and no longer recommended preliminary trial marriages for others. His atheism occasionally exposed him to public questioning. Once, in Mervyn's schooldays, he gave a lecture at Conway Hall and one of the audience said "Does the speaker believe that it would be a good thing if some religious leaders like Jesus Christ had been analysed?"

Failing to find a witty response Jones "slapped him down on the grounds that he was not asking the question for information."[366] His son felt that in such situations he lacked imagination.

There were occasions, when it seemed he had a "fear of not knowing."

He would, for instance, insist on doing the quiz in the Sunday newspaper and in order to shorten the boring ritual, Mervyn would sometimes look up the answers in advance. Jones senior would frequently say "We all, of course, know the answer to that one don't we," when in fact he did not know the answer. He had, Mervyn said, "in some respects a distinct chip on his shoulder which could make life difficult for his children."[367] His pretence of being a connoisseur of wines was easily exploded by the family but he was much too intelligent to expose this "weakness" in public. Seen in the social snobbery of his day, professional people who had broken out of the lower classes could ill afford such revelations.

He was also a collector. More or less identical possessions had to be multiplied. There were three penknives, several watches, many compasses and no less than twelve chess board sets, all indicative of an obsessional character.

But the ultimate paradox centred around sex. Here was a man preaching the gospel of sexual energy as the driving force, either directly or indirectly, of a large part of human behaviour, unable to reply directly to his children's sexual questions. He used "coded allusions" to reproductive processes which had symbolic validity but failed to convey the actual facts. When pressed on certain points he would say "We'll talk about that later."[368]

Not a musical man, he did have hundreds of records which he rarely had time to play and it was a special occasion when he went to a Queen's Hall concert with his wife. They had opposed views on opera. Jones occasionally succumbed to the more popular German and Italian operas but his wife was devoted to both. His attitude to women embraced an old fashioned gallantry which went through all the rituals of flirtation and was based on the Victorian notion of women as something special and apart, but with his wife he was – authoritarian. She was his helpmeet in life and he "ruled the roost."

His son remembers that he smoked "a particularly foul brand of Turkish cigarette" then very fashionable and usually exhausted twenty a day. Not in any sense a modish man, he dressed correctly for every occasion and seemed to have a passion for shirts, twenty or thirty of which, brand new with their covers unbroken, filled a complete drawer. He had encountered many of the

366. Interview, Mervyn Jones, November 14, 1980.
367. Ibid.
368. Ibid.

most interesting people of his time, from Shaw and Wells to Huxley and
Bertrand Russell, but he took no trouble to cultivate their acquaintance.

Mervyn remembers that his father saw himself in the role of elder statesman to the psycho-analytic movement, a person who could somehow
produce a compromise between opposing parties. This, according to
Mervyn, was rarely true because he set out with the conviction that "he was
always right." Such high aims were also inhibited by his attempts to control
the strong streak of ambition in his nature. This was one inspiration of the
constant overwork which sometimes threatened him with breakdown, but
Jones was tough, his ego powerfully organised and if his super ego could
occasionally he duped into high-powered acts of rationalisation, as the
common run of men go he was a highly principled person.

There were of course any number of self evident positive qualities: ha .
work, devotion to duty, consideration for his patients, concern for the future
of his family and an ability to outface the threat — constant at this time — of
financial disaster. He was tough, brave, adaptable to social changes.

Mervyn remembers the great trouble he took to assimilate refugees from
Nazi Germany into Britain and America and the complicated negotiations
which arose from the long drawn out attempts to set up Abraham's widow,
in comparative security.[369]

In the widespread correspondence he still conducted there was a letter to
Freud which said: "I am deeply moved even in these difficult days to help the
Abraham family and am sure we shall be able to do something practical in
this respect. I am negotiating with a friend of Eder's to find work for the boy
and with van Ophuijsen over the girl's future. I should imagine it impossible
for Mrs. Abraham to continue with her pension."[370] These were the days
when remnants of a belief that German civilised instincts would prevail
remained intact. Jones wrote: "There are formidable difficulties in the way,
both as regards admission to residence in England, especially when earning a
living, and even to leaving Germany. The German solution for what they
regard as superfluous Jews appears to be, not to send them away, but to keep
them in a cage until they starve. At the same time their guilt gives them a
certain sensitiveness to outside opinion. I know, for instance, that an interview between Lord Reading and the German Ambassador here produced a
deep impression. Therefore the furore will surely die down. . . . We are at the
moment trying to get permission for Schmideberg to live in England, and
hope to be able to do the same for two or three other colleagues from
Germany. Our Society is unanimous in wishing to help in every way it
can."[371] In the end Jones lent nearly all his savings to Abraham's widow to
enable her to keep her pension in operation and thereby became responsible
for all the taxes on her house.

By May, the B.B.C. relaxed its attitude to psycho-analysis and from
blacklisting Jones along with Bertrand Russell, launched a course of talks to

369. Ibid.
370. Jones to Freud, May 3, 1933.
371. Ibid, April 10, 1933.

be delivered by Professor Cyril Burt (a member of the London Society) and Jones himself. "My name" he wrote "was taken off the black list by the Archbishop of York."

The big event of May 1933 was the birth of a second son, announced in a letter to Freud[372]: *"Two* birthdays are the occasion of this letter. One, the most recent, came about this morning: a strong boy, called Lewis Ernest. Mother and son are very well, though the birth was not easy. . . .

"The other is of course your own [birthday]. . . ."

His letters to Freud continued to analyse theoretical differences between them and in January 1932 he wrote a somewhat acerbic note about feminine sexuality on which he had written a particularly penetrating paper.[373] "Your stimulating essays in the *Zeitschrift* gave me food for thought during the Christmas interval. The longer essay will of course occupy me more, as I am specially interested in its problem. As you can imagine, it was a surprise to find that my work and experience in them could be dismissed in a couple of sentences, and I think there must be some misunderstanding between the clitoritic and the phallic phases in your apprehension of what I wrote. It was, however gratifying to find you laying stress on the prolonged early mother attachment in women with a strong father-fixation (in my experience the same is true in cases, which perhaps you do not see so often, of strong father-aversion) and on the early aggressivity towards the mother, for in London we have for some time been emphasising these two points. But we do not find that this stage is entirely a matter between the girl and the mother *alone,* the phantasy of the father (especially of his penis in her womb) playing also a part of some importance."

Political struggles were still proceeding apace. The emphasis had once more shifted back to rivalries between America, England and Vienna with a concentrated correspondence between Jones in England and Eitingon in America. The Americans had launched a psycho-analytic quarterly which threatened to compete with the *International Journal* and Jones wrote to Freud[374]: "I am very concerned about both the fact and the form of the new American publishing undertaking, *The Psychoanalytic Quarterly.* It is in direct competition with the official English-speaking organ, the *Journal,* and, since we are dependent on American subscriptions, it may even constitute a threat to our existence. That this should have been done without consultation with me, who has been officially responsible for catering to the English-speaking public, or without letting me know, what was the nature of their dissatisfaction with my efforts, is unfortunate. . . ."

Another letter followed hot on the heels of the last[375]: "I have tried to cater for the Americans as well as for other countries in the *International Journal* (in spite of Mrs. Riviere's stern veto on American contributions). If the Americans had explained to me in what respects they regarded the *Journal* as inadequate to fulfil its function I am sure I should have been glad

372. Ibid, May 3, 1933.
373. Ibid, January 19, 1932.
374. Ibid, June 2, 1932.
375. Ibid, June 13, 1932.

to cooperate with them or make any concessions they wished, e.g. enlarging the size of the *Journal*, having an American co-Editor, a special section reserved for American contributions, or in any other way."

Then came this[376]: "I am sorry to say I was not able to get any satisfaction from Eitingon either from correspondence or during my visit to Berlin. He will never see what he does not want to see. I still find it deeply shocking that the President of the Association should have given his support to the enterprise of a small coterie in their competition with the Official Organ of the Association without first consulting with the Editor of that organ: . . . I have evidently too much trust in the good will of my generation. . . ."

Within a year the struggle had intensified. The Quarterly group, "flushed by their early and unexpected triumphs" had according to Jones become so troublesome that they threatened to paralyse the good working of the Society. Normally Jones could exert considerable influence on Brill but in the face of all these complications he failed to persuade him to suspend his resignation. This he felt would be a fatal blow to the Society: ". . . I therefore suggest that you make a personal appeal to him to continue his efforts to steer it until at least the paranoic Zilboorg be eliminated. I am afraid that nothing other than an appeal from you would be successful."[377]

Personal news continued to interlace professional discussion and Jones sustained attempts to assimilate one refugee after another came through clearly. Freud's son Ernst had already settled in London and Jones wrote "his vitality is inspiring to all those in contact with him." Abraham's son Gerd also arrived but work permits were proving very elusive.

An imposter revealed an unexpected streak of gullibility in the by now hard-bitten and disillusioned Jones. His receptionist suddenly announced one morning that "Professor Freud would like to see (you)." Controlling his astonishment Jones said calmly "By all means, show him in." "There appeared a man of about thirty-five who said his name was Marzel Freud, that he was nephew of yours, that he was a famous German painter and *Professor der bildenden Kunst* in the Academy at Karlsruhe."[378] Jones appears to have swallowed this story and promptly bought – "for a very high price" – several of his copper etchings, only to discover that Ernst denied all knowledge of such a relative. Jones had unmasked many a psychological con-man in his day. When it came to the arts he turned out to be a novice.

Jones had, for some time, been conducting a simultaneous correspondence – where did he find the time – with Anna Freud and his comments to her on the American scene were frank to the point of abuse: "The place seems to seethe with personal intrigue and the common aim of psychoanalysis put into the background. It is amazing what harm one psychotic such as Zilboorg can do in the Society."[379] In the end Zilboorg decided to resign all his many offices in America.

376. Ibid, June 21, 1932.
377. Ibid, September 18, 1933.
378. Ibid, July 17, 1933.
379. Jones to Anna Freud, October 25, 1933.

Almost simultaneously Anna wrote asking Jones to intervene in difficulties which had arisen in Holland and Germany, remarking at the end of her letter that Ernst's "children seem to be in a sort of school paradise in England."[380]

Notepaper headings now reflected the change in the composition of those managing the International Society. Jones was President, Brill Permanent Vice President, Eitingon Vice President, Anna Freud Honorary Secretary, Dr. J. H. W. Van Ophuijsen Honorary Treasurer, but behind these official titles it was Jones and Anna Freud who did most of the work.

Anna referred constantly to her father's health and her solicitude for every moment of his day came through clearly. Many minor references were suddenly dominated by a major one. "This is just to tell you that my father has been very ill since you last heard from him. On September 5th he had a heart attack."[381]

By 1934 Anna wrote saying what a relief it was not to be General Secretary any more and she was really grateful for Jones' "excellent idea of putting Glover in her place."[382] Edward Glover had by now become, in effect, joint manager of the British Society with Jones.

Throughout the twenties and thirties Jones was busy attacking any book which criticised Freud or psycho-analysis, and one such book, by Isidor Sadger, so incensed him that he went beyond all normal limits in a letter to Federn. He suggested that if necessary Sadger – who was Jewish – should be put in a concentration camp to prevent the book appearing:[383] His description of Sadger in his autobiography read: "He was a morose, pathetic figure very like a specially uncouth bear."[384]

During the summer of 1930 Freud was back in Berlin once more for further work intended to improve his monstrous prosthesis which muffled his voice and slurred his words, and there, William C. Bullitt, a United States diplomat, called on him. Bullitt found him sombre and depressed. He believed that death was approaching and since "he had written everything he had wished to write and his mind was emptied" his death would be unimportant to him or anyone else.[385] Attempting to lighten the gloom, Bullitt mentioned a project he had in mind which would include studies of the leading figures at the Paris Peace Conference in 1919. Whereupon Freud "rapidly asked a number of questions which I answered. Then he astonished me by saying he would like to collaborate with me in writing the Wilson chapter."[386]

The collaboration proved unfortunate with head-on collisions between the two men about "every sentence" and when Mrs. Wilson threatened a libel suit, publication for the finished book receded into the distance.

Freud had hoped that publication of the book – of which Jones privately disapproved – would give the Verlag a badly needed financial boost and now some new project which would serve the same purpose became necessary.

380. Anna Freud to Jones, October 18, 1933.   381. Ibid, September 20, 1933.
382. Ibid, October 1934.
383. Letter, Jones to Paul Federn, October 10, 1934; c.f. Letter from Jones to Max Eitingon, December 10, 1934; Anna Freud to Ernest Jones, December 31, 1932.
384. Jones: *Free Associations,* 169.
385. William C. Bullitt: *Foreword, Sigmund Freud* and William C. Bullitt, *Thomas Woodrow Wilson, 28th President of the United States, a Psychological Study,* VII.
386. Ibid.

This became the *New Introductory Lectures*, a series of seven lectures never originally intended to be delivered as lectures. Ronald Clark describes the true nature of the exercise: "By tailoring new material together with old and concluding with two lectures which concentrated on subjects whose links with psycho-analysis were slight, they skilfully disguised their conception as a pot-boiling act of goodwill." [387]

Talking to his wife about the project Jones at first expressed disapproval but when, within a year of its appearance in German, it was published in English, he felt that a new step towards real recognition and acceptance of psycho-analysis had been taken. [388]

Almost simultaneously with its English publication, differences over Melanie Klein's approach to pre-Oedipal analysis once more surfaced in Jones' correspondence with Freud. In April Jones had visited Freud and to his surprise had found him in far better spirits than he expected. "It was a pleasure of the highest order to see you looking so well and to enjoy talking with you again." Inevitably Freud brought up the theoretical question which most troubled him and Jones skilfully avoided any definite commitment, with the words: "Whether we have made a serious mistake or advanced your theory remains uncertain. That I am anxious to thrash it out in a friendly discussion I have already shown." [389]

In correspondence he wrote: "I was glad you liked my instinct paper but was very astonished at your thinking I had made such a mistake as to suppose you had used any of Melanie Klein's work as a starting point for any thoughts of yours. Of course I know very well that your exposition on the matter actually preceded her writing at all." Misunderstanding, Jones wrote, arose from one particular sentence which he would re-formulate:

"Detailed analytic studies, particularly those carried out on young children by Melanie Klein and others, have thrown a great deal of light on the sources of this severity and have led to the conception of a primitive aggressive instinct, non-sexual in character."

"To avoid the least chance of ambiguity I will re-write this sentence before publishing it. It does, it is true, come rather as an interpolation in the argument, but I wanted to deal with all the contributions made by psychoanalysis, not only your own. When writing it I was not actually thinking of you because I should not ascribe to you the belief in a primary aggressive instinct (that is rather my own view); yours I should describe as a belief in an internal Todestrieb which is *secondarily* exteriorised into an aggressive impulse." [390]

The whole Melanie Klein-Freud issue was disturbing everyone in the movement, not least Melanie Klein herself. Writing to his wife from York Terrace, Jones said "I am just back from two hours with Mrs. Klein (in the Garden Suburb, a German boarding house). She had evidently been quite crushed but she is a wonderful person and is working hard to fight back." [391]

387. Ronald Clark: *Freud, the Man and the Cause,* 477.
388. Interview, Mrs. Jones, November 18, 1980.
389. Jones to Freud, May 2, 1935.
390. Ibid.
391. Jones to Mrs. Katharine Jones, April 25, 1934.

As usual Jones was busy negotiating on all fronts. His letters to Freud dwindled away mainly, he said, because when he was writing to Anna he felt that he also addressed Freud. Rado came under scrutiny in his correspondence with Anna: "I think Rado's letter simply disgusting. Even New York cannot be quite such a lunatic asylum as he depicts it though he is evidently doing what he can to make it so."[392]

By February of the following year he insisted that Anna's presence in place of her father at the next Congress was so important that they must choose somewhere easily within her reach.[393] In the event they chose Marienbad and nothing of great consequence emerged from their discussions except the muffled thunder re-echoing from the Klein controversy.

Surprisingly, in view of what followed within a few years, Jones wrote to say that he had greatly enjoyed Anna's book, agreed with its conclusions and regarded it as beautifully written.[394]

By September his solicitude for Anna expressed itself in a mildly angry letter which repeated news he had garnered from Ernst Freud on the telephone. Anna had been ill and returned to work before she had fully recovered. "I am rather cross with you about that. What is the good of my giving you orders not to start work before at least October. Nevertheless I love you so much that I hope your wilfulness will meet with success . . . Glover and I are working at the Congress Report."[395]

In the Spring of 1937 he suffered from an aggregation of minor illnesses – influenza, neuralgia, otilis, wisdom tooth trouble and piles, and finally went off with Katherine for a holiday to Italy. "I visited all my old haunts in Florence and Rome and it was very instructive to compare one's judgment and perspective with that of twenty-five years ago."[396]

Attempts to accommodate the steadily increasing flood of refugees went on apace: "Eitingon tells me there is room for perhaps five more analysts in Palestine, a child analyst for Jerusalem . . . two analysts for Tel Aviv and two for Haifa one of whom should be female. I am informed however that immigrants to Palestine have to dispose of £1,000 and E. tells me he cannot lay hands on such a sum even temporarily."[397]

One of Jones' ex-patients next put forward Freud's name for Foreign Membership of The Royal Society and when they accepted his nomination Jones wrote with a dash of chauvinism "Congratulations. You have achieved the highest scientific honour in England and I should suppose the whole world."[398]

Despite the appalling events in Germany, the sweeping victories of Hitler and a considerable uneasiness in English diplomatic circles about the dangers to world peace, Jones continued reasonably optimistic for the future. His optimism included a glowing report about his family: "The children thrive and we are all in good health. Nesta May who has a passionate temperament has a pathological jealousy of her little brother and is being analysed by Dr.

392. Jones to Anna Freud, April 2, 1935.
393. Ibid, February 1936.
394. Ibid, June 28, 1936.
395. Ibid, September 25, 1936.
396. Ibid, April 15, 1937.
397. Ibid, April 20, 1938.
398. Jones to Freud, April 20, 1938.

Winnicot – our only man child analyst. Mervyn is precociously sitting for his matriculation examination in the summer having then reached the ripe age of fifteen. I intend to send him abroad for a year for languages between the school and the university: i.e. when he is seventeen."[399]

Mervyn recalls that his father was "never any good with children and even worse with his grandchildren." His overcrowded life allowed no time for games-playing, even if he had shown any inclination. "I went in awe of him but in fact I didn't see much of him. He was mainly interested in me intellectually. . . . The most he would do would be to plan motoring holidays with me but on those holidays he could get very short tempered as when I left some binoculars in a train and his outburst of anger scared me." The relationship between the children themselves was complicated because Nesta, the much loved darling of her father and mother, was really a replacement for Gwenith whose death had so disrupted their lives. Lewis, on the other hand, was an accident when Jones was fifty and did not want another child. Matters were further complicated by Nesta's pert, cheeky nature which frequently annoyed her father to the point where he "flipped his lid".

Late in 1937 Jones wrote to his wife "I was distressed but not surprised at your news about Mervyn and hope the enclosed letter may do him a little good. How wise of you to raise the question of Mrs. Klein. Indeed I am thinking rather seriously of going to her myself. . . ."[400]

Business it seems was bad in the autumn of that year. "Tomorrow I have a consultation, a rare event in these days. If it turns out to be 3gns. per hour I shall take him on: if a two guinea I shall postpone until I can consult you."

Mrs. Jones replied describing quarrels among the children and said that Ernest's letter had upset Mervyn. It was a letter in which Jones suggested that Mervyn should sit the matriculation examination again.

There was to be some argument about the further education of his two sons with Mervyn supporting his brother who did not want to go to Stowe public school and Katherine intervening to reduce the tensions.

The choice of two different schools for the boys was based on differing temperaments. Lewis was less rebellious, more amenable to conventional education than Mervyn and the choice of a well-ordered, famous public school, Stowe, no problem.

Jones was fifty four when Lewis was born and he recalls that he "only knew him as a old man." Lewis Jones wrote to me:

"One of his strongest character traits was his care for the esteem of fellow-humans. I remember years ago giving a lift to an RAF technician. My father naturally asked him about his work with which my father was unacquainted. To my amusement, my father bluffed successfully and pretended to knowledge he did not possess. After the airman had got out, my father said to me with a pleased smile 'I think I gave a good account of myself'.

"He was a good father in that he was generous and though we were not

399. Ibid, February 23, 1937.
400. Jones to Mrs. Katharine Jones, September 11, 1937.

close, I can recollect various talks and discussions. The enormous age gap came between us but we communicated, had holidays together though we were not intimate.

"His best points: Hard work, tenacity and integrity. Worst points: Ambition, ruthlessness and a hard streak/desire to get the better of all and sundry that I found unattractive."

Jones took his responsibilities as a parent very seriously and had the unusual gift of talking to a boy of twelve as if he were an adult, a habit Mervyn remembers gratefully. That did not remove the frictions between them and as Mervyn approached the appropriate age Jones investigated a number of progressive schools like Bryanston and Bedales, personally interviewing their head masters. Mervyn accompanied him on his trip to Abbotsholme where they found that the whole school had "gone to camp". The headmaster had left a map indicating his whereabouts and the map proved so accurate that they reached the camp without a hitch. Jones at once concluded that a man who could provide such a map "must be good" and decided that Abbotsholme should have "the honour of receiving his son", a phrase delivered with conscious irony.

Despite his unorthodox behaviour, Mervyn sailed through the school's curriculum successfully, only to be sent down on a relative triviality. On two occasions he overstayed his "outside pass" by a couple of hours and on the second occasion was made the instrument of the headmaster's need to tighten discipline, an incident which did not please Mervyn's meticulous father.

And then in 1939 Mrs. Jones set off for a trip to America in order to see her brother who had settled there, and took with her the seventeen-year-old Mervyn. For the first time in many years a disturbed note crept into one of her letters: "My darling true love, I was so glad to have your letter for the weekend left me none too happy. I stand separation from you very badly. It seems to me that we grow apart and that after an interval you are dissatisfied with me, a thing I find very hard to endure."[401]

As the threat of war became imminent she wrote in her diary[402] for September 1: "Wake up in terrible panic. Shall I ever see my home and my own ones again. I look forward for comfort in Mervyn who is puzzled." The intention was to send Mervyn to Oxford but his parents asked him whether he would prefer to stay in America and he found the prospect exciting. Mrs. Jones consulted Brill who tried to get him into Columbia but failed. Finally they settled on New York University.

Mrs. Jones was still in Washington when the news came that war had broken out. Deciding to return at once, she had some difficulty in finding a berth on the overcrowded ships but by September 13 she was writing in her diary: "Ireland should be reached by the small hours. And then for Southampton."[403] She had expected her husband to meet her at

401. Mrs. Katharine Jones to Ernest Jones, August 1938.
402. Mrs. Katharine Jones Diary, September 1, 1938.
403. Ibid, September 13, 1938.

Southampton but the next entry said: [Friday 15]:[404] "Isle of Wight. Southampton. No husband. After customs I ask for telegrams and am handed two asking me to go to Waterloo. Here also no one to meet me. Taxi through war-like London . . . in teeming rain to 42 where cook and . . . welcome me. Ernest is busy with patients . . . expecting me in the evening."

404. Ibid, September 15, 1938.

CHAPTER XXI

Jones Rescues Freud

AWAY IN AUSTRIA the climax came when Hitler ordered the Austrian Chancellor Kurt Schuschnigg to call off his plebiscite which would have determined Austria's fate independently. Freud heard the news and sent out the maid to buy a copy of *Abend,* the pro-Schussnigg paper. "After gently taking the paper from Paula's hands he read through the headlines" said Martin Freud "and then crumpling it in his fist he threw it into a corner of the room." In his diary he wrote the words "Finis Austriae." In London Jones heard the news with dismay and immediately decided to renew his appeals to Freud to leave Austria for the comparative safety of London.

The Nazis swept into Austria in full military force on March 14 and two days later Jones first telephoned Dorothy Burlingham, Anna's friend, who lived in the same apartment block, and Marie Bonaparte in Paris. Simultaneously John Cooper Wiley, the American Consul General in Vienna, was asked to keep a protective eye on Freud and his family. Freud's position was clearly desperate. His name appeared on Sir John Simon's 1936 list of celebrated Austrians who might need assistance if the Nazis invaded Austria but when an unidentified person sent the Prime Minister, Neville Chamberlain, a telegram – "Demand instant news of Professor Freud" – it was carefully minuted in the records "A past – or future – patient."[405] A member of Anna's circle believed that Jones himself had sent this telegram but he was never a man for rhetorical gestures and in the days following Austria's collapse he was far too busy lobbying, writing letters and at last travelling, to worry about anonymous telegrams. All planes to Vienna were cancelled but on March 15 Jones managed to fly as far as Prague where he hired a small monoplane and dramatically arrived – a single crusading Englishman – in the middle of the Nazi's storm troopers. "The airfield was stacked with German military planes and the air was full of them, assiduously intimidating the Viennese. The streets were full of roaring tanks and also of roaring people with their shouts of Heil Hitler'."[406] Katharine's sister still lived in Vienna and Jones made his way to her flat, where Anna Freud managed to reach him by telephone. They agreed that he should first go to the Verlag in the hope of saving the premises on the grounds that it was an

405. Foreign Office File No. 371, 22321 P.R.O., Quoted Clark.
406. Jones: *Freud, Life and Work,* Vol. III, 233.

international publishing house.

It needed very considerable courage to march into a building already occupied by storm troopers and request the preservation of the Verlag's equipment, books and papers. The stairs and rooms were occupied by villainous looking youths armed with daggers and pistols, Martin Freud was sitting in a corner under arrest and the Nazi "authorities" were engaged in counting the petty cash in a drawer.[407]

Jones' friendship with Earl de la Warr, Lord Privy Seal, and Sir Samuel Hoare, Home Secretary, had equipped him with special introductions to the British Embassy. The Foreign Office had cabled the British Ambassador in Vienna "Dr. Jones is anxious about the fate of Dr. Freud and if he applies to you for advice Lord Privy Seal would be grateful for anything you can do."

For some reason Jones ignored these overtures and set out on his lone quest but no sooner did he speak to the young thugs occupying the Verlag than his accent gave him away and he was put under arrest. Immediately he asked to be allowed to communicate with the Embassy only to be met with a torrent of abuse directed at England.

They released him within an hour and he at once made his way to Freud's home where a remarkable drama had just been played out. A gang of Nazis had invaded the house and begun ransacking the dining room where Mrs. Freud confronted them with the dignity of someone accustomed to civilised behaviour. She first invited the sentry to take a seat "instead of standing so uncomfortably" and when they demanded to see any money or valuables, she placed the household money on the table and said: "Won't the gentlemen help themselves." They insisted on opening the safe in another room and as they were trying to do so the door opened and there stood the frail figure of Freud, gaunt, white haired, apparently an inoffensive old gentleman. The sight of the marauders suddenly annoyed Freud and he brought himself to his full 5ft. 7in. with his eyes blazing like a prophet out of the Old Testament. Such was the impact of his combined personality, distaste and authority that the S.A. suddenly changed their minds. They would, they said, leave for the time being but would call again.[408]

Jones now entered into a prolonged argument with Freud, gradually wearing down his resistance and answering one by one his objections to leaving Vienna. Dominant among his arguments was his distaste for abandoning his native city at a time of disaster but Jones successfully countered this by quoting the analogy of Lightoller, the Second Officer of the Titanic who, when asked what happened to him during the disaster, said that he did not leave his ship but his ship left him.

There remained two big problems. First as Jones wrote: "It is hardly possibly nowadays for people to understand how ferocious every country was to would-be immigrants, so strong was the feeling about unemployment."[409] France hypocritically opened its frontiers wide to more or less

407. Ibid.
408. Brome: *Freud and His Early Circle*, 234.
409. Jones: *Freud, Life and Work*, Vol. III, 235.

anybody on condition that they did not earn a living but that in effect was inviting them to starve. And England. . . . There Jones successfully appealed to his friends the Earl de la Warr and Sir Samuel Hoare and within a short time the Home and Foreign Offices had smoothly interlocked to produce permits for the Freud family and a number of their friends.

It remained to overcome the last and most formidable difficulty: persuading the Germans to allow a Jew and an internationally known most distinguished Jew, to leave Austria unmolested. Whether Jones partly inspired what followed is in some doubt but the account he gives in the Freud biography implies that Bullitt, the American Ambassador in Paris, on his own initiative called President Roosevelt asking him to intervene. Roosevelt immediately instructed Cordell Hull to get his Secretary of State to tell his Charge d'Affaires in Vienna, Mr. Wiley, that he must use all influence possible to protect Freud. There followed an elaborate network of negotiations between Hugh Robert Wilson, the American Ambassador in Berlin, Princess Marie Bonaparte, Cordell Hull and Jones. Cordell Hull wired the American Ambassador in Berlin: "Wiley reported in a telegram from Vienna yesterday that he fears that Dr. Freud despite his age and illness is in danger. The President has instructed me to ask you to take the matter up personally and informally with the appropriate officials of the German Government. . . ."[410] Bullitt called on the German Ambassador, Graf von Welczeck, in Paris and re-emphasised what a scandal would result if the Nazis ill-treated Freud. Welczeck was himself Austrian, a cultured man, aware that Freud had made some not too clearly defined contribution to human thought, and he immediately contacted what Jones refers to as "the highest Nazi authorities."

Against this background Jones was working hectically in Vienna, coping with multiplying requests to help one person after another escape the slowly closing Nazi net. The situation of the English Society added fresh subtleties to the negotiations because there were analysts among the Viennese circle who were not exactly popular in London. Muller-Braunschweig, who had helped Jones deal with earlier refugees, arrived in Vienna from Berlin accompanied by a Nazi official with the intention of "liquidating the psycho-analytical situation." A hastily summoned meeting of the Board of the Vienna Society had decided that everyone must flee the country and accept any new home chosen by Freud as the seat of the Society, but how this was to be achieved in a city seething with openly anti-Semitic Nazis? Freud commented to Jones "After the destruction of the Temple in Jerusalem by Titus, Rabbi Jochanan ben Sakkai asked for permission to open a school, at Jabneh for the study of the Torah. We are going to do the same. We are after all used to persecution by our historical tradition and some of us by personal experience."

With the arrival of Princess Marie Bonaparte on March 17 Jones felt easy about leaving the exodus to Paris in her more than competent hands. The

410. Hull to Wilson March 16: 1938 (Nat. Archives).

question of permits to enter England needed urgent attention and had been further complicated by the large entourage Freud wanted to accompany him as part of his bargain for leaving Austria. He was still unpersuaded that his own fate mattered very much and only later did he reveal his underlying motive. "The advantage the emigration promises Anna" he wrote to Jones "justifies all our little sacrifices. For us old people (73–77–82) emigrating wouldn't have been worth while."[411]

As Ronald Clark disclosed in his definitive account of "the escape"[412] Wiley cabled Bullitt in some alarm on March 19. "Professor Freud wishes to take with him his family of ten, including three in laws, also maid, physician, latter's family of three, sixteen in all." Bullitt replied: "To support sixteen persons is of course entirely beyond any resources at my disposal. . . . At this distance it is impossible for me to give intelligent advice."[413] Apparently unaware that Freud had decided to settle in England, he was relieved when he learnt that only the problem of exit visas remained to be solved and immediately contacted von Stein who took the matter up with the Arch Fiend himself – Himmler.

Jones' meticulous attention to detail was matched by the close surveillance maintained under Roosevelt's instructions. On the 22nd Bullitt was advised: "Anna Freud just arrested. Have informed Berlin and von Stein." There followed some of the worst hours in Freud's life while he waited for fresh news. According to Jones he spent the whole day "pacing up and down, smoking an endless series of cigars to deaden his emotions." Five hours later Bullitt received a second message: "Anna Freud released."

Jones returned to London on March 22 and began a sustained campaign to muster as many famous names as possible to support the demand that Freud and his family be safely delivered to England. Sir Samuel Hoare, then the Home Secretary, was already an acquaintance of Jones, but Jones wanted the additional authority of a scientific body and – inevitably – he chose The Royal Society. His old friend Wilfred Trotter – now a member of the Council of The Royal Society – gave him a letter of introduction to Sir William Bragg, then the President. Jones saw him the following day and later wrote: "I was taken aback by discovering – though not for the first time – how naive in worldly matters distinguished scientists can be. He asked me: 'Do you really think the Germans are unkind to the Jews?' He was shocked when I described to him the bodily marks I had seen on friends who had got away from concentration camps."[414]

By now the Home Office had given Jones carte blanche to fill in permits for Freud, his family, servants, personal doctors and a certain number of pupils with their families: they were also to be allowed to work, a rare concession in those days.

Despite the concentration of international pressures at the highest level the remaining task – to persuade the Germans to release Freud and his entourage

411. Freud to Jones, May 13, 1938.
412. Ronald Clark: *Freud, the Man and the Cause,* 503/12; Wiley to Bullitt, March 19, 1938 (National Archives, Quoted Clark).
413. Ibid.
414. Jones: *Freud, Life and Work,* Vol. III, 237.

– was formidable. In the event the whole process took three months during which anxiety mounted, Martin Freud was frequently called to Gestapo Headquarters, and every possible source of money and possessions ruthlessly explored by the Germans. "The inquisition" Jones wrote "proceeded in great detail. When, for instance, the Nazis found that Martin Freud had for safety been keeping a store of Gesemelte Schriften in a neutral country, Switzerland, they insisted that he and his father issue instructions for them to be brought back to Vienna where they were more or less ceremoniously burned."[415]

On April 28 Freud wrote to Jones[416]: "Two letters from you to Anna and myself arrived today. They are so refreshingly kind that I am moved to write you at once without any external occasion but from an inner impulse." Freud was, he said, "sometimes perturbed by the idea that [Jones] might think that [Freud] believed he was simply doing his duty." "We recognise your friendliness, count on it and fully reciprocate it. This is a solitary expression of my feelings for between beloved friends much should be obvious and remain unexpressed." Freud said he continued to work at his Moses for an hour a day but he seriously doubted whether he would ever complete its third part.

Before Freud finally left Vienna he was asked to sign a document which read: "I Professor Freud, hereby confirm that after the Anschluss of Austria to the German Reich I have been treated by the German authorities and particularly by the Gestapo with all the respect and consideration due to my scientific reputation. . . ." Freud of course had no alternative but to sign, but his sense of irony which had persisted throughout the prolonged ordeal drove him to ask whether he might be allowed to add one sentence. The sentence read: "I can heartily recommend the Gestapo to anyone."

Freud left Vienna on June 4 and spent twelve hours in Marie Bonaparte's beautiful home in Paris before crossing by night on the ferryboat to Dover. So successful had Jones' negotiations been that they were accorded diplomatic privilege, and avoided the delays and irritations of passing through Customs. Even the train, under the influence of Earl de la Warr, arrived at a specially remote platform which defeated the waiting crowds and newspaper men. Jones with his wife were waiting to greet them "and the reunion was a moving scene. We made a quick getaway in my car and it was some time before the newspaper reporters caught us up. . . . I drove past Buckingham Palace and Burlington House to Piccadilly Circus and up Regent Street, Freud eagerly identifying each landmark and pointing it out to his wife."[417]

Jones at last made his way with "the precious cargo" to Freud's first home in London, a house rented by his son Ernst at 39, Elsworthy Road, Hampstead. Later they were to move to the now historic house at 23, Maresfield Gardens.

*   *   *

415. Ibid, 238.
416. Freud to Jones, April 28, 1938.
417. Jones: *Freud, Life and Work,* Vol. III, 243.

The tremendous upheaval caused by the war entered everybody's life and Jones was no exception, the underlying psychology producing the ironic situation where extravagant stresses gave people a new purpose in living which diminished neurotic indulgence. Jones wrote to his wife at The Plat[418]: "At moment therefore I have only six patients one of whom finishes at Xmas and at least two others next summer. Three of them now pay only 2 gns. (gone are the days when we tried to cut out all 3 gns. patients). The last new patient came over 18 months ago. I wonder if I shall get another. And what is the use of only one. At present it looks like being our last year! . . ."

"Last evening I was at the Freuds' till late at rather a critical time. . . . Exner [a radium specialist] and Schur [this Viennese doctor] were there. The latter was going to operate today but the place seemed so extensive that they telephoned Pichler who is expected to fly from Vienna tomorrow. He will go to the London Clinic. . . . Freud has had very little pain this time and is quite perky. He wants to change two things: the word dilettante about Shaw and the passage about religion in Russia. . . . He wants to call the book Moses and Monotheism which is a correct scientific description but Wolf points out that you can't sell a popular book under such a title and wants only Moses. I suggested Moses and God but the old man was in an obstinate mood. . . ."

To Freud Jones wrote on September 3, 1939 expressing gratitude for "all you have brought into my life." In the last war he said we were on opposite sides. "Now we are near to each other and united in our military sympathies." The letter ended "With my warmest and dearest regards, Your always affectionately Ernest Jones." Having read part of the typescript of *Moses and Monotheism* Jones decided to call on Freud and remonstrate with him personally over one sentence which expressed the Larmarckian view in universal terms. He found him frail, his speech halting, his manner slightly gruff, but nothing would persuade him to remove the offending sentence. "I told him he had of course the right to hold any opinion he liked in his own field, psychology, even if it ran counter to biological principles, but begged him to omit the passage where he applied it to the whole field of biological evolution since no responsible biologist regarded it as any longer tenable."[419] It was of no avail."

Freud managed to complete the third part of his Moses book before the major operation became necessary. He came through it with astonishing resilience. Another project, *An Outline of Psycho Analysis,* which he had begun while waiting to escape from Vienna, next received his full attention and by September he had finished sixty-three pages. There was a curious rivalry between Freud and Jones over the book. Jones had himself written a booklet simply called *Psycho-Analysis,* which appeared ten years earlier and Freud had then thanked him for saving him from duplicating the task. But now, in his last year of life, Freud revived the project. Alas, it was never finished.

418. Jones to Katharine Jones, September 6, 1938.
419. Jones: *Freud, Life and Work,* Vol. III, 336.

In March of 1939 the British Psycho-Analytical Society celebrated its 55th anniversary with a banquet which Freud was unable to attend. Freud wrote to Jones saying that when he had first written to Freud about founding a psycho-analytical society in London before the first world war he "could not foresee that a quarter of a century later [he] should be living so near to it and to [Jones] and still less could [he] have imagined it possible that in spite of being so near [he] should not be taking part in [their] gathering."[420]

It was the last letter he wrote to Jones.

Freud managed to continue his analytic work well into July but made one small concession to pain killing drugs – an occasional dose of aspirin. As he put it to Stefan Zweig: "I prefer to think in torment than not to be able to think clearly."

In August he rapidly deteriorated. "A distressing symptom" Jones wrote "was an unpleasant odour from his wound." Growing weaker day by day he spent most of his time at the window of his study from which he could "gaze at his beloved flowers in the garden."

On the day that Chamberlain declared Britain to be at war with Germany, he was lying on his couch in the garden, when the air raid siren sounded.

Complete composure in the face of death made no concessions to his rational belief that death was the end of individual life and even impatience or irritability were carefully controlled.

"On September 19," Jones wrote, "I was sent for to say goodbye to him and called him by name as he dozed. He opened his eyes, recognised me, and waved his hand, then dropping it with a highly expressive gesture that covered a wealth of meaning: greetings, farewell resignation. There was no need to exchange a word. In a second he fell asleep again."[421]

On September 21 Freud reminded Dr. Schur of the promise he had given to help him when continuing to live no longer made any sense to him. Schur gave Freud a third of a grain of morphia and he sighed with relief and "sank into a peaceful sleep." He died almost at midnight on September 23.

Mrs. Jones wrote in her diary: "We hear the sad news that Freud died last night."[422] Four days later: "We go up to town to Freud's cremation. Ernest makes a most beautiful speech and delivers it perfectly. . . . It is a terrible moment when the coffin as drawn by ghostly hands vanishes. . . . Call on the family in the afternoon. They are wonderfully collected. Help Anna and Ernst arrange the flowers."[423]

It is worth recording parts of Jones' funeral oration:

"As [a] close friend of Professor Freud and his family for more than 30 years it is my privilege to voice our last respects to him. I speak for his family and his friends gathered here and I also think of friends far away, of Brill, Eitingon, Hanns Sachs and others and of the shades of Abraham and Ferenczi.

"This one can say of him that as never man loved life more, so never man

420. Freud to Jones, March 7, 1939.
421. Jones: *Freud, Life and Work,* Vol. III, 262.
422. Mrs. Jones Diary, September 25, 1939.
423. Ibid, September 29, 1939.

feared death less. . . . We recall the rare spirits that transcend the smallness of life and give life its glory and show us the picture of true greatness. . . .''

So far it was a straightforward funeral oration but the obligatory rituals which sweep aside all criticism at such moments left ironic echoes in the words which followed: ''One feels that no-one could ever have lied to him. Not only that it would have been useless but any wish to do so would have melted in his presence. . . .'' Psycho-analytical history hardly bore out that claim.

Jones had some difficulty in controlling his voice as the last words came clearly:

''A great spirit has passed from the world. How can life keep its meaning for those to whom he was the centre of life? Yet we do not feel it as a real parting in the full sense for Freud has so inspired us with his personality.

''And so we take leave of a man whose like we shall not know again.''

CHAPTER XXII

The Melanie Klein Schism

JONES WAS SIXTY when war broke out, a battle-scarred veteran of every kind of struggle whose final ambitions were still unrealised. As we have seen the perverse logic of war reintroduced the missing purpose into so many lives that his patients fell away, communications with Europe broke down, and the American Society showed signs of rebelliousness as the Melanie Klein schism re-opened with renewed life in London.

Mrs. Jones recorded in her diary for 19, 20 and 21 September that she had spent these days in London with her husband and then returned to Elsted. Laconically she concluded the entry: "Ernest has only five patients now and we decided to settle in The Plat."[424]

On September 19 Jones struck a gloomier note: "I am terribly hit financially myself and the future is very dark. I am settling at my cottage in the country where I . . . have a couple of patients."[425]

Still a vigorous sixty, there were those who felt his retirement premature and his early attempts to absorb his restlessness were described by one friend as approaching the pathetic. He concentrated on his two patients, he gardened intensely, he became the Medical Officer of the Home Guard, he kept every possible line open to psycho-analytic struggles in London, but there was no major professional centre to his life. Unlike Jones, his wife was an opera devotee and she pleaded for the privilege of a small pied-à-terre in London from which she could sally forth to indulge this luxury, but her husband was adamant. Two homes were impossible. Jones had an old fashioned view of culture encompassing names like Shakespeare, Dostoievsky, Raphael and Beethoven, but music was not his forte and it seemed absurd to him to maintain an "opera establishment." As for modern painting and music – he had "no eye or ear for such rubbish." Even relatively mild innovators like Renoir were not, in his view, great painters.

His wife would say to her daughter-in-law Jeanne – "Ernest – is very nice – from two o'clock he lets me play my music" but Jeanne Jones always thought that her father-in-law was, as usual, studying his own convenience.

Two new psycho-analytic projects presently deflected and in one case absorbed his attention. Having successfully rushed through a resolution

424. Ibid, September 19, 20, 21, 1939.
425. Inteview Lancelot Whyte.

requiring members of psycho-analytic societies in the United States to subscribe to the *International Journal of Psycho-Analysis,* he was surprised when in 1938 signs of the new American rebellion became apparent. The *Journal* remained essentially a British production but the majority of its subscribers were American and Jones brought them under his umbrella by retaining the label International. Edward Glover later commented that "the skill with which he Jones maintained the international status of the Journal and secured the financial stability by rendering it an obligatory charge on English speaking membership of the Psycho-Analytical Association had to be seen to be believed.[426]

But in 1938/39 the Americans rebelled. Before he died Freud had suggested that the American group "will probably secede: we expect it."[427] William Gillespie described what followed as "a kind of Boston tea-party of psycho-analysis." Dominated by Jones in the role of George IV, the Americans rose and demanded independence with such vehemence that Jones had to accept defeat but out of defeat he constructed a half victory. The crucial meetings took place in Anna Freud's house with American "heavyweight representatives laying into Jones." Once more, Gillespie was surprised at the diplomacy Jones displayed in soothing frayed tempers. In the end it was agreed that there should be alternate European and American presidents.[428]

Arguments on theoretical differences were dropped when Hitler invaded Austria in 1938 but when the Viennese refugees joined the British Society they created fertile breeding ground for further dissension. The outbreak of war saw many analysts absorbed into the war machine, and when Jones retired to his country residence he left Edward Glover as his deputy to chair scientific and other committees. Glover was a shrewd, capable Scottish analyst who wrote well, had considerable polemical skills and did not hesitate to exploit them when challenged.

Dependent on your point of view it was fortunate or unfortunate that Glover did not share Jones' admiration for Melanie Klein and agreed with Anna Freud that classical psycho-analytic models could not accommodate what seemed to them such heresies. The atmosphere in the scientific meetings was increasingly unpleasant and as discontent mounted it became evident that they must formulate a clear training policy which accepted or rejected Melanie Klein's theories. A letter Jones now wrote to Anna Freud is worth quoting in its entirety because it brought to life the ferment which lay under the smooth official surfaces.

"You are quite wrong in saying that I attach no value to your judgment, and of course I should not have asked for it if that were so. It is true that I consider Mrs. Klein has made important contributions. How many of them are actually new is another matter, for I think one would find broad indications of most of them in earlier psycho-analytical writings; to determine this would be a piece of research well worth while. She undoubtedly magnifies the

426. Edward Glover: *In Praise of Ourselves; International Journal of Psycho-Analysis,* Vol. 50, Part 4 (1969).
427. Blanton: *Diary of My Analysis with Sigmund Freud,* 108.
428. Interview, Dr. William Gillespie, October 14, 1980.

newness of them, but it is undeniable, in my opinion, that she has forcibly brought to our attention the great importance of such mechanisms as introjection and projection and has, I think, demonstrated the existence of these and other mechanisms at an earlier age than was generally thought possible. That is how I should sum the matter up.

"These are however, all matters which will work themselves out in the course of time, the more easily if we concentrate on the scientific problems in place of the personal ones.

"I should not have said that scientific difficulties are at the basis of personal ones. Surely our psychological experience must teach us that the reverse is true.

"All this, however, is only one aspect of the discontent raging in the Society. They play for instance no part whatever with such people as Adrian Stephen or Barbara Low. It is an interesting situation, familiar sociologically, where a mood of rebelliousness – mainly induced in this instance, I think, by economic insecurity – draws into itself all other discontents from the most diverse and unco-ordinated sources. The practical problem is how best to cope with the situation and it is just there that I specially hope for your co-operation, both because of our success in working together in the past and because of our supreme devotion to the spirit of union as oposed to disunion, in our psycho-analytical organizations. I cannot believe, Anna, that I could appeal to you in vain on this fundamental issue.

"The immediate problem is the staffing of the Executive. Dr. Glover seems inclined to adopt a defiant attitude and insists that the present regime continue. Dr. Payne, who has done an enormous amount of hard work in the actual running of things, seems hurt at the signs of lack of appreciation. I can myself honestly say that I am above such reactions and am really only concerned with providing the most favourable opportunity for further co-operative work. Also I am very dissatisfied with the present unproductive activities of the Society, for which I hold Dr. Glover partly, though by no means wholly, to blame. By nature I believe in aristocratic leadership, but I think there are occasions, and I wonder if this is not one, where it is more successful to exert that leadership indirectly instead of overtly. Thus I am inclined to the solution of reducing the responsibility of officials, making their policies or decisions more a matter of business meetings, and having the officials re-elected annually. . . .

"I have expressed my opinions to you quite candidly and should now be very glad to hear yours. With kindest regards, Yours always. . . ."[429]

I have not been able to trace Anna's reply, but this letter has to be seen in another perspective. Since Freud's death the mantle had mutually descended on Anna Freud and Ernest Jones.

However, it was the controversy between Anna Freud and Mrs. Klein that became the focus of the "scientific life" of the Society and there were

429. Jones to Anna Freud, January 21, 1942.

increasing accusations that Klein's work was not consistent with Freud's.[430]

Jones had initiated the scientific meetings as far back as 1921 when Glugel gave the first paper on *A Psycho-Analytical Study of King Henry VIII.*[431] By the thirties these meetings were a key part of the intellectual vitality of the London Society and Glover steadily ascending in the hierarchy. By the late thirties he and Jones were the sole arbiters of new entrants into the profession and the preliminary interviews ranged from the efficient and rigorous to the austere and — sometimes — farcical.

Dr. Charles Rycroft remembers, as a young medical man, subjecting himself to Jones' scrutiny and when Jones discovered that he came from an upper class family he immediately said; "You will be going to St. Bartholomew's Hospital."

Rycroft: (puzzled) Why ever do you say that?

Jones, "Oh that's where all the upper class dilettantes go."[432]

Another candidate, a woman of thirty, revealed that she was thinking of getting married and Jones tartly commented: "It might be better to get that trauma out of the way before you attempt anything so serious as psycho-analytic training."

William Gillespie recalls that during his first interview Jones said to him — why did you go to Vienna — implying that London had more to offer than Vienna. The rigour of Jones' investigation reminded Gillespie of taking the Hippocratic oath. In the end he became a privileged member of the seminars which took place in the big dining room at Gloucester Terrace once a week with Jones in the chair. "Some people" Gillespie recalls "were frightened of Jones."

According to Paul Roazen "like Freud in the end Jones collected round him a group of especially talented female psycho-analysts. If Jones accepted a physician for membership he preferred a woman. He also encouraged lay people: Mrs. Joan Riviere for example was a brilliant Cambridge graduate. . . . A handsome woman with a fine mind, she engaged her power behind the throne and once tried to strike a bargain with Jones' second-in-command Edward Glover . . . to govern without Jones: but Glover refused to go along.[433]

Between February and June 1942 five Extraordinary Business Meetings were organised to thrash out a new approach to the Klein schism and Jones as chairman conducted these with courtesy and fairness as is evident from the minutes.

Melanie Klein had gone to Pitlochry in Scotland at the outbreak of war and there she continued her analysis of Dick, the aristocratic boy and Richard, another nine-year-old. This work became very important in the discussions which followed because it clarified the relationship between the depressive position and the Oedipus complex and formed the basis of Melanie Klein's famous paper *The Oedipus Complex in the Light of Early*

---

430. Hanna Segal: *Melanie Klein,* 91.
431. *International Journal of Psycho Analysis,* Vol. 60, 1979, Part 3, Pearl King.
432. Interview, Charles Rycroft, February 4, 1981.
433. Paul Roazen: *Freud and His Followers,* 350, c.f. Interview by Roazen, Edward Glover, August 25, 1965.

Anxieties, [434] Any attempt to condense the complexity of Mrs. Klein's model to introductory paragraphs must violate her thinking but at the risk of outraging all parties to the dispute, the four most important concepts were: first the capacity of the child to have a pre-verbal phantasy life (before the Oedipus complex) which was susceptible to analysis partly in child play: second the depressive position resulting from the child's double-bind relationship with the breast which at one moment it loved and the next hated and attacked, with guilt the inevitable result: third the paranoid-schitzoid attitude to reality deriving from his conditioning: and fourth – envy – in all its aspects as one of the most fundamental emotions which arises in earliest infancy and in its primitive form is directed at the feeding breast.

By 1942, when Melanie Klein had returned from Pitlochry to London, the Extraordinary Business Meetings decided that a series of controversial discussions were necessary to ventilate all points of view in order to arrive at a generally acceptable policy, especially for training purposes.

In his introduction to Melanie Klein's *Contributions to Psycho-Analysis* Jones summarised his own position. [435] "In England itself the storm was heightened by the advent of our Viennese colleagues whose life in their homeland had literally become impossible. They added to other criticisms the opinion that Mrs. Klein's conclusions not only diverged from but were incompatible with Freud's. This I find myself a grossly exaggerated statement. Not that it should be in any event a decisive consideration if experience showed that her conclusions were nearer the truth: I yield to no-one in my admiration for Freud's genius but on several occasions I have not hesitated to put forward reasons for thinking that certain of his inferences were imperfect."

Absolutely true of course and as balanced an assessment of his past criticism as anyone could produce: but Mrs. Klein had pushed the origins of neurosis back beyond the Oedipus complex, and seen in that perspective Jones' "imperfect inference" became disguised deviation.

The society, Jones continued in his introduction, had become so accustomed to regard Adler, Jung, Stekel and Rank as people who separated from Freud with subjective motives that they easily fell into the error of including Mrs. Klein in their class. "Yet, if psycho-analysis is to remain a branch of science it is evident that now that Freud's ability to continue his magnificent impetus has been extinguished, advance beyond the limits he reached is inevitable." It was in one sense a clarion call.

Four main papers were given during the Controversial Discussions one by Susan Isaacs *On the Nature and Functions of Phantasy:* another, *Some Aspects of the Role of Introjection and Projection* by Paula Heimann; a third, *Regression,* prepared cooperatively by Susan Isaacs and Paula Heimann and the last, *The Emotional Life and Ego Development of the Infant with Special Reference to the Depressive Position,* by Melanie Klein

434. Melanie Klein: *The Oedipus Complex in the Light of Early Anxieties,* 1945, *Writings* I, 370/419.
435. Melanie Klein's *Writings* III.

herself. In the debates which followed both sides quoted Freud extensively and it was illuminating to see how selected quotations were made to support opposing propositions, Kelin's adherents tending to invoke Freud's later and her opponents his earlier works. The full complexity of the discussions which ran on for many weeks can only be appreciated by studying the minutes or the *Scientific Bulletin* and brief extracts violate its subtelty, but a few quotations may illumine the major issues analysed and the atmosphere of the meetings.

At the first controversial meeting Dr. Susan Isaacs was at pains to remove conceptual inadequacies and to clarify psychical experience, perception and phantasy. She said: ". . . External perceptions thus begin to influence mental processes at a certain point (actually at birth but they are not then appreciated as such) but apart from the secondary pre-conscious and adaptations later developed, the psyche deals with external stimuli as with the instinctual ones under the dominance of the pleasure principle. . . .

"Klein has further shown in her analytic work with children of two years and over how the child's play exemplifies the dream mechanisms – symbolisation, condensation, dramatisation, displacement and the rest. . . .

"On the view I am here presenting, their phantasies are in their simplest beginnings *implicit meaning,* meaning latent impulse affect and sensation. . . . Phantasy resides in plastic images – visual, auditory, kinaesthetic, touch, taste, smell. . . .[436]

Anna Freud put her own position in these words: "The following seems to me an outstanding difference between Mrs. Klein's theories and psycho-analytic theory as I understand it. For Mrs. Klein object relationship begins with, or soon after birth, whereas I consider that there is a narcissistic and auto-erotic phase of several months' duration which precedes what we call object relationship in the proper sense even though the beginnings of relationship are slowly built up during this initial stage. . . .

"According to Mrs. Isaacs the newborn infant, already in the first six months lives, hates, desires, attacks, wishes to destroy and dismember the mother etc. He has feelings of guilt towards her, commits acts of aggression, of reparation and does things on her behalf and against her wishes. This means that his attitude towards her is that of a fully developed object-relationship. According to my own conception of this same period the infant is at this time exclusively concerned with his own well being. . . .

"The mother is important so far as she serves or disturbs this well being. She is an instrument of satisfaction or denial. . . ."[437]

Mrs. Susan Isaacs, replying to the discussion which followed, said: "I should be interested to know when Miss Freud and Mrs. Burlingham believe that the secondary processes begin to operate. Freud himself says in a passage which I shall quote in a moment 'so far as we know a psychic

436. *Scientific Bulletin,* Consecutive No. 288, No. 10 (1967), 16/18.
437. Ibid, 124.

apparatus processing only the primary process does not exist. . . .'

"By the time the infant is five to six months of age there is a high degree of integration and coordination. It seems to me entirely against the observable facts to hold that his mental life – even from three months on – is dominated wholly and entirely by the primary process and the 'free independent flow of instinctual urges without conflict or integration.' "[438]

Dr. Edward Glover was very much present at these meetings and made no bones about his strong view that heretical deviation was taking place. In a contribution to a symposium on Child Analysis[439] which Mrs. Isaacs now quoted, Glover had said: "In discussing the subject of child analysis . . . . I think it is possible that the idea of radical interference with the mental functioning of young children is calculated to arouse faint echoes of outworn conflicts. . . . Those who deal solely with adolescents and adults are of course entitled to hold themselves theoretical views on the subject but *those are at best pious opinions. . . .*"[440] (My italics.) This was an ironic reference reference to Mrs. Isaacs' view of his own opinions.

Mrs. Isaacs immediately disclaimed having any such attitude towards Glover or her opponents. She had, she claimed, simply said "that they were not in a favourable position to reject the evidence with which they may not have acquainted themselves in close enough detail."[441]

For a time the discussions remained cool and reasonably abstract but now Dr. Glover became very forceful:[442] "I think for example that Mrs. Isaacs' laudatory references to Freud's great discovery of the nature of psychic reality indicate merely her hope and belief that Freud's views on this subject can be made to support her own, viz that phantasy is the primary content of all mental processes and the psychic representative of instinct and that there is no impulse, no urge which is not experienced as unconscious phantasy. . . . I hold on the contrary that Freud's views on psychic reality do not support Mrs. Isaacs' theory of phantasy . . . and finally that Mrs. Isaacs' concept of phantasy is in opposition to Freud's basic concepts of the function of the psychic apparatus."

Susan Isaacs herself once more replied: "Dr. Glover like Dr. Friedlander makes some definite assertions about my views and those of Mrs. Klein which he could not substantiate by any quotation and which have no foundation in fact. Both of these speakers asserted that we have abandoned Freud's conception of the biological development of the libido. . . . There is not the slightest evidence for this assertion. . . . I agree with Dr. Brierley . . . that the infant's hallucination of the wished for sensations aroused by his first experience of the nipple is his first memory as well as his first phantasy. I have long thought that we as analysts should consider the phenomena studied by Jaensch and other experimental psychologists under the term eidetic imagery and see where these fitted in with our own views."

A much more detailed analysis of the Kleinian schism and the Contro-

438. Ibid, 93.
439. *International Journal,* VIII, July 3, 1977.
440. *Scientific Bulletin,* 288, No. 10 (1967), 96.
441. Ibid, 96/7.
442. Ibid, 107.

versial Discussions is given in Hanna Segal's Fontana book simply called *Klein* where she concludes:[443] ". . . the entire concept of regression is seen somewhat differently by Klein and her co-workers. For them the pre-genital stages play a far more important role in the genital organisation than was assumed by Freud. In clinical work they do not consider the appearance of pre-genital material as being necessarily evidence of regression. The early oral introjections of the good breast and the good penis are the basis of good genitality and the genital act contains all the symbolism of good mutual feeding."

Paula Heimann and Susan Isaacs gave a final summing up.[444] "While some analysts *think* of regression predominantly in terms of libido, we see *concurrent* changes in the destructive impulses as well, i.e. they return to earlier archaic aims. We hold that it is this recurrence of primitive destructive aims which is the chief causative factor in the outbreak of mental illness."

Jones kept in close touch with all these developments and wrote a number of letters to the contestants. In an early letter to Anna he described his position afresh: "Mrs. Klein is very worried. . . . She stands in a small minority in the Society with much opposition. My place as President is to bring about free and useful discussion to prevent unfair prejudice and to bring as much co-operation and harmony as is possible among psycho-analysts."[445] Yes − but he was very sympathetic to, if not a sponsor of, Mrs. Klein's views and to that extent his objectivity suffered.

As Hanna Segal wrote: "The Controversial Discussions occupied the British Society from January 1943 until May 1944 − eleven meetings in all. The discussions did not bring, as Jones had hoped, a better mutual understanding. On the contrary they seemed to have led to a still sharper polarization of view and sometimes degenerated into acrimony. From the scientific point of view the useful result of the discussions was that they compelled Mrs. Klein and her co-workers to a more rigorous formulation of their views."

Two final letters were exchanged between the joint "managers" of the London Society. One from Edward Glover was addressed to Jones as President of the International Psycho-Analytical Association of which body Glover had been reappointed secretary at the last Congress.[446] It has to be remembered that Glover had silently chafed for years as Jones' second-in-command and felt that Melanie Klein's theories were a challenge to his chances of leading the London Society.

His letter said that Jones as President in July 1944 must have been aware that he, Glover, had resigned his branch membership and branch office. "One of the main reasons was the fact that the British Psycho-Analytical Society is no longer a Freudian Society and is committed to teaching psycho-analytic candidates the Klein system of child psychology as part of psycho-analysis whereas in fact it constitutes a deviation from psycho-analysis."

443. Hanna Segal: *Melanie Klein,* 107-111.
444. Paula Heimann and Susan Isaacs: *Developments in Psycho Analysis,* 186.
445. Jones to Anna Freud, April 25, 1938.
446. Edward Glover to Jones, December 11, 1944.

Glover pointed out that he had at no time resigned his membership of the International Psycho-Analytical Association or the post of secretary of that body, but shortly after his resignation from the British Society he "learnt" from an indirect and unofficial source that [Jones] had "appointed" Anna Freud as Secretary of the International Association.

War and other complications had prevented Glover from calling a quorum of the International Council together, but now he was requesting an urgent meeting since that was the only proper body to deal with the situation. The request was heavily under-lined in his letter. Moreover, he added, such a situation could not be resolved by invoking the original statutes since these had undergone considerable modification by precedence.

A high degree of controlled anger broke through the letter and Jones opened his reply disingenuously: "I send at last the official reply you request to your letter but must add my surprise that you are not yet tired of psycho-analytic politics."

The letter then plunged into undisguised polemic. "Your request that I convene a meeting of the Council for a certain purpose raises at once the matter of your capacity to do so. . . . I do not see how you have any locus standi in the Association. The Congress of course ratified your election . . . and it would not occur to any one that a non member could hold any official position so that your resignation of membership automatically included that of officer."

The letter pressed on to explain that there was only one way in which someone could "become a member of the Association without being a member of its constituent branches, and that was by express permission from the President of the Association."

This marked the climax in their relationship. Jones and Glover more or less parted company and the Society began to split not in two but in three directions: first the exclusive followers of Anna Freud, second those of Melanie Klein and third the majority, a large group of British analysts prepared to accept some elements of Mrs. Klein's thinking but not all. The battles were over but reverberations rumbled on.

The person who suffered most in these struggles was Melanie Klein, a woman whose beauty was matched by her gentle personality. Like her opponent Edward Glover, in everyday life she was mild mannered but again like Glover when roused she became a different person. Klein's daughter Melitta Schmideberg had once sided with her mother against Freud in a manner which Freud found distasteful. Fratricidal strife became intense with Melitta, herself a doctor and analyst, married to another analyst undergoing analysis by yet another analyst, Dr. Glover, and slowly changing her views. She turned against her mother and privately expressed her opposition. Supported by their respective allies, mother and daughter next broke all the conventions by criticising each other in public. As Paul Roazen wrote: ''Klein personally suffered terribly under the attack and in particular from her daughter's behaviour. Feeling misunderstood Mrs. Klein could be angry and cruel. In later years her daughter grew alienated from the psycho-analysis for whose sake she had publicly criticised her mother.''[447]

---

447. Paul Roazen: *Freud and His Followers*, 486.

CHAPTER XXIII

He writes the Biography

WHEN JONES' SON Mervyn returned from America in November 1941 he volunteered for four different regiments only to be rejected, and began his war service as an "engineer" in a converted garage-factory. Finally his call-up papers came, he joined the Army and as the Allies advanced through Holland in October 1944 he was taken prisoner. It came as a great shock to his father. The pressures within the British and American Societies had put fresh strains on his ageing constitution and the threat of losing his son, patients and what control remained of the Movement combined to under-mine his resistance to many minor ailments.

A variety of illnesses overtook him in 1943 to 1944 and in December he was taken to University College Hospital from which he wrote a grumbling letter to his wife: "H. [meaning the doctor] has certainly bungled the situation and is very apologetic. It could all have been done easily in a week if had tested everything simultaneously. The lung condition is not serious and cannot explain the anaemia."[448] Later in the same year came something much more serious – a major heart attack which left him badly shaken. He wrote to Anna: "I've had a terrible winter . . . lying on a couch for six weeks. . . ." By February, Princess Marie Bonaparte was writing to condole with him and saying that the two opposing psycho-analytic schools would sooner or later burst asunder. She concluded: "Hoping that you have heard from your son and are steadily improving."[449]

By April he was writing a long letter to Anna complaining that her father had – unwittingly – done him a serious injustice in one of the last acts of his life. "I was indubitably the first person in this country (and so far as I know in the whole English speaking world) to assimilate your father's work and to practise psycho-analysis. In the conditions of forty years ago it was a considerable feat and I suppose my reputation rests largely on it."

"This honour your Father has strangely deprived me of in the preface he wrote for Dr. Eder's Memorial Volume. In view of my unfaltering devotion to him you will understand when I call the act a strange one. . . ."[450]

The facts, Jones said, were quite well known. In the pioneering days he had attempted to initiate Dr. Eder into the elements of psycho-analysis but

---

448. Jones to Mrs. Katharine Jones, December 12, 1944.
449. Marie Bonaparte to Jones, February 27, 1945.
450. Jones to Anna Freud, April 28, 1945.

Eder had been unfavourably impressed. When Eder joined Jung and "broke up our society by refusing to resign his office" it was no more than Freud expected. [451]

"Since your father was the last person in the world anyone could suspect of either ingratitude or untruthfulness the only possible supposition is that he allowed himself to be imposed on by one of two women, both of which must have known that the statements were untrue."

Jones was not surprised by their behaviour but "bewildered that neither you nor your Father did not think it worth while to verify."

His letter concluded "If your love of truth or desire to do justice . . . should move you to rectify the statement. . . ." Anna replied that she was very sorry to receive his letter but knew nothing about the origins of her father's statement in David Eder's book. However it should be easy to establish the true facts if they all collected the necessary dates. Could it be that there had been some mistake in the translation? [452] Jones wrote across the letter in pencil: "Answered that teachers usually ante-date pupils in this case by four years."

Another letter came from Anna suggesting that the priority reference made with her father's approval in David Eder's book "may have applied to the time when he was sole representative of analysis in England" while Jones remained in Toronto. [453] Certainly Jones was right. The facts clearly showed that no-one else in the English-speaking world could challenge his claim to being its first pioneer. In order to keep the record straight he wrote a short article in Volume XXVI of the *International Journal* for 1945. His summing up read: "Knowledge of Breuer and Freud's work was available in English periodicals in the nineties of the last century. The earliest publicists were F. W. H. Myers, Mitchell Clarke and Havelock Ellis – in that order. The first paper on psycho-analysis itself in English, an adverse one, was published by Dr. Putnam in Boston in 1906, *the first supporting it was by myself in 1909,* the first one in England – more favourable than Dr. Putman's – was by Dr. Mitchell in 1910." [454] (My italics).

Still hurt by Freud's apparent disloyalty Jones learnt from Anna that Loe Kann had died and in the midst of all his troubles it brought him to a halt. "A momentray flash of the past hit me so vividly I saw her face and heard her speak as if she were alive again. It was disturbing."

Illness, his son's capture, controversies and finally a heart attack certainly concentrated the fates against him in the winter of 1944. He lost weight, his face became gaunt, his body thin but as he recovered he was soon back once more working.

Within a year a different project of major proportions began to absorb more and more of his attention. It was to be the finest printed memorial to his remarkable career – *The Life and Work of Sigmund Freud.*

As we know Freud was no lover of biographies or biographers. Far back in

451. Ibid.
452. Anna Freud to Jones, May 7, 1945.
453. Ibid, August 26, 1945.
454. *International Journal of Psycho-Analysis,* Vol. 26 (1945), 10.

1885 he told Martha Bernays that he had carried out a threat which "some as yet unborn and unfortunate people" would one day resent.[455] The unborn people were of course biographers and the documents he destroyed "all my notes of the past fourteen years as well as letters, scientific excerpts and the manuscripts of my papers. . . . I couldn't have matured or died without worrying about who would get hold of those old papers. As for the biographers let them worry, we have no desire to make it too easy for them. Each one of them will be right in his opinion of The Development of the Hero and I am already looking forward to seeing them go astray."

He put the matter more explicitly to Fritz Wittels:[456]

"It seems to me that the public has no concern with my personality and can learn nothing from an account of it so long as my case (for manifold reasons) cannot be expounded without any reserves whatever."

When Arnold Zweig proposed writing Freud's life he received a short sharp lecture on the crimes of biographers: "Anyone turning biographer commits himself to lies, to concealment, to hypocrisy, to flattery and even to hiding his own lack of understanding for biographical truth is not to be had, and even if it were it couldn't be used."[457]

That last paragraph was prophetic. Even today there are many documents locked away in the American Freud Archives which cannot be used until the year 2020.

Why against all this scorn, contumely and resistance was an official biography ever written? First innumerable half-breed biographies had now proliferated, exemplifyng material which Freud deplored – half truths, half lies, distortions, concealment, hypocrisy and above all lack of understanding. Second, the citadel of Freud's silence resounded to attacks by journalists, novelists, biographers and film makers, all trying to break through eroding defences. The steady corruption of rumour and legend might leave an indelible hallmark on history and the time was ripe for the one man whose authenticity was unquestioning – Jones – to begin unravelling fact from fiction in order to keep the record straight.

Such was one aspect of the debate which took place between Jones, the Freud family, publishers and advisers. Another aspect was even more personal to Jones. In 1944 he had begun writing his own autobiography and prepared a manuscript draft of eleven chapters only to discover that the book would lose in value and integrity unless it frankly described the disagreements which accompanied the growth of psycho-analysis. To present these from his own angle might seem unduly subjective. Yet the facts, of which he had an unrivalled knowledge, were a part of scientific history. He decided therefore to embark on a work centred not on his own experiences but on psycho-analysis and its founder.[458]

There were rivals in the field. A number of distinguished writers would have given much to gain access to those huge dossiers which led into the

455. Freud to Martha Bernays, April 28, 1885; Letters 52/3.
456. Freud to Wittels, December 18, 1923.
457. Freud to Arnold Zweig, May 31, 1936.
458. Mervyn Jones Epilogue, Free Associations.

mind, heart and work of such a man as this. Jones gave the appearance to some colleagues of ambivalence about the biography. To at least one person he said that the prospect appalled him and he did not want to undertake it.[459] This reluctance was contradicted by a letter he wrote to an American publisher in which he said clearly that he and no-one else was the man for the job.

But where to begin in the never-ending forest of papers, documents, letters and personal testimony? First there were several days, coming and going between 23 Maresfield Gardens and The Plat, with Anna Freud subsequently superintending the removal of trunkloads of documents. Evidence on their availability is conflicting.

Unprofessional as a writer, untrained as an academic, Jones certainly lacked that sixth sense which, after long years of experience, can bring order to chaotic material and remains undismayed in a downpour of documents. No biographer ever finds himself working continuously in this happy state of ordered inspiration but experience does help.

And Jones? In the early stages he frequently sat back in despair in his study, contemplating the mountains of material which had a malignant life of their own and refused to come to heel. Should he order the material by subject, by people, events or just straightforward chronology?

Biography has undergone many mutations as a species. The pious three decker memorial by relatives or friends gave place to the Strachey debunking breed which was followed by shorter, sharper biographies in which the truth became a paramount but rarely achieved objective. There were deviant mutations like the *Quest for Corvo,* which Jones read and discarded: there were majestic tomes like Morley's *Gladstone* which he regarded as master-pieces of pompous evasion. Having examined all the options he settled – sensibly with such a complex and relatively technical subject – for the chronological approach, but that had a misleading simplicity.

The first attempts to order the papers by date broke down in confusion. On the second attempt he managed to put together material covering the earliest years and wondered whether he should begin writing immediately. This, fortunately, he rejected and first roughed out a chronological synopsis of Freud's career "as a kind of life raft to which he could cling" when the material threatened to overwhelm him. Already deeply launched into the actual writing, the death of Freud's wife Martha brought to light a mass of new material which made it necessary to begin all over again. Jones' wife Katharine made heroic contributions by translating hundreds of letters written in ancient Gothic script.

From the moment it was first agreed that he should carry out the project until the publication of the first volume, eight years elapsed and throughout those years he was in constant touch with Anna by phone, letter or in person but, she told me "I had no control over what he said and with Ernest Jones it

459. Interview, Edward Glover, December 5, 1956.

was the case that he wrote what he wanted to write. There was no censorship on my part but I certainly cleared up a great many points of fact for him."[460] This statement is contradicted from another source.

Was it symptomatic that after Freud's death the special ring which Freud had given Jones along with other members of the Inner Committee, was stolen one day from a box in the trunk of his car?[461] Did he acknowledge, by no longer wearing it, both the death of Freud and his own breakaway from what had undoubtedly been one of the most profound father fixations in psychoanalytic history? The trunk of his car: it could be seen as an ignominious resting place for such a highly charged symbol, but then Jones was in the habit of throwing valuable personal possessions into the boot of his car. Perhaps after all it amounted to nothing more than an unfortunate coincidence.

In these later years his values had hardened into a mould which some regarded as bourgeois. Over the years he had bought and sold property on a reasonable scale from the house in York Terrace to The Plat, the cottage at Gower to a villa at Menton. He always travelled first class and his main household would usually include a cook, two maids, and a gardener-housekeeper. Surrounded by the apparatus of middle class prosperity and respectability he no longer approved of illicit liaisons and when he discovered that his daughter Nesta was living with a man he commissioned Mervyn to instruct Lewis that they really must get married. When the happy pair refused he was visibly distressed.

He had also, at the age of 67, changed his attitude to his son Mervyn's choice of profession. Originally ridiculing the idea that anyone could "earn a living from writing" he wrote a letter one January day:

> I have just finished reading your book and feel impelled to write at once to say how good I find it. There are, of course, good things all through, in spite of the cuts, but the last part where you get on to the human soul shows you do not simply good writing but really great writing.
> 　　Stick to it. You have chosen the right profession.
> 　　　　　　　　　　　　　　　　　　Love from
> 　　　　　　　　　　　　　　　　　　Dad.

If he was no longer embroiled in quite the same way with psychoanalytic politics, another obsession had now taken their place: his biography of Freud. "'I don't believe" he said "that people who write biography – live with their subject – but I certainly found myself disturbed on occasion by the sense that the Herr Professor was looking over my shoulder – and once or twice I came uncomfortably close to hearing his muffled voice saying – I don't like that."[462]

The Plat became another smaller power house which reached out to all quarters of the earth sucking in material and he battled sometimes late at night to subdue the flood which was self multiplying.

460. Interview, Anna Freud, September 14, 1980.
461. Paul Roazen: *Freud and His Followers,* 344.
462. Interview, Jones, September 15, 1953.

In constant touch with Anna, sometimes one chapter, sometimes several went off for her — rumour has it approval — but she flatly contradicted this, substituting the word scrutiny.[463]

In September of 1953 when the first volume was about to appear she wrote to Ernest that she had been dreaming about her father's past and not her own.[464] "Like most children I have always been jealous of his past that I did not share and your descriptions bring home to me what a long and full life he had before my time." Jones replied: It must be unique for an author and translator to cooperate so closely as to do so in dream life.[465]

After the first volume had appeared she wrote: "I follow all the reviews of your book and I find the ambivalence of the reviewers very amusing, very interesting and very disappointing. It shows how much the former dislike of psycho analysis is still alive.[466]

Clearly Jones' absorption in writing the biography was frequently matched by Anna's, who wrote in January of 1954 that she had once more been dreaming about the work. They were both she said "trying to decipher a passage in my father's handwriting" and suddenly she unravelled it but in her moment of pride she realised it was his achievement, not hers, because he had "spotted the [original] mistake."[467]

By 1954 when he was well into the second volume and she had read several chapters she said that one in particular was "absolutely magnificent." She would "never have believed that anybody could do it or know so much about him. How do you do it. I just don't know."[468]

Throughout the last half of Jones' life, Mrs. Joan Riviere had played a significant part, appearing and reappearing for personal or professional reasons. Less well known was the part she played in Freud's life on which Jones did not enlarge in his biography. Now Anna wrote that she wondered about the reference to Mrs. Riviere among the women in Freud's life. "She must have played a part since I remember being very jealous of her (a sure sign!) But then what about Ruth Brunswick and perhaps even Jeanne Lampl?"[469]

Throughout the whole massive undertaking Jones had no secretary but in 1951 a letter to Anna revealed a concession which lightened what sometimes became a dismaying burden. "The Bollingen Foundation has sent me $2000 for research and I have engaged Mrs. Wagner for half time work."[470]

Some criticism appeared in Anna's letters for 1954.[471] She thought the second volume more cursory and hurried and chapter three seemed to her to give too much support to a mistaken myth: that Freud was "rather morose, impatient with others, hasty in judgment, occasionally, unjust." She reminded Jones that even when seriously ill he very often maintained a surprisingly gay and optimistic temper. There were only two periods in her recollection when he was definitely depressed: one in Marienbad and the other "following the death of Heinerle — Sophie's little boy."

463. Interview, Anna Freud, September 14, 1980. 468. Ibid, January 15, 1954.
464. Anna Freud to Jones, September 18, 1953.   469. Ibid, February 14, 1954.
465. Jones to Anna Freud, January 15, 1954.   470. Jones to Anna Freud, March 3, 1954.
466. Anna Freud to Jones, September 26, 1953.   471. Anna Freud to Jones, August 4, 1954.
467. Ibid, January 9, 1954.

Despite protestations to the contrary so close did Jones' identification with his subject become that he developed a pain in the right upper jaw which became so persistent that he went to see his dentist who could find nothing wrong with him. Nor was the illusion easily defeated. He would awake in the night clasping his jaw as if suffering from a substitute prosthesis and in the morning there were occasions when eating became a painful procedure. Anna worried about the persistence of the condition and wrote telling him that he must "please lose it soon".[472] Then came a letter to say that she was "cross with the *Observer* for their un-understanding review" which referred to a review by the Professor of Philosophy Stuart Hampshire.[473] These letters were all affectionate and frequently ended with the two words – love, Anna – the crises within the psycho-analytic movement through which they had both recently lived having left no permanent scars.

If Jones' mental life remained unimpaired and he maintained a modified correspondence with people all over the world, his physical health deteriorated. None the less he had confounded all predictions about the results of his serious coronary and within six weeks was walking around his beloved garden. His energy was not the same, skating had gone for ever and the house and garden more and more marked the limits of his everyday life, but his zest for living was unquenched.

In June of 1956 he sat in the garden one beautiful summer day, took his wife's hand and said "It's all been more than worth it." "Yes" she said.[474]

When I went to see him some years after his coronary, he took down a copy of Browning and said "I'm going to quote this in my autobiography." The passage read: "Little by little he sees fit to forgo claim after claim in the world, puts up with less and less share of its good as his proportion; and when the octogenarian asks barely a sup of gruel and a fire of dry sticks and thanks you as for his full allowance and right in the common good of life – hoping nobody may murder him – he who began by asking and expecting the whole of us to bow down in worship to him – why I say he is advanced far onward, very far . . ."

To another visitor he quoted Freud's famous remark: "I know nothing about it at all! Why I and incidentally my six adult children have to be thoroughly decent human beings is quite incomprehensible to me."[475]

He was shrunken but still spry, and he frequently wore a beautiful flower in his buttonhole, like a defiant emblem.

When his work on the Freud biography was nearing its end the time came for the celebration of the centenary of Freud's birth and he prepared four lectures which were subsequently published as his last book, *Four Centenary Addresses*. Now a frail old man of seventy-seven, the spirit driving him remained unimpaired but it was as if that spirit was too much for his physique and occasionally drove him to the point where he collapsed in a chair muttering "Oh God, I'm tired." Perhaps mistakenly, he accepted an

472. Ibid, October 25, 1955.
473. Ibid, October 11, 1955.
474. Interview, Mrs. Jones, November 1980.
475. Interview, Eva Rosenfeld, October 1969.

invitation to lecture in the States on Freud's centenary, and Anna wrote when she heard the news: "It's very brave of you to speak to the American psychiatrists about lay analysis. They will tear you to shreds and send the pieces back home."[476]

Coincidental with the centenary an emergency arose, when it was found that Jones had a growth in the gall bladder. A swift operation proved successful but the aftermath was unpleasant. In 1957 he developed a mysterious gastric complaint and his son Mervyn was called from the Labour Party Conference to see him. His father said, "I very nearly died."

Within a fortnight, instead of continuing his convalescence he had flown to America with his wife to carry out his lecture undertakings. The heavy programme of lectures, banquets, interviews, and television appearances was only slightly curtailed, and everything had to be geared to the central day of the centenary when he must be back in London to lecture and unveil a plaque at 23 Marefield Gardens where Freud had died.

Punctual to the last he arrived at the precise time and delivered a short oration which for once caused no controversy. He now predicted that he would "make it to eighty which might be a good or bad thing" but the approach of death did not in any way modify his rationalist view that once the black curtain had descended that was the end of the individual's life.

In June 1957 came a second coronary and although it was milder than the first, thereafter he was never in good health. Still he travelled the world and worked, still his drive – now diminished – kept him active in mind and spirit. He went off happily to Paris for his last Congress in August of 1957 and while there had a haemorrhage in the right eye. Thereafter reading was no longer easy. October brought a recurrence of the mysterious gastric complaint and his recovery seemed slow and partial. Sheer will-power drove him to get up and dress for Christmas and his seventy-ninth birthday. He seemed suddenly much weakened and early in the New Year he was forced to take to his bed again.

From there he wrote his last letter to his grandson, Mervyn Jones' son Conrad: "I was very sorry to hear of your accident. In one way you were a lucky boy for it gave you a chance early on to begin learning an important lesson which you will understand better when you are older. It is simply that those who are good at bearing pain or other trouble will get the most enjoyment and fun out of life . . . . Isn't it a good thing we have doctors."[477]

Throughout all these last illnesses Mrs. Katharine Jones became his devoted nurse and when it was discovered that the coronary had laid a false trail and something else must be responsible for his deteriorating condition she began to realise that this might be his last illness.

Towards the middle of January cancer of the liver was diagnosed and his condition grew worse. "He knew" his son wrote "that death was not far and faced it with the keen regret of one who has greatly loved life but entirely

476. Anna Freud to Jones, October 25, 1955.
477. Jones to Conrad Jones, January 27, 1958.

without fear and of course without any change in the view of the universe which he had expressed in his book."[478]

He continued working on his autobiography and one of his last acts was to dictate a sentence which simply said that he was one of the first to be inspired by the ideas of Freud. However it disturbed him that the sentence made no mention of Jung but when he re-examined it he thought that any insertion would upset the balance. He continued to manipulate words in an effort to get a combination of elegance and truth into the sentence. His son Mervyn suggested a footnote. "No – no" he said, his voice now weak, "It's too important for a footnote." They were almost the last words he spoke.[479]

His condition was now so serious that they removed him to the hospital from which his career had begun – University College. And there he decided one day that he had had enough of the long, clumsy process of natural dying, and would end his own life.[480] On February 11 he "took a pill" and within a short time he was dead.

Ernest Jones was cremated at Golders Green and by his express wish his relatives, friends and colleagues made no sentimental journey of his leaving this world, but some who were there found difficulty in controlling their grief. His ashes were preserved not as one might expect next to Freud's, but in the grave of his daughter Gwenith at the village of Cheriton, which is the next village to Llanmadoc where stood the cottage Ty Gwyn to which he so often returned in life to escape the harrassments of living and recover the peace of his roots.

The Times' obituary was surprisingly good since some members of its editorial staff had come close to sneering at psycho-analysis: "It was not only in the world of scientific achievement that Jones was outstanding. He had the qualities of leadership, courage and strength of character which showed themselves at their most brilliant when the Nazis invaded Austria and Freud himself and the large group of analysts in Vienna were in the gravest danger . . . . Besides all his organising activity Dr. Jones maintained a steady output of scientific contributions of the highest order from 1907 up to his last illness. It would require a large volume to do justice to Jones' many-sided achievements . . . .The passing of Dr. Jones will be mourned and his memory honoured not only in the world of psycho-analysis but by all for whom the proper study of mankind is man."[481]

478. Mervyn Jones: Epilogue, Free Associations.
479. Ibid.
480. Interview, Mrs. Katharine Jones, December 15, 1980.
481. Obituary, *The Times*, February 12, 1958.

Appendix

JONES'S THEORETICAL CONTRIBUTIONS to psycho-analysis are over-shadowed by his monumental biography of Freud and any examination of his published work has to begin with *Sigmund Freud life & Work*.

Jones declared his "biographical position" in his preface: "This is not intended to be a popular biography: several have been written already containing serious distortions and untruths. Its aims are simply to record the main facts of Freud's life while they are still accessible and — a more ambitious one — to try to relate his personality and the experiences of his life to the development of his ideas."

The first volume covered the years 1856 to 1900 from Freud's origins, boyhood and adolescence to the age of forty-four when he published what everyone regarded as his masterpiece — *The Interpretation of Dreams*. Unlike the second volume, the first had a narrative thrust which revealed so much new material about Freud's personal and professional life that a number of critics gave it high praise. Not so, however, *The Times:* ".... it all seems little more than the preface to the real story .... one is not surprised to read that [Freud] himself exhibited some neurotic symptoms, the precise nature of which Dr. Jones leaves rather obscure ...." In this volume Freud ".... was on the verge of exploring the whole range of infantile sexuality and completing his theory of dream psychology .... his two mightiest achievements ...." but "we will have to wait for the real person."[482]

Not until the last chapter of Volume One did Jones digress into discussion of Freud's Theory of the Mind, a device which made the remainder of the book assimilable — despite his protestations — to the ordinary reader.

Ronald Clark has since written a one-volume comprehensive biography of Freud which employs the techniques of the professional biographer and in the sweep of 650 pages he corrects many details of the received wisdom of Freud's life as recorded by Jones. Unavailable to Jones was information recently culled from birth, marriage, travel and death records by Freud's doctor, Schur, which threw new light on the Freud family legend in the first years of Freud's life. It is now known that in the earliest years Freud's home

482. *The Times,* September 19, 1953.

consisted of a single room in which the whole family lived, including the parents, Julius who died before he was two, and Anna born before Freud himself was two and half — a territorial restriction with inescapable psychological effects.

Jones claims in his first volume that Freud's wife "was the only person to whom he related the Gisela incident" (his calf love for Gisela Flüss) but Clark uncovered two more revealing accounts, one given to Gisela's brother Emil and the other to Silberstein, an early friend of Freud. As Clark comments "the incident could be written off as unimportant but for three things: Freud's life-long determination to expunge it from his memory; the virulence with which he responded to the news of Gisela's marriage and his revelation to Silberstein that there had in fact been another Leidenschaft (passion) and that he had "translated esteem for the mother into friendship for the daughter".[483] Clark comments "The absence of any reference to Frau Flüss in Freud's reminiscences should be noted together with the view that the theory of repression is the cornerstone on which the whole structure of psycho-analysis rests."

If Jones failed to trace the Silberstein letters he was not fooled about the importance of the Gisela incident and divined a mystery surrounding the details which accurately fitted the transference of esteem for the mother into friendship for the daughter. "I would venture to surmise" Jones wrote "it was his deep love for his mother."[484] Clark comments "Certainly Freud was a devoted son. But nowhere does he express for his mother the adulation reserved for Frau Flüss."[485] In fact there are several references in Freud's writings, not only to his love for his mother, but to seeing her naked and having erotic reactions to her. If Jones' documentation on the Flüss episodes is thin his general interpretation is accurate.

Jones also failed in the first volume to press home his research about the familiar case of Anna O, or Bertha Pappenheim. Describing the termination of the treatment in June 1882, Breuer said that she was "free from the innumerable disturbances which she had previously exhibited. After this she left Vienna and travelled for a while: but it was a considerable time before she regained her mental balance entirely. Since then she has enjoyed complete health."[486]

Professor Ellenberger wrote a definitive book *The Discovery of the Unconscious* and qualifies this picture — reproduced in Jones' biography — in considerable detail. He discovered that within a month of her discharge by Breuer she became a patient once more at the Belle Vue Sanatorium in Kreuzlingen, Switzerland, and remained a severe morphine addict until the end of October. Professor Ellenberger stated that while there, her hysterical symptoms persisted, she made many "disparaging judgments against the effectiveness of science in regard to her sufferings" and lacked "insight into the severity of her nervous condition."[487] When she finally left Belle Vue she

483. Ronald Clark: *Freud, the Man and the Cause*, 23.
484. Jones: *Freud, Life and Work*, Vol. II, 456.
485. Ronald Clark: *Freud, the Man and the Cause*, 23.
486. Breuer, *Studies*, 40.
487. Ellenberger: *The Discovery of the Unconscious*, 277.

still required heavy morphine sedation.

If Jones failed to discover these details the Freud-Jones version contained one sentence which once again redeemed its general accuracy. "The poor patient did not fare so well as one might gather from Breuer's published account. Relapses took place and she was moved to an institution in Gross Enzersdorf. A year after discontinuing the treatment Breuer confided to Freud that she was quite unhinged and that he wished she would die and so be released from her suffering. She improved however and gave up morphia."

Whatever the degree of the "cure" it does not appear to have had any direct connection with Breuer's treatment as indicated by Jones.

Turning to Jones' second volume, Clark claimed that it, too, was open to similar qualifications. Dr. Schur's remarkable material about the background of Freud's Irma dream was not included in Jones' biography or in the *Origins of Psycho Analysis*. Censorship removed the opening paragraph of Freud's letter to Fliess who had performed a sinus operation on "Irma" at Freud's instigation. This paragraph revealed that iodoform gauze had been unintentionally left in the patient's nose after the operation. Freud nearly fainted when he witnessed the subsequent removal of the gauze but he assured Fleiss that it was not his constitutional dislike of blood but the fact that they had misjudged Irma that upset him.

Jones gave Freud's interpretation of his Irma dream as a wish to exculpate himself from blame for her treatment. According to Clark, Freud was dominated by a desire to exonerate his friend Fleiss. Or could it be simply that he desired to shift and/or project the blame on to Fleiss?

Freudians who disentangle dogma from fact should long ago have worried about Jones' account of Freud's self-analysis – today considered a contradiction in terms – because the source of his infantile theories would be subject to his own resistance.

Freud reported to Fleiss, during the analysis, according to Jones, that "my primary originator of [neurosis] was an ugly, elderly but clever woman. I must have had the opportunity to see her nudam." She later became his instructress in sexual matters and chided him for his clumsiness. Clark comments: "For a forty-one year old remembering what happened at two and a half the 'must have' is no doubt a necessary qualification but it does suggest that the personal foundations on which Freud was to build so much should be regarded with caution."

Certainly, as Jones makes clear, the Oedipus complex was founded in part on Freud's love of his mother and jealousy of his father, recollected in dreams and analysis. How far was this reliable in modern analytic terms? Clark commented: "Whether these recollections – as recorded by Jones – were of what had taken place or what he thought had taken place no one can say with any certainty since his evidence was hardly more reliable than that which had supported the seduction theory."[488] But was his formulation of

488. Ronald Clark: *Freud, the Man and the Cause*, 167.

the seduction theory — that incest takes place on a surprisingly large scale — wrong? Jones tended to accept Freud's theory that guilt about incestuous activities was frequently a matter of intense *fantasies* expressing the desire without realisation, but statistical analysis of court cases showed that incest was far more frequent than Freud knew and since statistics failed to represent unrecorded cases, this tip of the iceberg might underpin his original conclusions.

Stuart Hampshire in his *Observer* review set the tone of respect surrounding the reception of the first volume and the opening shots against the second: "The second volume of this great biography has the title *Years of Maturity — 1901-1919*. In these years the psycho-analytic movement was created and consolidated by the range and speed of Freud's discoveries, and he emerged as a Moses figure determined that his disciples should follow the creed as laid down by the tablets."

It is important to remember that in the dissensions which engulfed the leading figures in the second volume, Freud — according to Jones — had one driving purpose. He wanted to reorganise the psycho-analytic movement with a new centre in the heart of Europe under a leader who did not generate the confused love and hate which had grown around his own person. Above all he wanted to create conditions which would preserve the purity of psycho-analytic practice as he saw it for the future. This meant accepting a minimum number of basic concepts without agreement on which analysts could not, he felt, work together. With such an approach in mind Jones found himself drawn into some rationalisations and omissions which the facts did not entirely justify.

As if to make amends for its dismissive review of the first volume *The Times* opened its review of Volume Two: "The second volume of Dr. Jones' masterly life of Freud takes him from his 45th to 63rd year a period in which he emerged from comparative obscurity into the light of fame (or as it sometimes seemed of infamy)."

The reviewer complained that the complexity of the case histories would mean little to the general reader and referred with inappropriate facetiousness to the Case of the Rat Man where the reader "is not even told if the rats were pink."

The note changed in the last few paragraphs. Readers, they said, would be tempted to "turn to the last chapter first, where, in response to certain criticisms of his first volume Dr. Jones sets himself to paint a portrait of the whole man in the round. This is a fine piece of work. Freud emerges as a man like other men but on a grander scale."[489]

If it remained true that Jones was not altogether successful in holding the life and work together in the second volume, everywhere the volume continued to carry the authority of first hand knowledge and there was a certain charm in the "steady and intimate admiration."

489. *The Times,* September 22, 1955.

Jones opened his chapter – *Dissensions* – with the words: "This is a painful and difficult topic to expound: painful because of the distress the dissensions caused at the time and of the unpleasant consequences which lasted for many years after: difficult because it is hard to convey their inner-meaning to the outside world and because the personal motives of the dissidents cannot even yet be fully exposed."[490]

This disarming preamble did not prevent Jones from sometimes converting resistance to Freudian ideology into the personal neurosis of Freud's opponents. As we have seen it was a habit not uncommon among certain members of the early circle. There were also signs of omission.

Paul Roazen has written an interesting book on Victor Tausk whose dramatic suicide was carried out with such determination that he simultaneously shot and strangled himself. This does not appear in Jones' account. Nor does the circumstantially brutal letter written by Freud to Lou Andreas Salome about the suicide: ". . . so he fought out his day of life with the father ghost. I confess I do not really miss him; I had long taken him to be useless, indeed a threat to the future. I had a chance to cast a few glances into the substructure on which his proud sublimations rested: and would long since have dropped him had you not so boosted him in my esteem."[491]

Of course this letter can be read both as brutally frank and as an example of Freud's belief that what he wrote should correspond to what he believed. Moreover Freud's obituary of Tausk [492] was a splendidly generous and adequate account of his career.

As for the general picture of Freud in Volume Two, Stuart Hampshire felt that "the story of these middle years certainly does make him seem more than ever single minded, bleak, strong and orderly. There is a heavy bourgeois calm as the Professor climbs his mountains in his holidays, collects his antiquities and proclaims the proper patriotism at the outbreak of war. But Dr. Jones admits also the other side, the buried life of fantasy and projection which comes out in the studies."[493]

Stuart Hampshire complained that Jones presented Freud's *Totem and Taboo* without sufficient apology but despite the scorn poured on Freud's primal horde theory Levi-Strauss underpinned his formulation in *La Pensée Sauvage*.

More vulnerable is the account of the famous Schreber case, a lengthy study published in 1911 and fatally based not on clinical material but an autobiographical book written by the patient after he had partially recovered. Jones accepted Freud's interpretation of the case as a man suffering from acute paranoia, resulting from an upsurge of unconscious homosexuality which Schreber found himself unable to accept. Macapline and Hunter's analysis of Schreber's life claimed that a much more persuasive explanation of Schreber's breakdown could be based on his failure to father a son, and Morton Schatzman has convincingly linked Schreber's delusions

490. Jones: *Freud, Life and Work*, Vol. II, 142.
491. Freud to Lou Andreas Salome, August 1, 1919.
492. *Victor Tausk, Standard Edition*, Vol. 17, 273/5.
493. Stuart Hampshire: *Observer*, October 19, 1955.

to his upbringing by a tyrannical father. Contradictory theories now proliferate. It is easy with hindsight to criticise Jones' presentation of case histories, but frequently he was not in possession of material which made a fuller account possible.

The first half of the third volume gave a detached and sometimes moving account of those confused years after the break-up of the early circle and the reunion of surviving members following World War I. The sub-titles – Progress and Misfortune – Fame and Suffering – The Last Years in Vienna – covered a period full of the horror of Freud's slow destruction by cancer and his gradual emergence into the kind of international recognition which no amount of criticism could destroy.

Jones took the easy way out. He gave a chronological account which carried the authority of his personal vision and a nice balance of detachment and admiration made that section a pleasure to read. He crowded all the technical material into the second half of the book which gave the whole structure a broken-backed effect but made the first half easy reading.

Perhaps *The Times Literary Supplement* review is the best summing up of what remains the most detailed, original and irreplaceable account of Freud's life and work:

"The standard set by Dr. Jones in the earlier instalments of his biography is fully maintained . . . He has gathered his material with skill and care and presented it as a well organised narrative. In spite of his great devotion to Freud his personal judgments are shrewd and fair. Indeed several episodes which might be thought to show Freud in an unsympathetic light (e.g. his reaction to the news of Adler's death) find mention. Dr. Jones has also handled the awkward problem of his own relation to Freud with sincerity and candour. He is not afraid to set out their differences whether personal or scientific or to relate disagreements in which he was involved. On occasion Dr. Jones would seem less than fair to himself . . . Indeed in the semi-auto-bio-graphical parts of his narrative Dr. Jones displays a tolerance and detachment which even a fellow psycho-analyst might envy. With the completion of this outstanding biography . . ."[494]

For the rest, academic analysis is out of place with Jones' biography of Freud. The sweep of its one thousand five hundred pages carries the reader over lack of refined research into sheer admiration for such a remarkable monument to one of the most original thinkers of the twentieth century. It is thorough and rambling, authentic and devoted, personal and detached but no-one else could have constructed its many complex chambers or arranged such an illuminating tour of all its idiosyncrasies. All hail therefore to the supreme example of Jones' written work and his ten year struggle with mountainous material.

*   *   *

Characteristically, Jones' theoretical contributions to psycho-analysis are under-estimated and it comes as a surprise to the uninitiate to realise that he wrote over two hundred papers and twelve books.

His papers covered three areas from the historical and interpretive to the original and scientific, with a wide scattering of administrative contributions. Throughout, he remains unswervingly devoted to the concept of a dynamically repressed unconscious. Any modification in theory or practice of this approach he regarded with scepticism. His medical training emphasised the biological basis of psycho-analysis which he valued as a method of scientific investigation more than for its therapeutic applications.

Like Freud, his physiological grounding was centred on a modernisation of the Helmholtz school which has been so much misunderstood in psycho-analytic literature. Professor Paul Cranefield began a paper, *Freud and the School of Helmholtz,* with the remark "there never was a school of Helmholtz", but certainly a small group of physiologists led by Emil de Bois-Reymond, whose earliest disciple was Ernest Brucke, believed that "life" could be explained in mechanistic terms. Jones tended to accept the over-simplified view that Hemholtz's group was exclusively devoted to the study of molecular mechanisms. In fact, as Cranfield points out, they were deeply interested in the more complex phenomena of the mind, as indeed was Jones.

One of Jones first papers,[495] *Rationalisation in Everyday Life*, presented in 1908, simultaneously illustrated Freud's main hypothesis and Jones' dynamic approach to conscious and unconscious pheonomena.

I do not share the received view that another early paper, *On the Nightmare,* (1910) was one of his better efforts. The impressive range of literary and medical evidence in the paper was not matched by the quality of psychological interpretation. Medically, Jones concluded that sleep does not protect a person from increased blood pressure during nightmares which could precipitate cerebral haemorrhage.

Psychologically, the paper over-simplified. Exemplifying the disciple who insists on forcing the evidence into the mould of his theory, he concludes that "the malady known as Nightmare is always an expression of intense mental conflict centering about some form of repressed sexual desire." Spelt out in greater detail: "Nightmares are an expression of violent conflict between a certain unconscious sexual desire and intense fear, the unconscious desire being specifically the feminine or masochistic component of the sexual instinct. In other words in men, nightmares are caused by repressed homosexuality, in women by repressed heterosexuality." (c.f. Charles Rycroft's The Innocence of Dreams 99-103)

"The definite proof of this conclusion", Jones wrote, " is best obtained by the psychoanalysis of a number of cases." Some cases however refuse to conform to the sexual component of this formula.

Expository though many of these early papers were, they continuously

495. Jones: *Rationalisation in Everyday Life (Journal of Abnormal Psychology);* 3, No. 2.

added fresh clinical evidence to Freud's theories and occasionally hinted at re-formulation. In papers like *The Relationship Between Dreams and Psychoneurotic Symptoms,* [496] based mainly on Chapter Seven of *The Interpretation of Dreams,* Jones contributed rich and penetrating clinical observations.

Freud's *Three Essays on the Theory of Sexuality* proposed a development theory concentrated mainly on regression and fixation, but it slowly emerged that definitive personality traits could be attributed to the persistence of primal impulses and the defences they created. Jones' expositions and developments of these theories followed Freud's work, as when Freud's paper *Character and Anal Eroticism* in 1908 was taken up in Jones' paper *Hate and Anal Eroticism in the Obsessional Neurosis* in 1918. [497] There were even occasions when he anticipated Freud's work, as witness his paper *The God Complex* published in German one year before Freud's paper *On Narcissism. The God Complex,* as Zetzel, wrote, "Contains a beautifully accurate description of the superficially well adjusted narcissistic character which illustrates Jones 'insight into the pathology of the so-called "normal". It also contains a concise delineation of the psychology of the academic psychologist as apt today as it was at the time it was written."[498]

His paper *The Pathology of Morbid Anxiety*[499] showed marked deviations from Freud's original formulation but remained within the widest boundaries of Freud's approach. According to Freud's original definition, anxiety arose as a "physiological discharge of ungratified sexual desire". Jones' paper insisted that this formulation underestimated the relation between anxiety and fear. "Desire" he wrote, "that can find no direct expression is introverted and the dread that arises is really the patient's dread of an outburst of his own buried desire. In other words morbid anxiety serves the same biological function as normal fear in that it protects the organism against processes of which it is afraid."

These papers all stressed the importance of internal factors in coping with reality and especially the forces of hate and aggression. There were three underlying assumptions: the biological basis from which everything sprang; the importance of aggressive impulses and the determinant role of innate factors.

Freud's paper *On Narcissism* had important implications for war psychology and Jones' paper *War Shock and Freud's Theory of the Neuroses* brought out similar narcissistic features. Freud's paper was seminal, producing a modification of instinct theory and the introduction of the death wish. There followed his paper *Inhibitions, Symptoms and Anxiety* which became a crucial watershed in the development of ego psychology. It was from this period that Jones' divergencies became more marked and slowly cohered around three main theoretical concepts. First the origin and nature of the super-ego, second the concept of the death instinct and third the early

496. Jones: *The Relationship between Dreams and Psycho-Neurotic Symptoms (American Journal of Insanity, 1911).*
497. Jones: *Hate and Anal Eroticism in Obsessional Neuroses, Papers on Psycho Analysis.*
498. *International Journal of Psycho Analysis,* Vol. 39 (1958), 311/318.
499. Jones: *The Pathology of Morbid Anxiety (Journal of Abnormal Psychology, 1911).*

development of female sexuality.

Freud had related the origins of the super-ego to the genital-oedipal situation, placing the emphasis on environmental structures. Jones worked within a similar framework but emphasised aggressive pre-genital drives. Jones attempted to reconcile these differences and although he failed, he drew attention to an important factor in his conclusions.

The super-ego, he wrote, was to become . . . ". . . the nodal point where we may expect all the obscure problems of the oedipal complex and narcissism on the one hand, and hate and sadism on the other, to meet."

His paper *Psycho-Analysis and the Instincts* revealed his resistance to the death instinct as an "integral part of psycho-analysis since it represents a personal train of thought rather than a direct inference from verifiable data." Rejecting the psychic reality of a self-directed death instinct, Jones still accepted the importance of innate aggression. The proposition that our life consisted of "nothing but a struggle between love and hate" received his full approval.

*   *   *

To understand the intrinsic nature of Jones' work it is necessary to select three important papers and analyse them in greater detail. Outstanding, of course, was Jones' paper on *Hamlet and the Oedipus Complex*[500] which aroused ridicule among Shakespearian scholars, admiration among analysts and every variety of reaction among reviewers.

At the very outset Jones paper violates every canon in modern critical theory and structuralists like Roland Barthes would regard his opening paragraphs as travesties of the truth. "It has been found that with poetic creations the critical procedure cannot halt at the work of art itself: to isolate this from its creator is to impose artificial limits to our understanding of it."[501]

In total contradiction, Barthes' first and cardinal act was to take the author to the top of the Eiffel Tower and ceremoniously push him off, the removal of anything so irrelevant as the author-in-himself, being a prime condition of properly understanding his work.

It is no fault of Jones that these refinements of literary analysis were not current in his day and he could not therefore be acused of lacking modern scholarship, but even in his day there were those like Wilson Knight who claimed that he was not completely up to date.

If such refinements did not trouble Jones it would be a mistake to imagine that his paper lacked scholarship. At the outset he attacked the naive belief that poetic ideas arise in their finished form ". . . from a quasi-divine source rather than as elaborations of simple and familiar elements devoid in themselves of glamour or aesthetic beauty".[502]

500. Jones: *Hamlet and the Oedipus Complex,* 1948.
501. Ibid, 7.
502. Ibid.

When D'Annunzio made his artist-hero think of the extraordinary moments during which his hand wrote immortal verse born of some "impetuous deity blindly obeyed", Jones regarded it as pure rubbish.

Creative inspiration derived in Jones' view from the unconscious and consisted of material which had to be "extensively transformed and purified before it [could] be presented to consciousness."[503]

Thus the particular problem of Hamlet was intimately related to problems which frequently presented themselves in Jones' work. This problem – or central mystery as Jones called it – concerned the prolonged hesitation shown by Hamlet in seeking to revenge his father's murder. Many other major problems in the play have exercised Shakepearian scholars but it quickly became evident why Jones isolated this one.

"Some of the most competent literary authorities have freely acknowledged the inadequacy of . . . the solutions . . . that have hitherto been suggested and when judged by psychological standards their inadequacy is still more evident."

What is it, Jones asked, which inhibited Hamlet's will to slay Claudius without hesitation and led to vacillations which could only be explained by the most powerful psychological paralysis? Extensive analytic experience had shown that certain kinds of mental processes were more inaccessible to consciousness than others and Freud had demonstrated a mechanism of repression which was partly responsible for this phenomena. "A little consideration of the genetic aspects of the matter will make it comprehensible that the trends most likely to be repressed are those belonging to what are called the natural instincts. As the herd unquestionably selects from the natural instincts the sexual one on which to lay its heaviest ban, so it is the various psycho-sexual trends that are most often repressed by the individual."[504]

Whereas the pious task laid on him by Hamlet's father – the positive striving towards vengeance – was a social and moral act of which his consciousness approved, the equally powerful striving against the act arose from some hidden instinctual source in Hamlet's psyche.

What, Jones asked, was Hamlet's precise attitude towards the object of his vengeance, Claudius, and what the nature of the crimes which had to be avenged. First Claudius' incest with the Queen and second the murder of his father, but the intensity of his reaction to the two crimes was of a different order. "Whereas the murder of his father evokes in him indignation and a plain recognition of his obvious duty to revenge it, his mother's guilty conduct awakes in him the intensest horror." Thrown into the deepest depression by his mother's posting in haste to those incestuous sheets, in Hamlet's eyes his mother's lust dishonoured his father's memory, but his reaction goes beyond conventional depression and he thinks of actual suicide. As the psychiatrist Connolly had previously written: "The circum-

503. Ibid, 8.
504. Ibid, 11.

stances are not such as would turn a healthy mind to the contemplation of suicide, the last resource of those whose reason has been overwhelmed by calamity and despair:'' but this pinpoints the precipitating not the predisposing cause.

"Therefore" Jones wrote "if Hamlet has been plunged into this abnormal state by the news of his mother's second marriage it must be because that news has awakened a slumbering memory . . . which is so painful that it may not become conscious."[(505)] Normally, a son might be jealous of sharing his mother's affections with a stepfather, but such jealousy would be conscious and the motive sought by Jones was unconscious.

Psycho-analytic experience revealed that the origin of material subsequently repressed by adult consciousness could be found in childhood experience. Supposing, Jones wrote, that Hamlet as a child had bitterly resented sharing his mother's affections even with his own father, had regarded him as a rival and secretly desired his removal. "The actual realisation of his early wish, in the death of his father at the hands of a jealous rival would have produced in the form of depression and aggression, guilt and sadism, an obscure aftermath of his childhood's conflict.''

Children frequently regard as gratuitously cruel the frustration of desires which seem to them of unblemished authenticity and the agent of the supposed cruelty is frequently the parent. Above all the division of affection between father-mother-child is most strongly resented, and aggressive fantasies towards the father sometimes culminate in a desire for his removal or death. "When the attraction exercised by the mother is excessive it may exert a controlling influence over the boy's later destiny'' Jones wrote.

He was now heading fast towards the crux of his argument. Maternal influences could impart feminine traits to a son and many references had been made in the literature to the author of Hamlet as Gentle Will dominated by Frank Harris' claim that: "Whenever we get under the skin it is Shakespeare's femininity which startles us.'' Unaware of the cavalier nature of Harris' scholarship and the flagrant plagiarism he practised, Jones found himself in doubtful company but there were differential sources for similar statements.

Then came this: "When the weaning from the deep love of the mother is incomplete, it frequently produces bachelors in adult life or makes it impossible for the fully grown man to marry any woman who does not resemble his mother.'' Far worse – a fact not mentioned but fully understood by Jones – impotence frequently supervened with mother substitutes because the re-awakened incest taboo defeated consummation.

Jones continued: "When the aroused feeling is intensely repressed and associated with shame, guilt, and similar reactions the submergence may be so complete as to render the person incapable of experiencing any feeling at all of attraction for the opposite sex . . . This may declare itself in pronounced

505. Ibid, 15.

mysogeny or even, when combined with other factors, in actual homo-sexuality."[506]

So far, straightforward logic carries Jones' argument forward convincingly but now comes a crystallisation which literary scholars were predisposed to resist. As a boy Hamlet had undergone the profoundly conflicting experience of erotic affection from his mother and a desire to remove and or destroy his father. With the death of his father and the mother's second marriage the "association of the idea of sexuality with his mother, buried since infancy, can no longer be concealed from his consciousness, and the desire to destroy the father has in fact been carried out by another who is also a relative."

"Without his being in the least aware of it these ancient desires ringing in his mind, are once more struggling to find conscious expression and need such an expenditure of energy again to repress them" that vacillation breaks his resolution. Shakespeare's own father — according to Jones — had died the year the before the play was written which reinforced his theory. Now the central mystery of the play has been laid bare and explained by psycho-analytic insight.

This condensation violates the subtlety of Jones' long paper. Without reproducing it, step by step, the whole cannot satisfactorily be conveyed. For instance the simple love-of-mother, death-of-father equation is spelt out in refinements which make the paper much more satisfying. Thus: "Much as he hates [his uncle] he can never denounce him with the ardent indignation that boils straight from his blood when he reproached his mother, for the more vigorously he denounces his uncle the more powerfully does he stimulate to activity his own unconscious and repressed complexes."

Fundamentally — and here Jones strains credibility — having identified himself with his uncle's erotic life, the incestuous guilt thus generated turns the death wish against his uncle into a death wish against himself. This inexorably follows the law according to which "all neurotics ultimately direct against themselves death wishes relating to others. In the last analysis Hamlet deals himself the punishment of death because death represents the most absolute form of castration."

Let it be said at once that the thirty-five page paper is well written, reveals a wide range of literary reference, carries great plausibility, and was eventually developed into a book. Inevitably there are flaws. First, considerable doubt exists whether Shakespeare's father did in fact die in the year before Shake-speare wrote the play. There is evidence to show that his father was still alive when the play was first performed but the evidence is inconclusive. Seen from the playwright's point of view Hamlet's prolonged hesitation was a necessary part of the plot without which the action would have come to an abrupt end and the play collapsed.

Repressed homosexuality? It was a fashionable complaint when Jones

506. Ibid, 20/21.

wrote his paper. Applied to Hamlet it suffered from an excessive desire to meet all requirements of the Master's model. Shorn of that final Freudian adornment, the case would have carried greater conviction. Alternative psychological explanations include the simple fact that even in those bloody and murderous days, the act of taking another man's life, and that man a relative, was not carried out without some qualms of conscience, and those qualms may have had socio-cultural roots which were far removed from the Oedipal Complex. Such explanations did not convince Ernest Jones. Socio-cultural patterns he believed were rooted in psychological realities, an attempt to codify the id and ego in civilised form, but the instinct to aggression was a two-edged force in the blind evolutionary machinery. It could be invoked to destroy an enemy for the simple purpose of survival and as such lay deeper than the complications imposed on its expression by the Oedipal Complex.

Jones' Hamlet paper remained in complete agreement with Freud but as we have seen there were others where he deviated. The Kleinian "rebellion" we have already examined in detail. The Lamarckian debate is more difficult to follow. Jones spent many hours searching the record for allusions to Darwin's writings: "Freud has told us" he wrote 'that learning of Darwin's work on evolution had been a main motive in deciding his choice of a scientific career;"[507] but when did this learning take place? The only book of Darwin's which Freud actually possessed was *The Descent of Man* but twice in the *Studies on Hysteria* he refers to Darwin's *The Expression of the Emotions in Man and Mammals*. That such an omnivorous reader missed *The Origin of Species* seems impossible but the record of his reading is much clearer – not unexpectedly – with Lamarck. Early in the first world war Freud and Ferenczi considered collaborating on a book which would unravel the interlocking relationship between psycho-analysis and Lamarck and in 1916, when his practice was failing, Freud wrote to Ferenczi reviving the idea.[508]

"He ordered books on the subject from the University Library and said he could at once see a number of promising ideas, the truth of which he was already convinced of."[509] Although Ferenczi's enthusiasm diminished Freud promptly sent him an outline of the proposed work with a letter which said that he "was busy reading Lamarck's *Philisophie Zoologique*"[510] In the intervening months interest in the project fluctuated and finally waned.

Everyone is familiar with the Lamarckian proposition that an interlocking chain of repeated experiences backed by effort on the part of the organism may modify the organism in such a way as to transmit that modification to its offspring. Darwin alternatively maintained that acquired characteristics and variations in the species were due to natural selection and chance mutations. Freud now wrote to Abraham of Lamarckism: "Its essential content is that the omnipotence of thoughts was once a reality . . . Our intention is to base

507. Jones: *Freud, Life and Work,* Vol. 3, 332.
508. Freud to Ferenczi, December 22, 1916.
509. Jones: *Freud, Life and Work,* Vol. III, 334/5.
510. Freud to Ferenczi, January 1, 1917.

Lamarck's ideas completely on our own theories and to show that the concept of need which creates and modifies organs is nothing else than the power unconscious ideas have over the body of which we see the remains in hysteria — in short 'the omnipotence of thoughts'. Fitness would then be really explained psycho-analytically: it would be the completion of psycho-analysis. Two great principles of change (of progress) would emerge: one through adaption of one's own body, the later one through alteration of the outer world (autoplastic and heteroplastic)."[511]

Jones' first general answer to this was to quote Julian Huxley the modern biologist: "With the knowledge that has been amassed since Darwin's time it is no longer possible to believe that evolution is brought about through the so-called inheritance of acquired characters — the direct effect of use or disuse of organs or of changes in the environment . . . All the theories lumped together under the heads of biogenesis and Lamarckism are invalidated . . . They are no longer deserve to be called scientific theories but can be seen as speculations without due basis of reality or old superstitions disguised in modern dress."[512]

Jones next refuted what he regarded as dangerous distortions of the facts in Freud's book *Moses and Monotheism*. There Freud suggested that the excessive sense of guilt haunting Jewish history and its concomitant ethical ideals were due to unconscious memories inherited from their forefathers of the terible day when they arose and slew the father of the race, Moses. "This" he said "was a powerful reinforcement of universal process." Innumerable repetitions of this act down the ages had created the so-called original sin of the theologians and its mental inheritance led to the re-enactment in every new generation of similar tragedies.

Jones' answer to this was simple and devastating. "Now this implies that the conscious attitudes of the primitive man made on him such a profound impression as to reverberate throughout his body producing perhaps through Darwin's "gemmules" a corresponding impression on his seminiferous tubules so that when — perhaps years later — they produced spermatozoa each of these had been modified in such a way as to create, when united with an ovum, a child who bore within him the memory of his father's experience."

Jones' continued: "Freud must have been familiar with the overwhelming evidence Weismann among others had brought forward showing that the germ cells are totally immune from the influence of any changes in the soma. For some reason he chose to ignore it."[513]

"For some reason" was disingenuous. Lyschenko invoked Lamarck to support Marx and Freud was clearly invoking Lamarck to give biological respectability to his psycho-analytic theories.

As we have seen Jones personally argued the point with Freud but Freud's only reply was to reaffirm his position. "This state of affairs is made more

511. Freud to Abraham, November 11, 1917.
512. Julian Huxley: *Evolution in Action*, 40.
513. Jones: *Freud, Life and Work*, Vol. III, 334.

difficult it is true by the present attitude of biological science, which rejects the idea of acquired qualities being transmitted to descendants. I admit in all modesty that in spite of this I cannot picture biological development proceeding without taking this factor into account.[514]

Qualifications of the anti-inheritance school have appeared very recently in the work of an Australian geneticist who has shown that when rats' resistance to organ transplants are immunised, that immunity may be passed on to their offspring. Whether genetic engineering which deliberately interferes with gene structures is equivalent to the gradual modification of organs through the impact of a million repeated experiences, is seriously in doubt. Conceptual confusions bedevil the proposition but Professor Medawar has taken it seriously enough to offer laboratory facilities for checking the experiments.

Occultism was another aspect of Freud's work and beliefs which aroused Jones' criticism, and sometimes ire. In 1932, among Freud's *New Introductory Lectures*, was one entitled *Dreams and Occultism* which began with a very persuasive account of the prejudices against such phenomenon. It is "easy to dismiss data of the kind Freud invoked" Jones wrote, but when it came to the explanation of the origins of such beliefs he omitted the obvious and basic one – primitive animism. Inanimate objects became animate, babbling brooks had tongues, trees spoke and thunder was the voice of God. Unravelled, such phenomena were easily shown to have a physical basis into which human characteristics were projected, leading into a belief in ghosts, poltergeists, telepathy and thought transference. No new and special dimension was required to explain the conjuring trick.[515]

In his lecture Freud recounted three cases where extra-sensory predictions had come true; the first concerned a woman who was to bear two children by the time she became thirty-two; the second a student whose brother-in-law was to be poisoned from eating crabs and a third the story of a young man who frequented graphologists to get a correct reading of his handwriting. Significantly Jones added "the only new case related was the one the notes of which [Freud] had forgotten to bring to the lecture."

Freud commented: "If we had to deal with only *one* case like that of my patient we should turn away from it with a shrug of the shoulders . . . But I can assure you that this is not the only case in my experience." Then came the psycho-analytic explanation. "I have collected a whole set of such prophecies and I have the impression that in every instance the fortune teller has only given impression to the thoughts and particularly to the secret wishes of his clients: so that we are justified in analysing such prophesies as if they were the subjective productions, fantasies or dreams of the people concerned."[516]

Not another faculty, but psycho-analytic thought projection was at the root of telepathy in Freud's view. Once again Jones found conceptual

514. G.W. XVI, 207, S.E. XXIII.
515. Interview, Michael Balint, December 1957.
516. Jones: *Freud, Life and Work,* Vol. III, 434.

inadequacies in this explanation. Psycho-analytical introjection and projection were different from thought communication in telepathy.

Jones put some emphasis on the fact that Freud forgot to bring to the lecture the notes of the missing case. This case concerned a play on the name of David Forsyth, a member of the London Society, and turned on whether a jealous patient had guessed that Dr. Forsyth had visited Freud just before he himself had arrived.'' Foresight, Forsyte, Forsyth . . . all these near misses were given by the jealous patient as the name of the next patient, and Foresight turned out to be the nickname which David Forsyth's sweetheart had given him in earlier days. Jones tartly commented: ''Many would consider the case the most tenuous related. At all events there were so many alternative explanations to telepathy that it is not surprising Freud forgot to lay it before us at our meeting.''

Jones then suggested that Freud had ''unconsciously touched up the story''. There was he said ''one minor error I can myself correct. Freud said I had been in Vienna a month before Forsyth's visit. In fact it was the same week for I dined with Forsyth in Zurich when I was returning from Vienna and he on his way there.''

Jones was horrified at the idea that Freud might be so carried away by telepathic persuasions that he would incorporate telepathy into psycho-analytic treatment, and recalled a relevant incident in his own career. ''A lady who consulted me explained that she could not leave her home a hundred miles away for long and suggested that I devote an hour to analyse her in her absence. When I expressed my regret that her plan was not feasible she gave a sigh and said 'No I suppose you haven't yet got so far in your work!' ''[517]

It was at this time that Jones' old friend Ferenczi geuinely believed he was being psycho-analysed by messages transmitted telepathically across the Atlantic from an ex-patient. Jones commented ironically: ''How right Freud was when he wrote of telepathy: 'It is only the first step that counts. The rest follows.' '' If Freud has been accused of having his feet sunk deeply in the mud of materialism then Jones' beliefs in the same philosophy could be said to be engulfing.

Jones' paper on *The Early Development of Female Sexuality* subtly infiltrated Freud's position without directly invoking his name at the points of strongest disagreement. He opens by agreeing with an American rebel, Karen Horney, that men were accustomed to adopt an unduly phallo-centric view of the early development of female sexuality, but warned that both sexes had a bias in favour of their own sexually determined views.

The immediate stimulus to his paper had been his simultaneous analysis of five cases of manifest homosexuality in women. They were all deep analyses, three of which were completed and the other two taken to an advanced stage. Three patients were in their twenties, two in their thirties, and only two of the

517. Ibid, 435.

five were openly hostile towards men. "It was not possible to establish any consistent rule in respect of their conscious attitude towards the parents", all varieties occurring from the "negative towards the father with either negative or positive towards the mother and vice versa." One consistent factor did stand out: "in all cases there was evidence of an unusually strong infantile fixation" towards the mother and this was "definitely connected with the oral stage". So far the picture seemed clear-cut but now Jones introduced fresh qualifications which seemed to contradict his statement that no consistent rule on parent attitudes could be established. "This (the mother fixation) was always succeeded by a strong father fixation whether it was temporary or permanent in consciousness."[518]

Lost in a forest of further subtleties the central core of Jones' argument seemed too revolutionary for him to commit it plainly to paper: that a girl child becomes aware of the vulva-vagina, before penis-castration.

Clinically no case history runs a straight and simple course but there were elements in this paper which complicated matters to the point of obscurity. Jones asks the question – what precisely in women corresponds with the fear of castration in men and what differentiates the development of homosexual from that of heterosexual women?

Answering the first question Jones came to the conclusion that the concept castration "hindered our appreciation of the fundamental conflicts. We have here, in fact, an example of what Karen Horney has indicated as an unconscious bias in approaching such studies too much from the male point of view." This was pure anti-Freudianism.

Castration, Jones argued, was equivalent to the complete abolition of sexuality. For women, he wrote, the whole penis idea is partial and mostly secondary in nature, once more qualifying Freud. We need a new vocabulary, he said "For the main blow of total extinction we might do well to use a separate term, such as the Greek word 'aphanisis' ".

Jones suggested that the "fundamental fear which lies at the basis of all neurosis" was the fear of aphanisis, "the total and, of course permanent extinction of the capacity . . . of sexual enjoyment." Jones claimed that this principle was exemplified in parents' sexual precepts for their children. "Their attitude is quite uncompromising: children are not to be permitted any sexual gratification. And we know that to the child the idea of indefinite postponement is much the same as that of permanent refusal."

Masturbation represented another point of difference with Freud. Freud believed that masturbation was undesirable if not bad for three reasons: (1) The organic consequences connected with excessive indulgence combined with inadequate satisfaction; (2) the habitiual attitude of seeking gratification without making any efforts in the outer world (finding a partner etc); (3) because it favoured infantile aims and the retention of physical infantilism."[519]

518. Jones: *Papers on Psycho-Analysis*, 439.
519. Jones: *Freud, Life and Work*, Vol. II, 337.

According to Jones, Freud saw masturbation "as the basis of the psycho-neuroses", a proposition now replaced by aphanisis in Jones' thinking. It was of minor importance that he also found no evidence of *organic* consequences from excessive masturbation.

Jones argued that the whole question had been wrongly formulated which led to confused answers. The male dread of being castrated might or might not have a precise female counterpart but this dread was only a special case in both sexes of the same thing – aphanisis.

He then reconstructed the male train of sexual thought: "I wish to obtain gratification by committing a particular act but I dare not do so because I fear that it would be followed by the punishment of aphanisis, by castration which would mean for me the permanent extinction of sexual pleasure."

Jones shared aspects of Freud's male chauvinism, and believed that women were something special and apart from men with inbuilt characteristics which went deeper than gender into biological role prescription. Hence he now spoke of "the corresponding thought in the female, with her *more passive nature*" as "*characteristically different.*" (My italics).

He spelt it out thus: I wish to obtain gratification through a particular experience but I dare not take any steps towards bringing it about, such as asking for it, and thus confessing my guilty wish because I fear that to do this would be followed by aphanisis."

Imaginative reconstructions of female sexual responses is a dangerous business but what a woman driven to take the sexual initiative might fear is first rebuff, second social disapproval and third guilt, but that this should be rooted in fear of obliterating sexuality forever, seems somewhat extravagant.

The whole paper puts the emphasis on sexual not socio-economic origins of behaviour patterns and would infuriate modern feminists. Thus: "It leads directly to a greater dependence (as distinct from desire) of the female on the willingness and moral approbation of the partner than we usually find in the male where, characteristically the coresponding sensitiveness occurs in respect of another authoritative male. Hence among other things the more familiar reproaches and need for reassurance on the woman's part."

Social and sexual values change as do male and female role prescriptions. Retrospectively it is easy to dismiss the basis of Jones' paper as out-dated, but in his day such stereotypes were not only acceptable but underpinned by Freud himself.

He did not hesitate to carry his approach to its logical conclusion. It was well known, Jones said, that the morality of the world was essentially a male creation and "what is more curious" the "moral ideas of women are mainly copied from those of men." This he claimed "must be connected with the fact . . . that the super-ego of women is like that of men, predominately derived from reactions to the father."[520]

520. Jones: *Papers on Psycho-Analysis,* 441.

Momentarily, Jones diverged into a fascinating analysis of the purpose of guilt in dealing with privation (ungratified libido) but it is irrelevant to his main theme. He then recapitulated the stages of sexual development in the young girl beginning with the oral stage: "The view commonly accepted is that the nipple or artificial teat is replaced, after a little dallying with the thumb, by the clitoris as the chief source of pleasure just as it is with boys by the penis. Freud concluded that dissatisfactions with this solution among girls led to the wish for a baby gradually replacing the desire for a penis."

Then came the crucial deviation: "My own analyses, as do Melanie Klein's early analyses, indicate that in addition to this stage there are more direct transitions between the oral and Oedipus stages. " The tendencies derived from the former stage "bifurcate easily into clitoris and fellatio directions, i.e. into digital plucking at the clitoris and into fellatio phantasies respectively . . . ."[(521)]

In the deeper thickets of psycho-analytic theorising condensation means violation and it is impossible satisfactorily to convey the twists and turns throughout this paper which revealed immense intellectual ingenuity if some of its more extreme propositions found tortured formulations. What are we to make of the following? "We have thus obtained a generalisation which applies in a unitary manner to boy and girl alike: *faced with aphanisis as the result of inevitable privation they must renounce either their sex or their incest:* (Jones' italics) what cannot be retained except at the price of neurosis is hetero-erotic and allo-erotic incest, i.e. any incestuous-object relationship. In both cases the situation of prime difficulty is the simple but fundamental one of union between penis and vagina."[(522)]

Jones attempts to clarify the whole paper in a brief summary but anyone who wants to grasp his proceeding argument should manfully make their way through its intricacies. It is certainly an important paper because it finally questions a basic Freudian assumption but there is a sense in which it becomes the victim of its own subtlety. Simplified to the point of distortion, the summing up can be condensed in this form: Privation of sexual wishes evokes in the child the fear of aphanisis which Jones equates with dread of frustration. Guilt arises from within as a defence against aphanisis rather than "as an imposition from without." The oral-erotic stage in the girl "develops directly into the fellatio-clitoris stage and then into the anal-erotic stage where the mouth, anus and vagina . . . . form an equivalent series for the female organ." Repressing incest wishes the girl regresses to the auto-erotic, penis envy, pre Oedipal stage. As a defence against them "the penis envy met with clinically is principally derived from this reaction on the allo-erotic plane, the identification with the father essentially representing denial of femininity."

Any summing up would be incomplete without making the point towards

521. Ibid, 443.
522. Ibid, 445.

which the whole paper built: "Freud's 'phallic phase' in girls is probably a secondary defensive construction rather than a true development stage."

Against the received wisdom Jones' paper *The Theory of Symbolism* seemed more significant than *The Early Development of Female Sexuality*. His attention was directed to the subject by the strong resistance encountered from patients when interpreting symbols, and their use in critical attacks upon Freud's theories.

It has long been recognised that the absence in Freud's work of any account of cognitive development or the development of symbolism is a gap in the model which requires repair. How do functions like reasoning, perception and memory develop and mature, and how does the psyche acquire and employ symbolic representation? The New York school of ego psychology and the English school derivative from Melanie Klein have both recognised these deficiences but the man – after Jones – who has spent a life-time grappling with re-definitions is the legendary Frenchman Jacques Lacan. Before attempting to bring his thinking into some coherent relation-ship with Jones, let us first examine Jones' paper.

Among the maze of meanings given to the word symbolism, what attributes, Jones asked, could be found in common. "1. A symbol is a representation or substitute of some other idea from which, in the context, it derives a secondary significance not inherent in itself. . . . 2. A symbol represents the primary element it contains by having something in common with it. 3. A symbol is characteristically sensorial and concrete whereas the idea may be a *relatively* abstract and complex one. The symbol thus tends to be shorter and more condensed than the idea represented. 4. Symbolic modes of thought are the more primitive, both ontogenetically and phylo-gentically and represent a reversion to some simpler and earlier stage of mental development."

Elaborating the latent content of which the symbol was the manifest expression Jones referred to a frequently recurring element of wit. Different disciplines describe symbols in varying terms, the artist invoking "spon-taneous visual explosions" which cannot be put into words and the literary critic insisting that symbolic resonances are not susceptible of conceptualisa-tion. Indeed the negative literary definition in poetry for instance would probably claim that an effective symbol cannot be put into other words without omitting overtones which are vital to its poetic meaning.

Preliminary attributions of one kind or another were followed by a bold statement of Jones' main theme. "The thesis will here be maintained that true symbolism in the strict sense is to be distinguished from other forms in indirect representation." This was not merely a matter of convenience but intended to clarify the differences between "the most primitive levels in mental development and their relation to conscious thought."

There remained considerable groundwork before approaching this objective. Symbol must be distinguished from simile, and simile from metaphor because the intricacies of language had subtly blended one with the other.[523]

There followed a long quotation from Rank and Sachs which carried his argument forward with greater clarity[524]: "A final means of expression of repressed material, one which lends itself to very general use on account of its special suitability for disguising the unconscious and adapting it (by compromise formations) to new contents of consciousness is the Symbol. By this we understand a special kind of indirect representation which is distinguished by certain peculiarities from the simile, metaphor, allegory, illusion and other forms of pictorial representation of thought material. . . . The symbol represents an almost ideal union of all these means of expression: it is a substitutive, perceptual replacement-expression for something hidden with which it has evident characteristics in common or is coupled by internal associative connections. Its essence lies in its having two or more meanings as indeed it itself originates in a kind of condensation or amalgamation of individual characteristic elements. Its tendency from the conceptual to the perceptual indicates its nearness to primitive thought: by this relationship symbolisation essentially belongs to the unconscious, though, in its function as compromise it in no way lacks conscious determining factors which in varying degrees condition both the formation of symbols and the understanding of them."

Verbosity at its best? Perhaps, but it brought Jones close to the heart of his paper. The characteristic, he argued, which most sharply distinguished what he believed to be true symbolism from similar processes was the representation of unconscious material. However this was no ordinary unconscious material. Paradoxically the concepts symbolised may be known to the individual but *"the affect investing the concept is in a state of repression and so is unconscious."* (My italics.) Whatever the mysterious processes which created symbolisation they too were carried out unconsciously and the *meaning* of the *symbol* remained unconscious. "The actual comparison between the idea symbolised and the symbol has never been present to consciousness at all. Clearly all such symbols were open to multiple interpretation as when a room may symbolise a womb, a prison or a cave . . . . When these points are appreciated it will be seen that there is little scope for arbitrariness in the interpretation of symbols."

Carrying his argument into phylogenetic parallels Jones makes an important point which has since become a commonplace in structural thinking: the ubiquity of symbols throughout different levels of civilisation and in different races and cultures. "A symbol which we today find, for instance, in an obscene joke, is also to be found in a mythical cult of ancient Greece and another that we come across only in dream analysis was used thousands of years ago in the sacred books of the East."

This phenomenon was represented in Jung's archetypes which cut across

523. Ibid, 91.
524. Ibid, 96; Rank and Sachs, *Die Bedeutung der Psychoanalyse für die Geisteswissenschaften S. 11, 1913.*

all boundaries in the collective unconscious but Jones would hate to be reminded of the analogy and certainly had a very different approach.

Now came the big and in some senses unanswerable question — how were symbols generated? Jones' point of departure was that "in symbolism a comparison between two ideas of a kind that is alien to the conscious mind is established unconsciously and then one of these — which for the sake of convenience may be called the secondary idea — may unknowingly be substituted for and so represent the first or primary idea." Clumsily formulated, it made a fundamental point but begged the question — why did two ideas which the conscious mind finds dissimilar become identified in the unconscious. Why also, as Jones asked, "does the one idea symbolise the other and never the reverse?"

He now invoked the authority of Freud to push the argument forward. "What today is symbolically connected was possibly in primeval times united in conceptual and linguistic identity. The symbolic relationship being the remains and sign of an identity that once existed."

Clinical experience reinforced this conclusion. The primitive mind — as observed in primal people, children and the insane — tended to fuse different ideas. Three factors were at work. First the intellectual incapacity for discrimination, second the psycho-analytic pleasure-pain principle and third the reality principle. The first was reinforced by Jones' statement: "I will only point out that the many significations of the individual dream images (Freud's overdetermination) is a sign of the lack of clarity and definition in dream thought. Because of the defective sensibility which prevails in dreams, the contents . . . can become compounded at least in symbolic form."

The second factor was explicable in terms of the pleasure-pain principle because "when the primitive mind is presented with new experiences it seizes on resemblances. These resemblances, according to Jones, are selected on the basis of what most interests the psyche, but he fails to realise that this begs the question — why does A interest it more than B? Throughout these passages large assumptions are made about the way in which the primitive mind works without any anthropological evidence but it is just possible that Levi-Strauss structuralists today would formulate similar propositions on quite different evidence. Characteristically all attempts to analyse the workings of primitive minds, whether by anthropologists or psycho-analysts, tend to be highly speculative and if Jones had limited his thesis to children whose clinical case histories were available, it would have carried more conviction. Alternatively, a deeper analysis of resemblences between primitive and childish minds would be more acceptable than speculation about the workings of neurological machinery of which we know very little.

Jones pressed on regardless: "Symbolism thus appears as the unconscious precipitate of primitive means of adaptation to reality that have become superfluous . . . . a sort of lumber room of civilisation to which the adult readily flees in states of reduced or deficient capacity for adaptation to reality in order to regain his old forgotten playthings of childhood." States such as, for instance, overtake poets when inspired to find beautifully resonant symbols to express what they mean by – say – sublimity.

Thus the symbols which in primitive life had an intrinsic meaning and value of their own became for later generations simple symbols recovered from their past.

Clinically this interpretation was very important. When, in analysis, a patient discovered the "true" meaning of a symbol – its roots in the unconscious – "he often strives to weaken and explain away the significance .... by trying to give it some other 'functional' more general (and therefore more harmless) interpretation."

This down-graded the symbolism to the metaphorical and made it easier for the patient to cope. Metaphorically, there was a relationship to the fundamental meaning of the symbol, but its acceptance indicated powerful resistance to the deeper meaning and thus to the assimilation of the unconscious. Some patients developed great facility in replacing symbolism with metaphorical meanings in dream interpretation. Thus every boat race became the ambition to succeed on the river of life, money spilt became a "symbol" of a wish to be profligate, revolvers fired "symbols" of power. "If now the psycho-analyst allows himself to be deceived by these defensive interpretations and refrains from overcoming the patient's resistances he will assuredly never reach a knowledge of his unconscious."

"So far all is clear," Jones wrote but sensing unexplained complexities he proceeded to give some concrete examples. According to Jung and Silberer a dream about a serpent may symbolise the abstract idea of sexuality more than a concrete idea of a penis but Freudian psycho-analysis insists that snakes symbolise the phallus. Thus Jung-Silberer dream-interpretation would be in terms of secondary generalisation instead of its primary unconscious meaning. A wedding ring to Jones was an emblem but not a symbol of marriage. Yet a bracelet offered as a pre-engagement present became an unconscious symbol of the female organ. There seemed some logical confusion here.

There followed a remarkable prophecy from Jones which gave his proposition a touch of scientific prediction. Modern economists he claimed understood wealth as "a lien on future labour" .... which could be represented by any number of emblems apart from a gold standard. Actual coins in Jones' dictionary were unconscious symbols of excrement and this particularly applied to gold coins. "The ideas of possession and wealth, therefore, obstinately adhere to the idea of 'money' and gold for definite psychological reasons, and people simply will not give up the 'economists' fallacy' of confounding money with wealth."

Jones was no economist, had little knowledge of Treasury tactics, and was not given to gambling on the Stock Exchange, but he concluded: ''This superstitious attitude will cost England in particular many sacrifices after the war when efforts will probably be made at all costs to reintroduce the gold standard.'' Written in 1915, the prediction came true in 1923.

For the rest, to oversimplify grossly, symbolism meant to Jones a regression to a simpler and more primitive mode of apprehension, where only that which is repressed is symbolised. When the regression was relatively superficial, remaining conscious or preconscious, it maintained metaphorical expression which in effect was functional. When the power of the complex drove regression to deeper levels the result was symbolism in the true analytical meaning of that word.

In a short chapter in *Ecrits* the French analyst Lacan paid tribute to Ernest Jones and discussed his theory of symbolism. Lacan believed that Jones did not foresee the danger of ''psychologisation'' making psycho-analysis more complicated. Jones, he said, wanted to support Freud and was against the hermeneutisation of psycho-analysis. As if unaware of the irony that his own hermeneutics frequently disappeared in clouds of obscurity he complained that Jones found difficulty in establishing his conclusions.

Any attempt to reproduce Lacan's re-interpretations in less than six hundred pages is doomed to failure. Many a splendid intellectual enterprise has set out with this objective and foundered within a few chapters. Anthony Wilden wrote a book *The Language of the Self* in which the commentary is more elaborate and muddied than the text it examines. Excellent translations of *Ecrits* and the *Four Fundamental Concepts of Psycho-Analysis* have recently appeared but alas, English is not a good vehicle for carrying the remote abstractions characteristic of a psycho-analytic writer who rarely invokes clinical evidence and has somehow removed from Freud's model one crucial element commonly called affect.

Lacan's attempt to elucidate and elaborate the broad outlines of the model left by Freud gives symbolism clear priority over cognitive development. The child is seen acquiring symbolism in two stages. First, an improvising pre-symbolic stage named by Lacan, The Imaginery, followed by symbolism proper, an entity which bears little resemblence to anything so precisely definable as that put forward by Ernest Jones.

The whole force of Lacan's argument leads in one direction: the progression towards the use of language. Initially at the mercy of unmediated instinct, the child graduates from birth through The Imagery, Symbolic and Mirror image stages into a full-blown semiotically-structured, language-using human being. Differing from Jones general approach, Lacan sees the infant's entry into symbolism proper beginning with a similar single event – the *stade du miroir*. Jones faithfully reproduced Freud's account of the origins of human culture in the primal horde, the sons of which rose and slew the primal father. That catastrophe was matched in

Lacan's thinking by the shock of the child's discovery of its mirror image. First formulated as long ago as 1936, this hypothesis has been heavily reworked since without gaining any greater validity since Lacan fails to produce any supporting clinical evidence.

In the first stage of symbol acquisition – the Imagery stage – the child is involved in a two-term or dyadic relation and in the second, the Symbolic stage, a three-term or triadic relation. The two terms of the Imagery stage are a straightforward relationship between the infant and the image, but in the three-term stage, relationships become much more complex. The first term necessarily retains the infant but the image transforms into the sign, and the third and crucial term becomes The Other. For those in tune with Lacan's thinking The Other is an immensely rich concept which embraces wide-ranging connotations but to over-simplify it can be said to be that which mediates between a child and the world it inhabits. Immediately multiple elaborations become necessary. The Other is an already existing system of rules into which the infant is born, a system which denies the egocentric discourse of Piaget. Fundamentally Lacan argues that the infant emerges into full blown individuality but language splits the inner world from the outer. "I" as a pronoun is divided from the self which it describes, and leads into the illusory ego which creates ego psychology. Lacan's analysis of the "good" effects of language are relatively clear but when he borrows Hegel to illustrate the bad and alienating effects, clarity disappears. Introspective language may falsify internal reality and language distort meaning but the way in which this happens remains obscure.

Perhaps the differences between Jones and Lacan can – very roughly – be put this way: In contradiction to Lacan, Jones believed that, biologically, the unconscious involved pre-language symbols of birth, death, the father, phallus etc. Instead, Lacan saw the unconscious as semiotically structured in terms of metonomy and metaphor. For Lacan, *Verschiebung* (displacement) corresponds to metonymy and *Verdichtung* (condensation) to metaphor.

Jones believed that whatever the dictionary of symbols said, everyone created their own because each individual gave them personal meaning. Lacan saw it differently. In the end if Jones' paper did not revolutionise psycho-analytical thinking it clarified many confusions, and offered a useful tool to future practice.

Many other papers among the multitude he produced are worth close exegesis but in the end his main contribution was to give one of the few authentic outlines of Freud's psychology – as in *The Psychopathology of Everyday Life* and *Freud's Theory of Dreams*. He also threw detailed light on many unexplored questions. No-one should underestimate his positive contribution and the divergences were easily assimilated into a comprehensive exposition which remained faithful to Freud.

For the rest, reality-corespondence is the trap into which all model makers fall. The implicit assumption that metapsychology corresponds to some reality in the human psyche runs powerfully through the work of Freud, Jung and Ernest Jones. Even physics nowadays has modified its old reality-correspondence claim and when less empirically based "sciences" claim similar validation it becomes a dangerous exercise. English psycho-analysis, at least, has its clinical evidence to support the multiplication of models, but on the wilder shores of France theoretical propositions proliferate untroubled by clinical facts. Unfortunately the word "reality" itself begs the question it sets out to answer.

Index

Abraham, Gerd, 185
Abraham, Karl, 49, 52, 76, 99, 106, 107, 108, 109, 169, 198, 231; differences with Jung & Freud, 54-5, 56; Ernest Jones' respect for, 55; to Freud on Rank, 145; Ernest Jones to Freud on, 163; death, 163; Ernest Jones helps widow & family, 163, 183
Adlar, Alfred, ii, 52, 58, 76, 77, 178, 204, 224; Ernest Jones on, 58; at Clark University, 73; break with Freud, 80, 98
Adler, Alexandra, ii
Adlerian school competition with Freudians & Jungians, 107
aetheism, 10-11, 182
Allen & Unwin, 152, 159
Alzheimer, 47, 60
American Journal of Abnormal Psychology, 65
American Journal of Insanity, The, 91
American Psycho-Analytic Society, 71, 73, 210
American Therapeutic Congress, 66
Ames, Richard, 80, 146-7
Anna Ocase 220-1
Assagioli, 59

Bad Homberg Congress, 130
Balint, Dr. Michael, ii, 61, 86, 97, 120, 169, 171, 172, 173, 176, 177
Barthes, Roland, 227
BBC talks on Psycho-analysis (Ernest Jones and Burt), 183-4
Beevor, Dr. C. E., 22, 25, 30
Bennet, Dr. E. A., ii
Berlin Congress, 130
Bernays, Edward, 133
Bernays, Martha, 212
Berne, Ernest Jones in, 122
Bicêtre Hospital, Paris, 62
Binswanger, 95, 96
Bleuler, Prof. Manfred, ii, 47-8, 54, 55, 56, 81

Bodkin, Sir Archibald, 41
Bollinger Foundation, 215
Bolton, Dr. Charles, 25
Bonaparte, Princess Marie, 175, 177, 192, 194, 196, 210
Bones, Dr. Harry, 147
Boston, Mass., Ernest Jones in, 65, 66
Bradford, Dr. Rose, 24-5, 33
Bragg, Sir William, 195
Brain, 45
Bramwell, Milne, 43
Bremen, meeting of Freud, Jung and Ferenczi in, 71-2
Breuer, Josef, 211, 220, 221
Brierley, Dr. 206
Brill, A. A., i, 48, 49, 52, 56-7, 58, 59, 65, 66, 67, 71, 72, 73, 80, 108, 128, 129, 139, 147, 154, 160-1, 175, 176, 185, 198
British Association for the Advancement of Science, 105
British Medical Association, 105, 107, 164, 166
British Medical Journal, 41-2
British Psycho-Analytic Society, 121-2, 143, 168, 202, 207-8, 210; Ernest Jones President of, 138; Glover joint manager with Ernest Jones, 186; 55th anniversary, 198; Controversial Discussions, 204-5, 207
British Psychological Society, 105
Brome, Vincent, meeting, with Ernest Jones, iii-vii; biography of Havelock Ellis, iii
Brompton Chest Hospital, 28
Brown, William, 167
Bruce, Hon. Dr. Herbert A., 92
Brunswick, Ruth, 137, 215
Bryan, Dr. Douglas, 122, 128, 134, 143
Budapest Congress (1918), 123, 173
Budapest group of analysts, 107
Budapest Medical Society, 93
Budge, Wallis, 106
Bullitt, William C., 186, 194, 195
Burgholzi, The, 47, 48, 49, 61

Burlingham, Dorothy, 192, 205
Burt, Prof. Cyril, 122, 184

Campbell, C. Macfie, 70
Campbell, Harry, 93
Canadian Medical Association, 152
Chadwick, Miss, 156
Charing Cross Hospital, 36
child analysis, 152, 153, 156, 187, 206; see also Klein, Melanie
Christian Science, Ernest Jones on, 168
Clark, Ronald, 95, 187, 195; biography of Freud, 219-20, 221
Clark University, Mass., Freud at, 72-3
Clarke, Dr. C. K., 50, 51, 63, 68, 78, 92-3
Collins, Mrs. Joseph, 69
Comparative Philosophy, Board of Studies for, 26
Connolly, 228-9
Cranefield, Prof. Paul, 225

Daily Graphic enquiry into psycho-analysis, 109
Darwin, Charles, 231, 232
Davies, T. G., 10
de Bois-Reymond, Emil, 225
de Forest, Izette, ii, 175
de la Warr, Earl, 193, 194, 196
de Taves, Judith, ii
Dreadnought Seamen's Hospital, 36

Ebing, Kraft, E
Eder, Dr. David, 121, 210-11
Eder, Dr. M. D., 36, 37, 105, 106
Edmunds, Mr., 5
Eitingon, Max, 109, 110, 139, 154, 161, 174, 176, 184, 185, 186, 188, 198; rivalry with Ferenczi for Presidency, 175-6
Ellen, Tom, 44-5
Ellis, Havelock, v, 39, 60, 78; Ernest Jones on, iii-vii, 23, 52
Exner, 197

Fabian Society, 37
Falconer, Sir Robert, 64, 68, 92
Farringdon Dispensary, 36
Federn, 58, 154
Ferenczi, Sandor, 52, 59, 70, 71-4, 76, 86, 88-9, 93, 98, 99, 107-8, 109, 123, 130, 132, 138-9, 145, 146, 147, 152, 154, 168, 170-4, 175, 176-7, 178, 195, 231, 234
Fliess, 97, 221
Flugel, Prof. J. C., 122, 128, 132, 134, 167, 203
Flüss, Gisela, 220
Forsdike, 21
Forsyth, Dr. David, 36, 234

France, Ernest Jones in, 62
Freud, Anna, i, ii, 6, 8, 58, 60, 68, 134, 154, 186, 192, 195, 196, 198, 201; on Ernest Jones and Loe Kann, 37-8, 51, 59, 83; Ernest Jones on her book, 155, 157; attack on Melanie Klein, 156-7, 202-9; at Oxford Congress, 162; correspondence with Ernest Jones, 185-6, 188, 201-2, 207, 210; and Ernest Jones' biography of Freud, 213, 215
Freud, Ernst, 185, 186, 188, 196, 198
Freud, Martha (Mrs. Sigmund Freud), 57, 71, 193, 196, 213
Freud, Martin, 192, 193, 196
Freud, Sophie, 164
Freud, Sigmund
    Ernert Jones' relationship with, i, 74, 83, 96; Ernest Jones' first meeting with, 52-4; Ernest Jones' biography of, see under Jones, Ernest; published works: Freud, Life and Work; Ernest Jones on, 57, 58, 72, 74, 77; on Ernest Jones, 58-9, 62, 74; conflict with Ernest Jones over Joan Riviere, 131-2, 135-7, 142-3; differences with Ernest Jones, 150, 168; Ernest Jones and his works, 128, 133, 152; Ernest Jones rescues from Nazis, 192-6; death, and Ernest Jones' funeral oration on, 198-9
Friedlander, 206
Frink, Horace, 128, 147, 160
Fromm, Erich, 146, 147, 148, 175

Gillespie, Dr. William, ii, 203
Glover, Dr. Edward, ii, 153-4, 164, 186, 201, 202; part in Klein controversy, 206, 207; split with Ernest Jones, 207-8
Glover, Dr. James, 122, 143
Gordon, Dr. 68
Greenland, Prof. Cyril, ii, 90-1, 92, 152
Groddeck, 130, 169
Gross, Otto, 60-1

Hale, Nathan, G., Jr., 65
Hall, Prof. G. Stanley, 57, 70, 71, 72-3
Hamburg Congress, 153
Hampshire, Stuart, on Ernest Jones' biography of Freud, 222, 223
Harris, Frank, 229
Hart, Bernard, 33, 45
Hartman, 60
Harvard   University   Psychological Laboratory, 71
Hattie, Dr. W. H., 78
Haycroft, Prof. J. B., 14
Heimann, Paula, v, 59, 204, 207
Hella, Hugo, 134
Heller, Eric, 134, 136, 137

Helmholtz, 225
Hill, Maude, Ernest Jones and, 32–3, 35
Hiller, Eric, 112, 123, 127, 128, 138, 142
Hinkle, 80
Hirschfield, Magnus, 80
Hitschmann, 58
Hitzig, 19
Hoare, Sir Samuel, 193, 194, 195
Hoch, Dr. August, 70, 78
Hogarth Press, 128
Hopkinson, Pryns, 153
Horney, Karen, 235
Horsley, Sir Victor, 25, 26, 30, 102
Hospital for Sick Children, Ernest Jones'
  assistantship at, 32
Hughes, Prof. A. W., 13
Hull, Cordell, 194
Huxley, Julian, 183, 232
Huxley, T. H., 12, 14, 15, 19
hypnotic techniques, 44, 45

Innsbruck Congress, 130, 162
Institute of Psycho-Analysis, i, 128, 138, 153,
  159, 168
International Congress of Neurology, 47
International Journal of Psycho-Analysis,
  162, 177, 184–5, 201, 211; founded by Ernest Jones, 122
International Psycho-Analytical Association, i, 122, 185, 207–8; Ferenczi's plan to
  wind up, 107–8; Jung resigns from Presidency, 108; dissension among Committee,
  134–5, 138–9, 145, 146
    Congresses:
    (1908) 52–6; (1910) 76–7; (1911) 80–2;
    (1913) 98–100, 145; (1918) 123; (1920) 130;
    (1925) 153; (1927) 162; (1929) 162
    Correspondenzblatt, 82
    Zentralblatt, 77, 82, 99
International Psycho-Analytical Library
  Series, 128, 157, 168
International Psycho-Analytical Press, The,
  128
International Psychoanalytischer Verlag,
  127, 128, 138, 186, 192–3
Internationale Zeitschrift für Psychoanalyse,
  95, 108, 128, 162, 184
Isaacs, Susan, 156, 204–6, 207

Jahrbuch für psychoanalystiche und psychopathologische Forschungen, 54, 77, 80, 106,
  107
James, Allsop, 27
James, William, 34, 43, 73
Janet, Pierre, 44, 45, 62; Ernest Jones un-
  masks talking cure, 46

Jennings, 18, 19
Jokl, Katharine, (Later Mrs. Ernest Jones)
  (2nd wife), 124–6; see also Jones, Katharine
Jones, Conrad (grandson), 217
Jones, Elizabeth (sister), 4, 35, 40, 64, 78, 89
Jones Ernest:
  Birth, 1; Childhood, 2–5, 8–9; Early Sex
  Experiences, 3–5, 11; Early Education, 5–
  6, 9–12; Motives for Selecting Medicine,
  8–9; Student in London, 13–23; Medical
  training, 18–23; House Physician, 24–29;
  Harley Street, 35; Relationship with
  Wilfred Trotter, 26–7, 29, 34, 36–7, 38–40,
  45, 54, 78–9, 89, 93–4; North Eastern Hospital For Children, 28–9, 30; First Indecency Charge, 39–40; Second Indecency
  Charge, 49–50; First Meeting With Freud,
  52–4; Subsequent relationship with Freud
  see Freud, Sigmund; West End Hospital
  for Nervous Diseases, 36, 49, 59, 62; Asked
  to resign from, 50; Goes to Canada, 51; In
  Canada, 63–79, 82, 89; First meeting with
  Jung, 47; Subsequent relations with Jung,
  see C. G. Jung; Involvement psycho-analytic movement, 52–6, 70; Hostility towards, 93–4; American-European Conflict, 133, 157–8; Contention over medical
  training, 150; Leaves Canada, 90; Appearance, 90, 96, 149; Character, 149, 160, 182,
  189; Private Practice, 93, 102, 105, 132,
  141; First meeting with Loe Kann, 37;
  Subsequent relationship with Loe Kann,
  see Kann, Loe; First Marriage Morfydd
  Owen, 112–13; Second Marriage Katharine Jokl, 124–7, 179–80; Subsequent relations with, see Jones Katharine; First
  meeting Joan Riviere, 113; Subsequent relations with Joan Riviere, see Joan Riviere; Illnesses, 5–6, 101, 103–4, 106, 143–
  4, 163, 169, 188, 210–11, 216–18; Finances,
  179–80, 181, 200; Recreations, 7, 10, 20,
  182, 200; Dreams, 181; Family Life, 179–
  191; Edits International Journal of
  Psycho-Analysis, 128, 133, 141, 144; Criticism of Journal, 134–6; Acting President
  of International Psycho-Analytical Association, 123; President of I.P.A., 176, 180,
  186; Analytic technique, 149–50; First
  meeting with Melanie Klein, 150; Subsequent relations with Melanie Klein, see
  Klein, Melanie; First appearance of Anna
  Freud, 58; Subsequent relations with
  Anna Freud, see Freud Anna; Rescues
  Freud From Nazis, 192–6; Writes Freud
  Biography, 219–224; Last Years, 210, 218;
  Death, 218

Jones Ernest—*contd.*
  works cited:
  Essays on Applied Psycho-Analysis, 53;
  Free Associations, ii, 1, 2, 3, 4, 5, 7, 8, 14,
  19, 20, 25, 27-8, 31, 32, 34, 35, 36, 40, 43,
  44, 45-6, 51, 52, 57, 60, 61, 63, 65, 86, 102,
  103, 139, 212, 218; *Freud, Life and Work*,
  47, 48, 72, 76, 96, 97, 194, 211-16, 219-24;
  reviews quoted, 219, 222, 223, 224; *Freud's
  Theory of Dreams*, 243; *God Complex, The*,
  226; *Hamlet and the Oedipus Complex*, 75,
  227-31; *Hate and Anal Eroticism in the
  Obsessional Neurosis*, 226; *Hemiplegia,
  The Onset of*, 45; *Inhibitions, Symptoms
  and Anxiety*, 226-7; *Madonna* essay, 106;
  *Modern Conception of the Psycho-Neu-
  roses*, 78; *On the Nightmare*, 225; *Papers
  on Psycho-Analysis*, 138; *Pathology of
  Morbid Anxiety, The*, 226; *Psycho-Analysis*, 197; *Psycho-Analysis and the Instincts*,
  227; *Psycho-Analysis in Psycho-Therapy*,
  74; *Psycho-Analytic Notes on a Case of
  Hypomania*, 90-1; *Psychopathology of Ev-
  eryday Life*, 243; *Rationalisation in Everyday Life*, 53, 73, 225; *Relationship between
  Dreams and Psychoneurotic Symptoms*,
  226; *Symbolism, The Theory of*, 238-43;
  *War Shock and Freud's Theory of the Neu-
  roses*, 226
Jones, Gwenith (daughter), 140-2, 189, 218;
  Death, 163; Ernest Jones' grief over,
  165-6
Jones, Herbert, 88, 104, 112; marries Loe
  Kann, 105
Jones, Jeanne (daughter-in-law), ii, 200
Jones, Katharine (2nd wife), i, 124, 140, 141-
  2, 144, 162, 179-81, 190; correspondence
  with Ernest Jones, quoted, 124-6, 132,
  142, 162, 164, 165, 176, 179, 181, 187, 189,
  197; visits Freud, 164; diary quoted, 190,
  191, 198, 210; translation of Freud letters,
  213
Jones, Lewis Ernest (son), ii, 184, 189, 214;
  on his father, 189-90
Jones, Mary Ann May (mother), 1, 5, 8, 9,
  31, 62; influence on Ernest Jones, 6; relationship with Ernest Jones, 2, 4; death, 78
Jones, Mervyn (son), ii, 4, 6, 141, 162, 164,
  189, 190, 210, 211, 214, 217, 218; on Ernest
  Jones, 102, 155-6, 180, 181-3, 189-90;
  analysed by Klein, 155, 169
Jones, Morfydd (1st wife), 112-13, 126; Ernest Jones' grief on her death, 113
Jones, Nesta May (daughter), 165, 189, 214;
  analysed by Winnicot, 188-9
Jones, Sybil (sister), 4-5
Jones, Thomas (father), i, 1-2, 5, 6, 7, 8, 9,

13, 18, 27, 38, 62, 104, 113, 165; influence
  on Ernest Jones, 2; Ernest Jones' relationship with, 22-3, 31
Jones, Prof. Viriamus, 12
Journal of Abnormal Psychology, 44
Jung, Carl Gustav, i, ii, 48, 52, 53-4, 61, 62,
  71-4, 76, 77, 80, 105, 106, 108, 110, 178,
  204, 211, 239, 241, 244; Ernest Jones'
  meetings with, 47-8; Ernest Jones on, 48,
  55, 97; to Freud on Ernest Jones, 49, 66-7;
  differences with Freud and Abraham, 54-
  5; at Weimar Congress, 80, 81, 82;
  President of International P.A.A., 99;
  differences with Freud, 94-100; at 1913
  Congress, 98-100; lectures in London,
  107; withdraws from International Association, 108; lectures in Vienna, 169
Jung, Frau Emma, 73, 80, 176
Jungian school, competition with Adlerians
  and Freudians, 107

Kann, Loe (later Mrs. Herbert Jones), 37-9,
  40, 50-1, 59, 60, 61, 62, 64-5, 69, 75, 79,
  88, 89, 96, 111, 112, 126; Ernest Jones to
  Freud on, 69-70, 82-3; Ernest Jones con-
  sults Freud on, 79, 82; analysed by Freud,
  83-5, 86-7, 104-5; returns to Ernest Jones,
  104; marriage, 105; death, 211
Keller, Rev., 80
Kerr, Dr., 39
King, Pearl, 149
Klages, Ludwig, 60
Klein, Melanie, 150, 189, 200, 231, 237, 238;
  invited to London by Ernest Jones, 152;
  Ernest Jones-Freud correspondence on,
  152-3, 154, 155, 156, 187; analyses Ernest
  Jones' children, 154-5, 169; controversy
  with Anna Freud, 156-7, 168, 187, 188,
  202-9; Ernest Jones to Anna Freud on,
  201-2, 207; Ernest Jones' introduction to
  her book, 204; criticised by daughter,
  208-9
Kline, Paul, 99
Knight, Wilson, 227
Kraepelin, Prof., 47, 59; Ernest Jones at his
  Clinic, 47, 60
Krafft-Ebbing, 60, 78
Krauss, 11
Kreuzlingen incident, 95, 96; sanatorium at,
  220

Lacan, Jacques, 238, 242
Laennec, 22
Lamarck, Jean-Baptiste, 168, 231
Lamarckism, Freud on, 231-2
Lambert, Archdeacon J. Malet, 109
Lampl, Jeanne, 215

Lancet, The, 25
Lawrence, D. H., 103
Lawrence, Frieda, 103
lay analysis, 153; Ernest Jones to Freud on, 154
Lina, Ernest Jones' relationship with, 86–7, 104, 111–12, 126
Lipps, 60
Llandovery College, Ernest Jones at, 7, 9–12
London Psycho Analytic Society, 105, 107, 121; reconstituted (1919) as British Psycho-Analytical Society
Long Grove adolescent unit, 33
Low, Barbara, 140, 156, 162, 167, 202
Lucerne Congress, 130
Lyceum Club, 167
Lyschenko, 232

Maberly, Dr. Alan, ii
McCarthy, Molly (Mrs. Desmond McCarthy), 159
McClellan, Rev., 9
McDougall, William, 167
Maeder, Alphonse, 48
Main, Tom, 59
Marie, Prof. Pierre, 62
Marienbad Congress, 130, 188
Marx, Karl, 232
Medawar, Prof., 233
Menton, Ernest Jones' villa at, 214
Meyer, Adolf, 69, 78, 82
Money-Kyrle, 27, 143
Moore, Dr. J., ii, 38
Moorfields Eye Hospital, 32
Muller-Braunschweig, 194
Munich Congress, 98–100, 145
Münsterberg, Hugo, 71
Myers, Frederic, 43

New York Psycho Analytic Society, 48, 71, 133, 146, 153, 160
Nuremberg Congress, 76–7

Oberndorf, 128, 160
Observer, The, review of Freud biography, 222, 223
occultism, Ernest Jones on, 233
Oedipus complex, 121, 156, 176, 221, 231
Ontario Hospital for the Insane, Bulletin of, 74, 90, 91
Ophingsen, 154
Oppenheim, Prof., 93
Order of the Rings, 178
Osler, Sir William, 51
Owen, Morfydd (later Mrs. Ernest Jones), 112
Oxford Congress, 130, 162

Paris Congress, 130, 217
Parker, Prof., 12
Pathological Society of London, 25
Payne, Dr., 202
Pearson, Prof. Karl, 39
Penrose, Lionel, 159
Pfister, Rev. 80
Piaget, 243
Plaut, 47
Prince, Morton, 34, 44, 65, 66, 70, 73
psycho-analysis its gradual acceptance by military establishment 1914–18 war, 102; attempts to discredit, 168
Psychoanalytic Quarterly, The, 184
Putnam, Dr. James Jackson, i, 65, 67, 68, 70, 78, 80, 81, 94, 152

Rado, 188
Rank, Otto, 52, 58, 81, 98, 109, 122, 123, 125, 126, 127, 136, 144–5, 146, 147, 148, 151, 160–1, 178, 204, 239; quarrels with Ernest Jones, 130–1, 132–3, 134, 138–9, 143
Rank, Mrs., 176
Rat Man, case of, 52–3, 222
refugee analysts from Nazi Germany, Ernest Jones' help for, 188
Reik, Theodore, 153
religion, Ernest Jones' attitude to, 3, 5, 10–11
Richards, T. S. (housemaster), 9–10
Rickman, Dr. John, 122, 128, 134, 135, 142, 143, 153, 159, 168
Riggall, Dr., 122
Riklin, Franz, 48, 82, 96
Ringer, Dr. Sidney, 22
Riviere, Diana, ii, 113, 114
Riviere, Joan, ii, 113, 120, 122, 131, 143, 156, 167, 172, 184, 215; analysed by Ernest Jones, 114–19; letters to Ernest Jones, quoted, 114–19; Ernest Jones' conflict with Freud over, 131–2, 135–7; Roazen on, 203
Roazen, Paul, 149, 150, 161,177, 203, 209, 223
Roosevelt, Franklin D., 194
Rosenfeld, Dr. Eva, v, 125
Rowlandson, Janet, 119–20
Royal Army Medical Corps, 102
Royal Society, The, 22, 188, 195
Royal Society of Medicine, 93, 105
Russell, Betrand, vi, 183
Rycroft, Dr. Charles, v, 203, 225

Sachs, Hanns, 58, 106, 109, 123, 124, 163, 198, 239
Sadger, Isidor, 58, 76, 186
St. Bartholomew's Hospital, 19, 33, 203

Salome, Lou Andreas, 98, 99, 107, 108, 137, 223
Salzburg Congresses, 52-6, 80, 146
San Cristoforo, Committee meeting at, 139
Savill, Dr., 49, 50
Schmideberg, Melitta, 208
Schreber case, 81, 223-4
Schur, Dr. (Freud's doctor), 197, 198, 219, 221
Searl, 156
Segal, Hanna, 207
sexual offences, Ernest Jones charged with, 39-41, 49-50, 67
sexuality, 182, 234-8
Sharpe, Ella, 122, 156
Shakespeare, William, *see under* Jones, Ernest: published works: *Hamlet and the Oedipus Complex*
Shaw, Bernard, 37, 183
Silberer, 241
Silberstein-Freud correspondence, 220
Steiner, Ricardo, ii
Stekel, Wilhelm, 52, 58, 75, 76, 77, 80, 81, 95, 178, 204
Stephen, Adrian, 159, 202
Stephen, Karin, 159
Stoddart, Dr., 33, 122
Strachey, Alix, ii, 122, 144, 152, 159
Strachey, James, 122, 134, 142, 144
Suttie, Ian, 144
Swiss Psycho-Analytical Society, 130
Switzerland, Ernest Jones in, 122-3, 124
symbolism, 238-43

Tausk, Victor, 223
telepathy, 234
The Hague Congress, 130
Thompson, Dr. Clara, 12, 176, 177
Times, The, leading article and correspondence on psycho-analysis, 109; obituary of Ernest Jones, 218; reviews of Freud biography, 219, 222
Times Literary Supplement, review of Freud biography, 224
Trotter, Wilfred, 26-7, 29, 34, 36, 37, 38, 39, 40, 45, 54, 78-9, 89, 93-4, 113; moves to Harley St. with Ernest Jones, 35; draws Ernest Jones' attention to Freud, 45; marries Ernest Jones' sister, 78-9

Ty Gwyn (Ernest Jones' cottage in Wales), 180-1, 214, 218

United States of America, Ernest Jones in, 65, 66, 217; conflict between American and European analysts, 133, 157-8, 160-2, 184; Katharine J. and Mervyn in, 190
University College, London, 39

van Emden, 80
van Ophuijsen, Dr. J. H. W., 186
Varendonck, 134
Veraguth, 48
Vienna Psycho-Analytical Society, 153, 194
Virchow, 19
von Freund, 127
von Monakow, 48

Wagner, Mrs, 215
War neuroses, Ernest Jones' treatment of, 102-3
Ward, Bertie, 19, 20, 33
Webb, Sidney, 37
Weimar Congress, 79, 80-2
Wells, H. G., 12, 13, 37, 183
Welsh Medical Dinner Society, 19
Welxzeck, Graf von, 194
Westermarck, 91
Whyte, Lancelot, ii, 44, 45, 55, 57, 119
Wiesbaden Congress, 130, 171, 172, 174, 176
Wilden, Anthony, 242
Wiley, John Cooper, 192, 194, 195
Wilson, Hugh Robert, 194
Wilson, Woodrow, 186
Winnicot, 189
Wittels, Fritz, 54, 57-8, 212
Woolf, Leonard, 152, 159
Woolf, Virginia, 159

Zeitschrift, see *Internationale Zeitschrift für Psychoanalyse*
Zentralblatt für Psychoanalyse, 77, 82, 95
Zetzel, 226
Zilboorg, 185
Zweig, Arnold, 212
Zweig, Stefan, 198